CHRISTINA OF DENMARK

DUCHESS OF MILAN AND LORRAINE

1522—1590

AMS PRESS
NEW YORK

Photo-Hanfstaengl.

Christina, Duchess of Milan.
by
Hans Holbein.
National Gallery.

CHRISTINA OF DENMARK
DUCHESS OF MILAN AND
LORRAINE

1522—1590

BY JULIA CARTWRIGHT
(MRS. ADY)

AUTHOR OF "ISABELLA D'ESTE," "BALDASSARRE CASTIGLIONE,"
"THE PAINTERS OF FLORENCE," ETC.

> " Dieu, qu'il la fait bon regarder,
> La gracieuse, bonne et belle !
> Pour les grans biens qui sont en elle,
> Chacun est prest de la louer.
>   Qui se pourrait d'elle lasser ?
> Toujours sa beauté renouvelle.
> Dieu, qu'il la fait bon regarder,
> La gracieuse, bonne et belle !
>   Par deça, ne delà la mer,
> Ne sçay Dame ne Damoiselle ·
> Qui soit en tous biens parfais telle ;
> C'est un songe que d'y penser,
>   Dieu, qu'il la fait bon regarder !"
>   CHARLES D'ORLÉANS

NEW YORK
E. P. DUTTON AND COMPANY
1913

Library of Congress Cataloging in Publication Data

Ady, Julia Mary (Cartwright) d. 1924.
  Christina of Denmark.

  Bibliography: p.
  1. Christine, consort of Francis I, Duke of
Lorraine, 1522-1590.
D226.8.C5A63 1973   944'.38'0280924 [B]   73-154140
ISBN 0-404-09205-5

From the edition of 1913, New York
First AMS edition published in 1973
Manufactured in the United States of America

AMS PRESS INC.
NEW YORK, N. Y.   10003

PREFACE

CHRISTINA OF DENMARK is known to the world by
Holbein's famous portrait in the National Gallery.
The great Court painter, who was sent to Brussels
by Henry VIII. to take the likeness of the Emperor's
niece, did his work well. With unerring skill he has
rendered the " singular good countenance," the clear
brown eyes with their frank, honest gaze, the smile
hovering about " the faire red lips," the slender
fingers of the nervously clasped hands, which Brantôme and his royal mistress, Catherine de' Medici,
thought " the most beautiful hands in the world."
And in a wonderful way he has caught the subtle
charm of the young Duchess's personality, and made
it live on his canvas. What wonder that Henry fell
in love with the picture, and vowed that he would have
the Duchess, if she came to him without a farthing!
But for all these brave words the masterful King's
wooing failed. The ghost of his wronged wife,
Katherine of Aragon, the smoke of plundered abbeys,
and the blood of martyred friars, came between him
and his destined bride, and Christina was never
numbered in the roll of Henry VIII.'s wives. This
splendid, if perilous, adventure was denied her. But
many strange experiences marked the course of her
chequered life, and neither beauty nor virtue could
save her from the shafts of envious Fortune. Her

troubles began from the cradle. When she was little
more than a year old, her father, King Christian II.,
was deposed by his subjects, and her mother, the
gentle Isabella of Austria, died in exile of a broken
heart. She lost her first husband, Francesco Sforza,
at the end of eighteen months. Her second husband,
Francis Duke of Lorraine, died in 1545, leaving her once
more a widow at the age of twenty-three. Her only son
was torn from her arms while still a boy by a foreign
invader, Henry II., and she herself was driven into
exile. Seven years later she was deprived of the
regency of the Netherlands, just when the coveted
prize seemed within her grasp, and the last days of
her existence were embittered by the greed and
injustice of her cousin, Philip II.

Yet, in spite of hard blows and cruel losses, Christina's
life was not all unhappy. The blue bird—the symbol
of perpetual happiness in the faery lore of her own
Lorraine—may have eluded her grasp, but she filled
a great position nobly, and tasted some of the deepest
and truest of human joys. Men and women of all
descriptions adored her, and she had a genius for
friendship which survived the charms of youth and
endured to her dying day. A woman of strong
affections and resolute will, she inherited a considerable share of the aptitude for government that distinguished the women of the Habsburg race. Her
relationship with Charles V. and residence at the
Court of Brussels brought her into close connection
with political events during the long struggle with
France, and it was in a great measure due to her
exertions that the peace which ended this Sixty Years'
War was finally concluded at Câteau-Cambrésis in
1559.

Holbein's Duchess, it is evident, was a striking figure, and her life deserves more attention than it has hitherto received. Brantôme honoured her with a place in his gallery of fair ladies, and the sketch which he has drawn, although inaccurate in many details, remains true in its main outlines. But with this exception Christina's history has never yet been written. The chief sources from which her biography is drawn are the State Archives of Milan and Brussels, supplemented by documents in the Record Office, the Bibliothèque Nationale, the Biblioteca Zelada near Pavia, and the extremely interesting collection of Guise letters in the Balcarres Manuscripts, which has been preserved in the Advocates' Library at Edinburgh. A considerable amount of information, as will be seen from the Bibliography at the end of this volume, has been collected from contemporary memoirs, from the histories of Bucholtz and Henne, and the voluminous correspondence of Cardinal Granvelle and Philip II., as well as from Tudor, Spanish, and Venetian State Papers.

In conclusion, I have to acknowledge the kind help which I have received in my researches from Monsignor Rodolfo Maiocchi, Rector of the Borromeo College at Pavia, from Signor O. F. Tencajoli, and from the keepers of English and foreign archives, among whom I must especially name Signor Achille Giussani, of the Archivio di Stato at Milan, Monsieur Gaillard, Director of the Brussels Archives, and Mr. Hubert Hall. My sincere thanks are due to Count Antonio Cavagna Sangiuliani for giving me permission to make use of manuscripts in his library at Zelada; to Monsieur Leon Cardon for leave to reproduce four of the Habsburg portraits in his fine collection at

Brussels; and to Mr. Henry Oppenheimer for allowing me to publish his beautiful and unique medal of the Duchess of Milan. I must also thank Sir Kenneth Mackenzie and the Trustees of the Advocates' Library for permission to print a selection from the Balcarres Manuscripts, and Mr. Campbell Dodgson and Mr. G. F. Hill for the kindness with which they have placed the treasures of the British Museum at my disposal. Lastly, a debt of gratitude, which I can never sufficiently express, is due to Dr. Hagberg-Wright and the staff of the London Library for the invaluable help which they have given me in this, as in all my other works.

JULIA CARTWRIGHT.

OCKHAM,
Midsummer Day, 1913.

CONTENTS

LIST OF ILLUSTRATIONS

xi

xii   LIST OF ILLUSTRATIONS

CHRISTINA OF DENMARK

BOOK I

ISABELLA OF AUSTRIA, QUEEN OF DENMARK,
THE MOTHER OF CHRISTINA

1507—1514

I.

THE 19th of July, 1507, was a memorable day in the history of Malines. A solemn requiem Mass was sung that morning in the ancient church of S. Rombaut for the soul of Philip, King of Castille and Archduke of Austria, and, by right of his mother, Duke of Burgundy and Count of Flanders and Brabant. The news of this young monarch's sudden death at Burgos had spread consternation throughout the Netherlands, where the handsome, free-handed Prince was very popular with the subjects who enjoyed peace and prosperity under his rule. " Never," wrote a contemporary chronicler, " was there such lamentation made for any King, Duke, or Count, as for our good King Philip. There was no church or monastery in the whole land where solemn Masses were not said for the repose of his soul, and the mourning was greatest in the city of Antwerp, where all the people assembled for the yearly Fair wept over this noble young Prince who had died at the age of twenty-eight." [1] The King's corpse was laid in the dark

[1] L. Gachard, " Voyages des Souverains des Pays-Bas," i. 455.

vaults of Miraflores, where his widow, the unhappy Queen Juana, kept watch by her husband's grave night and day ; while, in obedience to his last wishes, his heart was brought to the Netherlands and buried in his mother's tomb at Bruges. Now the States-General and nobles were summoned by Margaret of Austria, the newly-proclaimed Governess of the Netherlands, to attend her brother's funeral at Malines.

From the gates of the Keyserhof, through the narrow streets of the old Flemish city, the long procession wound its way : Knights of the Golden Fleece, nobles, deputies, Bishops and clergy, merchants, artisans, and beggars, all clad in deep mourning. Twelve heralds, followed by a crowd of gentlemen with lighted torches, bore the armour and banners of the dead King to the portals of S. Rombaut. There an immense catafalque, draped with cloth of gold and blazing with wax lights, had been erected in the centre of the nave. Three golden crowns, symbols of the three realms over which Philip held sway, hung from the vault, and the glittering array of gold and silver images on the high-altar stood out against the sable draperies on the walls. A funeral oration was pronounced by the late King's confessor, the Bishop of Arras chanted the requiem Mass, and when the last blessing had been given, Golden Fleece threw his staff on the floor, crying: " The King is dead !"[1] At the sound of these thrice-repeated words the heralds lowered their banners to the ground, and there was a moment of profound silence, only broken by the

---

[1] "Bulletins de la Commission Royale d'Histoire," 2ⁱᵉᵐᵉ série, v. 113-119. Jehan Le Maire, " Les Funéraux de Feu Don Philippe."

sound of weeping. Then Golden Fleece cried in a ringing voice: "Charles, Archduke of Austria !" and all eyes were turned to the fair, slender boy, who, robed in a long black mantle, knelt alone before the altar. " My lord lives! long may he live !" cried the King-at-Arms; and a great shout went up on all sides: " Long live Charles, Archduke of Austria and Prince of Castille !" A sword blessed by the Bishop of Arras was placed in the boy's hands, and the heralds of Burgundy, Flanders, Holland, and Friesland, raising their fallen pennons, each in turn proclaimed the titles of the youthful Prince, who was to be known to the world as Charles V.

No one wept more bitterly for King Philip than his only sister, Margaret, the widowed Duchess of Savoy, as she knelt in her oratory close to the great church. Although only twenty-seven, she had known many sorrows. After being wedded to the Dauphin at two years old, and educated at the French Court till she reached the age of thirteen, she was rejected by Charles VIII. in favour of Anne of Brittany, and sent back to her father, the Emperor Maximilian. Three years afterwards she went to Spain as the bride of Don Juan, the heir to the crowns of Castille and Aragon, only to lose her husband and infant son within a few months of each other. In 1501 she became the wife of Duke Philibert of Savoy, with whom she spent the three happiest years of her life. But in September, 1504, the young Duke died of pleurisy, the result of a chill which he caught out hunting, and his heart-broken widow returned once more to her father's Court.

On the death of Philip in the following year, Maximilian prevailed upon his daughter to undertake the government of the Netherlands, and in April, 1507, Margaret was proclaimed Regent, and took up her abode at Malines. She was a singularly able and gifted woman, and her personal charms and rich dowry soon attracted new suitors. Before she became Regent she had received proposals of marriage from Henry VII. of England, which Maximilian urged her to accept, saying that she might divide the year between England and the Netherlands. Louis XII., who in his boyhood had played with the Archduchess at Amboise, would also gladly have made her his second wife, but, as he remarked: " Madame Marguerite's father has arranged marriages for her three times over, and each time she has fared badly." Margaret herself was quite decided on the subject, and declared that she would never marry again. Henceforth she devoted herself exclusively to the administration of the Netherlands and the guardianship of her brother's young family. Of the six children which Juana of Castille had borne him, two remained in Spain, the younger boy Ferdinand and the infant Katherine, who did not see the light until months after her father's death. But the elder boy, Charles, and his three sisters, grew up under their aunt's eye in the picturesque old palace at Malines, which is still known as the Keyserhof, or Cour de l'Empereur. The eldest girl, Eleanor, afterwards Queen of Portugal and France, was two years older than her brother; the second, Isabella, the future Queen of Denmark, born on the 15th of August, 1501, was nearly six; and Mary, the Queen of Hungary, who was to play so great a part in the history of the Netherlands, had only just completed her first year. Margaret, whose own child hardly survived its birth, lavished all a

CHARLES V. (1515)
By Bernard van Orley (Cardon Collection)

To face p. 4

mother's affection on her youthful nephew and nieces. If the boy was naturally the chief object of her care, the little girls held a place very near to her heart. This was especially the case with " Madame Isabeau," her godchild, who was born when Margaret was living at Malines before her second marriage. A gentle and charming child, Isabella won the hearts of all, and became fondly attached to the brother who was so nearly her own age.

Margaret's letters to the Emperor abound in allusions to these children, whose welfare was a matter of deep interest to their grandfather. In the midst of the most anxious affairs of State, when he was presiding over turbulent Diets or warring beyond the Alps, Maximilian was always eager for news of " our very dear and well-beloved children." The arrangements of their household, the choice of their tutors and companions, their childish maladies and amusements, were all fully reported to him. One unlucky day, when the royal children had just recovered from measles, Madame Isabeau caught the smallpox, and gave it to Madame Marie. Then Madame Leonore complained of her head, and since Margaret had been told that the malady was very contagious, and especially dangerous in winter, she felt it advisable to keep her nephew at Brussels out of reach of infection. But this precaution proved fruitless, for presently the boy sickened and became dangerously ill. Great was the alarm which his condition excited, and it was only at the end of three weeks that Margaret was able to inform the Emperor, who was in Italy fighting against the Venetians, that his grandson was out of danger.[1]

[1] E. Le Glay, " Correspondance de l'Empereur Maximilien I. et de Marguerite d'Autriche," i. 203.

The education of Charles and his sisters was the subject of their guardian's most anxious consideration. A lady of Navarre, Dame Anne de Beaumont, took charge of the little girls from their infancy, and watched over them with a tenderness which earned their lifelong gratitude. The old King of Aragon rewarded this lady with the Order of S. Iago, while Margaret begged that she might be allowed to spend her old age in one of the Archduke's houses at Ghent, seeing that she had served " Mesdames mes nièces " so long and so well, and had been but poorly paid for her trouble. Among their teachers was Louis Vives, the learned friend of Erasmus, who afterwards became tutor to their cousin, the Princess Mary of England, and took Sir Thomas More's daughters as his models. Vives taught his pupils Greek and Latin, and made them study the Gospels, and St. Paul's Epistles, as well as some parts of the Old Testament. French romances, then so much in vogue, were banished from their schoolroom, and the only tales which they were allowed to read were those of Joseph and his brethren, of the Roman matron Lucretia, and the well-known story of Griselda. Madame Leonore was fond of reading at a very early age, but Madame Isabeau was more occupied with her dolls, and is represented holding one in her arms in the triptych of Charles and his sisters at Vienna. All the children were very fond of music, in which they were daily instructed by the Archduchess's organist, and there is a charming portrait of Eleanor playing on the clavichord in Monsieur Cardon's collection at Brussels. When, in 1508, the Spanish Legate, Cardinal Carvajal, visited Malines, Charles and his sisters were confirmed by him in the palace chapel,

ELEANOR OF AUSTRIA, QUEEN OF PORTUGAL AND FRANCE
By Bernard van Orley (Cardon Collection)

To face p. 6

and the Archduke addressed a letter of thanks to
Pope Julius II. in his childish round hand.

Margaret was careful to provide her young charges
with suitable companions. A niece of Madame de
Beaumont and a Spanish girl of noble birth were
brought up with the Archduchesses, while the sons
of the Marquis of Brandenburg and Duke of Saxe-
Lauenburg were among Charles's playmates. Another
youth whom the Emperor sent to be educated at
Malines in 1509 was his godson, Maximilian Sforza,
the eldest son of the unfortunate Duke Lodovico and
Beatrice d'Este. While his younger brother, Francesco, afterwards the husband of Christina of Denmark, remained at Innsbruck with his cousin, the
Empress Bianca, Maximilian grew up with Charles,
and throughout his life never ceased to regard
Margaret as a second mother. The young Duke of
Milan's name often figures in the Archduchess's correspondence with her father. One day Maximilian
tells her to borrow 3,000 livres from the Fuggers, and
give them to the Duke, who has not enough to buy
his own clothes, let alone those of his servants.[1]
At another time we find Margaret appealing to her
father to settle the disputes of precedence which
have arisen between the Dukes of Milan and Saxe-
Lauenburg, upon which Maximilian replied that they
were too young to think of such matters, and that
for the present they had better take the place of
honour on alternate days.

It was a free and joyous life which these young
Princes and Princesses led at the Court of Malines.
If they were kept strictly to their lessons, they also
had plenty of amusements. They played games,

[1] Le Glay, i. 393.

shot with bows and arrows, and looked on at stag-
hunts from the balcony of the Swan, an old hostelry
in the market-place. Charles had a little chariot,
drawn by two ponies, in which he often drove his
sisters through the town and out into the open
country. Above all they enjoyed the visits which
they paid to the Castle of Vueren, near Brussels,
where Charles often went by his grandfather's orders
to enjoy fresh air and take hunting expeditions.
The old Emperor was delighted to hear of his
grandson's taste for sport, and wrote from Augsburg that, if the Archduke had not been fond of
hunting, people would have suspected him of being
a bastard.[1]

When, in 1512, Maximilian came to Brussels, and
Charles was sent to meet him, he begged Margaret to
bring the three Princesses, without delay, to " amuse
themselves in the park at Vueren," and sent the
haunch of a stag which he had killed that day as a
present to his " dear little daughters." At the
children's urgent entreaty, the Emperor himself rode
out to join them at supper, and invited them to a
banquet in the palace at Brussels on Midsummer
Day. When the English Ambassador, Sir Edward
Poynings, came to pay the Emperor his respects, he
found His Majesty in riding-boots, standing at the
palace gates, with the Lady Regent, the Lord Prince
and his sisters, looking on at a great bonfire in the
square. The Ambassador and his colleague, Spinelli,
were both invited to return to the palace for supper,
and had a long conversation with the Lady Margaret,
in whom they found the same perfect friend as ever,
" while the Prince and his sisters danced gaily with

[1] Le Glay, i. 241.

the other young folk till between nine and ten
o'clock." [1]

But this merry party was soon to break up. Before
the end of the year Maximilian Sforza crossed the
Brenner, and entered Milan amidst the acclamations
of his father's old subjects, and eighteen months later
two of the young Archduchesses were wedded to
foreign Kings.

II.

While her nieces were still children Margaret was
busy with plans for their marriage. Her views for
them were ambitious and frankly expressed. " All
your granddaughters," she wrote to her father,
" should marry Kings." The old Emperor himself
was an inveterate matchmaker, and the House of
Austria had been proverbially fortunate in its alliances. *Tu felix Austria nube* had passed into a
common saying. By his marriage with Mary of Burgundy, Maximilian entered on the vast inheritance of
Charles the Bold, and his grandson was heir to the
throne of Spain by right of his mother Juana. In
1509 proposals for two of the Archduchesses came
from Portugal, and Margaret urged her father to
accept these offers, remarking shrewdly that King
Emanuel was a wealthy monarch, and that there
were few marriageable Princes in Europe. If both
Madame Leonore and Madame Marie were betrothed
to the two Portuguese Princes, there would still
be two of her nieces to contract other alliances.
But Maximilian's thoughts were too much occupied
with his war against Venice to consider these proposals seriously, and the matter was allowed to

[1] Calendar of State Papers, Henry VIII., i. 369.

drop.[1] Meanwhile Madame Isabeau's hand was in great request. In March, 1510, Maximilian received offers of marriage for his second granddaughter from the King of Navarre's son, Henri d Albret, but this project was nipped in the bud by the jealousy of Isabella's other grandfather, Ferdinand of Aragon, and Francis I.'s sister, Margaret, Duchess of Alençon, became Queen of Navarre in her stead. A new and strange husband for the nine-year-old Princess was now proposed by the Regent herself. This was none other than Charles of Egmont, Duke of Guelders, the turbulent neighbour who had been a thorn in Margaret's side ever since she became Governess of the Netherlands. It is difficult to believe that Margaret ever really intended to give her beloved niece to the man whom she openly denounced as " a brigand and a felon," but it was necessary to cajole Guelders for the moment, and conferences were held in which every detail of the marriage treaty was discussed, and the dowry and fortune of the bride and the portions of her sons and daughters were all minutely arranged. But when the deputies of Guelders asked that Madame Isabeau should be given up to the Duke at once to be educated at his Court, the Regent met their demands with a flat refusal. The negotiations were broken off, and war began again.[2] Another matrimonial project, which had been discussed ever since King Philip's lifetime, was the union of the Archduchess Eleanor with the young Duke Antoine of Lorraine. Maximilian seems to have been really eager for this marriage, which he regarded as a means of detaching a neighbouring Prince from the French alliance, but was so dilatory in the matter that

[1] Le Glay, i. 165.   [2] Le Glay, i. 281, 399-441.

Margaret wrote him a sharp letter, asking him if he ever meant to marry his granddaughters. Upon this the affronted Emperor rebuked her for these undutiful remarks, and asked peevishly " if she held him for a Frenchman who changed his mind every day."[1] But in spite of these protestations he took no further steps in the matter, and in 1515 Duke Antoine married Renée de Bourbon, a Princess of the blood royal of France.

The marriage of Louis XII. to Henry VIII.'s handsome sister Mary was a more serious blow. Six years before the English Princess had been wedded by proxy to the Archduke Charles, and Margaret, whose heart was set on this alliance, vainly pressed her father to conclude the treaty. Meanwhile, in January, 1514, Anne of Brittany died, and the widowed King sent offers of marriage, first to Margaret herself, and then to her niece Eleanor.[2] A few months later news reached Brussels that Louis had made a treaty with Henry, and was about to wed the Princess Mary. So the Archduke lost his promised bride, and his sister was once more cheated of a husband. The Lady Regent was deeply hurt, but found some consolation for her wounded feelings in the double marriage that was arranged in the course of the same year between the Archduke Ferdinand and Anna, daughter of Ladislaus, King of Hungary, and between this monarch's son Louis and the Archduchess Mary. In May, 1514, the little Princess was sent to be educated with her future sister-in-law at Vienna, where the wedding was celebrated a year afterwards.[3]

[1] Le Glay, ii. 205.

[2] H. Ulmann, " Kaiser Maximilian," ii. 484, 498.

[3] Le Glay, ii. 252 ; A. Henne, "Histoire du Règne de Charles V.," i. 96.

At the same time marriage proposals for another of his granddaughters reached Maximilian from a new and unexpected quarter. The young King of Denmark, Christian II., on succeeding to the throne, declined the French marriage which had been arranged for him by his father, and conceived the ambitious design of allying himself with the Imperial Family. In March, 1514, two Danish Ambassadors, the Bishop of Schleswig and the Court-Marshal Magnus Giœ, were introduced into Maximilian's presence by Christian's uncle, the Elector of Saxony, and asked for the Archduchess Eleanor's hand on behalf of their royal master. The prospect of an alliance with Denmark met with the Emperor's approval, and could not fail to be popular in the Low Countries as a means of opening the Baltic to the merchants of Bruges and Amsterdam. Accordingly the envoys met with a friendly reception, and were told that, although the elder Archduchess was already promised to the Duke of Lorraine, the Emperor would gladly give King Christian the hand of her sister Isabella. The contract was signed at Linz on the 29th of April, 1514, and the dowry of the Princess was fixed at 250,000 florins, an enormous sum for those times. Only three-fifths of his sister's fortune, however, was to be paid by Charles, and the remainder by her grandfather, the King of Aragon.[1]

From Linz the Ambassadors travelled by slow stages to Brussels, where they were received with great honour. But Margaret was scarcely prepared for the proposal which they made, that the wedding might take place on the following day, when King Christian was to be crowned at Copenhagen. It was,

---

[1] Le Glay, ii. 383.

ISABELLA OF AUSTRIA, QUEEN OF DENMARK
By Bernard van Orley (Cardon Collection)

To face p. 12

however, impossible to refuse such a request, and on Trinity Sunday, the 11th of June, the marriage was solemnized with due splendour. At ten o'clock a brilliant assembly met in the great hall of the palace, which had been hung for the occasion with the famous tapestries of the Golden Fleece, and Magnus Giœ, who represented the King, appeared, supported by the Duke of Saxe-Lauenburg and the Marquis of Brandenburg. Presently a flourish of trumpets announced the bride's coming, and Charles led in his sister, a tall, slender maiden of thirteen, robed in white, with a crown of pearls and rubies on her fair locks. " Madame Isabeau," as Margaret wrote with motherly pride to her father, " was certainly good to see." [1] They took their places under a baldacchino near the altar, followed by the Regent, who led her niece Eleanor by the hand. The Archbishop of Cambray, clad in rich vestments of purple and gold, performed the nuptial rites, and the Danish Ambassador placed a costly ring, bearing three gold crowns set round with large sapphires and the motto *Ave Maria gratia plena*, on the finger of the bride, who plighted her faith in the following words:

" Je, Isabelle d'Autriche et de Bourgogne, donne ma foi à très hautt et très puissant Prince et Seigneur, Christierne roy de Danemarck, et à toy Magnus Giœ, son vrai et léal procureur, et je le prens par toy en époux et mari légitime." [2]

Then the Mass of the Holy Ghost was chanted, the Spanish Ambassador being seated at the Archduke's side, and the others according to their rank, all but the English Envoy, who refused to be present owing

---

[1] Le Glay, ii. 256.

[2] J. Altmeyer, " Isabelle d'Autriche," 53.

to a dispute as to precedence. Afterwards the guests
were entertained by the Regent at a banquet, followed
by a tournament and a state ball, which, was kept up
far into the night. Finally all the chief personages
present escorted the bride with lighted torches to her
chamber, and Magnus Giœ, in full armour, lay down
on the nuptial bed at her side in the presence of this
august company. Then, rising to his feet, he made
a deep obeisance to the young Queen and retired.
During the next three days a succession of jousts and
banquets took place, and on the Feast of Corpus
Christi a public reception was held in the palace, at
which the bride appeared wearing the ring of the
three kingdoms and a jewelled necklace sent her by
King Christian. Unfortunately, the Archduke danced
so vigorously on the night of the wedding that this
unwonted exertion brought on a sharp attack of
fever.

" Monseigneur," wrote his aunt to the Emperor,
" fulfilled all his duties to perfection, and showed
himself so good a brother that he overtaxed his
strength, and fell ill the day after the wedding.
Not," she hastened to add, " that his sickness is in any
way serious, but that the slightest ailment in a
Prince of his condition is apt to make one anxious."[1]

On the 4th of July the Danish Ambassadors took
their leave, but Isabella remained in her home for
another year. She and Eleanor shared in the fêtes
which celebrated the Archduke's coming of age, and
were present at his *Joyeuse Entrée* into Brussels.
But in the midst of these festivities the Danish fleet,
with the Archbishop of Drondtheim on board, arrived
at Veeren in Zeeland, and on the 16th of July, 1515,

---

[1] Le Glay, ii. 257.

the poor young Queen took leave of her family with
bitter tears, and sailed for Copenhagen. On the day
of Isabella's christening, fourteen years before, the
ceremony had been marred by a terrific thunderstorm,
and now the same ill-luck attended her wedding
journey. A violent tempest scattered the Danish
fleet off the shores of Jutland, and the vessel which
bore the Queen narrowly escaped shipwreck. When
at length she had landed safely at Helsingfors, she
wrote a touching little letter to the Regent:

" MADAME, MY AUNT AND GOOD MOTHER,
    " I must tell you that we landed here last
Saturday, after having been in great peril and distress
at sea for the last ten days. But God kept me from
harm, for which I am very thankful. Next Thursday
we start for Copenhagen, which is a day's journey
from here. I have been rather ill, and feel weak still,
but hope soon to be well. Madame, if I could choose
for myself I should be with you now ; for to be parted
from you is the most grievous thing in the world to
me, and the more so as I do not know when there is
any hope of seeing you again. So I can only beg you,
my dearest aunt and mother, to keep me in your
heart, and tell me if there is anything that you wish
me to do, and you shall always be obeyed, God helping
me. That He may give you a long and happy life is
the prayer of your humble and dutiful niece
                                          " ISABEAU.[1]
    " August 7, 1515."

Two days later Isabella continued her journey to
Hvidore, the royal country-house near Copenhagen.
There she was received by King Christian, who rode
at her side, a splendid figure in gold brocade and
shining armour, when on the following day she made
her state entry into the capital in torrents of rain.
On the 12th of August the wedding was celebrated

    [1] Altmeyer, " Isabelle d'Autriche," 43.

in the great hall of the ancient castle, which had been rebuilt by King Christian's father, and was followed by the coronation of the young Queen. But Isabella was so much exhausted by the fatigue which she had undergone, that before the conclusion of the ceremony she fell fainting into the arms of her ladies. Her illness threw a gloom over the wedding festivities, and seemed a forecast of the misfortunes that were to darken the course of her married life and turn her story into a grim tragedy.

BOOK II

CHRISTIAN II., KING OF DENMARK, THE FATHER OF CHRISTINA

1513—1523

I.

CHRISTIAN II., King of Denmark, Sweden, and Nor
way, as the proud title ran, was in many respects a
remarkable man. His life and character have been
the subject of much controversy. Some historians
have held him up to admiration as a patriot and
martyr who suffered for his love of freedom and
justice. Others have condemned him as a cruel and
vindictive tyrant, whose crimes deserved the hard
fate which befell him. Both verdicts are justified
in the main. On the one hand, he was an able and
enlightened ruler, who protected the liberties of his
poorer subjects, encouraged trade and learning, and
introduced many salutary reforms. On the other,
he was a man of violent passions, crafty and unscrupulous in his dealings, cruel and bloodthirsty in
avenging wrongs. His career naturally invites comparison with that of Lodovico Sforza, whose son
became the husband of his daughter Christina. Both
Princes were men of great ability and splendid
dreams. In their zeal for the promotion of commerce
and agriculture, in their love of art and letters, both
were in advance of the age in which they lived.

Again, their vices and crimes, the cunning ways and unscrupulous measures by which they sought to attain their ends, were curiously the same. No doubt Christian II., born and bred as he was among the rude Norsemen, belonged to a coarser strain than the cultured Duke of Milan, and is hardly to be judged by the same standard. But the two Princes resembled each other closely, and the fate which eventually overtook them was practically the same. Both of these able and distinguished men lost their States in the prime of life, and were doomed to end their days in captivity. This cruel doom has atoned in a great measure for their guilt in the eyes of posterity, and even in their lifetime their hard fate aroused general compassion.

Certainly no one could have foreseen the dismal fate which lay in store for Christian II. when he ascended the throne. Seldom has a new reign opened with fairer promise. His father, good King Hans, died in 1513, lamented by all his subjects, and leaving his successor a prosperous and united kingdom. Christian was thirty-two, and had already shown his courage and ability in quelling a revolt in Norway. A man of noble and commanding presence, with blue eyes and long fair hair, he seemed a born leader of men, while his keen intelligence, genial manners, and human interest in those about him, early won the affection of his subjects. Unfortunately his own passions proved his worst enemies. In Norway he had fallen in love with a beautiful girl named Dyveke—the Dove —whose mother, a designing Dutchwoman named Sigebritt Willems, kept a tavern at Bergen. On his accession he brought Dyveke and her mother to Hvidore, and gave them a house in the neighbour-

hood. This illicit connection excited great scandal
at Court, and the Chancellor, Archbishop Walkendorf
of Drondtheim, exhorted the King earnestly to put
away his mistress on his marriage. Even before
Isabella left Brussels, the Archbishop wrote glowing
accounts of her beauty and goodness to his master,
and told the King of the romantic attachment which
she cherished for her unknown lord. After her arrival
at Copenhagen he did his utmost to insure her comfort, and see that she was treated with proper respect.

For a time Christian seems to have been genuinely
in love with his young wife, whose innocent charm
won all hearts in her new home. In his anxiety to
please her, he furnished his ancestral castle anew,
and sent to Germany for musicians, fearing that the
rude voices of Danish singers might sound harsh in
her ears. A young Fleming, Cornelius Scepperus,
was appointed to be his private secretary, and the
Fuggers of Antwerp were invited to found a bank at
Copenhagen. At the same time twenty-four Dutch
families, from Waterland in Holland, were brought
over in Danish ships, and induced to settle on the
island of Amager, opposite the capital, in order that
the royal table might be supplied with butter and
cheese made in the Dutch fashion. This colony,
imported by Christian II., grew and flourished, and
to this day their descendants occupy Amager, where
peasant women clad in the national costume of
short woollen skirts, blue caps, and red ribbons, are
still to be seen. Unfortunately, the influence which
Sigebritt and her daughter had acquired over the King
was too strong to be resisted. Before long they returned to Court, and, to the indignation of Isabella's
servants, Sigebritt was appointed Mistress of her

household. Rumours of the slights to which the young Queen was exposed soon reached the Netherlands, and when Maximilian informed Margaret that he intended to marry her niece Eleanor to the King of Poland, she replied with some asperity that she could only hope the marriage would turn out better than that of her unhappy sister. The Emperor expressed much surprise at these words, saying that he considered his granddaughter to be very well married, since the King of Denmark was a monarch of the proudest lineage, and endowed with noble manners and rare gifts, if his people were still somewhat rude and barbarous.[1] But, in spite of Maximilian's protests, the reports of King Christian's misconduct soon became too persistent to be ignored. When, in October, 1516, Charles, who had assumed the title of King of Spain on his grandfather Ferdinand's death, held his first Chapter of the Golden Fleece, the Knights with one accord refused to admit the King of Denmark to their Order, because he was accused of adultery and illtreated his wife.[2] At length Maximilian was moved to take action, and wrote to his grandson Charles in sufficiently plain language, saying:

" The shameful life which our brother and son-inlaw, the King of Denmark, is leading with a concubine, to the great sorrow and vexation of his wife, our daughter and your sister, is condemned by all his relatives ; and in order to constrain him to abandon this disorderly way of living, and be a better husband to our said daughter, we are sending Messire Sigismund Herbesteiner to remonstrate with him, and have begged Duke Frederic of Saxony, his uncle, who

[1] Le Glay, ii. 336.
[2] De Reiffenberg, " Histoire de l'Ordre de la Toison d'Or, "307.

arranged the marriage, to send one of his servants on the same errand. And we desire you to send one of your chief councillors to help carry out our orders, and induce the King to put away his concubine and behave in a more reasonable and honourable manner."[1]

But none of these remonstrances produced any effect on the misguided King. When Herbesteiner reproached him with sacrificing the laws of God and honour and the Emperor's friendship to a low-born woman, he shook his fist in the imperial Envoy's face, and bade him begone from his presence.[2] At the same time he showed his resentment in a more dangerous way by making a treaty with France and closing the Sound to Dutch ships. He even seized several trading vessels on pretence that the Queen's dowry had not been paid, and when Archbishop Walkendorf ventured to expostulate with him on his misconduct, banished the prelate from Court.[3]

Meanwhile Isabella herself bore neglect and insults with the same uncomplaining sweetness. But we see how much she suffered from a private letter which she wrote to her sister Eleanor about this time. This attractive Princess, who at the age of eighteen still remained unmarried, had fallen in love with her brother's brilliant friend, Frederic, Count Palatine, the most accomplished knight at Court, and the idol of all the ladies. The mutual attachment between the Palatine and the Archduchess was the talk of the whole Court, and met with Margaret's private approval, although it was kept a secret from Charles and his Ministers. Eleanor confided this romantic story

---

[1] Le Glay, ii. 337.
[2] L. Van Bergh, " Correspondance de M. d'Autriche," ii. 135.
[3] Ulmann, ii. 510.

to her absent sister, and expressed a secret hope
that the popular Count Palatine might succeed her
aunt as Regent when the young King left Brussels
for Spain. In reply Isabella sent Eleanor the
warmest congratulations on her intended marriage,
rejoicing that her sister at least would not be forced
to leave home, and would be united to a husband
whom she really loved. The poor young Queen proceeded to lament her own sad fate in the following
strain:

" It is hard enough to marry a man whose face you
have never seen, whom you do not know or love, and
worse still to be required to leave home and kindred,
and follow a stranger to the ends of the earth, without
even being able to speak his language."[1]

She goes on to describe the misery of her life, even
though she bears the title of Queen. What is she, in
fact, but a prisoner in a foreign land ? She is never
allowed to go out or appear in public, while her lord
the King spends his time in royal progresses and
hunting-parties, and amuses himself after his fashion,
apart from her. Far better would it be for Eleanor
to follow her own inclination, and choose a husband
who belongs to her own country and speaks her
language, even if he were not of kingly rank. Unfortunately, the pretty romance which excited Isabella's sympathy was doomed to an untimely end.
The death of Mary of Castille, Queen of Portugal, in
May, 1517, left King Emanuel a widower for the
second time. He had married two of Charles's aunts
in turn, and was now over fifty, and a hunchback
into the bargain. None the less, the plan of a

---

[1] Hubertus Leodius Thomas, "Spiegel des Humors grosser
Potentaten," 79. E. Moeller, " Éléonore d'Autriche," 307.

marriage between him and his niece Eleanor was now
revived, and in August these proposals reached the
young King at the seaport of Middelburg, where he
and his sister were awaiting a favourable wind to set
sail for Spain. Filled with alarm, Frederic implored
Eleanor to take a bold step, confess her love to Charles,
and seek his consent to her marriage with his old
friend. In a letter signed with his name, and still
preserved in the Archives of Simancas, the Palatine
begged his love to lose no time if she would escape
from the snare laid for them both by "the Uncle of
Portugal."

" Ma mignonne," he wrote, " si vous voulez, nous
pouvez être la cause de mon bien ou de mon mal.
C'est pourquoi je vous supplie d'avoir bon courage
pour vous et pour moi. Cela peut se faire si vous
voulez. Car je suis prêt, et ne demande autre chose,
sinon que je sois à vous, et vous à moi."[1]

Accordingly, on the Feast of the Assumption
Eleanor approached her brother after hearing Mass in
the abbey chapel. But while she was gathering all
her courage to speak, Charles caught sight of the
Palatine's letter in her bosom, and, snatching it from
his sister's hands, broke into furious reproaches,
swearing that he would avenge this insult with the
traitor's blood. As Spinelli, the English Envoy,
remarked, " The letter was but honest, concerning
matters of love and marriage,"[2] but the young King
would listen to no excuses, and, in spite of the Regent's
intervention, Frederic was banished from Court in
disgrace. A fortnight later Charles and his sister

[1] Moeller, 327. L. Mignet, " Rivalité de Francis I. et
Charles V.," i. 140.
[2] Calendar of State Papers, Henry VIII., ii. 2, 1151. H. Baumgarten, " Geschichte Karl V.," i. 58.

sailed for Castille, and in the following summer
Madame Léonore became the bride of " l'Oncle de
Portugal," King Emanuel.

II.

The death of Christian II.'s mistress, Dyveke, in
the summer of 1517 produced a change in the situation
at Copenhagen. This unfortunate girl, a victim of
her ambitious mother's designs, died very suddenly
one afternoon after eating cherries in the royal
gardens. The King's suspicions fell on his steward,
Torben Axe, who was brutally put to death in spite
of his protestations of innocence. But the Queen's
position was distinctly improved. Christian now
treated his wife with marked kindness, and appointed
her Regent when, early in the following year, he went
to Sweden to put down a rising of the nobles.
Sigebritt Willems's influence, however, still remained
paramount, and, in a letter to the Queen from Sweden,
Christian begged her to consult the Dutchwoman in
any difficulty, and ended by wishing her and " Mother
Sigebritt " a thousand good-nights. Stranger still to
relate, when, on the 21st of February, Isabella gave
birth to a son, the infant Prince was entrusted to
Sigebritt's care.

This happy event, combined with Isabella's unfailing affection for her wayward lord, led to improved
relations between Christian and his wife's family
After the death of Maximilian, Charles became anxious
to secure his brother-in-law's support in the imperial
election, and in February, 1519, a treaty was concluded between the two monarchs at Brussels.[1]

[1] Henne. ii. 249.

The Danish Envoys, Anton de Metz and Hermann Willems, Sigebritt's brother, received rich presents from Margaret, who was once more acting as Regent of the Netherlands, and she even sent a silver-gilt cup to the hated Dutchwoman herself.[1] A month later the King of Denmark was elected Knight of the Golden Fleece at a Chapter of the Order held at Barcelona, and in a letter which Charles addressed to him he expressed his pleasure at hearing good accounts of his sister and little nephew, and promised to pay the arrears of Isabella's dowry as soon as possible.[2]

On the 28th of June, 1519, Charles was elected King of the Romans, and the formal announcement of his election was brought to Barcelona by Eleanor's rejected suitor, the Palatine Frederic, whom he received with open arms. A few days after this auspicious event the Queen of Denmark, on the 4th of July, 1519, gave birth to twin sons, who received the names of Philip and Maximilian. Both, however, died within a week of their baptism, upon which Sigebritt is said to have remarked that this was a good thing, since Denmark was too small a realm to support so many Princes.

With the help of Dutch ships and gold, Christian succeeded in subduing the Swedish rebels, and was crowned with great solemnity in the Cathedral of Upsala on the 4th of November, 1520. But the rejoicings on this occasion were marred by the execution of ninety Swedish nobles and two Bishops, who were treacherously put to death by the King's orders. This act, which earned for Christian the title of the

---

[1] Archives du Royaume: Bruxelles Régistre des Revenus et Dépenses de Charles V., ii. 72.

[2] J. Altmeyer, 46.

Nero of the North, is said to have been instigated by
Sigebritt and her nephew Slagbök, a Westphalian
barber, who had been raised from this low estate to
be Archbishop of Lunden. The insolent conduct of
these evil counsellors naturally increased the King's
unpopularity in all parts of the kingdom. Yet at
the same time Christian II. showed himself to be an
excellent and enlightened ruler. He administered
justice strictly, and introduced many salutary reforms.

The common practice of buying and selling serfs was
prohibited, Burgomasters and Town Councils were
appointed to carry out the laws, and a system of
tolls and customs was established. Schools and hospitals were founded, inns were opened in every town
and village for the convenience of travellers, piracy
and brigandage were sternly repressed. An Act was
passed ordering that all cargoes recovered from
wrecks were to be placed in the nearest church, and,
if not claimed by the end of the year, divided between
the Crown and the Church. When the Bishops
complained of the loss thus inflicted on them, the
King told them to go home and learn the Eighth
Commandment. Still greater was the opposition
aroused when he attempted to reform clerical abuses.
Early in life Christian showed strong leanings towards
the doctrines of Luther, and on his return from
Sweden he asked his uncle, the Elector of Saxony,
to send him a Lutheran preacher from Wittenberg.
Although these efforts at proselytizing met with little
success, the King openly professed his sympathy with
the new Gospel. He had the Bible translated into
Danish, bade the Bishops dismiss their vast house-
holds, issued edicts allowing priests to marry, and

ordered the begging friars to stay at home and earn their bread by honest labour.[1] All these reforms could not be effected without vigorous opposition, and the discontent among the nobles and clergy became every day more active. In the spring of 1521 a young Swedish noble, Gustavus Wasa, raised the standard of revolt in Dalecarlia, and led his peasant bands against Stockholm. Upon this Christian decided to pay a visit to the Low Countries to meet the new Emperor, who was coming to be crowned at Aix-la-Chapelle, and seek his help against the citizens of Lübeck and the Swedish rebels. The government was once more placed in the hands of Isabella. A few months before this, on the 10th of November, 1520, while Christian was absent in Sweden, the Queen had given birth to a daughter, named Dorothea after the King's grandmother, the able and ambitious Princess of Brandenburg, who married two Kings of Denmark in succession. Now she followed her husband with wistful thoughts as he started on his journey, attended only by his Chamberlain, Anton de Metz, and three servants, and rode all the way to her old home in the Netherlands.

On the 20th of June nine Danish ships sailed into the port of Antwerp, and a few days afterwards Christian II. rode into the town. His fine presence and the courage which he had shown in riding through Germany with this small escort excited general admiration.

" I noted," wrote Albert Dürer in his Journal, " how much the people of Antwerp marvelled at the sight of this manly and handsome Prince, who had come hither through his enemies' country, with these few attendants."[2]

[1] F. Dahlmann, " Geschichte von Dänemark," iii. 359.
[2] M. Conway, " Literary Remains of Albert Dürer," 124.

The Nuremberg master had been spending the winter in the Low Countries, paying his respects to the Regent at Malines, and conversing with Erasmus of Rotterdam and Lucas van Leyden. He was starting on his journey home, when, on the Feast of the Visitation, he was sent for by the King of Denmark, who received him very graciously, and asked him to dine at his table and to take his portrait. So great was the interest which Christian showed in the painter's work, that Dürer gave him a fine set of his prints, which are still preserved in the museum at Copenhagen, and accepted an invitation to accompany him to Brussels the next day. Thus Albert Dürer was a witness of the meeting between Christian and his brother-in-law Charles V., who had just arrived from his coronation at Aix-la-Chapelle, and had been received with great rejoicing by his subjects. At five that summer evening Charles rode out from Brussels at the head of a brilliant cavalcade, and met his royal brother-in-law in a meadow, where they embraced each other and conversed with the help of an interpreter, Christian speaking in German, and Charles in French. They entered Brussels after sunset, and found the streets hung with tapestries and lighted with innumerable torches and bonfires. The Emperor escorted Christian to the Count of Nassau's palace on the top of the hill, which Dürer describes as the finest house that he had ever seen. The next morning Charles brought his guest to the palace gates, where the Regent and Germaine de Foix, King Ferdinand's widow, were awaiting them, and for the first time Margaret came face to face with her niece's husband. Christian kissed the two ladies in French fashion, and after dinner the two

Princes spent the evening dancing with the Court
ladies.

" Now," wrote the Venetian Ambassador, Gaspare
Contarini, " at two hours after dark, they are still
dancing, for young monarchs such as these are not
easily tired."[1]

The impression which the Danish King made on the
learned Italian was very favourable. He describes
him as a fine-looking Prince, with an earnest, animated expression, long locks, and a beard curled after
the Italian fashion. In his black satin doublet,
Spanish cloak, and jewelled cap, he looked every
inch a King. On the Sunday after his arrival
Christian entertained the Emperor, the Lady Margaret, and the Queen-Dowager of Spain, at dinner.
Albert Dürer was present on this occasion, and was
afterwards employed to paint a portrait of the King
in oils, for which Christian gave him thirty florins,
an act of liberality which contrasted favourably with
Margaret's parsimony. " The Lady Margaret in particular," remarks the painter in his Journal, " gave
me nothing for what I made and presented to her."
Another personage in whose society the King took
pleasure was Erasmus, who discussed the reform of
the Church with him, and was much struck by the
monarch's enlightened opinions. On the 12th of July
Christian accompanied his brother-in-law to Antwerp,
to lay the foundations of the new choir of Our Lady's
Church, and went on to Ghent, where he paid formal
homage for the duchy of Holstein, and was confirmed
in his rights over the Hanse towns, but could not
persuade Charles to join him in making war on the
friendly citizens of Lübeck. At Ghent the King

---

[1] Venetian State Papers, iii. 139.

sent for the English Ambassador, Sir Robert Wingfield, with whom he had a long and friendly conversation, expressing great anxiety to meet King Henry VIII. In reply, Wingfield told him that he would soon have the opportunity of seeing the English monarch's powerful Minister, Cardinal Wolsey, to whom he could speak as frankly as to the King himself.[1] Accordingly, on the 5th of August Christian accompanied Charles and Margaret to the Prinzenhof at Bruges, where Wolsey joined them a week later. The regal state of the English Cardinal formed a striking contrast to the King's simplicity. He arrived with a train of over a thousand followers, clad in red satin, and twenty English nobles, wearing gold chains, walked at his horse's side. On Sunday he rode to Mass with the Emperor, and dined with Charles and Margaret, " praising the delicate and sumptuous manner " in which he was entertained. When the King of Denmark sent to ask him to come to his lodgings, the Cardinal demurred, saying that, as he represented His Majesty of England, the King must be the first to visit him, but that if Christian preferred he would meet him in the palace garden. Christian, however, waived ceremony, and called on Wolsey the next morning. The interview was a very friendly one. Christian expressed his anxiety to enter into a close alliance with England, and begged King Henry to be a good uncle to his young kinsman, James V. of Scotland. Wolsey on his part was much impressed by the King's good sense and peaceable intentions.

" Surely, Sir," he wrote to his royal master, " the King of Denmark, though in appearance he should be judged to be a rash man, yet he is right wise, sober,

[1] Calendar of State Papers, Henry VIII., iii. 2, 555, 561, 582.

CHRISTIAN II., KING OF DENMARK

To face p. 30

and discreet, minding the establishing of good peace
betwixt Christian Princes, wherein he right substanti-
ally declared his mind to me at good length."[1]

But the next day the King sent the Cardinal word
that he had received such bad news from his own
country that he must return without delay. He
actually left Bruges that day, and was escorted to the
city gates by the Papal Nuncio Caracciolo and Contarini, who took leave of the King, and returned to
dine with Erasmus and his English friend, *Messer
Toma Moro*.[2] Unfortunately, Christian's visit to
the Low Countries produced no good result, and there
was some justification for the Imperial Chancellor's
cynical remark: " It would have been better to keep
the King here, where he can do no harm, than to let
him go home to make fresh mischief."[3] He left
Bruges dissatisfied with the Emperor, and on reaching
Copenhagen his first act was to dismiss the Queen's
confessor, Mansueri. When the Emperor begged
him to leave his sister free in matters of conscience,
he broke into a passionate fit of rage, tore the Golden
Fleece from his neck, and trampled it underfoot,
cursing his meddlesome brother-in-law. What was
worse, he seized several Dutch ships in the Sound,
and drew upon himself the serious displeasure of the
Regent and her Council.

Meanwhile Gustavus Wasa had laid siege to Stockholm, and there was a rising in Jutland. A Papal
Legate arrived at Copenhagen to inquire into the
judicial murder of the Swedish Bishops and demand
the punishment of Slagbök. The unfortunate Arch-

---

[1] Calendar of State Papers, Henry VIII., iii. 2, 614.
[2] Venetian State Papers, iii. 162.
[3] Calendar of State Papers, Henry VIII., iii. 2, 576.

bishop was made a scapegoat, and put to death in January, 1522. Stones were thrown at Sigebritt when she drove out in the royal carriage, and one day she was thrown into a pond by some peasants, and only rescued with difficulty. Even Christian began to realize the danger of the situation, and wrote to Isabella from Jutland, begging her to " bid Mother Sigebritt hold her tongue, and not set foot outside the castle, if she wished him to return home alive." In another letter, written on the 4th of February, 1522, from the Convent of Dalin, the King congratulates his wife on her safe deliverance, and the birth of " a marvellously handsome child."[1] This is the only intimation we have of the birth of Isabella's second daughter, Christina. The exact date is not to be found in the Danish archives, and has hitherto eluded all research. The child who saw the light in these troubled times received the name of Christina from her grandmother, the Queen-Dowager of Denmark, a Princess of Saxon birth, who still resided at King Hans's favourite palace of Odensee. All we know of Queen Christina is that, on the 2nd of April, 1515, two years after her husband's death, she addressed an urgent prayer to King Henry VIII., begging him to send her a relic of St. Thomas of Canterbury.[2] We are not told if a phial containing a drop of the saint's blood was sent to Denmark in response to this entreaty, but the request is of interest as a proof of the English martyr's widespread renown.

A few weeks after the birth of her little daughter Isabella wrote a touching appeal to her aunt, imploring the Regent's help against the Danish rebels:

[1] Altmeyer, 23. Reedtz Manuscripts, xiii. 28.
[2] Calendar of State Papers, Henry VIII., ii. 191.

" We have sad news from my lord in Jutland. The nobles there have rebelled against him, and seek to deprive him and our children of their crown and their lives. So we entreat you to come to our help, that we may chastise these rebels."[1]

Anton de Metz was sent to Brussels on the same errand, but could obtain small hopes of assistance. The Regent's Council complained that King Christian had damaged the trade of the Low Countries and ill-treated their sailors, and the temper of the Court was reflected in Sir Robert Wingfield's despatches to England.

" The Easterlings," remarked the Ambassador, " handle the King of Denmark roughly, and his own people are said to have killed the Woman of Holland, who was mother to his Dove, as the King's mistress was called, whereby it appeareth that ill life and like governance often cometh to a bad end."[2]

King Christian's affairs, as Wingfield truly said, were in an evil plight. In June Stockholm surrendered to Gustavus Wasa, and the citizens of Lübeck sent a fleet to burn Helsingfors and threaten Copenhagen. To add to the unfortunate King's difficulties, his uncle Frederic, Duke of Holstein, who had always nursed a grievance against his elder brother, the late King Hans, now took up a hostile attitude, and made common cause with the rebels. On the 20th of January, 1523, the nobles of Jutland met at Viborg, deposed Christian II. formally, and elected his uncle Frederic to be King in his stead. In vain Christian endeavoured to raise fresh forces, and sent desperate appeals to his kinsfolk in the Low Countries and Germany, and to his allies in England and Scotland.

[1] Altmeyer, " Isabelle d'Autriche," 23.
[2] Calendar of State Papers, Henry VIII., iii. 2, 1086.

Margaret replied curtly that the Emperor himself needed all the men and ammunition that could be obtained in those parts. The young King of Scotland's Chancellor, the Archbishop of Glasgow, sent a sympathetic message, regretting that the enmity of England prevented him from helping King Christian against his rebel subjects. When the Dean of Roskild appeared in London with a letter from the Danish monarch, begging King Henry to induce Margaret to help him against the Easterlings, Wolsey sent a splendid barge to conduct the Ambassador to Greenwich, but gave him little encouragement beyond fair words. " So I hope," wrote Sir Robert Wingfield, who, in spite of Christian's civilities at Ghent, had little pity for him, " that this wicked King will fail."[1]

The unhappy monarch was at his wits' end. Yet many of his subjects were still loyal. The bulk of the middle and lower classes, the burghers, artisans, and country-folk, looked on him as their best friend; and when he appeared at the fair of Ringsted, a thousand strong arms were raised, and a thousand lusty voices swore fealty to Christian, the peasants' King. Copenhagen was strongly fortified, and as long as he stayed there he was safe from his foes. But an unaccountable panic seized him. Whether, as in the case of Lodovico Sforza, whom he resembled in so many ways, remorse for past crimes enfeebled his will, or whether his nerves gave way, he could not summon up courage to meet his foes, and decided to fly. A fleet of twenty ships was equipped, fully supplied with arms and ammunition, and laden with the crown

[1] Calendar of State Papers, Henry VIII., iii. 2, 1189. Altmeyer, " Relations Commerciales du Danemark et des Pays-bas," 105.

jewels, archives, and treasures. The Queen and her
young children—the five-year-old Prince John, the
two little Princesses, Dorothea and Christina (a babe
of fifteen months)—went on board the finest vessel of
the fleet, the *Great Mary*, and Mother Sigebritt was
hidden in a chest to save her from the fury of the
people, who regarded her as the chief cause of the
King's unpopularity. But the greatest compassion
was felt for Isabella and her innocent babes; and
even the usurper Frederic wrote to beg the Queen
to remain in Denmark, assuring her that she and her
children would be perfectly safe. On the 14th of
April the fleet set sail. An immense crowd assembled on the ramparts to see the last of the royal
family. The King made a farewell speech, exhorting
the garrison to remain loyal to his cause, and promising to return in three months with reinforcements.
Then the ships weighed anchor, and neither Isabella
nor her children ever saw the shores of Denmark
again.

BOOK III

KINGS IN EXILE

1523—1531

I.

THE troubles of the Danish royal family were not over when they left Copenhagen. A violent storm scattered the fleet in the North Sea, and drove several of the ships on the Norwegian coast, where many of them were lost with all their cargo. The remaining eleven or twelve ships entered the harbour of Veeren, in Walcheren, on the 1st of May. Here the King and Queen were kindly received by Adolf of Burgundy, the Admiral of the Dutch fleet, who kept them for a week in his own house, and then escorted them to the Regent's Court at Malines. Margaret welcomed her niece with all her old affection, and took her and the royal children into her own house. But she met the King's prayer for help coldly, saying that it was beyond her power to give him either men or money. The moment, it is true, was singularly unpropitious. Not only were all the Emperor's resources needed to carry on his deadly struggle with France, but nearer home the Regent was engaged in a fierce conflict with her old enemy, Charles of Guelders, for the possession of Friesland. As Adolf of Burgundy wrote to Wolsey: " We need help so much ourselves that

we are hardly in condition to help others."[1] Christian
soon realized this, and determined to apply to
Henry VIII., relying on his former assurances of
brotherly affection, and feeling confident of Wolsey's
support. The scheme met with Margaret's approval,
and, since Isabella had only brought one Dutch maid
and the children's nurses from Copenhagen, the
Regent lent her several ladies, in order that she
might appear in due state at the English Court.[2]

On the 5th of June the King and Queen left Malines
with a suite of eighty persons and fifty horses, and,
after waiting some time at Calais to hear the latest
news from Denmark, crossed the Channel, and reached
Greenwich on the 19th. Wolsey had already told
the Imperial Ambassador, De Praet, that the King
of Denmark would receive little encouragement from
his master, and had expressed a hope that he would
not give them the trouble of coming to England.
He met the royal travellers, however, at the riverside,
and conducted them to the palace, where they dined
in the great hall with the King on the following day,
Henry leading Christian by the hand, and Queen
Katherine following with Isabella and her sister-in-
law, Mary, Duchess of Suffolk, the widow of
Louis XII., who was still known as *la Reine blanche*.
From Greenwich the King and Queen of Denmark
moved to Bath Place, where they were lodged at
Henry's expense. Katherine welcomed her great-niece
with motherly affection, but both Henry and Wolsey
told Christian plainly that he had made a fatal mistake in deserting his loyal subjects, and advised him to
return at once and encourage them by his presence

[1] Calendar of State Papers, iii. 2, 1270.
[2] Altmeyer, "Relations Commerciales," 108.

All the English monarch would do was to send Envoys to Denmark to urge the usurper Frederic and his supporters to return to their allegiance.

" For," as Henry himself wrote to the Emperor, " this perfidity of the King's subjects is a most fatal example, if for the most trifling cause a Prince is to be called in question, and expelled and put from his crown."[1]

The futility of these measures was evident to De Praet, who wrote to Charles at Toledo, saying that unless he took up the exiled monarch's cause for his sister's sake he would never recover his kingdom. Copenhagen was now besieged by land and sea, and if the garrison were not relieved by Michaelmas they would be forced to surrender, and Christian's last hope would be gone. The King himself, De Praet owned, seemed little changed, and he advised the Emperor to insist on Sigebritt's removal before giving him any help.

" Your Majesty," wrote the Ambassador, " ought first of all to have the Woman of Holland sought out and punished, an act which in my small opinion would acquire great merit in the eyes of both God and man."[2]

At Isabella's request, both Margaret and King Henry had spoken strongly to Christian on this subject, but he still persisted in his infatuation, and it was not till after he had left the Netherlands, and his wife and aunt were dead, that this miserable woman was arrested in Ghent and burnt as a witch.[3]

As for the Queen, no words could express De Praet's admiration for her angelic goodness. " It is indeed

[1] State Papers, Record Office, vi. 139, 155-158. Calendar of State Papers, iii. 2, 1293, 1329.
[2] J. Altmeyer, " Relations," etc., 108.
[3] D. Schäfer, " Geschichte von Dänemark, iv. 26.

grievous," he wrote, " to see this poor lady in so melancholy a plight, and I cannot marvel too much at her virtues and heroic patience." Henry was equally moved, and wrote to Charles in the warmest terms of his sister's noble qualities, but did not disguise his contempt for her husband.[1]

There was, clearly, nothing more to be gained by remaining in England, and on the 5th of July the King and Queen returned to the Low Countries. Isabella joined her children at Malines, and Christian went to Antwerp to equip ships for the relief of Copenhagen. But he soon quarrelled with Margaret, and left suddenly for Germany. In September he appeared at Berlin, having ridden from Brussels attended by only two servants, and succeeded in raising a force of 25,000 men, with the help of his brother-in-law, the Marquis of Brandenburg, and Duke Henry of Brunswick. But when the troops assembled on the banks of the Elbe, King Christian was unable to fulfil his promises or provide the money demanded by the leaders, and he was glad to escape with his life from the angry hordes of soldiers clamouring for pay. By the end of the year Copenhagen capitulated, and in the following August the usurper Frederic was elected King by the General Assembly, and solemnly crowned in the Frauenkirche.[2] The crimes of the unhappy Christian recoiled on his own head, and in the Act of Deprivation by which he was formally deposed, it was expressly stated that his neglect of his noble and virtuous wife, and infatuation for the adventuress Sigebritt and her daughter, had estranged the hearts of his people. But through all these troubles Isabella

---

[1] State Papers, Record Office, viii. 141, 156.
[2] Altmeyer, " Relations," etc., 112; Schäfer, iv. 44, 48.

clung to him with unchanging faithfulness. She
followed him first to Berlin, then to Saxony, where
he sought his uncle's help. In March she went to
Nuremberg on a visit to her brother, King Ferdinand,
and pleaded her husband and children's cause before
the Diet in so eloquent a manner that the assembled
Princes were moved to tears.

"Everyone here," wrote Hannart, the minister
whom Charles V. had sent to his sister's help, "is
full of compassion for the Queen, but no one places
the least trust in the King. If it were not for her
sake, not a single man would saddle a horse on his
behalf."

Hannart, in fact, confessed that he had done his
utmost to keep Christian away from Nuremberg,
feeling sure that his presence would do more harm
than good. Even Isabella's entreaties were of no
avail. She begged her brother in vain for the loan of
20,000 florins to satisfy the Duke of Brunswick, whose
angry threats filled her with alarm.

"I am always afraid some harm may happen to
you when I am away," she wrote to her husband.
"I long to join you, and would rather suffer at your
side than live in comfort away from you."[1]

But Christian, as Hannart remarked in a letter to
the Regent Margaret, had few friends. Even his
servants did not attempt to deny the charges that
were brought against him, and the Queen alone, like
the loyal wife that she was, sought to explain and
excuse his conduct.

To add to Isabella's troubles, her brother Ferdinand
was seriously annoyed at the leanings to the Lutheran
faith which she now displayed. Christian's Protestant

---

[1] Altmeyer, "Isabelle d'Autriche," 30.

tendencies had been greatly strengthened by his residence in Saxony during the winter of 1523. He heard Luther preach at Wittenberg, and spent much time in his company, dining frequently with him and Spalatin, the Court chaplain, and making friends with the painter Lucas Cranach. The fine portrait of King Christian by this artist forms the frontispiece of a Danish version of the New Testament published by Hans Mikkelsen, the Burgomaster of Malmoë, who shared his royal master's exile. When the Marquis Joachim of Brandenburg remonstrated with his brother-in-law for his intimacy with the heretic Luther, Christian replied that he would rather lose all three of his kingdoms than forsake this truly Apostolic man.[1] Isabella's naturally religious nature was deeply impressed by these new influences, and both she and her sister-in-law, Elizabeth of Brandenburg, secretly embraced the reformed doctrine. At Nuremberg she attended the sermons of the Lutheran doctor Osiander, and received Communion in both kinds from his hands on Maundy Thursday, to the great indignation of King Ferdinand, who told her he could not own a heretic as his sister. Isabella replied gently that if he cast her off God would take care of her. Luther on his part was moved by the apparent sincerity of his royal convert.

" Strange indeed are the ways of God !" he wrote to Spalatin. " His grace penetrates into the most unlikely places, and may even bring this rare wild game, a King and Queen, safely into the heavenly net."[2]

[1] " Relations," etc., 126; C. Förstemann, " Neues Urkundenbuch z. Geschichte d. Reformation," i. 269.

[2] J. Köstlin, "Leben Luthers," i. 66; C. Förstemann, i. 169.

While Luther addressed a strong remonstrance to
the newly-elected King of Denmark and the citizens
of Lübeck, Christian's Chancellor, Cornelius Scepperus,
drew up an eloquent memorial to Pope Clement VII.
on the exiled King's behalf, and travelled to Spain to
seek the Emperor's help. By Hannart's exertions a
Congress was held at Hamburg in April, which was
attended by representatives of the Emperor, the
Regent of the Netherlands, the Imperial Electors and
Princes, as well as by deputies from Denmark,
England, Poland, and Lübeck. Isabella accompanied
her husband on this occasion, at Hannart's request.

" I hear on all sides," he wrote to Charles, " that
the people of Denmark would gladly welcome the
return of the Queen and her children if the King
would not meddle with public affairs, and a good
Governor appointed by Your Majesty should act as
Regent until the young Prince is of age."[1]

But when, by way of compromise, some members
of the Congress proposed that Frederic should retain
the throne, and recognize Prince John as his successor,
Christian rejected this offer angrily, and negotiations
were soon broken off. Both Charles and Margaret
now gave up all hope of effecting Christian's restoration, and concluded a treaty in the following August
with King Frederic, by which his title was recognized,
and the Baltic was once more opened to the merchants
of the Low Countries.

II.

The exiled monarch, now compelled to realize
the hopelessness of his cause, returned sorrowfully
with his wife to the Low Countries, and Isabella had

[1] K. Lanz, " Correspondenz Karls V.," i. 108.

at least the joy of embracing her children once more. During this long absence the faithful servants who had followed their King and Queen into exile had kept her well supplied with news of their health and progress.

" Prince John," wrote Nicolas Petri, Canon of Lunden, " learns quickly, and begins to speak French. He is already a great favourite with the Lady Margaret. His sisters, the Princesses, are very well, and are both very pretty children. The youngest, Madame Christine, has just been weaned. Madame Marguerite says that she will soon be receiving proposals of marriage for the elder one. These are good omens, for which God be praised. It is a real pleasure to be with these children, they are so good and charming. If only Your Grace could see them, you would soon forget all your troubles."[1]

But not all Margaret's affection for Isabella and her children could reconcile her to the King's presence. Christian was, it must be confessed, a troublesome guest. His restless brain was always busy with new plots and intrigues. At first he announced his intention of taking Isabella to visit the Emperor in Spain, but, after spending some weeks in Zeeland fitting out ships, he suddenly changed his mind, and took Isabella, whose health had suffered from all the hardships and anxiety that she had undergone, to drink the waters at Aix-la-Chapelle. On his return he wished to settle at Ghent, but the Regent and her Council, fearing that his presence would excite sedition in this city, suggested that the Castle of Gemappes should be offered him instead. Charles replied that if the King lived at Gemappes he would certainly spoil his hunting, and thought that Lille or Bruges would be

[1] Altmeyer, " Isabelle d'Autriche," 26.

a better place. In the end Lierre, a pleasant city
halfway between Malines and Antwerp, was chosen
for the exiled Princes' home. Towards the end of
1524 Christian and his family took up their abode in
the old castle which still goes by the name of *Het Hof
van Danemarken*, or *Cour de Danemarck*. A guard of
fifty halberdiers and a considerable household was
assigned to them by the Emperor's order. A monthly
allowance of 500 crowns was granted to the King,
while the Queen received a yearly sum of 2,000 crowns
pour employer en ses menus plaisirs. But Christian's
reckless and disorderly conduct soon landed him in
fresh difficulties. Isabella cut up her husband's old
robes to make clothes for her little girls, and was
reduced to such penury that she was compelled to
pledge, not only her jewels, but the children's toys.
Meanwhile Margaret's letters to her imperial nephew
were filled with complaints of the Danish King's
extravagance. She declared that he was spending
800 crowns a month, and perpetually asking for more.
When she sent her *maître d'hôtel*, Monsieur de
Souvastre, to set his affairs in order, he was con-
fronted with a long list of unpaid bills from doctors,
apothecaries, saddlers, masons, carpenters, tailors,
and poulterers. But accounts of the straits to which
the Queen and her children were reduced had evidently reached Spain, and Charles felt it necessary to
remind his aunt gently that, after all, Isabella was
his own sister, and that many pensioners whom he
had never seen received many thousands of crowns a
year from his purse.[1]

Another cause of perpetual irritation was the

---

[1] Lanz, i. 145, 150, 195; Archives du Royaume : Revenus et
Dépenses de Charles V., 1520-1530, Rég. 1709; Schäfer, iv. 89.

favour shown by the King to the Lutherans, whom the
Regent was trying to drive out of Flanders. The
Court of Lierre became the refuge of all who professed the new doctrine. Margaret insisted on the
banishment of several of the King's servants, including
the chaplain, Hans Monboë, and Prince John's tutor,
Nicolas Petri, and sent others to prison. But these
high-handed acts only strengthened Christian's zeal
in the cause of reform. " The word of God," he wrote
to his friend Spalatin, "waxes powerful in the Netherlands, and thrives on the blood of the martyrs."[1]
The letters which he addressed to his old subjects
were couched in the same strain. He confessed his
past sins, and prayed that he might be restored to
his kingdom, like David of old, declaring that his
sole wish was to live for Christ and do good to his
enemies. At the same time he hired freebooters to
ravage the coast of Denmark, and provoked King
Frederic to close the Sound, an act which aroused
widespread discontent in the Low Countries. In
August, 1525, he sent a herald to England, begging
King Henry and his good friend the Cardinal to
intercede with the Regent, and induce her to lend
him men and money for a fresh expedition. But
Margaret turned a deaf ear to all entreaties, and
when Isabella's physician recommended her to try
the waters of Aix-la-Chapelle again, she declined to
sanction this journey on the score of expense. She
sent her own doctor, however, to Lierre, and at his
suggestion the invalid was moved for change of air
to Swynaerde, the Abbot of St. Peter's country-house
near Ghent. But Isabella's ills were beyond the
reach of human skill, and she soon became too weak

[1] J. H. Schlegel, " Geschichte der Könige v. Dänemark," 123.

to leave her room. On the 12th of December
Christian sent for his old chaplain from Wittenberg,
begging him to return without delay.

" DEAR BROTHER IN CHRIST," he wrote,
    " Here we forget Christ, and have no one to
preach the word of God. I implore you to come and
give us the comfort of the Gospel. Greet our brothers
and sisters."

Upon receiving this summons, Monboë and Hans
Mikkelsen hastened to Ghent, at the peril of their
lives, and administered spiritual consolation to the
dying Queen. On the 19th of January she received
the last Sacraments from the priest of Swynaerde, and
saw Monsieur de Souvastre, by whom she sent her
aunt affectionate messages, commending her poor
children to Margaret's care. A few hours afterwards
she passed quietly away. Both Catholics and Lutherans bore witness to her angelic patience, and a letter
which Christian addressed to Luther, ten days later,
gives a touching account of his wife's last moments:

"As her weakness increased, Frau Margaret sent
her servant, Philippe de Souvastre, and other excellent
persons, to admonish her after the fashion of the
Popish Anti-Christ's faith and the religion of his sect.
But Almighty God in His mercy deprived my wife
of her powers of speech, so that she made no reply,
and they gave up speaking, and only anointed her
with oil. But before this she had received the Blessed
Sacrament in the most devout manner, with ardent
longing, firm faith, and stedfast courage ; and when
one of our preachers exhorted her, in the words of
the Gospel, to stand fast in the faith, she confessed
her firm trust in God, and paid no heed to the super-
stitious mutterings of the others. After this she
became speechless, but gave many signs of true faith
to the end, and took her last farewell of this world
on the 19th of January. May God Almighty be

gracious to her soul, and grant her eternal rest ! We are strong in the sure and certain hope that she has entered into eternal bliss, unto which God bring us all !"[1]

On the 4th of February the dead Queen, who had not yet completed her twenty-fifth year, was buried with great pomp in the cloisters of the Abbey of St. Peter at Ghent, where a stately marble tomb was raised over her ashes. The painter Mabuse was employed to design the monument, as we learn from a letter which the King addressed to the Abbot of St. Peter's in 1528, complaining of his delay in completing the work. A Latin inscription by Cornelius Scepperus, giving Isabella's titles in full, and recording her virtues and the sufferings which she had endured during her short life, was placed on the monument, which is described by an English traveller of the sixteenth century, Philip Skippon.[2] Unfortunately, the tomb was rifled by the mob at the time of the French Revolution, but the ashes of the Queen were carefully preserved by a pious Curé, and afterwards restored to their former resting-place.

Isabella's early death was deeply lamented, not only in the Low Countries, where she was so beloved, but in her husband's kingdoms. Funeral services were held throughout the land, and all men wept for the good Princess " who had been the mother of her people." On all sides testimonies to her worth were paid. Henry of England wrote to King Christian that the late Queen had been as dear to him as a sister, and Luther paid an eloquent tribute to her memory in his treatise on Holy Women:

[1] Schlegel, 124-126.
[2] Churchill, " Travels," vi. 348.

" Of such Kings' daughters there was indeed one,
of the noblest birth, Isabella, Queen of Denmark, a
Princess of the royal house of Spain. She embraced
the Gospel with great ardour, and confessed the faith
openly. And because of this she died in want and
misery. For had she consented to renounce her faith,
she would have received far more help and much
greater kindness in this life."[1]

III.

The news of the Queen of Denmark's death reached
her brother, the Emperor, on the eve of his marriage
to Isabella of Portugal. Guillaume des Barres, the
bearer of Margaret's letters, found him at a village
in Andalusia, on his way to Seville, where the wedding
was to take place on the following day, and had a long
interview with his imperial master before he left his
bed on the 9th of March. Charles spoke with deep feeling of his sister, and inquired anxiously if the Regent
had been able to obtain possession of her children—
" a thing," wrote Des Barres, " which His Majesty
desires greatly, because of the King's heretical leanings."[2]

Margaret had certainly not been remiss in this
matter. But Christian was more intractable than
ever. He took his children to Ghent immediately
after their mother's death, and refused to give them
up until the Regent had paid all his debts, including
7,000 florins for the funeral expenses, and 2,000 more
which he owed to the landlord of the Falcon at Lierre
for Rhine-wine and fodder. His language became
every day more violent. He threatened to cut off
the Governor of Antwerp's head, and appealed to his

[1] Altmeyer, " Isabelle," 35; " Relations," 160.
[2] Altmeyer, " Relations," etc., 166.

comrades of the Golden Fleece for the redress of his supposed grievances. At length Margaret, seeing that none of her Court officials and Councillors could bring him to reason, rode to Lierre herself on the 2nd of March, and made a last attempt to obtain possession of the children *par voye aimable*. The King, she found, had already packed up his furniture and plate, even the chalice which was used in the royal chapel, and was about to start for Germany.

After prolonged discussion, the Regent succeeded in persuading Christian to leave his children with her, on condition that she paid his debts in Lierre, and provided for the late Queen's funeral expenses—" a thing which must be done," she wrote to Charles, " out of sheer decency." But she quite refused the King's demand for an increased allowance, saying that he could not require more money than he had received in his wife's lifetime. Christian then left the Netherlands for Saxony, saying that he intended to raise a fresh army and invade Denmark. " He is confident of recovering his kingdoms," wrote Margaret to the Emperor, " but my own impression is that his exploits will be confined to plundering and injuring your subjects." This prophecy was literally fulfilled, and during the next four years the peaceful folk in Friesland were harassed by turbulent freebooters in the King of Denmark's pay, while pirates ravaged the coasts of the North Sea, and led the Hanse cities to make severe reprisals on the Dutch ships.

Margaret's chief object, however, was attained. On the 5th of March she returned to Malines with the Prince of Denmark and his little sisters. " Henceforth, Monseigneur," she wrote to Charles, " you will have to be both father and mother to these poor children, and must treat them as your own."[1] The Regent herself nobly fulfilled the sacred trust committed to her by the dying Queen. From this time until her own death, four and a half years later, Isabella's children were the objects of her unceasing care, and lacked nothing that money could provide or love suggest. They lived under her own roof in the Palace of Malines, that city of wide streets and canals, with the fine market-place and imposing cathedral, which many called the finest town in Flanders. Margaret's first care was to arrange the royal children's household. Prince John was placed in the charge of a governess, Mademoiselle Rolande de Serclaes, who superintended his meals and taught him " Christian religion and good manners," while he had for his tutor Cornelius Agrippa, the distinguished scholar and defender of women's rights, who dedicated his book, "On the Pre-excellence of Women," to the Regent. In Lent the Prince and his sisters received regular instruction in the palace chapel, and one year Friar Jehan de Salis received thirty-six livres for preaching a course of Lent sermons before the Prince and Princesses of Denmark. Margaret herself kept a watchful eye on the children. A hundred entries in her household accounts show how carefully she chose their nurses and companions, their clothes and playthings. One of her first gifts to the Prince was a handsome pony, richly harnessed with black and gold trappings. Another was a dwarf page, who became his constant playfellow, and in his turn received good Ypres cloth and damask for his own wear. Italian merchants from Antwerp often came to lay their wares before the Regent.

[1] Lanz, i. 195.

We find her choosing black velvet and white satin for Prince John's doublet, and pearl buttons and gold fringe to trim his sleeves, and ordering the goldsmith, Master Leonard of Augsburg, to supply an antique silver dagger and an image of Hercules for the Prince's cap. Or else a merchant is desired to send her two pairs of cuffs of exquisitely fine " toile de Cambray," embroidered with gold thread, for the young Princesses' wear,[1] and twenty gold balls for the fringe of their bed. Amid all the anxious cares of State which filled her time, this great lady seldom allowed a day to pass without seeing her nephew and nieces. Their innocent prattle and merry laughter cheered her lonely hours, while the Prince and his sisters found plenty to amuse them in their great-aunt's rooms. The halls were hung with costly Arras tapestries of David killing Goliath, stories of Alexander and Esther, hunting scenes and Greek fables, or adorned with paintings by the best masters. Van Eyck's " Merchant of Lucca, Arnolfini with his Wife," and " Virgin of the Fountain," Rogier Van der Weyden's and Memling's Madonnas, Jerome Bosch's " St. Anthony," Jacopo de' Barbari's " Crucifixion," were all here, as well as Michel van Coxien's little Virgin with the sleeping Child in her arms, which Margaret called her *mignonne*.[2] The library contained a complete collection of family portraits, chiefly the work of the Court painter, Bernard van Orley or Jehan Mabuse.

Among these were pictures of Margaret's parents, Maximilian and Mary of Burgundy; of her second

---

[1] Archives du Royaume, Bruxelles. Régistre des Dépenses, etc., Nos. 1799, 1800, 1803.

[2] L. de Laborde, " Inventaire "; Henne, iv. 387-390.

husband, Monsieur de Savoie, a brilliant cavalier
clad in a crimson mantle sown with daisies in allusion to his wife's name; and of her brother, King
Philip, with his children, the young Archduke Charles
and the future Queens of France and Denmark.
Prince John and his sisters would recognize the portraits of their own father and mother, King Christian
and his gentle wife, which hung over the mantel-
piece, together with those of their great-grandparents,
Ferdinand and Isabella, the Kings of France and
England, and the Grand Turk. But better in the
children's eyes than all the pictures and bronzes, the
marble busts and ivories, the silver mirrors and
chandeliers, better even than the Chinese dragons
and stuffed birds-of-Paradise from the New World,
were the live pets with which their aunt loved to be
surrounded. The famous green parrot which once
belonged to Mary of Burgundy had lately died, to
her great sorrow. Margaret herself had written its
epitaph, and the Court poet, Jehan Le Maire, had
sung the bird's descent into the Elysian fields, and its
converse with Charon and Mercury, in his elegy of
" L'Amant Vert." But in its stead she had cages
full of parakeets and singing birds, which were carefully tended by her ladies, and fed with white loaves
newly baked every morning. There was an Italian
greyhound in a white fur tippet, and a number of
toy-dogs in baskets lined with swansdown, and a
marmoset that she had bought from a French pedlar,
which afforded the Court ladies as much amusement
as the royal children. Nor were other diversions
wanting. Margaret was very fond of music, and not
only kept a troop of viol and tambourine players, but
often sent for the town band of Ghent and Brussels,

or the Prince of Orange's fife and organ players, to
beguile her evenings. Sometimes the children of
S. Rombaut and the choir-boys of Notre Dame du
Sablon in Brussels would sing chorales during dinner,
or strolling players and German marionettés, Italian
jugglers, or Poles and Hungarians with tame bears,
would be allowed to perform in her presence. On one
occasion a famous lute-player from the Court of
Whitehall was sent over by King Henry, and received
seven gold crowns for his pains. Another time three
Savoyards were rewarded with a handful of gold
pieces for the tricks with which they had amused the
Court after supper. And every May Day the archers
of the guard marched in procession to plant hawthorn-
bushes covered with blossom under the palace
windows.[1]

In these pleasant surroundings the children of Denmark grew up under the same roof as their mother
and aunts before them, leading the same joyous and
natural life. No wonder that through all her troubled
life Christina looked back fondly to these early times,
and never forgot the happy days which she had spent
at Malines. There is a charming picture, now at
Hampton Court, of the three children, painted by
Mabuse soon after their mother's death, and sent
to King Henry VIII., whose favour Christian II. was
once more trying to obtain.[2]

[1] Henne, iv. 387-391.
[2] This painting is mentioned in one of Henry VIII.'s catalogues
as " A table with the pictures of the three children of the King of
Denmark, with a curtain of white and yellow sarcenet." In
Charles I.'s inventory it is described as " A Whitehall piece,
curiously painted by Mabusius, wherein two men children and
one woman child are playing with some oranges in their hands
by a green table, little half-figures upon a board in a wooden

5

The three children are standing at a table covered
with a green cloth, on which apples and cherries are
laid. Prince John, a manly boy with a thoughtful,
attractive face, wearing a black velvet suit and cap
and a gold chain round his neck, is in the centre
between his sisters. On his right, Dorothea, a pretty
child with brown eyes and golden curls frizzled all
over her head, reaches out her hand towards the
fruit, while on his left the little Christina grasps an
apple firmly in one hand, and lays the other con-
fidingly on her brother's arm. Both little girls are
dressed in black velvet with white ermine sleeves,
probably made out of their father's old robes. But
while Dorothea's curly head is uncovered, Christina
wears a tight-fitting hood edged with pearls, drawn
closely over her baby face. Her tiny features are
full of character, and the large brown eyes, with their
earnest gaze, and small fingers clasping the apple,
already reveal the courage and resolution for which
she was to be distinguished in days to come.

At this early period of their lives it was, naturally
enough, Prince John who chiefly occupied his guardian's thoughts. A boy of rare promise, studious,
intelligent, and affectionate, he had inherited much
of his mother's charm, and soon became a great
favourite at Court. Margaret was never tired of

frame." At the sale of the King's effects it was called a Mabuse,
and valued at £10. In 1743 the same picture hung in Queen
Caroline's closet at Kensington Palace, and was described by
Vertue as " Prince Arthur and his sisters, children of Henry VII."
Five years later it was removed to Windsor and engraved under
this name. Sir George Scharf was the first to correct this obvious
error and restore the original title (see " Archæologia," xxxix. 245).
Old copies of the picture, mostly dating from the seventeenth
century, are to be seen at Wilton, Longford, Corsham, and other
places.

THE CHILDREN OF CHRISTIAN II, KING OF DENMARK

By Jean Mabuse (Hampton Court Palace)

To face p. 54

describing his talents and progress to the Emperor, who took keen interest in his young nephew, and was particularly glad to hear how fond he was of riding.

" MADAME MY GOOD AUNT," he wrote,
     " I hear with great pleasure of the kindness shown by M. de Brégilles, the Master of your Household, to my nephew, the Prince of Denmark, and am very grateful to him for teaching the boy to ride and mounting him so well.   And you will please tell Brégilles that I beg him to go on from good to better, and train the boy in all honest and manly exercises, as well as in noble and virtuous conduct, for you know that he is likely to follow whatever example is set before him in his youth.   And I have no doubt that, not only in this case, but in all others, you will not cease to watch over him.
                         " Your good nephew,
                              "CHARLES."[1]

When in July, 1528, Margaret's servant Montfort was sent on an important mission to Spain, the Emperor's first anxiety was to hear full accounts of Prince John and his sisters from the Envoy's lips. He expressed great satisfaction with all Montfort told him, saying that he entertained the highest hopes of his nephew, and would far rather support his claim to Denmark than help his father to recover the throne —" the more so," he added, " since we hear that King Christian, to our sorrow, still adheres to the false doctrine of Luther."

IV.

King Christian, as the Emperor hinted, was still a thorn in the Regent's side.   Although, since his wife's death, most of his time had been spent in Germany,

---

[1] Altmeyer, " Isabelle d'Autriche," 52.

he remained a perpetual source of annoyance. In July, 1528, he induced his sister Elizabeth to leave her husband, Joachim of Brandenburg, and escape with him to Saxony. All Germany rang with this new scandal, and while the Marquis appealed to Margaret, begging her to stop Christian's allowance as the only means of bringing him to his senses, Elizabeth, who had secretly embraced the reformed faith, implored the Emperor's protection against her husband, and refused to return to Berlin. At the same time the King did his utmost to stir up discontent round Lierre, and raised bands of freebooters in Holland, whose lawless depredations were a constant source of vexation to Charles's loyal subjects. When the Regent protested, he replied that he had nothing to do with these levies, and that his intentions were absolutely innocent, assurances which, Margaret remarked, would not deceive a child. Under these circumstances, relations between the two became daily more strained. " Margaret loves me not, and has never loved me," wrote Christian to his Lutheran friends, while the Regent turned to Charles in her despair, saying: " Monseigneur, if the King of Denmark comes here, I simply do not know what I am to do with him !"[1]

Suddenly a new turn in the tide altered the whole aspect of affairs. On the 3rd of August, 1529, the Peace of Cambray was finally concluded. The long war, which had drained the Emperor's resources, was at an end, and his hands were once more free. Christian lost no time in taking advantage of this opportunity to secure his powerful kinsman's help. He addressed urgent petitions to the Emperor and

[1] Lanz, i. 283; Henne. iv. 337.

King Ferdinand, and sent an Envoy to plead his
cause at Bologna, where on the 24th of February,
1530, Charles V. received the imperial crown from
the hands of Pope Clement VII. But the only condition on which the exiled monarch could be admitted
into the new confederation was his return to the
Catholic Church. For this, too, Christian seems to have
been prepared. On the 2nd of February he signed
an agreement at Lierre, in which he promised to obey
the Emperor's wishes, and to hold fast the Catholic
faith, if he should be restored to the throne of Denmark. When Charles crossed the Brenner, Christian
hastened to meet him at Innsbruck, and, throwing
himself at the foot of Cardinal Campeggio, craved the
Holy Father's pardon for his past errors, and received
absolution. But, in spite of this public recantation,
the King still secretly preferred the reformed faith,
and continued to correspond with his Lutheran friends.
On the 25th of June he arrived at Malines with letters
of credit for 24,000 florins, which he had received
from the Emperor as the price of his submission.
But the Council refused to give him a farthing without
the Regent's consent, and Margaret declined to see
him, pleading illness as her excuse. Although only
fifty years of age, she had long been in failing health,
and only awaited the Emperor's coming to lay down her
arduous office and retire to a convent at Bruges. An
unforeseen accident hastened her end. She hurt her
foot by treading on the broken pieces of a crystal
goblet, blood-poisoning came on, and she died in her
sleep on the 30th of November, without ever seeing
her nephew again. The touching letter in which she
bade him farewell was written a few hours before her
death:

" MONSEIGNEUR,

" The hour has come when I can no longer write with my own hand, for I am so dangerously ill that I fear my remaining hours will be few. But my conscience is tranquil, and I am ready to accept God's will, and have no regrets saving that I am deprived of your presence, and am unable to see you and speak with you before I die. . . . I leave you your provinces, greatly increased in extent since your departure, and resign the government, which I trust I have discharged in such a way as to merit a Divine reward, and earn the goodwill of your subjects as well as your approval. And above all, Monseigneur, I recommend you to live at peace, more especially with the Kings of France and England. Finally I beg of you, by the love which you have been pleased to bear me, remember the salvation of my soul and my recommendations on behalf of my poor servants. And so I bid you once more farewell, praying, Monseigneur, that you may enjoy a long life and great prosperity.   " Your very humble aunt,
" MARGARET."[1]

" From Malines the last day of November, 1530."

This letter reached the Emperor at Cologne together with the news of Margaret's death, and a solemn requiem was chanted for her soul in the cathedral. Charles and his subjects fully realized the great loss which his *pays de par-deça* had suffered by his aunt's death.

" All the provinces," said Cornelius Agrippa, in the funeral oration which he pronounced in S. Rombaut of Malines, " all the cities, and all the villages, are plunged in tears and sorrow. For no greater loss could have befallen us and our country."

The young Prince of Denmark, whom Margaret had loved so well, was chief mourner on this occasion,

[1] Lanz, i. 408; Gachard, " Analecta Belgica," i. 378.

and rode at the head of the procession which bore her remains to Bruges. Here they were laid in the Convent of the Annunciation until the magnificent shrine that she had begun at Brou in Savoy was ready to receive her ashes and those of her husband. When, in the following March, the Emperor came to Malines, Prince John welcomed him in a Latin speech, in which he made a pathetic allusion to the loss which he and his sisters had sustained in the death of one who had been to them the wisest and tenderest of mothers. Then, turning to his uncle with charming grace, he begged the Emperor to have compassion upon him and his orphaned sisters, and allow them to remain at his Court until their father should be restored to his rightful throne. The young Prince's simple eloquence produced a deep impression. The Emperor with tears in his eyes embraced him, and the magistrates of Malines presented him with a barrel of Rhenish wine in token of their regard.[1]

Fortunately for the children of Denmark, as well as for the provinces which Margaret had ruled so well, another Habsburg Princess was found to take her place. This was the Emperor's sister Mary, whose gallant husband, King Louis of Hungary, had fallen on the field of Mohacz four years before, fighting against the Turks. The widowed Queen, although only twenty-one, had shown admirable presence of mind, and it was largely due to her tact and popularity that her brother Ferdinand and his wife Anna, the dead King's sister, were recognized as joint Sovereigns of Bohemia and Hungary. Her own hand was sought in marriage by many Princes, including the young King James V. of Scotland and her sister

[1] Schlegel, 126; Altmeyer, " Relations," etc., 186.

Eleanor's old lover, the Palatine Frederic, whose romantic imagination was deeply impressed by the young Queen's heroic bearing. But Mary positively refused to take another husband, saying that, having found perfect happiness in her first marriage, she had no wish to try a second. To the end of her life she remained true to her dead lord, and never put off her widow's weeds. But her courage and spirit were as high as ever. She was passionately fond of hunting, and amazed the hardest riders by being all day in the saddle without showing any trace of fatigue. Her powers of mind were no less remarkable. She was the ablest of the whole family, and the wisdom of her judgments was equalled by the frankness with which she expressed them. Like all the Habsburg ladies, she was highly educated, and spoke Latin as well as any doctor in Louvain, according to Erasmus, who inscribed her name on the first page of his " Veuve Chrétienne." Mary shared her sister Isabella's sympathy with the reformers, and accepted the dedication of Luther's " Commentary on the Four Psalms of Consolation." When this excited her brother Ferdinand's displeasure, she told him that authors must do as they please in these matters, and that he might trust her not to tarnish the fair name of their house. " God," she added, " would doubtless give her grace to die a good Christian."[1]

In the spring of 1530 Mary met Charles at Innsbruck, and accompanied him to Augsburg. When, a few months later, the news of Margaret's death reached him at Cologne, the Emperor begged her to become Regent of the Low Countries and share the burden of government with him. But Mary had no

[1] Altmeyer, " Relations," 190.

wish to enter public life, and asked her brother's leave to retire to Spain and devote herself to the care of their unhappy mother, Queen Juana. For some time she resisted the entreaties of both her brothers, and it was only a strong sense of duty which finally overcame her reluctance to assume so arduous and ungrateful a task. When at length she consented, she made it a condition that she should not be troubled with offers of marriage, and pointed out that her Lutheran sympathies might well arouse suspicion in the Netherlands. But Charles brushed these objections lightly aside, saying that no one should disturb her peace, and that he should never have trusted her with so important a post if he had regarded her Lutheran tendencies seriously. All he asked was that the Queen should not bring her German servants to the Low Countries, lest they should arouse the jealousy of his Flemish courtiers.

Mary scrupulously fulfilled these conditions, and on the 23rd of January, 1531, the new Regent entered Louvain in state, and was presented to the Council by the Emperor, as Governess of the Netherlands. Two months later she accompanied Charles to Malines, where for the first time she embraced her little nieces. For the present, however, Dorothea and Christina, who were only nine and ten years old, remained at Malines, while Prince John accompanied his uncle and aunt on a progress through the provinces.

Mary soon realized all the difficulties of the task that she had undertaken with so much reluctance.

" The Emperor," she wrote to Ferdinand from Brussels, " has fastened the rope round my neck, but I find public affairs in a great tangle, and if His

Majesty does not reduce them to some degree of order before his departure, I shall find myself in a very tight place."[1]

The Treasury was exhausted, the people groaned under the load of taxation, and the prodigal generosity of the late Regent had not succeeded in suppressing strife and jealousy among the nobles. As Mary wrote many years afterwards to her nephew, Philip II.:

" No doubt our aunt, Madame Marguerite, ruled the Netherlands long and well; but when she grew old and ailing she was obliged to leave the task to others, and when the Emperor returned there after her death, he found the nobles at variance, justice little respected, and all classes disaffected to the imperial service."[2]

But the young Regent brought all her spirit and energy to the task, and with her brother's help succeeded in reforming the gravest abuses and restoring some order into the finances. The gravest difficulty with which she had to contend was the presence of the King of Denmark. Since Margaret's death this monarch had grown bolder and more insolent in his demands. With the help of his old ally, Duke Henry of Brunswick, he collected 6,000 men-at-arms and invaded Holland, spreading fire and sword wherever he went. In vain Charles remonstrated with him on the suffering which he inflicted on peaceable citizens. Christian only replied with an insolent letter, which convinced the Emperor more than ever of " the man's little sense and honesty." He now feared that the King would seize one of the forts in Holland and remain there all the winter, feeding his soldiers at the expense of the unfortunate peasantry, and infecting

---

[1] T. Juste, " Les Pays-Bas sous Charles V.," 35.
[2] L. Gachard, " Retraite et Mort de Charles V.," i. 348.

them with Lutheran heresy. Under these circumstances Charles felt that it was impossible to desert his
sister, and decided to put off his departure for Germany until he had got rid of this troublesome guest.
At length, on the 26th of October, Christian sailed
from Medemblik, in North Holland, with twenty-five
ships and 7,000 men.

" He has done infinite damage to my provinces of
Holland and Utrecht," wrote Charles to Ferdinand,
" treating them as if they were enemies, and forcing
them to provide him with boats and provisions,
besides seizing the supplies which I had collected for
my own journey."[1]

So great were the straits to which Charles found
himself reduced that he was compelled to raise a fresh
loan in order to defray the expenses of his journey
to Spires. But at least the hated adventurer was
gone, and as a fair wind sprang up, and the sails of
King Christian's fleet dropped below the horizon, the
Emperor and his subjects felt that they could breathe
freely.

" The King of Dacia," wrote the Italian traveller
Mario Savorgnano, from Brussels, on the 6th of
November, " has sailed with twenty big ships, thus
relieving this land from a heavy burden. He goes
to recover his kingdom of Denmark, a land lying
north of the Cymbric Chersonesus. . . . But I am
sure that when the people come face to face with
these mercenaries, especially those who have been
in Italy and have there learnt to rob, sack, burn, and
leave no cruelty undone, in their greed for gold, they
will rise and drive out the invaders."[2]

This time Christian determined not to attempt a
landing in Denmark, but to sail straight to Norway,
where he had always been more popular than in any

[1] Lanz, i. 572.   [2] M. Sanuto, " Diarii," lv. 174.

other part of his dominions, and still numbered many partisans. His expectations were not disappointed. When he landed, on the 5th of November, the peasantry and burghers flocked to his standard. The Archbishop of Drondtheim and the clergy declared in his favour, and the States-General, which met in January, 1532, at Oslo, the old capital, renewed their oaths of allegiance to him as their rightful King. But the strong forts of Bergen and Aggershus, at the gates of the town, closed their gates against him, and his army soon began to dwindle away for want of supplies. Early in the spring a strong fleet, fitted out by King Frederic, with the help of the citizens of Lübeck, appeared before Oslo, and set fire to Christian's ships in the harbour, while a Danish army, under Knut Gyldenstern, advanced from the south. Once more the King's nerve failed him. He met the Danish captain in a meadow outside Oslo, and, after prolonged negotiations, agreed to lay down his arms and go to Copenhagen, to confer with his uncle. The next day he disbanded his forces and took leave of his loyal supporters. Thus, without striking a blow, he delivered Norway into the usurper's hands, and surrendered his last claim to the three kingdoms.[1]

In return for his submission, Gyldenstern had promised the King honourable entertainment and given him a written safe-conduct. Trusting in these assurances, Christian went on board a Danish ship, and on the 24th of July arrived before Copenhagen. As the ship sailed up the Sound in the early summer morning, people flocked from all parts to see their old King, and many of the women and children wept aloud. His fate, they realized, was already sealed.

---

[1] Schäfer, iv. 178-194.

Before the arrival of the fleet, a conference had been held between Frederic and the Swedish and Hanse deputies, who agreed that so dangerous a foe must not be allowed to remain at liberty, and condemned the unfortunate monarch to perpetual imprisonment in the island fortress of Sonderburg. In vain Christian demanded to be set on shore and conducted into his uncle's presence. He was told that the King would meet him in the Castle of Flensburg in Schleswig. But when, instead of sailing in this direction, the ship which bore him entered the narrow Alsener Sound, and the walls of Sonderburg came in sight, the unhappy King saw the trap into which he had fallen, and broke into transports of rage. But it was too late, and he was powerless in the hands of his enemies. No indignity was spared him by his captors. As he entered the lonely cell in the highest turret of the castle, Knut Gyldenstern, who is said to have been one of his mistress Dyveke's lovers, plucked the fallen monarch by the beard, and tore the jewel of the Golden Fleece from his neck. None of the old servants who had clung to their exiled Prince so faithfully were allowed to share his prison, and for many years a pet dwarf was his sole companion.[1]

In this foul and treacherous manner King Christian II. was betrayed into the hands of his foes and doomed to lifelong captivity. And, by a strange fate, in these early days of August, at the very moment when the iron gates of Sonderburg closed behind him, his only son, the rightful heir to the three kingdoms, died far away in Southern Germany, within the walls of the imperial city of Regensburg.

[1] Schlegel, 127-219.

Meanwhile the news of Christian's unexpected success in Norway had reached Brussels and excited great surprise.

" The King of Denmark," wrote Mary of Hungary to her brother Ferdinand, " has done so well by his rashness that he has actually recovered possession of one of his kingdoms, and his friends hope that he may be able to stay there."[1]

This was towards the end of December, when the imperial family had assembled in the palace to keep Christmas. Prince John had won golden opinions on the progress which he had made with his uncle and aunt, and was as much beloved by the Emperor, wrote Mario Savorgnano, as if he were his own son. Now his little sisters were brought to Brussels by their uncle's command to share in the festivities. Early in January, 1532, Charles heard that his sister, Queen Katherine of Portugal, had given birth to a son, and the happy event was celebrated by a grand tournament on the square in front of the Portuguese Ambassador's house. The Emperor, accompanied by the Queen of Hungary and the Prince and Princesses of Denmark, looked on at the jousts and sword and torch dances from a balcony draped with white and green velvet, and at nine o'clock sat down to a sumptuous banquet. The Queen was seated at the head of the table, opposite the fireplace, with the Emperor on her right and Princess Dorothea at his side. Prince John was on his aunt's left, and the youthful Christina, who made her first appearance in public on this occasion, sat between her brother and the Portuguese Ambassador. Henry of Nassau, the Prince of Bisignano, and Ferrante Gonzaga, were at

[1] T. Juste. " Les Pays-Bas sous Charles V.," 49.

the same board, while Nassau's son, the young Prince René, who had lately inherited the principality of Orange from his maternal uncle, sat with the Queen's ladies at another table. Charles was in high spirits. He talked and laughed with all the lords and ladies who were present during the interminable number of courses of meat, fish, game, wines, cakes, and fruits, that were served in succession, with brief interludes of music. When, at eleven, the Emperor rose from table, an Italian comedy was acted, in which Ferrante Gonzaga and several Italian and Spanish noblemen took part. Then King Cupid appeared, riding in a triumphal car, and a troop of Loves danced hand in hand, until, at a sign from Charles, the actors removed their masks. A collation of confetti and Madeira and Valencia wines was then served at a buffet laden with costly gold and silver cups and precious bowls of Oriental porcelain. When all the guests had ate and drunk their fill, the finest crystal vases and bottles of perfume were presented to the Queen and Princesses, and the other ladies received gifts from the Ambassador. The royal guests joined with great spirit in the dancing which followed, and did not retire till two o'clock.[1] Concerts and suppers, jousts and dances, succeeded each other throughout the week, and the Emperor gave splendid presents to the Ambassador of Portugal, and sent cordial congratulations to his royal brother-in-law on the birth of his son and heir.

A fortnight later Charles left Brussels, taking Prince John with him, and travelled by slow stages to Regensburg, where the Imperial Diet was opened in May. Here the Court remained during the next

[1] M. Sanuto, lv. 417-419.

three months, and the young Prince was sent to receive the Count Palatine, the Archbishop of Mainz, and other Princes of the Empire, who arrived in turn to take part in the assembly. Unluckily the weather proved very disagreeable. " Never," exclaimed the Venetian Ambassador, " was there such a detestable climate !" A long continuance of heavy rains and unusual heat was followed by some bitterly cold days, which produced serious illness. Princes and nobles, Ambassadors and servants, all succumbed in turn to the same epidemic. The Venetian took to his bed, and four of his servants became seriously ill. The Emperor himself was invalided, and left the town to take waters and change of air in a neighbouring village. " There is hardly a house in the Court," wrote the Mantuan Envoy," where some person is not ill. Most people recover, but a good many die, especially those who are young." Among the victims was Prince John of Denmark. Charles returned to find his nephew in high fever and delirium. He was deeply distressed, and when the poor boy became unconscious, and the doctors gave no hope, he left the town again, saying that he could not bear to see the child die. The Prince never recovered consciousness, and passed away at two o'clock on the morning of the 12th of August.

" The poor little Prince of Denmark died last night," wrote the Mantuan Ambassador, " to the infinite distress of the whole Court, and above all of Cæsar, who bore him singular affection, not only on account of the close ties of blood between them, but because of the young Prince's charming nature and winning manners, which made him beloved by everyone and gave rise to the highest hopes."[1]

[1] M. Sanuto, lvi. 813-823.

By the Emperor's orders an imposing funeral service was held at Regensburg, after which the Prince's body was taken to Ghent and buried in his mother's grave. Charles himself wrote to break the sad news to Mary of Hungary and her poor little nieces:

" MADAME MY GOOD SISTER,
" This is only to inform you of the loss we have suffered in the death of our little nephew of Denmark, whom it pleased God to take to Himself on Sunday morning, the day before yesterday, after he had been ill of internal catarrh for a whole week. This has caused me the greatest grief that I have ever known. For he was the dearest little fellow, of his age, that it was possible to see, and I have felt this loss more than I did that of my son, for he was older, and I knew him better and loved him as if he had been my own child. But we must bow to the Divine will. Although I know that God might have allowed this to happen anywhere, I cannot help feeling that if I had left the boy at home with you he might not have died. At least his father will be sure to say so. I expect you know where he is said to be. Without offence to God, I could wish he were in his son's place, and his son well received in his own kingdom. All the same, without pretending to be the judge, perhaps the King has not deserved to be there, and the little rogue is better off where he is than where I should have liked to see him, and smiles at my wish for him, for he was certainly not guilty of any great sins. He died in so Christian a manner that, if he had committed as many as I have, there would have been good hope of his soul's weal, and with his last breath he called on Jesus. I am writing to my little nieces, as you see, to comfort them. I am sure that you will try and do the same. The best remedy will be to find them two husbands."[1]

When Charles wrote these touching words, he had not yet heard of the disastrous end to King Christian's campaign, and believed the Prince's father to be in

[1] Lanz, ii. 3.

6

possession of the Norwegian capital. But he added a postscript to his letter, telling the Queen of a report which had just arrived, that the King had been taken prisoner by his foes. Four days later this report was confirmed by letters from Lübeck merchants, and no further doubt could be entertained of the doom which had overtaken the unhappy monarch. His melancholy fate excited little compassion, either in Germany or in the Netherlands. Luther, to his credit, addressed an earnest appeal to King Frederic congratulating him on his victory, and begging him to take example by Christ, who died for His murderers, and have pity on the unfortunate captive. But in reply Frederic issued an apology, in which he brought the gravest charges against the deposed King, and accused him of having preferred a low woman of worthless character to the noblest and most virtuous of Queens. Before long the old commercial treaties between Denmark and the Low Countries were renewed, and the Baltic trade was resumed on the understanding that no attempt was made to revive King Christian's claims.

The prisoner of Sonderburg was forgotten by the world, and the one being who loved him best on earth, his sister Elizabeth of Brandenburg, could only commend his little daughters sadly to the Regent, and beg her to have compassion on these desolate children. Mary replied in a letter full of feeling, assuring Elizabeth that she need have no fear on this score, and that her little nieces should be treated as if they were her own daughters. She kept her word nobly.[1]

[1] Altmeyer, " Relations," etc., 206.

BOOK IV

CHRISTINA, DUCHESS OF MILAN
1533—1535

I.

In the letter which the Emperor wrote to Mary of
Hungary on his nephew's death, he remarked that
the best way of consoling his little nieces for their
brother's loss would be to find them husbands. The
marriages of these youthful Princesses had already
engaged his attention for some time past. While
Christina was still a babe in her nurse's arms, the
Regent Margaret had been planning marriages for
her great-nieces. In 1527 Wolsey proposed King
Henry's illegitimate son, the Duke of Richmond, as
an eligible suitor for one of them, but the idea of
such a union was scouted by the imperial family.[1]
A marriage between Dorothea and her second cousin,
King James V. of Scotland, was discussed during many
years, and only abandoned eventually owing to the
fickle character of the young monarch. After Prince
John's death, this Princess inherited her brother's
claims to the Danish throne, and King Frederic went
so far as to propose that she should wed his younger
son John, offering to recognize him as heir to Denmark,
and leave the duchies of Schleswig - Holstein to his

[1] Calendar of Spanish State Papers, ii. 146.

elder son Christian. But the Emperor and Mary of
Hungary were both reluctant to treat with the
usurper who had deposed their brother-in-law, and
the death of Frederic in April, 1533, put an end to
the scheme.[1]

Another suitor now came forward in the person of
Francesco Sforza, Duke of Milan. This Prince was
the younger brother of Massimiliano Sforza, who as
a boy had spent several years at the Court of Malines,
and had been deposed by Francis I. after a brief reign
of three years. Born at Milan on the 4th of February,
1495, when his father, Lodovico, was at the height of
his glory, and named after his grandfather, the great
Condottiere, Francesco II. had been the sport of
Fortune from his childhood. Before he was two
years old, his mother, the brilliant Duchess Beatrice,
died, and when he was five his father lost both
throne and freedom. While the unfortunate Moro
ended his days in the dungeons of Loches, his young
children were brought up in Germany by their cousin
Bianca, the second wife of the Emperor Maximilian.
Francesco spent most of his time at Innsbruck, and,
after the brief interlude of his brother's reign at
Milan, retired once more to Trent. His opportunity
came in 1521, when Leo X., in his dread of France,
joined with Charles V. to place the younger Sforza
on his father's throne. A gallant soldier and cultivated man, Francesco II. won the hearts of all his
subjects, who rejoiced to see a Sforza Duke again
among them. But misfortune dogged his footsteps.
In 1523 Milan was once more taken by the French,
and after their defeat at Pavia the Duke incurred
the Emperor's displeasure, and was deprived of his

[1] Schäfer, iv. 204, 209.

State, chiefly owing to the intrigues of his Chancellor, Morone, with Pope Clement VII. It was only in December, 1529, when Charles came to Bologna for his coronation, that, at the intercession of the Pope and the Venetians, he consented to pardon Francesco, and give him the investiture of Milan for the enormous sum of 900,000 ducats. But it was a barren realm to which the Duke returned. His subjects were ruined by years of warfare, his own health had suffered severely from the hardships which he had undergone, and he had been dangerously wounded by the poisoned dagger of an assassin. At thirty-eight he was a broken man, prematurely old and grey. The Venetian chronicler Marino Sanuto, who saw the Duke at Venice in October, 1530, describes him as looking very melancholy, and being only able to walk and move his hands with difficulty.[1] He applied himself, however, manfully to the almost hopeless task of relieving the distress of his subjects and restoring order and prosperity. With great difficulty he succeeded in raising 400,000 ducats, the first instalment of the payment for the investiture of Milan, upon which the Castello was restored to him. His loyalty and modesty had gone far to recover the Emperor's confidence, and Charles treated him with marked favour and kindness.

This encouraged Francesco to aspire to the hand of a Princess of the imperial house. His subjects were exceedingly anxious to see their Duke married, and already more than one suitable bride had been proposed. But Margherita Paleologa, the heiress of Montferrat, whom her mother would gladly have given Francesco in marriage, was wedded to his

[1] " Diarii," liii. 231.

cousin Federico, Duke of Mantua, in October, 1531, and the Pope's niece, the Duchessina Caterina de' Medici, another prize who had been dangled before the Duke of Milan's eyes, was betrothed to the Duke of Orleans in the following year. Before this event was announced, in January, 1532, the Milanese Ambassador, Camillo Ghilino, who had accompanied Charles to Brussels, ventured to ask the Emperor, on his master's behalf, for the hand of one of his nieces. Charles was evidently not averse to the proposal. It was part of his policy to consolidate the different Italian dynasties, and he was alive to the advantage of drawing the Duke of Milan into his family circle. But he returned an evasive answer, saying that Princess Dorothea was already destined for the King of Scotland, while her sister Christina was too young, and that he could arrange nothing without the consent of her father, the King of Denmark, who had gone to Norway to try and recover his kingdom.[1] When Francesco met Charles at Bologna in the following December, and was admitted to the newly-formed League of Italian States, he renewed his suit, and once more asked for Christina's hand. On the 10th of March Charles came to Milan, and spent four days in the Castello, after which he accompanied the Duke on a hunting-party at Vigevano, and enjoyed excellent sport, killing two wild-boars and three stags with his own hand.[2] During this visit the marriage was arranged, and on the 10th of June, 1533, the contract was signed at Barcelona by the Emperor on the one hand, and the Chancellor of Milan, Count Taverna, and the ducal Chamberlain,

[1] Altmeyer, " Relations," etc., 298; Sanuto, lv. 389, 414.
[2] Sanuto, lvii. 610, 637.

Count Tommaso Gallerati, on the other. Christina was to receive 100,000 ducats out of the sum due to the Emperor, as her dowry, and in the event of Dorothea succeeding to the throne of Denmark another 100,000 was to be settled on her. Hawkins, the English Ambassador, who wrote home from Barcelona to announce the conclusion of the marriage, remarked that the Milanese had left well pleased, but that the Duke was somewhat to be pitied, since he was only to have the younger sister, and no fortune with her. " Dower getteth he none."[1]

In spite of this drawback, the Milanese received the news with great rejoicing, and any regret which they might have felt at the substitution of the younger for the elder sister was dispelled by the Spaniards in the Emperor's suite, who informed the Duke's Ambassadors that Christina was taller and far more beautiful than Dorothea. Francesco himself wrote to an old friend in Cremona, Giorgio Guazzo, saying that he would lose no time in telling him of his great good fortune in winning so high-born and attractive a young lady for his bride.[2] At the same time he agreed with the Emperor to send Count Massimiliano Stampa, his intimate friend, to the Netherlands, to wed the Princess in his name, and bring her to Milan that autumn. Meanwhile the news of the marriage was received with much less satisfaction in the Low Countries. Mary had taken the motherless children to her heart, and was especially attached to Christina, who resembled her in character and tastes. She inherited the family passion for riding and hunting, and combined her aunt's intelligence and ability with

---

[1] State Papers, Record Office, vii. 465.
[2] M. Sanuto, lvii. 157; A. Campo, " Storia di Cremona," 107.

her mother's sweetness of disposition. The idea of marrying this charming child of eleven to a half-paralyzed invalid old enough to be her father was repulsive, and Mary did not hesitate to protest against the Emperor's decision with characteristic frankness.

" MONSEIGNEUR," she wrote to Charles on the 25th of August, " I have received Your Majesty's letters with the copy of the treaty which you have been pleased to make between our niece, Madame Chrétienne, and the Duke of Milan, on which point I must once for all relieve my conscience. I will at least show you the difficulties which to my mind lie in the way, so that Your Majesty may consider if any remedy can be devised before the matter is finally arranged. As for our said niece, I have no doubt that she will agree to whatever you please to wish, since she regards you as her lord and father, in whom she places absolute trust, and is ready to obey you as your very humble daughter and slave. The child is so good and willing there will be no need for any persuasion on my part, either as regards the Count's coming or anything else that you may please to command; but on the other hand, Monseigneur, since the words of the treaty clearly show that the marriage is to be consummated immediately, and she will have to take her departure without delay, I must point out that she is not yet old enough for this, being only eleven years and a half, and I hold that it would be contrary to the laws of God and reason to marry her at so tender an age. She is still quite a child, and, whatever may be the custom in yonder country, you are exposing her to the risk of bearing a child at this tender age, and of losing both her own life and that of her issue. Monseigneur, I am saying more than I ought to say, and speaking with a freedom which I can only beg you to forgive, because both my conscience and the love which I bear the child constrain me to write thus. On the other hand, seeing that this treaty requires the two sisters to make certain promises, I do not think that she is old enough to enter into these engagements, while her sister, although turned twelve, is very young of her age, and should hardly make these promises without the consent of her father, who is still living. I know that I am meddling with other people's business by writing to you of those matters which are not, strictly speaking, my affair. But I feel that I must send you these warnings, not from any wish to prevent the marriage, if Your Majesty thinks it well, but in order to give you a reason for breaking it off, if any difficulties should arise. For it seems to me, that as people often try to discover the fifth wheel in the coach, where there is no reason to make any difficulty, it would be easy to find some excuse for embroiling matters, when so good a cause exists. I quite understand that it may not be easy to alter the treaty at this hour, but, since I had not the opportunity of speaking to you on the subject before, I feel it to be my duty to warn you of these things, and to remind you of the child's tender age, of which Your Majesty may not have been aware. However this may be, Monseigneur, I have written this to fulfil my duty to God, as well as to Your Majesty, my niece, and the whole world, and can only beg you not to take what I have said in bad part, or to believe that any other cause could have led me to speak so plainly ; and I take my Creator to witness that this is true, begging Him to give you health and long life, and grant your good and virtuous desires :

> " Your very humble and obedient sister,
> " MARIE.

"From Ghent, August 25, 1533."[1]

Charles answered the Queen's protest in the following brief letter, which showed that his mind was made up, and that he would allow no change in his plans :

" MADAME MY GOOD SISTER,
    " I have received your letter, and will only reply briefly, as I am writing to you at length on other matters by my secretary, and also because my niece's

[1] Lanz, ii. 87, 88.

affair is rather a matter for priests and lawyers than for me, and I have desired Granvelle to satisfy your objections. So I will only tell you that, as the children's father is more dead to them than if he had ceased to live, I signed the marriage treaty before I left Barcelona. As for the question of issue, I fear that the Duke's advanced years will prove a greater barrier than my niece's tender youth. I am sure that you will act in accordance with my wishes, and I beg you to do this once more.

"From Monzone, September 11, 1533."[1]

There was clearly nothing more to be said; but Mary had secretly determined, whatever happened, not to allow the actual marriage to take place until the following year, and in the end she had her way.

II.

When the Emperor wrote this letter to his sister, Count Massimiliano had already started on his journey. He left Milan on the eve of St. Bartholomew, taking Count Francesco Sfondrati of Cremona and Pier Francesco Bottigella of Pavia with him, and travelled by Trent and Spires to Louvain, where he arrived on the 12th of September. The next day he was conducted to Ghent by Monsieur de Courrières, the Captain of the Archers' Guard, and met at the palace gates by Monsieur de Molembais, the Queen's Grand Falconer, who informed him that Her Majesty was laid up, owing to a slight accident out hunting, and could not receive him at present. After many delays, Stampa at length succeeded in obtaining an audience, and begged the Queen earnestly to satisfy his master's impatience, and allow the marriage to

[1] Lanz, ii. 89.

be concluded without delay. Mary replied very civilly
that, since this was Cæsar's will, she would certainly
put no obstacle in the way, but explained that affairs
of State compelled her to visit certain frontier towns,
and begged the Count to await her return to Brussels.
She then sent for the Princesses, and Stampa was
presented and allowed to kiss their hands. But, as he
only saw them for five minutes, all he could tell his
master was that Christina seemed very bright and
lively, and was much better-looking than her sister.[1]

In spite of the courtesy with which he was enter-
tained by De Courrières and the Duke of Aerschot,
Stampa clearly saw that it was Mary's intention to
delay the marriage as long as possible, and began to
despair of ever attaining his object. Fortunately,
by the end of the week the Emperor's confidential
Chamberlain, Louis de Praet, arrived at Ghent.
De Praet had been Ambassador in England and
France, and was now sent from Spain to represent
His Majesty at the wedding and escort the bride to
Milan. When he had seen Stampa's copy of the
Treaty of Barcelona, he advised him to join the Queen
at Lille and deliver his credentials. Here the Count
accordingly presented himself on the 18th of September, and was graciously received by Mary, who
assured him that the affair which lay so near his
heart would shortly be arranged. He was conducted into a room where he found the Princesses
and their governess, Madame de Fiennes, and conversed with them for half an hour. When the Queen
rose to attend vespers, she touched the Count's sleeve
and made him walk at her side as far as the chapel,
and thanked him for the fine horse which the Duke

[1] Archivio di Stato, Milan, Carteggio Diplomatico, 1533.

had sent her, telling him how fond she was of hunting. The next day Stampa was invited to supper, and afterwards ventured to ask if he might see the Princesses dance. To this request the Queen gave her consent. The flutes and tambourines struck up a merry tune, and the Princesses danced first a *ballo al francese*, then a *branle*, and a variety of French and German dances, in which the gentlemen and ladies-in-waiting took part. The Count was about to take his leave, since the hour was already late, when De Praet told him he must first see the Princesses dance a *ballo all'italiano*, upon which the two sisters rose and, joining hands, danced an Italian ballet with charming grace. The Ambassador was delighted, and wrote to tell his master what a favourable impression Christina had made upon him and his companions:

" She is hardly shorter than her sister, and much handsomer and more graceful, and is indeed as well built and attractive a maiden as you could wish to see. God grant this may lead to a happy marriage !"[1]

The next morning business began in good earnest. Prolonged negotiations were held between Stampa and the Queen's Councillors—Aerschot, De Praet, and other nobles—and the rights of the Princess Dorothea and the condition of Denmark were fully discussed. While the Count was at dinner, De Praet came in, and, to his surprise, informed him that Her Majesty wished the wedding to be celebrated on the following Sunday, the 28th of September. The Count asked nothing better, and hastened to send the good news to Milan.

On Saturday evening Christina signed the marriage

[1] Archivio di Stato, Milano, Carteggio Diplomatico, 1533.

contract before an illustrious assembly in a hall of
the palace at Lille, which was hung with black and
gold damask for the occasion, and between four and
five on Sunday afternoon the wedding was solemnized
by the Bishop of Tournay in the chapel. Count
Massimiliano, gallantly arrayed in cloth of gold, was
conducted to the altar by De Praet and the great
officers of State; the violins and drums sounded, and
the bridal procession entered, the Queen leading her
niece by the hand. " As the Bishop placed the
nuptial ring on the bride's finger," wrote Stampa to
his lord, " she received it with evident pleasure, and
all the Court displayed great satisfaction."

When the ceremony was over, the bride retired, and
Stampa spent some time in conversation with the
Queen, vainly endeavouring to persuade her to fix
a date for the Duchess's journey. But on this point
Mary was inflexible. De Praet, who visited him the
next day, explained that the Queen could not allow
this youthful lady to be exposed to the perils and
fatigue of so long a journey in winter, and that her
departure must therefore be put off till the following
spring. This was a grievous disappointment to the
Count, who knew how anxious the Duke was to see
his wife. But he had to accept the situation, and
could only try and console his master by repeating
the Queen's assurances of good-will and affection.

She even begged the Count to join her in a hunting
expedition at Brussels in the following week. But
this Stampa firmly declined, saying that he must
return to Milan without delay. On the same evening
he had the honour of a parting interview with the
Duchess, and presented her with a fine diamond
and ruby ring and a length of costly brocade in her

lord's name. Christina's eyes sparkled with delight at the sight of these gifts, and she thanked Count Massimiliano with a warmth which captivated him. Then he took leave of the Queen, who started at break of day in torrents of rain, to hunt on her way to Brussels, leaving the Princesses to return by Tournay. The Count himself went to Antwerp to raise money for his journey, and despatched a messenger to Milan with full accounts of the wedding.

" All this Court and the Queen herself," he wrote, " are delighted with this happy event. And Your Excellency may rejoice with good reason, and may rest assured that you have the fairest, most charming and gallant bride that any man could desire."[1]

These despatches reached Milan on the 13th of October, and were received with acclamation. Guns were fired from the Castello, the bells of all the churches were rung, and the Senate went in solemn procession to give thanks to God in the Duomo. " It was indeed good tidings of great joy," wrote the chronicler Burigozzo, " and such rejoicing had not been known in Milan for many years."[2] Francesco's own satisfaction was considerably diminished by hearing that his bride was not to set out on her journey until the following February. But he took the Queen's decision in good part, and wrote to express his eternal gratitude to her and Cæsar for giving him their niece.

" However anxious I naturally am to have my wife with me," he added, " I recognize the gravity of the reasons which have made you put off her journey to a more convenient season, and think, as you say, this should take place next February."[3]

---

[1] Carteggio Diplomatico, 1533, Archivio di Stato, Milan.

[2] G. M. Burigozzo, " Cronaca Milanese," 1500-1544, p. 516 : "Archivio Storico Italiano," iii. (1842).

[3] Potenze Sovrane, 1533-34, Archivio di Stato, Milan.

The Duke sent this letter by a special messenger, and received in reply the following brief note in Italian from Christina:

" MOST ILLUSTRIOUS CONSORT,
    " It gave me great pleasure to hear of Your Excellency's good health from Messer Sasso, and I can assure you that my wish to join you is no less ardent than your own. But it is only reasonable that we should bow to the decision of the Most Serene Queen, who orders everything wisely and well. I will only add how sincerely I hope that you will keep well, and love me as much as I love you.
        " Your Excellency's most loving consort,
                " CHRISTIERNA, DUCHESS OF MILAN.
    "From Brussels, November 4, 1533."[1]

On the last day of January, 1534, the Duke held a Council of State to consider the best means of raising the £100,000 due to Cæsar, which was assigned to his niece for dower, and the citizens agreed cheerfully to new taxes on grain and wine in order to provide the necessary amount. But it was not until the 31st of March that Francesco was able to issue a proclamation informing the Milanese that his wife had started on her journey. The Duchess, he told them, would be among them by the end of April, and he could count on his loyal subjects to receive her with due honour; but, knowing as he did their poverty, he begged that the customary wedding gift should be omitted. The Milanese responded with enthusiasm to their Duke's appeal, and prepared to give his bride a worthy reception. Their example was followed by the citizens of Novara, Vigevano, and the other towns along the route between Savoy and Milan. The roads, which were said to be

---

[1] Autografi di Principi Sforza, Archivio di Stato, Milan.

the worst in the duchy, were mended, triumphal
arches were erected, and lodgings were prepared for
her reception. The following quaintly-worded memorandum was drawn up by Councillor Pier Francesco
Bottigella, to whom these arrangements were entrusted :

" (1) Mend the roads and clean the streets through
which the Lady Duchess will pass, and hang the
walls with tapestries and carpets, the largest and
widest that you can find. (2) Paint her arms on all
the gates through which she passes. (3) Provide a
baldacchino to be carried over her head. (4) See
that lodgings are prepared for her at Novara, either
in the Bishop's palace or in the ducal hunting-lodge,
and let these be cleansed and decorated. (5) Prepare
rooms in the town for the Duchess's household.
(6) Let this also be done in the Castello Vecchio at
Vigevano. (7) Desire that no gifts of any kind
should be made to the Duchess at Novara, Vigevano,
or any other place."[1]

When these instructions had been duly carried out,
Bottigella, who had accompanied Stampa on his
mission to the Low Countries, and was already
acquainted with the chief members of the Duchess's
suite, set out for Chambéry by the Duke's orders, to
meet the bride on the frontiers of Savoy and escort
her across the Alps.

III.

Christina had now completed her twelfth year,
and Mary of Hungary could no longer invent any
excuse to delay her journey to Milan. The bridal
party finally set out on the 11th of March, conducted
by Monseigneur de Praet, the Emperor's representa-

---

[1] Potenze Sovrane, Archivio di Stato, Milan.

tive, and Camillo Ghilino, the Duke's Ambassador, with an escort of 130 horse. Madame de Souvastre, one of Maximilian's illegitimate daughters, whose husband had been one of the late Regent's confidential servants, was appointed mistress of the Duchess's household, which consisted of six maids of honour, six waiting-women, four pages, and ten gentlemen. Christina herself rode in a black velvet litter, drawn by four horses and attended by six footmen, and her ladies travelled in similar fashion, followed by twenty mules and three waggons with the baggage. Mary had taken care that the bride's trousseau was worthy of a daughter of the imperial house, and the chests were filled with sumptuous robes of cloth of gold and silver, of silk, satin, and velvet, costly furs, jewels and pearls, together with furniture and plate for her table and chapel, and liveries and trappings for her servants and horses. The Duchess's own lackeys and all the gentlemen in attendance wore coats and doublets of black velvet, and the other servants, we learn from John Hackett, the English Ambassador at Brussels, were clad in suits of "medley grey," trimmed with velvet, all "very well accounted."[1] The imposing cortège travelled by slow stages through the friendly duchy of Lorraine and across the plains of the imperial county of Burgundy, taking journeys of twelve or fifteen miles a day, until, on the 12th of April, it halted at Chambéry, the frontier town of Savoy. The reigning Duke, Charles III., was the Emperor's brother-in-law and stanch ally, and the travellers were hospitably entertained in his ancestral castle on the heights. Here Bottigella was introduced into

[1] State Papers, Record Office, vii. 545.

Christina's presence by his old friend Camillo Ghilino, and found her on the way to attend Mass in the castle chapel.

" The Duchess," wrote the Councillor to his lord, " received me in the most friendly manner, and asked eagerly after you, and was especially anxious to know where you were now. I told her that you were at Vigevano, but would shortly return to Milan, to prepare for her arrival. Mass was just beginning, so I had to take my leave, but hope for another opportunity of conversing with her before long, and can see how eager she is to ask a hundred questions. She is very well and lively, and does not seem any the worse for the long journey. She has grown a great deal since I saw her last September, and is as beautiful as the sun. M. de Praet hopes to reach Turin in seven days, and will start again to-morrow."[1]

The most arduous part of the journey now lay before the travellers. Leaving Chambéry, they penetrated into the heart of the Alps, through the narrow gorge of the Isère, between precipitous ravines with castles crowning the rocks on either side, until they reached the impregnable fortress of Montmélian, the ancient bulwark of Savoy, which had resisted all the assaults of the French. After spending the night here, they rode up the green pastures and pine-clad slopes of S. Jean de Maurienne, and began the ascent of the Mont Cenis, over " those troublesome and horrid ways " of which English travellers complained so bitterly, where loose stones and tumbled rocks made riding almost impossible. " These ways, indeed," wrote Coryat, " are the worst I ever travelled in my life, so much so that the roads of Savoy may be proverbially spoken of as the owls of Athens, the pears of Calabria, or the quails of Delos."[2] On the

[1] Potenze Sovrane, Archivio di Stato, Milan.
[2] T. Coryat, " Crudities," i. 215; "Hardwick Papers," i. 85.

summit of the pass De Praet and his companions saw with interest the Chapel of Our Lady of the Snows, where a few years before the famous Constable of Bourbon had offered up his sword on the altar of the Virgin, as he led the imperial armies across the Alps. Then they came down into a smiling green valley, with walnut woods and rushing streams, and saw the medieval towers of Susa at their feet. Here they were met by the Emperor's Ambassador at the Court of Savoy, who came to pay his respects to the Duchess, bringing with him two elegant litters of crimson brocade, sent by Charles's sister-in-law, Beatrix of Portugal, Duchess of Savoy, for Christina's use. At Rivoli, two stages farther on, fifty Councillors from Turin, with the Bishop of Vercelli at their head, appeared on horseback to escort the Duchess to the city gates. Here Christina mounted her horse and rode up the steep ascent to the citadel, with De Praet walking at her side. The beautiful Duchess Beatrix herself awaited her guest at the castle gates, and, embracing Christina affectionately, led her by the hand up the grand staircase into the best suite of rooms in the palace. The travellers spent two days in these comfortable quarters, and enjoyed the brief interval of rest, although the Duchess, as Bottigella was careful to tell the Duke, seemed the least tired of the whole party, and was in blooming health and high spirits.

On the following Sunday Christina rode into Novara, on a brilliant spring morning, and was lodged in the Bishop's palace, and received with the greatest enthusiasm by her lord's subjects. At Vigevano, the birthplace and favourite home of Lodovico Sforza, the nobles, with Massimiliano Stampa at their head, rode out to welcome the Duke's bride, and carried a rich baldacchino over her head. Nevertheless, halfway between Novara and Vigevano, De Praet complained to the Count that neither the reception of the Duchess nor the rooms prepared for her were sufficiently honourable—" in fact, he found fault with everything." The Count expressed some surprise, since both the Emperor Maximilian and Charles V. himself had stayed at Vigevano, and the latter had greatly admired the buildings and gardens laid out by Bramante and Leonardo. But, to pacify the exacting priest, Stampa proposed that the Duchess should only take her *déjeuner* in the castle, and push on to his own villa of Cussago, where she was to spend some days before entering Milan. But De Praet replied that the Duchess, not being yet accustomed to this climate, felt the heat of the sun, and must on no account ride any farther till evening. So all the Count could do was to send Bottigella on to see that the Castello was adorned with wreaths of flowers and verdure, and that a good bed was prepared for the Duchess.[1]

At least, De Praet could find nothing to grumble at in Stampa's country-house at Cussago, the ducal palace and hunting-grounds which had been given him by Francesco II. in reward for his unwavering loyalty. The beauty of the spot, the delicious gardens with their sunny lawns and sparkling fountains, their rose and myrtle bowers, their bosquets and running streams, enchanted the travellers from the north. The villa had been adorned with frescoes and marble doorways by the best Lombard masters of the Moro's Court, and was once the favourite country-house of Beatrice d'Este, the present Duke's

[1] Potenze Sovrane, Archivio di Stato, Milan.

mother, who often rode out from Milan to hunt in the forests of the Brianza or play at ball on the terraces. Now her son's child-bride saw these green lawns in all the loveliness of early summer, and the frescoed halls rang once more to the sound of mirth and laughter. Music and dancing enlivened the days, and a drama—*La Sposa Sagace*—was acted one evening to amuse Christina. At nightfall the guns of the Castello, firing salutes in her honour, were heard in the distance, and the bonfires on the towers of Milan lit up the evening sky with crimson glow. Count Massimiliano took care that nothing should be lacking to the enjoyment of the Duchess, and begged De Praet to attend to her comfort in every particular, but, as he told the Duke, it was not always easy to satisfy these gentlemen.

One day Christina and her ladies received a visit from the great Captain Antonio de Leyva, the Duke's old enemy, who now came, cap in hand, to pay homage to the Emperor's niece. Another day there was a still greater stir at the villa, for the Duke himself appeared unexpectedly, having ridden out almost alone, to pay a surprise visit to his bride. The first sight of her future lord must have given Christina a shock, and her ladies whispered to each other that this wan, grey-haired man, who could not walk without the help of a stick, was hardly a fit match for their fair young Princess. But Francesco's chivalrous courtesy and gentleness went far to atone for his physical defects, and nothing could exceed the kindness which he showed his youthful bride. After all, she was but a child, and the sight of this new world that was laid at her feet with all its beauties and treasures was enough to dazzle her eyes and please her innocent fancy.

On Sunday, the 3rd of May, the Duchess made her state entry into Milan. Early in the afternoon she rode in her litter to S. Eustorgio, the Dominican convent outside the Ticino gate, where she was received by the Duke's half-brother, Giovanni Paolo Sforza, mounted on a superb charger, and attended by all his kinsmen, clad in white and gold. After paying her devotions at the marble shrine of S. Pietro Martive, the Prior and friars conducted her to partake of refreshments in the guests' hall, and receive the homage of the Bishop and clergy, of the magistrates and senators. At six o'clock, after vespers, the procession started from the Porta Ticinese. First came the armourers and their apprentices, in companies of 200, with coloured flags in their hands and plumes to match in their caps. One troop was in blue, the other in green. At the head of the first rode Alessandro Missaglia, a splendid figure, wearing a silver helmet and shining armour over his turquoise velvet vest, and mounted on a horse with richly damascened harness. The green troop was led by Girolamo Negriolo, the other famous Milanese armourer. Then came 300 archers in pale blue silk, and six bands of trumpeters and drummers, followed by a great company of the noblest gentlemen of Milan, all clad in white, with flowing plumes in their hats and lances in their hands, riding horses draped with silver brocade. Visconti, Trivulzio, Borromeo, Somaglia— all the proudest names of Milan were there, and in the rear rode the veteran Antonio de Leyva, with the Emperor's representative, De Praet, at his side.

Immediately behind them, under a white and gold velvet baldacchino, borne by the doctors of the University, rode the bride, mounted on a white horse with glittering trappings, and wearing a rich white brocade robe and a long veil over her flowing hair— " a vision more divine than human," exclaims the chronicler who witnessed the sight; " only," he adds in an undertone, " she is still very young." At the sight of the lovely child the multitude broke into shouts of joy, and the clashing of bells, the blare of trumpets, and sound of guns, welcomed the coming of the Duchess. Close behind her rode Cardinal Ercole Gonzaga, the Duke's cousin, and on either side a guard of twelve noble youths, with white ostrich feathers in their caps, so that Her Excellency " appeared to be surrounded with a forest of waving plumes." In the rear came Madame de Souvastre and her ladies in litters, followed by a crowd of senators, bishops, and magistrates.

Six triumphal arches, adorned with statues and paintings, lined the route. Peace with her olive-branch, Plenty with the cornucopia, Prosperity bearing a caduceus, Joy crowned with flowers, welcomed the bride in turn. Everywhere the imperial eagles were seen together with the Sforza arms, and countless mottoes with courtly allusions to the golden age that had at length dawned for distracted Milan. " Thy coming, O Christina, confirms the peace of Italy !" On the piazza of the Duomo, a pageant of the Seasons greeted her—Spring with arms full of roses, Summer laden with ripe ears of corn, Autumn bearing purple grapes, and Winter wrapt in snowy fur; while Minerva was seen closing the doors of the Temple of Janus, and Juno and Hymen, with outstretched arms, hailed Francesco, the son of the great Lodovico, and Christina, the daughter of Dacia and Austria. At the steps of

the Duomo the long procession halted.   Cardinal
Gonzaga helped the Duchess to alight, and led her to
the altar, where she knelt in silent prayer, kissed the
pax held up to her by the Archbishop, and received
his benediction.   The walls of the long nave were
hung with tapestries, and the choir draped with cloth
of gold and adorned with statues of the patron saints
of Milan.   " When you entered the doors," wrote
the chronicler, " you seemed to be in Paradise."

Then the Duchess mounted her horse again, and
the procession passed up the Goldsmiths' Street to
the Castello.   Here the decorations were still more
sumptuous.   One imposing arch was adorned with
a painting of St. John leaning on the bosom of Christ,
copied from Leonardo's " Cenacolo " in the refectory of
S. Maria delle Grazie.   Another bore a figure of Christ
with the orb and sceptre, and the words " Mercy and
Truth have kissed each other."   On the piazza in
front of the Castello, a colossal fountain was
erected, and winged children spouted wine and
perfumed water.   The Castello itself had been elabor-
ately adorned.   The arms of Denmark and Milan were
carved in fine marble over the portals, the walls were
hung with blue draperies studded with golden stars
and wreathed with garlands of myrtle and ivy, and on
either side of the central doorway two giant warriors
leaning on clubs supported a tablet crowned with the
imperial eagles, and inscribed with the words: " The
wisest of Princes to-day weds the fairest of Virgins,
and brings us the promise of perpetual peace."[1]

[1] M. Guazzo, " Historie d'Italia," 272-275; P. Avenati, " Entrata Solemne di Cristina di Spagna "; MS. Continuazione della
Storia di Corio, O. 240 (Biblioteca Ambrosiana).

CHRISTINA, DUCHESS OF MILAN (1534)

(Oppenheimer Collection)

FRANCESCO SFORZA, DUKE OF MILAN (1534)

(British Museum)

To face p. 92

As the procession reached the gates of the Castello, a triumphant burst of martial music was sounded by the trumpeters on the topmost tower, and Count Massimiliano, the Castellan, presented the golden keys of the gates to the Duchess, on bended knee. Christina received them with a gracious smile, and, accepting his hand, alighted from her horse, amid the cheers of the populace, who, rushing in on all sides, seized the baldacchino, tore the costly brocade into ribbons, and divided the spoil. Meanwhile the Duke, leaning on a stick, received his wife with a deep reverence, and led her by the hand into the beautiful suite of rooms, hung with mulberry-coloured velvet and cloth of gold, which had been prepared for her use.[1] Cardinal Gonzaga and De Praet supped with the bride and bridegroom that evening, to the sweet melodies of the Duke's flutes and viols. The gates of the Castello were closed, enormous bonfires blazed on the walls, and rockets went up to heaven from the top of the great tower. Thousands of torches illumined the darkness, and the streets were thronged with gay crowds, who gladly took advantage of the Duke's permission and gave themselves up to mirth and revelry all night long. Long was that day remembered in Milan. Old men who could recall the reign of Lodovico, and had witnessed the coming of Beatrice and the marriage of Bianca, wept, and thanked God that they had lived to see this day. But their joy was destined to be of short duration.

[1] C. Magenta, " I Visconti e gli Sforza nel Castello di Pavia," i. 750; Nubilonio, " Cronaca di Vigevano," 131.

IV.

At six o'clock on the evening of the 4th of May the marriage of the Duke was finally celebrated in the hall of the Rocchetta, which was hung with cloth of gold beautifully decorated with garlands of flowers. Among the illustrious guests present were the Cardinal of Mantua, the Legate Caracciolo, Antonio de Leyva, and the chief nobles and senators. The Bishops of Modena and Vigevano chanted the nuptial Mass, and Monseigneur de Praet delivered a lengthy oration, which sorely tried the patience of his hearers. No sooner had he uttered the last words than the Duke took the bride's hand, and brought the ceremony to an abrupt conclusion by leading her into the banquet-hall. There a supper of delicate viands, fruit, and wines, was prepared, and the guests were entertained with music and songs during the evening.[1]

Letters of congratulation now poured in from all the Courts of Europe. Christina's own relatives— Ferdinand and Anna, the King and Queen of Hungary and Bohemia, the King and Queen of Portugal, the Elector of Saxony and the Marquis of Brandenburg— all congratulated the Duchess on her safe arrival and happy marriage; while the Pope, the Doge of Venice, and other Italian Princes, sent the Duke cordial messages. One of the most interesting letters which the bridegroom received was an autograph epistle from his cousin, Bona Sforza, Queen of Poland, who would probably herself have been Duchess of Milan if Massimiliano Sforza had reigned longer. It had been the earnest wish of her widowed mother, Isabella of Aragon, to effect this union, and it was

[1] MS. Continuazione di Corio, O. 240 (Biblioteca Ambrosiana).

only after the French conquest of Milan in 1515 that her daughter became the wife of King Sigismund. From her distant home Bona kept up an active correspondence with her Italian relatives, and now sent Francesco the following friendly letter:

" DEAREST AND MOST ILLUSTRIOUS COUSIN,
" I rejoice sincerely to hear that your most illustrious wife has reached Milan safely. I feel the greatest joy at your happy marriage, and trust that Heaven will send you a fine son. My husband and children join with me in wishing you every possible happiness.
" BONA, QUEEN.

" From Cracow, July 15, 1534." [1]

Another of Francesco's illustrious kinsfolk, Alfonso d'Este, Duke of Ferrara, came to Milan in person to offer his congratulations to his nephew, although he preferred to remain incognito, and his name does not figure among the guests who were present at the wedding festivities. But Ferrarese chroniclers record that the Duke went to Milan on the 30th of April, to attend the wedding of Duke Francesco Sforza, who took for wife Madame Christierna, daughter of the King of Dacia, and returned home on the 6th of May.[2] Forty-four years before, Alfonso, then a boy of fourteen, had accompanied his sister Beatrice to Milan for her marriage, and escorted his own bride, Anna Sforza, back to Ferrara. Now his long and troubled life was drawing to a close, and he died a few months after this last journey to Milan, on the 31st of October, 1534. By his last will he left two of his best horses and a pair of falcons to his beloved nephew, the Duke of Milan.[3] Some writers have

---

[1] Autografi di Principi: Sforza, Archivio di Stato, Milan.
[2] F. Roddi, " Annali di Ferrara " (Harleian MSS. 3310).
[3] E. Gardiner, " A King of Court Poets," 355.

conjectured that Alfonso brought his favourite
painter, Titian, to Milan, and that the Venetian
master painted portraits of the Duke and Duchess
on this occasion.[1] No record of Titian's visit, however, has been discovered, and he probably painted
the portraits of Francesco and Christina from drawings sent to him at Venice.

Titian's friend, Pietro Aretino, was in constant
correspondence with Count Massimiliano Stampa,
who rewarded his literary efforts with gifts of gold
chains, velvet caps, and embroidered doublets. " I
shall be clad in your presents all through the summer
months," he wrote in a letter, signing himself, " Your
younger brother and devoted servant." Aretino
was not only profuse in thanks to this noble patron,
but sent him choice works of art, mirrors of Oriental
crystal, medals engraved by Anichino, and, best of
all, a little painting of the youthful Baptist clasping
a lamb, " so life-like that a sheep would bleat at the
sight of it." [2] The wily Venetian was exceedingly
anxious to ingratiate himself with the Duke of Milan,
and not only dedicated a " Paraphase " to him on
his marriage, but, according to Vasari, painted
portraits of both the Duke and Duchess. These
pictures were reproduced by Campo in the " History
of Cremona," which he published in 1585, while
Christina was still living. The portrait of Francesco
was at that time the property of the Milanese noble
Mario Amigone, while that of Christina hung in the
house of Don Antonio Lomboni, President of the
Magistrates.[3] This last portrait was afterwards sent
to Florence by order of the Grand-Duke Ferdinand,

[1] Crowe and Cavalcaselle, " Titian," i. 355.
[2] P. Aretino, " Lettere," i. 214.   [3] A. Campo, 107.

who married the Duchess's granddaughter, Christine of Lorraine.

" I send Your Highness," wrote Guido Mazzenta in January, 1604, " the portrait of the Most Serene Lady, Christina, Queen of Denmark, and grandmother of the Most Serene Grand-Duchess, painted by Titian, by order of Duke Francesco Sforza, when he brought her to Milan as his bride."[1]

Unfortunately, this precious portrait was afterwards sent to Madrid, where it is said to have perished in a fire. In Campo's engraving the youthful Duchess wears a jewelled cap and pearl necklace, with an ermine cape on her shoulders. Her serene air and thoughtful expression recall Holbein's famous picture, and give an impression of quiet happiness and content which agrees with all that we know of her short married life.

The change was great from Malines and Brussels, and Christina often missed her old playmates. But her simple, docile nature became easily accustomed to these new surroundings, and the affectionate little letters which she sent to her aunt and sister all breathe the same strain. " We are as happy and contented as possible," she writes to Dorothea ; and when Camillo Ghilino was starting for Germany, she sends a few words, at her lord's suggestion, to be forwarded to Flanders, just to tell her aunt how much she loves and thinks of her.[2]

Certainly, when we compare her lot with that of her mother, and remember the hardships and sorrows which the young Queen had to endure, Christina may well have counted herself fortunate. Her husband treated his child - wife with the greatest

[1] Gaye, " Carteggio," iii. 531.
[2] Autografi di Principi : Sforza, Archivio di Stato, Milan.

kindness. Her smallest wish was gratified, her tastes were consulted in every particular. The rooms which she occupied in the Rocchetta, where his mother, Duchess Beatrice, had lived, were hung with rich crimson velvet ; the walls of her bedroom were draped with pale blue silk; a new loggia was built, looking out on the gardens and moat waters. The breaches which French and Spanish guns had made in the walls were repaired, and the Castello resumed its old aspect. Three state carriages, lined with costly brocades and drawn by four horses draped with cloth of gold, were prepared by the Duke for his wife, and were first used by the Duchess on Ascension Day, when, ten days after her wedding, she made her first appearance in public. As she drove to the Duomo, followed by the Legate and Ambassadors, and escorted by a brilliant cavalcade of nobles, the streets were thronged with eager crowds, who greeted her with acclamation, and waited for hours to catch a sight of her face. On Corpus Christi, again, a few weeks later, the Duke and Duchess both came to see the long procession of Bishops and priests pass through the streets, bearing the host under a stately canopy from the Duomo to the ancient shrine of S. Ambrogio.

The popularity of the young Duchess soon became unbounded. Her tall figure, dark eyes, and fair hair, excited the admiration of all her subjects, while her frank and kindly manners won every heart. Although prices went up in Milan that year, and the tolls on corn and wine were doubled, the people paid these dues cheerfully, and, when they sat down to a scanty meal, remarked that they must pay for Her Excellency's dinner.[1]   Fortunately, by the end of the

---

[1] Burigozzo, 521.

year there was a considerable fall in prices, and a general sense of relief and security prevailed.

To the Duke himself, as well as to his people, the coming of the Duchess brought new life. For a time his failing health revived in the sunshine of her presence. He threw himself with energy into the task of beautifying Milan and completing the façade of the Duomo. At the same time he employed painters to decorate the Castello and Duomo of Vigevano, and an illuminated book of the Gospels, adorned with exquisite miniatures and bearing his arms and those of the Duchess, may still be seen in the Brera.

Hunting-parties were held for Christina's amusement both at Vigevano and in Count Massimiliano's woods at Cussago. Madame de Souvastre and most of the Duchess's Flemish attendants had returned to the Netherlands with De Praet, and Francesco took great pains to provide his wife with a congenial lady-in-waiting.. His choice fell on Francesca Paleologa, a lady of the noble house of Montferrat, and cousin of the newly-married Duchess of Mantua. Her husband, Constantine Comnenus, titular Prince of Macedonia, had served under the Pope and Emperor; and her daughter, Deianira, had lately married Count Gaspare Trivulzio, a former partisan of the French, who was now a loyal subject of the Duke. From this time the Princess of Macedonia became Christina's inseparable companion, and remained devotedly attached to the Duchess throughout her long life. At the same time Francesco appointed one of his secretaries, Benedetto da Corte of Pavia, to be master of the Duchess's household, and to teach her Italian, which she was soon able to speak and write fluently.

The Milanese archives contain several charming
little notes written in Christina's large, round hand
to the Duke during a brief visit which he paid to
Vigevano, for change of air, in the summer of 1535:

" MY LORD AND DEAREST HUSBAND,
        " I have received your dear letters, and rejoice
to hear of your welfare. This has been a great
comfort to me, but it will be a far greater pleasure to
see you again. I look forward to your return with
such impatience that a single hour seems as long
as a whole year. May God keep you safe and bring
you home again very soon, for I can enjoy nothing
without Your Excellency. I am very well, thank
God, and commend myself humbly to your good
graces. Signora Francesca is also well, and com-
mends herself to Your Highness.
                " Your very humble wife,
                        " CHRISTIERNA.
    " Milan, June 7, 1535.
    " The bearer of this letter has been very good to
me."

Francesco's health had lately given fresh cause for
anxiety. He suffered from catarrh and fever, and
was frequently confined to his bed. A Pavian Envoy
who had been promised an audience had to leave
the Castello without seeing His Excellency, and a
visit which he and the Duchess had intended to pay
to Pavia in the spring was put off, to the great disappointment of the loyal citizens. Now his absence
was prolonged owing to a fresh attack of illness, and
the young wife wrote again at the end of the month,
lamenting the delay and expressing the same impatience for his return:

" MY DEAREST HUSBAND,
        " I was delighted, as I always am, with your
dear letter of the 20th instant, but should have been

much better pleased to see you and enjoy the pleasure
of your presence, as I hoped to do by this time,
especially as these Signors assured me that your
absence would be short. But they were, it is plain,
quite wrong. However, I must be reasonable, and
if your prolonged absence is necessary I will not
complain. I thank you for your kind excuses and
explanations, but I will not thank you for saying that
I need not trouble to write to you with my own
hand, because this at least is labour well spent, and
I am only happy when I can talk with Your Excellency or write to you, now that I cannot enjoy your
company. I commend myself infinitely to your remembrance, and trust God may long preserve you,
and grant you a safe and speedy return.
            " Your very humble wife,
                             " CHRISTIERNA.
    " From Milan, June, 1535."[1]

But the warm-hearted young wife's wish remained
unfulfilled, and four months after these lines were
written Christina was a widow.

V.

The chief event of Christina's brief married life
was the marriage of her elder sister, the Princess of
Denmark. Dorothea was by this time an attractive
girl of fourteen, shorter and slighter than her sister,
and inferior to her in force of character, but full of
brightness and gaiety. She was very popular in her
old home at Malines, and often shot with a crossbow
at the meetings of the Guild of Archers. Several
marriages had been proposed for her, and King
James of Scotland had repeatedly asked for her
hand; but the Emperor hesitated to accept his
advances, from fear of offending King Francis,

[1] Autografi di Principi: Sforza, Archivio di Stato (see
Appendix I.).

whose daughter Magdalen had long been pledged to
this fickle monarch, while the difficulty of providing
a dower and outfit for another portionless niece, made
Mary reluctant to conclude a second marriage. But,
a few months after Christina's marriage, a new suitor
for Dorothea's hand came forward in the person of
the Count Palatine, who had vainly aspired to wed
both Eleanor of Austria and Mary of Hungary.
Frederic's loyal support of Charles's claims to the
imperial crown, and his gallant defence of Vienna
against the Turks, had been scurvily rewarded, and
hitherto all his attempts to find another bride had
been foiled. When, in 1526, after the King of
Portugal's death, he approached his old love, the
widowed Queen Eleanor, his advances were coldly
repelled ; and when he asked King Ferdinand for one
of his daughters, he was told that she was too young
for him. After Mary of Hungary's refusal, he left
the Imperial Court in anger, and told Charles V. that
he would take a French wife;[1] but Isabel of Navarre,
Margaret of Montferrat, and the King of Poland's
daughter, all eluded his efforts, and when he asked
for Mary Tudor's hand, King Henry told him that
he could not insult his good friend and cousin by
offering him a bride born out of wedlock.[2] Now Ferdinand, unwilling to lose so valuable an ally, suddenly
proposed that the Palatine should marry his niece
Dorothea, saying that both he and Charles would
rejoice to see him reigning over the three northern
kingdoms. At first Frederic hesitated, saying that
he was a grey-headed man of fifty, little fitted to be
the husband of so young a lady, and had no wish
to reign over the turbulent Norsemen. Mary, how-

[1] Lanz, i. 419.   [2] H. Thomas, 310.

ever, welcomed her brother's proposal, regarding it
as a means of strengthening the Emperor's cause in
Northern Europe. In Denmark the succession of
Frederic's son Christian III. was disputed, and a
Hanseatic fleet had seized Copenhagen, while Christopher of Oldenburg, a cousin of the captive King,
had invaded Jutland. With the help of these allies
it might be possible for the Palatine to recover his
wife's inheritance. But the execution of this plan
was full of difficulties, as Prince John's old tutor,
the wise Archbishop of Lunden, told Charles V. in a
letter which he addressed to him in the autumn of
1534:

" MOST SACRED CÆSAR,—I know Denmark well, and
am convinced that the Danes will never recognize
Christian II. as their King. Count Christopher's
expedition will prove a mere flash in the pan, and
when he can no longer pay his men, the peasants,
who flocked to his banner at the sound of their old
King's name, will return to their hearths. Then the
nobles will have their revenge, and the proud Lübeck
citizens will seize Denmark and establish the Lutheran
religion in the name of Christopher or King Henry of
England, or any other Prince, as long as he is not
Your Majesty; and if they succeed, the trade of the
Low Countries will be ruined."[1]

The bait held out to the Palatine, however, proved
too alluring, and he easily fell a victim to the snare.
The Emperor sent him flattering messages by Hubert,
the faithful servant who has left us so delightful a
chronicle of his master's doings, and promised his
niece a dowry of 50,000 crowns. It was late on
New Year's Eve when Hubert reached his master's
house at Neumarkt, on his return from Spain, and
Frederic was already in bed; but he sent for him, and

[1] Altmeyer, " Relations Commerciales," etc., 317; Lanz, ii. 120.

bade him tell his news in three words. The messenger exclaimed joyfully: " I bring my lord a royal bride, a most gracious Kaiser, and a sufficient dowry." Upon which the Palatine thanked God, and bade Hubert go to the cellar and help himself to food and drink.[1]

One of Charles's most trusted Flemish servants, Nicholas de Marnol, was now sent to Milan, to obtain the consent of the Duke and Duchess to Dorothea's marriage. After a perilous journey over the Alps in snow and floods, Marnol reached Milan on the 10th of January, 1535, and received a cordial welcome. Francesco approved warmly of a union which would insure the Princess's happiness and serve to confirm the peace of Germany, but quite declined to accept the Emperor's suggestion that he should help to provide a pension for Christina's brother-in-law, saying that this was impossible, and that His Majesty would be the first to recognize the futility of making promises which cannot be kept.

After a short stay at Milan, Marnol went on to Vienna, and advised the Palatine to go to Spain himself if he wished to settle the matter. Frederic, always glad of an excuse for a journey, travelled by way of Brussels and France to Saragossa, and accompanied the Emperor to Barcelona, where Charles signed the marriage contract on the eve of sailing for Africa.

On the 18th of May, 1535, the marriage was solemnized at Brussels, and Frederic consented to leave his bride with her aunt until her outfit was completed. Queen Eleanor expressed the liveliest interest in her old lover's marriage, and insisted on

[1] H. Thomas, 328.

seeing Dorothea before she went to Germany. At
length the wedding-party reached Heidelberg, on the
8th of September, where the gallant bridegroom,
who, in Hubert's words, " loved to shine," rode out
in rich attire to meet his bride, and escorted her with
martial music and pomp worthy of a King's daughter
to the famous castle on the heights. The next day
the nuptial Mass was celebrated by the Bishop of
Spires, and a series of splendid entertainments were
given by Frederic's brother, the Elector Louis, after
which the Count took his bride to his own home at
Neumarkt, in the Upper Palatinate.[1]

" Now at length," wrote Hubert, " my lord thought
that he had attained a haven of rest, and found a
blessed end to all his troubles; but he was grievously
mistaken, and soon realized that he had embarked
on a new and tempestuous ocean."[2]

The splendid prospects of recovering his wife's
kingdom were destined to prove utterly fallacious,
and only involved him in heavy expenses and perpetual intrigues. The Emperor, as he soon discovered, " had no great affection for the enterprise
of Denmark,"[3] and before long Copenhagen surrendered, and Charles and Mary were compelled to
come to terms with Christian III. and acknowledge
his title. Fortunately, in all other respects his
marriage proved a happy one. Dorothea was greatly
beloved by her husband's family and subjects, and made
him a devoted wife, although, as Hubert soon found
out, she was as great a spendthrift as her lord, and confessed that she was never happy until she had spent
her last penny.[4] The very frivolity of her nature

[1] Henne, vi. 132. [2] H. Thomas, 350.
[3] Lanz, ii. 659. [4] H. Thomas, 350.

suited the volatile Count. She shared his love of adventure, and was always ready to accompany him on perilous journeys, to climb mountains or ford rivers, with the same unquenchable courage and gaiety of heart. Even when, in her anxiety to bear a child, she imitated the example of Frederic's mother, the old Countess Palatine, and went on pilgrimages and wore holy girdles, "this was done without any spirit of devotion, but with great mirth and laughter. And how little," adds the chronicler, "either pilgrimages or girdles profited her, we all know."[1]

VI.

Before the Palatine and his bride reached Heidelberg, Europe was thrilled by the news of the capture of Tunis, and the flight of the hated Barbarossa before his conqueror. It was the proudest moment of the Emperor's life. Twenty thousand Christian captives were released that day, and went home to spread the fame of their great deliverer throughout the civilized world. The news reached Milan on the 2nd of August, and was hailed with universal joy. *Te Deums* were chanted in the Duomo, bells were rung in all the churches, and the guns of the Castello boomed in honour of the great event. Camillo Ghilino was immediately sent by the Duke to congratulate the Emperor on his victory, and thank His Majesty once more for all the happiness which the generous gift of his niece had brought Francesco and his people.[2]

The late Pope, Clement VII., had already expressed his intention of rewarding Ghilino's services with a Cardinal's hat, and his successor, Paul III., would

---

[1] " Zimmer'sche Chronik," iv. 145. [2] Burigozzo, 525.

FREDERIC, COUNT PALATINE
Ascribed to A. Dürer (Darmstadt)

To face p. 106

probably have kept his promise, but the Ambassador fell ill in Sicily, and died at Palermo in September, to the Duke's great sorrow.[1]   Soon after receiving the news, Francesco himself fell ill of fever, and once more lost the use of his limbs.   All through October he grew steadily worse, and by the end of the month the people of Milan learnt that their beloved Prince was at the point of death.   On Monday, the Feast of All Saints, the public anxiety was at its height, and silent crowds waited all day at the gates of the Castello to hear the latest reports.   At length, early in the morning of All Souls' Day, they learnt that the last Sforza Duke was no more.   Christina watched by his bedside to the end, and wept bitterly, for, in the chronicler's words, " they had loved each other well."[2]   All Milan shared in her grief, and nothing but sobbing and wailing was heard in the streets.   Everyone lamented the good Duke, and grieved for the troubles and misery which his death would bring on the land.   But the city remained tranquil, and there was no tumult or rioting.   This was chiefly due to Stampa, who, by the Duke's last orders, took charge of the Duchess, and administered public affairs in her name, until instructions could be received from Cæsar.

A messenger was despatched without delay to the Emperor at Palermo, with letters from the Count and a touching little note from Christina, informing her uncle how her dear lord's weakness had gradually increased, until in the early morning he passed to a better life.   The dead Prince lay in state for three days in the ducal chapel, clad in robes of crimson velvet and ermine, on a bier surrounded by lighted

[1] G. Ghilino, " Annali di Alessandria," 141.
[2] Potenze Sovrane, Archivio di Stato.

tapers. But the funeral was put off till the 19th of November, in order, writes the chronicler, to give the people time to show the love they bore their lamented master, and also because of the difficulty of obtaining sufficient black cloth to drape the walls of the Castello and put the Court in mourning. It was a sad time for the young widow. During three weeks not a ray of light was allowed to penetrate the gloom of the funereal hall where she sat with her ladies, while solemn requiems and Masses were chanted in the chapel.

It had been Francesco's wish to sleep with his parents in the Church of S. Maria delle Grazie, where the effigies of Lodovico and his lost Beatrice had been carved in marble. But when this became known there was a general outcry. The people would not allow their beloved Duke to be buried anywhere but in the Duomo with the great Francesco and the other Sforza Princes. So it was decided only to bury the Duke's heart in the Dominican church. His body was laid in a leaden casket covered with black velvet, and a wax effigy, wearing the ducal crown and robes, was exposed to public view.

Late on Friday, the 19th of November, an imposing funeral procession passed from the Castello to the Duomo, through the same streets which, only eighteen months before, had been decked in festive array to receive the late Duke's bride. First came the Bishops and clergy with candles and crosses, then the senators, magistrates, and nobles, wearing long black mantles and hoods. After them gentlemen bearing the ducal standard, cap, and baton, and Francesco's sword and helmet, and what moved the spectators more than all, the white mule which he had ridden daily, led by four pages, " looking just as it did when His Excellency was alive, only that the saddle was empty." Then the bier was carried past, under a gold canopy, and the wax effigy of the dead man, was seen clad in gold brocade and ermine, with a vest of crimson velvet and red shoes and stockings. Immediately behind rode the chief mourner, Giovanni Paolo Sforza, followed by Antonio de Leyva, the Imperial and Venetian Ambassadors, the Chancellor Taverna, Count Massimiliano Stampa, and the chief Ministers and officials. After them came a vast multitude of poor, all in mourning, bearing lighted tapers, and weeping as they went. A catafalque, surrounded with burning torches, had been erected in the centre of the Duomo, and here, under a canopy of black velvet, the Duke's effigy was laid on a couch of gold brocade, with his sword at his side and the ducal cap and baton at his feet—" a thing," says the chronicler, " truly marvellous to see."[1]

The next morning the funeral rites were celebrated in the presence of an immense concourse of people, and a Latin oration was delivered by Messer Gualtiero di Corbetta. During three days requiems were chanted at every altar in the Duomo, and the great bell, which had never been rung before, was tolled for the space of three hours, accompanied by all the bells of the other churches in Milan. " And there was no one with heart so hard that he was not moved to tears that day," writes Burigozzo, the chronicler who was a living witness of the love which the citizens bore to their dead Duke.[2] At the end of the week the casket containing Francesco's remains was finally laid in a richly carved sarcophagus, which had been

[1] Burigozzo, 525   [2] *Ibid.*, 529.

originally intended to receive the ashes of Gaston de
Foix, the victor of Ravenna, and which was now
placed against the wall of the choir, " for a perpetual
memorial in the sight of all Milan."[1]

No one loved the Duke better and lamented his
loss more truly than Count Massimiliano Stampa, and
Pietro Aretino, who realized this, condoled with his
noble friend, and at the same time paid an eloquent
tribute to the dead Prince, in the following letter :

" The Duke is dead, and I feel that this sad event
has not only taken away all your happiness, but part
of your own soul. I know the close intimacy in
which you lived, nourished in your infancy at the
same breast, and bound together in one heart and
soul. But you must take comfort, remembering that
His Excellency may well be called fortunate in his
end. His wanderings began when he was barely six
years old, and he was driven into exile before he
was old enough to remember his native land. After
so many wars and labours, after experiencing famine
and sickness himself, and seeing the cruel misery and
affliction endured by his subjects, he lived to see
perfect tranquillity restored in his dominions, and
to enjoy the passionate affection of all Milan. Now,
secure in the friendship of Cæsar and the love of Italy,
he has given back his spirit to God who gave it.
Rejoice, therefore, and render praise and glory to
Francesco Sforza's name, because by his wisdom and
virtue he conquered fortune, and has died a Prince
on his throne, reigning in peace and happiness over
his native land. So, my dear lord, I beg you dry
your tears, and meet those who love you as I do
with a serene brow. The fame of your learning
and greatness is known everywhere. Rise above the
blows of fate, and console yourself with the thought
of your Duke's blessed end. There lies His Excellency's corpse. Give it honourable burial, and I
meanwhile will not cease to celebrate him dead and
you who are alive."[2]

[1] M. Guazzo, 312.   [2] P. Aretino, " Lettere," i. 43.

BOOK V

THE WIDOW OF MILAN

1535—1538

I.

CHRISTINA'S short married life was over. At the end of eighteen months she found herself a widow, before she had completed her fourteenth year. But the brief interval which had elapsed since she left Flanders had sufficed to turn the child into a woman. From the moment of the Duke's death, her good sense and discretion won golden opinions from the grey-headed statesmen around her. The senators and Ambassadors, the deputies from Pavia and the other Lombard cities, who came to offer their condolences, were deeply moved at the sight of this Princess, whose heavy mourning and widow's weeds contrasted strangely with her extreme youth. The dignity and grace of her bearing charmed them still more, and all the Milanese asked was to keep their Duchess among them. By the terms of the late Duke's investiture, if he died without children, the duchy of Milan was to revert to the Emperor, but the city of Tortona was settled on the Duchess. By Francesco's will the town and Castello of Vigevano, which he had done so much to beautify, were also bequeathed to her. Immediately after the Duke's funeral, in obedience to his dying lord's order, Stampa hoisted the imperial standard on the Castello of Milan, but refused to allow Antonio de Leyva to take possession of the citadel until he received orders from Cæsar himself. This was faithfully reported to the Emperor by Christina, who gave her uncle a full account of the steps which she had taken to administer affairs as her lord's representative, adding:

" If I have failed in any part of my duty or done anything contrary to Your Majesty's wishes, I beg you to excuse my ignorance, assuring you that I have acted by the advice of my late husband's Councillors, and with no regard to my own interests, but with the sole object of promoting Your Majesty's honour and service, and remain
" Your very humble and obedient servant,
" CHRÉTIENNE.
" November 20, 1535."[1]

The messenger whom Stampa sent to Palermo on the day of the Duke's death missed the Emperor, who had already left for Messina, and the news did not reach him until he had landed in Calabria, on his way to Naples. It was not till the 27th of November that a horseman bearing letters from Cæsar arrived in Milan. Here intense anxiety prevailed among all classes, and the Spaniards were as much hated as the Duke and Duchess had been beloved. Accordingly, the relief was great when it became known that, although Signor Antonio de Leyva was appointed Governor-General, Stampa was to retain his post as Castellan, and the Duchess was to remain in the Castello.

" The Duchess remains Duchess," wrote the chronicler, " and all the other officials retain their places. Above all, Count Massimiliano keeps his office, and the city is perfectly quiet."[2]

---

[1] Potenze Sovrane, 1535, Archivio di Stato.   [2] Burigozzo, 528.

Stampa now made a last effort to maintain the independence of Milan. He proposed that the widowed Duchess should be given in marriage to the Duke of Savoy's eldest son, Louis, a Prince of her own age, who was being educated at his imperial uncle's Court. A petition to this effect, signed by Chancellor Taverna and all the leading senators, was addressed to the Emperor, and Giovanni Paolo Sforza was sent to Rome to meet His Majesty and obtain the Pope's support.

" Gian Paolo Sforza and Taverna," wrote the Venetian Envoy, Lorenzo Bragadin, " have begged Cæsar to give the hand of his niece, the widow, to the Duke of Savoy's son, and this is the wish of all the people of Milan."[1]

Unfortunately, Giovanni Paolo fell ill on the journey, and breathed his last in a village of the Apennines, and before Charles left Naples he heard that the promising young Prince of Piedmont had died on Christmas Day at Madrid. His brother, Emanuel Philibert, was a child of seven, and although his ambitious mother, Duchess Beatrix, hastened to put forward his claim, nothing more was heard of the scheme.

By this time another marriage for Christina was being seriously discussed at the Imperial Court. Even before the Duke's death, the French King had done his best to provoke a quarrel with him, and had begun to make active preparations for war. Hardly had Francesco breathed his last, than he openly renewed his old claim to Milan, and sent an Ambassador to the Emperor at Naples, demanding the duchy for his second son, Henry, Duke of Orleans, the husband

[1] G. de Leva, " Storia Documentata di Carlo V.," etc., iii. 152.

of Catherine de' Medici. This plan, which would have made the French supreme in North Italy, could not be entertained for a moment, but Charles, in his anxiety to avoid war, was ready to accept almost any other alternative. When his sister Eleanor implored him to agree to her husband's proposal, and, by way of cementing the alliance, give " the little widow of Milan" in marriage to the King's third son, the Duke of Angoulême, he replied that he would gladly treat of the proposed marriage, but only on condition that Angoulême, not Orleans, was put in possession of Milan.

The union of the French Prince with Christina now became the subject of prolonged negotiations between the two Courts. The Imperial Chancellor, Granvelle, drew up a long and careful memorandum, dwelling on the obvious advantages of the scheme, on the virtues and charms of the young Duchess, on her large dowry and great popularity in Milan, and Charles told Francis plainly that he would agree to no scheme by which the widowed Duchess was removed from the State, " where she was so much beloved and honoured, and where the people placed all their hopes of tranquillity in her presence." One great object of these negotiations, he wrote, " is to find a noble and suitable husband for our niece, the Widow of Milan, who is to us almost a daughter, and who has always shown herself so discreet and so obedient to our wishes."[1]

Both the Pope and the Venetians supported this scheme as the best means of avoiding war and preserving the independence of Milan. At the same time Pope Paul did not fail to put in a plea for his

---

[1] Granvelle, " Papiers d'État," ii. 407, 446, 435.

own kinsman, the son of his niece Cecilia Farnese, and Count Bosio Sforza, a descendant of Francesco I.'s half-brother. Bosio had been a loyal supporter of the late Duke, but died soon after Christina's marriage, leaving a son of fifteen, who was brought up at the Court of Milan. The Pope himself addressed a grateful letter to Christina, thanking her for the kindness which she had shown the boy, and throwing out a hint that a marriage with her young Sforza cousin might be possible. Another husband whom Granvelle proposed for her was Duke Alexander of Florence, but, fortunately, Charles decided to give him his own illegitimate daughter Margaret, and Christina thus escaped union with this reckless and profligate Prince, who was soon afterwards murdered by his kinsman.[1] Meanwhile the Scottish Ambassadors at the French Court made proposals to the Emperor on behalf of their King, James V., who had not yet made up his mind to wed Magdalen of Valois, and these negotiations were only interrupted by the high-handed action of King Henry's new favourite, Thomas Cromwell. Thus, a few weeks after the Duke of Milan's death his widow's hand had become the subject of animated controversy in all the Courts of Europe.[2]

But while others were negotiating the French were arming. On the 6th of March, the first day of Carnival, news reached Milan that a French army had crossed the Alps. The strong citadel of Montmelian was betrayed by the treachery of a Neapolitan captain, and after a gallant defence the Duke of

[1] Granvelle, ii. 407.
[2] Calendar of Spanish State Papers, v. 1, 586; Granvelle, ii. 417.

Savoy was compelled to evacuate Turin, and take refuge with his wife and children at Vercelli. All hope of peace was now over, and, in a consistory held in the Vatican on the 8th of April, the Emperor appealed to the Pope to bear witness how earnestly he had tried to prevent war, and how fruitless his efforts had proved. At Granvelle's suggestion, he determined to carry the war into the enemy's country, and, following in the steps of Charles VIII., crossed the Apennines, and marched by the Emilian Way and along the banks of the Po towards Asti.

The dread of a French invasion had united all parties in Milan. The citizens forgot their hatred of the Spaniards in their terror of another siege, and cheerfully submitted to fresh taxes to pay the defending army. It was a late spring that year in Lombardy, the weather was bitterly cold, and by the end of April the vines had only put forth tiny shoots, and the roses were not yet in flower. Nothing was heard in the streets but the din of approaching warfare, and the tramp of armed *Landsknechten* marching from Tyrol on their way to the frontier. But in the last days of April Christina's dull life was brightened by the sudden arrival of the Duchess of Savoy, who fled from the camp at Vercelli to take refuge in the Castello of Milan. Times were altered since the two Princesses had met at Turin, and the Duchess Beatrix, who had welcomed the little bride so warmly, was sadly changed in body and mind. She had lost her eldest son, and been driven out of her home by foreign invaders, never to return there again in her lifetime. With her she brought her two remaining children, the little Princess Catherine and Emanuel Philibert, who was one day to become famous as the bravest captain in Europe. And she also brought a treasure which excited the utmost enthusiasm among the Milanese—the Holy Shroud of St. Joseph of Arimathea, which had been preserved for centuries at Chambéry. Crowds flocked to the Duomo when Beatrix's Franciscan confessor preached, in the hope of seeing the precious Shroud; but the Duchess would not allow the relic to leave the Castello, and on the 7th it was exposed on the ramparts to the view of an enormous multitude assembled in the piazza.[1]

A week later Francesco Sforza's cousin, Ferrante Gonzaga, and the Duke of Savoy, came to Milan, but soon left for the camp. Beatrix then obtained permission to pay the Emperor a visit on his journey north, and by Charles's express request took Christina with her. On the 18th of May the magistrates of Pavia received orders from the Duchess of Milan's *maggiordomo*, Benedetto da Corte, to prepare lodgings for Her Excellency and the Duchess of Savoy, as near to each other as possible.[2] The Castello of Pavia had suffered terribly in the siege by Lautrec in 1528, but a few rooms were hastily furnished, and on the 20th Beatrix and Christina arrived, escorted by Count Massimiliano and several courtiers. Early on the following morning the two Duchesses rode out to Arena on the Po, where they found the Emperor awaiting them. Charles was unfeignedly glad to see both his sister-in-law and the niece whom he had left as a child at Brussels four years before, and welcomed them affectionately.[3] But the inter-

---

[1] Burigozzo, 532.
[2] Museo Civico di Storia Patria, Pavia, 546.
[3] L. Gachard, " Voyages des Souverains des Pays-Bas," ii. 133.

view was a short one, and the next day he continued his journey to Asti, where he joined Antonio de Leyva and Ferrante Gonzaga, and prepared to invade Provence.

Meanwhile Beatrix and Christina returned to Milan, and spent the summer together in the Castello. A close friendship sprang up between the two Duchesses. Beatrix took a motherly interest in her young companion, and the children's presence helped to cheer these anxious months. At first the Emperor's arms were entirely successful. The French retired before him to Avignon, laying the country waste, and he met with no opposition until he reached Aix, which resisted all his attacks. During the long siege which followed, his soldiers suffered severely from disease and famine, and many youths of the noblest Milanese families were among the victims.[1] Early in September, while Christina's own secretary, Belcorpo, was robbed and murdered on his way to the camp, Antonio de Leyva, the redoubtable Commander-in-Chief, died, and was buried in S. Eustorgio at Milan. The Papal Legate, Cardinal Caracciolo, a Neapolitan by birth, was appointed to succeed him as Viceroy of Milan. He had only just assumed the reins of office, and paid his first visit to the young Duchess, when he received a summons from the Emperor to join him at Genoa. Finding it impossible to reduce Aix, Charles had determined to abandon the campaign, and on the 16th of November a three months' truce was signed between the two monarchs. The Emperor was anxious to return to Spain, where his presence was sorely needed. But before his departure he sent for the Cardinal, desiring him to leave some

[1] Calendar of Spanish State Papers, v. 2, 230.

trusty lieutenant to govern the State in his absence,
and take charge of his niece the Duchess. Accordingly, Caracciolo went to Genoa on the 4th of October,
accompanied by Beatrix of Savoy, who, after a long
interview with the Emperor, joined her husband at
Nice, the only city which still belonged to him.
Soon after this her health gave way under the prolonged strain, and this once brilliant and beautiful
woman died in January, 1538, as she said herself, of
a broken heart.

Christina, now left alone at Milan, wrote a long
letter to the Cardinal, whom she addressed in the
language of a caressing child, saying that he was
dear to her as a father, and seeking his help for two
objects which lay very near her heart.

" The true affection," she writes, " which Your
Excellency has shown me, and the kind remembrance of me which you always keep, makes me
anxious for your health and welfare. So I beg
you to tell me how you have prospered on your
journey, and if you are well in health."

She then begs her friend the Cardinal to use his
influence with the Emperor on behalf of her sister
Dorothea, " the person now nearest and dearest to
her on earth," who is in need of her powerful uncle's
help. Probably the Palatine was, as usual, endeavouring to recover arrears of the pension due to him by
the Emperor, and to obtain compensation for the
costs which he had incurred in the disastrous expedition against Copenhagen. Hubert had lately
been sent to Charles with this object, and had at the
same time suggested that, if the Emperor needed a
Viceroy for Milan, no one could be more suitable
than his lord. But whatever the precise object of

Dorothea's request may have been, Christina's intercession, it is to be feared, availed her little.

The Duchess's other petition was more easily granted.

" As a whole year," she wrote, " will soon have elapsed since the death of my dearest husband, of blessed memory, I beg you to entreat His Majesty, in my name, to be pleased to give orders that this anniversary may be observed in a due and fitting manner. And I am quite certain that he will not refuse to hear this my prayer."[1]

It would indeed have been impossible for the Emperor to refuse so reasonable a request, and the anniversary of the late Duke's death was observed with due ceremonial in all the churches of Milan. But the days of the young Duchess's abode in this city were fast drawing to a close. Before Charles left Italy he had determined to place a strong Spanish garrison in the Castello, to defend Milan against the risk of a French invasion, and had only delayed to take this step from fear of exciting discontent in the city. Stampa had hitherto succeeded in warding off the blow, but now he was forced to bow to the imperial command, and surrender the Castello to a foreign captain.

Charles, it must be owned, did his best to soften the blow. He made the Count a present of the rich fief of Soncino in the province of Cremona, and sent him as a parting gift the costly plate which had belonged to the late Duke, with a cordial invitation to follow him to Spain. But we see, from a letter which Stampa's friend Aretino sent him, how sorely this vexed his noble heart.

[1] Autografi di Principi, Archivio di Stato (see Appendix II.).

" I will not grieve, my illustrious friend," wrote the time-serving Venetian, " if you have to give up the Castello, which you held for love of His Excellency, of happy memory, because to my mind it was a prison for your genius. Dry your tears, and console yourself with the reflection that now at least you are a free man. His Majesty is relieved from the jealousy of his Spanish servants, and you are saved from further anxieties on this subject. Now you can, if you choose, follow him to Spain, and lay down your office with honour unstained, and then return to Milan to live in freedom and contentment."[1]

This was poor comfort for Massimiliano, but the Emperor's will was not to be gainsaid, and the Count could only lay down his office and take leave of the young Duchess, assuring her of his undying loyalty and faithfulness. Charles had not forgotten his niece, and before he sailed for Barcelona on the 15th of November he sent one of his oldest and most trusted servants, Jean de Montmorency, Sieur de Courrières, the Captain of the Archers' Guard, to take charge of the Duchess, and eventually conduct her to Flanders. But while negotiations for her second marriage were still pending, it was felt desirable that she should remain in Lombardy ; and since the Castello would no longer be a fit place for her, Montmorency was ordered to escort her to Pavia. On the 10th of December, 1536, De Courrières arrived with fifty archers of the Imperial Guard, and, after a brief consultation with the Cardinal and Stampa, decided to take the Duchess to Pavia without delay.[2]

The leaves of the trees in the gardens were turning yellow, and a pale wintry sun shone down on the

---

[1] Aretino, " Lettere," i. 45.

[2] " Correspondance de Charles V. avec J. de Montmorency, Seigneur de Courrières," Papiers d'État de l'Audience, No. 82. p. 1, Archives du Royaume, Bruxelles.

Castello, which Christina had first seen in the joyous
May-time, when a little procession of black-robed
ladies, with their attendants, issued from the
Rocchetta, and mounted the horses and litters in
waiting for them. A few bystanders saluted them
reverently, and followed them with wistful eyes as
they rode out of the gates, down the street leading to
the Porta Ticinese, until they were out of sight.

A few days later Count Massimiliano Stampa
marched out of the Castello at the head of his troops,
and gave up the keys, which he had received from the
last Sforza Duke, to the Spanish Captain Alvarez de
Luna, who entered the gates amid the curses and
groans of the citizens. Henceforth the life of Milan
as an independent State was over, and the yoke of
Spain descended on the ancient capital of Lombardy.

II.

The city of Pavia had always been loyal to the
House of Sforza. In no part of the duchy was there
greater rejoicing on the restoration of Duke Francesco II.; nowhere was his premature death more
deeply lamented. Several of Christina's most faithful
servants were natives of Pavia; among others, Benedetto da Corte, the master of her household, and Bottigella, who had been so active in the preparations for
her reception. Now the people of Pavia welcomed her
coming warmly, and exerted themselves to see that
nothing was lacking to her comfort. But the city
and Castello had suffered terribly in the protracted
struggle with France. The palace which had been
the pride of the Sforza Dukes was stripped of its
fairest treasures. The frescoes and tapestries were

destroyed, the famous library was now in the castle of Blois, and a great part of the walls had been thrown down by French guns and allowed to crumble to pieces. So dilapidated was the state of the building that it was difficult to find habitable rooms for the Duchess and her suite.

On the 21st of December, ten days after Christina's arrival, she was forced to address a request to the chief magistrate, Lodovico Pellizone, begging that her bedroom might be supplied with a wooden ceiling, as the room was lofty and bitterly cold in this winter season. Pellizone wrote without delay to the Governor of Milan, but received no reply, and on New Year's Day Montmorency himself wrote to remind the Cardinal of the Duchess's request, urging that the work might be done without delay, and putting in a plea for a better provision of mattresses to accommodate the members of her household. Still no redress was obtained, and at length the Captain of the Archers took the law into his own hands, and sent for carpenters to panel the Duchess's bedroom.[1] But in spite of these drawbacks, in spite of the wind that whistled through the long corridors and the comfortless air of the empty halls, Christina's health and spirits were excellent. Her spirits quickly recovered their natural buoyancy in these new surroundings, her eyes shone with the old brightness, and the sound of merry laughter was once more heard in the spacious halls and desolate gardens. On the 3rd of January, only two days after Montmorency addressed his fruitless remonstrance to the Viceroy, Christina herself wrote a letter to the same illustrious personage in a very different strain. She

[1] Carteggio con Montmorency, Archivio di Stato, Milan.

had, it appears, seen a very handsome white horse in the hostelry of the Fountain in Pavia, and was seized with a passionate desire to have the palfrey for her own use. So she wrote in the most persuasive language to her good Father the Cardinal, begging his leave to buy the horse, which she is convinced will suit her exactly. But, since she fears that her monthly allowance will not suffice to defray the cost, she begs His Eminence to advance the necessary sum, and charge it to the extraordinary expenses for which she is not responsible. This letter, written in her large round hand, was sent to Milan by one of the Duchess's lackeys, with the words " Cito, cito " on the cover, and an urgent plea for an immediate answer.[1] The kindly old Cardinal, who had a soft side for the youthful Princess, could hardly refuse so pressing a request, and Christina probably bought the white horse, and had the pleasure of mounting it when she rode out to visit the friars of the Certosa or hunted in their park.

She had another good friend and devoted servant in the Sieur de Courrières—Monsignor di Corea, as he was called in Italy. This gallant gentleman had grown up in close intimacy with the Emperor from his boyhood. He accompanied Charles to Spain as cupbearer, and was appointed Captain of the Archers' Guard on attaining his majority. In 1535 he followed his master to Africa at the head of a chosen band of archers, fifty of whom remained with him as an escort for the Duchess. By Charles's orders, he sent constant reports to His Majesty from Pavia. The correspondence fills a whole volume, and is extremely interesting

[1] Autografi di Principi, Archivio di Stato, Milan (see Appendix III.).

if only because it shows the familiarity with which the great Emperor treated his old servant, and the freedom which Montmorency allowed himself in addressing his master.

On the 15th of February, Charles wrote from Valladolid, thanking De Courrières cordially for the services which he had rendered the Duchess, approving highly of her residence at Pavia, and promising to pay for the maintenance of his archers. He alludes pleasantly to Montmorency's meeting with another of his confidential servants, Simonet, whom he had left at Milan.

" Simonet was right to put off his return to Flanders until the worst rigours of winter were over, and was fortunate in meeting you, for old folks of the same country are very glad to meet in foreign lands, even if they are not natives of Brabant. Farewell, *cher et féal*, for the present, and God have you in His holy keeping !"

Five weeks later he wrote again, expressing his satisfaction at hearing of his dear niece's health and happiness, and saying how entirely he trusted Montmorency to provide for her comfort.

" At the same time," he continued, " we cannot help feeling, both with regard to the Duchess's widowed condition and the troubled state of Italy, that she would be better with our sister, the Queen of Hungary, in our own country, *par-deça*, where some suitable marriage might be found for her. Accordingly we have written to our sister on the subject, and desired Cardinal Caracciolo to make all needful preparation for her journey. You had better see that she has a proper escort and all else that is necessary to her comfort, without making these things public, until we hear from our sister."[1]

---

[1] Papiers d'État, 82. 2, 12, Archives du Royaume.

Mary on her part was most anxious for her niece's return, and lost no time in letting Charles know how impatiently she expected her. But, with characteristic dilatoriness, the Imperial Council, which met at Monzone on the 2nd of June, pronounced that it was highly expedient for the Widow of Milan to go to Flanders, but that the Queen's wishes must first of all be consulted.[1] Meanwhile Count Massimiliano Stampa returned from Spain with instructions from the Emperor to make arrangements for the Duchess's journey with the Cardinal and Montmorency, and Charles wrote again to beg the Captain to start without delay. But this, as Montmorency replied, was not so easy. Three months' pay was due to his men, and in his penniless condition it was hard to provide them with food or their horses with fodder.

" I will do my utmost, Sire," he wrote on the 15th of June, " but some things are impossible. As I told you when you left me at Genoa, six months' wages were due to me, and I can only beg you to have pity on your poor Captain ; for we are in sore straits, and you alone can help us, for, as the Scripture saith, *Tua est potentia*."

At the same time, like the brave soldier that he was, the writer cannot refrain from expressing his joy at the good news of the capture of S. Pol, which had just arrived from Flanders.

" Sire, I hear grand news from S. Pol, and am sure, when you return to your Low Countries, you will find that the Queen has been very vigilant in charge of your affairs, and will be welcomed by very humble and loyal subjects. But you will have something to say to the citizens of Ghent, for I fear those gentlemen are not as wise as they might be. Sire, I hear that, after the surrender of Hesdin, your sister the Queen

[1] Calendar of Spanish State Papers, v. 2, 353.

of France came to the camp in rich attire, with a
number of ladies all in white. Such insolence cannot
last long, as S. Pol—both the town and the Apostle—
bear witness. I hear that Madame the new Duchesse
d'Étampes was nowhere. *Sic transit gloria mundi.*
All this Latin is to show Your Majesty that I have not
wasted my time in Pavia, any more than Don Beltrami
did at Louvain. Once more I beg you to have pity
on *La Chrétiennete*, who needs your help more than
ever."

But the summer months went by, and still no orders
and no money came from Spain. Pavia became
unhealthy, and the Duchess and all the members of
her household fell ill of fever.

" Hardly one has escaped," wrote Montmorency
on the 22nd of August, " but now, thank God, my
Lady has recovered, and I am trying to raise money
to carry out your orders, although I fear my purse is
not long enough to feed my poor archers."[1]

A month later the Captain went to Milan to expedite
matters, but as yet could hear nothing from Spain,
and on his return to Pavia early in October, he addressed long remonstrances both to Charles and
Granvelle.

" Sire," wrote the irate Captain, " I have been
ordered to take my Lady Duchess to Flanders, but
not a word has been said as to the route that I am to
take. Since it is your pleasure, it shall be done ; but
if any harm comes to her in Germany, seeing the poor
escort we shall have, who will be to blame ? My
fear is that, as we pass through the duchy of Würtemberg, the Duke's son may fall upon us with his
Landsknechten, and my Lady would certainly not
be a bad match for him ! Your Majesty has not
given me a single letter or warrant for the journey,
and has not written me a word. And when I get
par-deça, I know not what I am to do or say. My

[1] Papiers d'État, 82, 8-10.

Lady, too, is much surprised not to have received a
letter from Your Majesty before her departure, but
of this, of course, I have no right to speak."

In a postscript he adds that he has raised 500 gold
crowns, and given each of his men 10 crowns to buy
new saddles, as they hope to start on the 15th of
October. He ends by humbly reminding His Majesty
that he is growing old, and is almost fifty, and that
if he does not soon take a wife it will be too late.

" All this coming and going ages a man, and before
long I shall be as wrinkled as the rest. So when I
reach the Queen, I hope some little token of honour
may be given me, that men may see Your Majesty
has not wholly forgotten me. And you will, I hope,
tell me what I am to do when I have taken Her
Excellency to Flanders, as I have written to Granvelle
repeatedly, and had no answer, but suppose he is busy
with great affairs. And I pray that all prosperity may
attend Your Majesty, and that this year, which has
begun so well, may end by seeing you back in
Piedmont."[1]

On the 14th of October Christina herself wrote to
inform the Emperor of her intended departure, and
of the good order of her affairs, thanks to the Cardinal
and Seigneur de Courrières. " We hope to start to-
morrow, and travel by way of Mantua and Trent, and
through Germany, taking whichever seems to be the
shortest and safest route." There had, it appears,
been much discussion over the revenues assigned
to the Duchess as her dower, and in the end she
was deprived of the town and Castello of Vigevano,
which the Duke had left her by his will. But by the
terms of her marriage contract she remained absolute
mistress of the city of Tortona, and informed the
Emperor that, acting on the advice of the Cardinal, as

---

[1] Papiers d'État, 82, 12.

Lady of Tortona, she had appointed a certain Gabriele Panigarola to be Governor of the town, and begged his approval. At the same time she sent her uncle a memorial, drawn up by Montmorency, explaining that, since she had not received the arrears of her dowry, she was not able to pay her servants, and had been forced to contract many debts at Pavia, and to spend money on the repair of the rooms which she occupied in the Castello.

Many last requests were addressed to the Duchess by the poor and needy whom she had befriended, and from her own servants, who with one voice begged to be allowed to follow her to Flanders. One of the most pressing came from an old Milanese couple, whose son, Niccolò Belloni, was Christina's secretary, and at their earnest prayer she decided to allow the young man to remain in her service as one of the four Italians who accompanied her to Flanders by the Emperor's orders. And the last letter which the Duchess wrote to the Cardinal, on the eve of her departure, was to plead for a community of noble ladies in Pavia who were reduced to dire poverty owing to the late wars, and begged humbly for a remission of taxes.[1] During the ten months which she had spent at Pavia the young Duchess had made herself beloved by all classes of people, and her departure was lamented by the whole city.

III.

On the 15th of October Christina and her suite left Pavia, and started on their long-deferred journey to Flanders. When she first set foot in Italy as a bride, three and a half years before, the Lombard plains

[1] Autografi di Principi, Archivio di Stato, Milan.

were in the first flush of spring, roses and myrtles were breaking into bloom, and the flowers sprang up under her feet. Now the autumn rains fell in such torrents that Cardinal Caracciolo was seriously alarmed, and wrote to Benedetto da Corte and Monsignore di Corea, asking if it might not be well to delay their departure. The first idea had been to go from Pavia to Cremona in a single day, but the bad roads and swollen rivers increased the difficulties of travel, and the Cardinal wrote to implore Messer Benedetto and Corea not to undertake such long journeys, lest the Duchess should be overtired. So the party only rode as far as Codogno, the castle of Count Gaspare Trivulzio, where he and his beautiful wife, Deianira, received them joyfully, and entertained them " as magnificently as if they had been invited to a wedding." Christina's lady-in-waiting, the Princess of Macedonia, rejoiced to be under her daughter's roof, and Benedetto da Corte wrote to tell the Cardinal that nothing could exceed the splendour and hospitality of Count Gaspare's reception. On the 18th the travellers rode along the plains flooded by the swollen Po till they reached Cremona, the dower city of Bianca Visconti, where she had been married to the great Condottiere Francesco Sforza, and which had clung with unswerving loyalty to the fortunes of his house. Here the Castellan came out to meet the Duchess, at the head of the chief citizens, and escorted her to the Castello under the shadow of the famous Torrazza, where she and all her suite found the best of cheer. The next morning the travellers resumed their way, and crossed the rushing Oglio, under the castle of the Gonzagas of Bozzolo, and rode along the green meadows by

Castiglione's country home, where his aged mother
was still living. The great courtier's name was
familiar to all Charles V.'s servants, and Montmorency,
who had known him in Spain, may have paused to
look at the fair sepulchral chapel which Giulio
Romano had lately reared in the pilgrimage church
of S. Maria delle Grazie. At Mantua another splendid
welcome awaited Christina. The Gonzaga Princes
never forgot their close relationship to the Sforzas,
and while the reigning Duchess welcomed the Princess
of Macedonia as a kinswoman, the old Marchesana,
Isabella, rejoiced to embrace her nephew's wife, and
looked with affection on this youthful Duchess who
bore the same title as her long-lost Beatrice.

The next morning Benedetto da Corte sent the Cardinal a glowing account of their journey, which, in
spite of the weather, had been one triumphal progress:

" REVERENDISSIMO,
        " Her Excellency arrived safely here at Mantua
yesterday with all her company, horses, and carriages,
and was received most royally, as has, indeed, been
the case in every place where we have halted on our
way. Her whole household has been entertained
with the best fare, and with little damage to our
purses. . . . The kindness with which we have been
received has made these perpetual rains tolerable.
We are quite accustomed to them, and shall not be
afraid of the next tempest ! We are resting here on
this sixth day of our journey at the entreaty of these
illustrious Princes. On Sunday, please God, we shall
reach Verona, and I have sent to ask the Governor
to prepare convenient lodgings for Her Excellency.
His Reverence the Cardinal of Trent has sent a
messenger here to-night to inquire how many we
number, and so we go on gaily from stage to stage.
Once we have reached Trent, we shall seem to be in
sight of the Rhine, and can pursue our way at less
peril to our lives, and, let us hope, to the greater

advantage of His Majesty's service. I kiss Your Reverence's hand, and so also does Monsignore di Corea.

"Mantova, October 20." [1]

"BENEDETTO DA CORTE.

The Cardinal's worst anxieties were relieved by the receipt of Benedetto's letter, and he sent a reply to the Castle of Trent thanking him and Monsignore di Corea for their trouble, and expressing great satisfaction to hear of their prosperous journey. The travellers now turned their steps northwards, and, after spending a night in the city of the Scaligeri, followed the Adige through the rocky defile known as La Chiusa di Verona. As they passed through the fortified gates at the farther end of the ravine, a salute from the guns made them aware that they had entered Austrian territory. A few miles farther they were met by the Cardinal-Bishop, Bernhard von Clès, who had ridden out with a great train to welcome the Duchess. A strong Imperialist no less than an active reformer, Bernhard von Clès had been raised to the cardinalate at Charles's coronation, and was now Vice-Chancellor of the Empire.[2] He had lately received a visit from Christina's uncle, King Ferdinand, and his wife, Anna, who honoured his niece's wedding with their presence, and the sumptuous rooms which they had occupied were now placed at Christina's disposal. " Nothing was lacking," wrote Benedetto da Corte, " which could please the eye or delight the mind." The splendour of the episcopal palace and the open-handed liberality of the Cardinal made a great impression on Mont-

---

[1] "Carteggio con Montmorency, Conte di Corea," 1537-38, Archivio di Stato, Milan.
[2] L. Pastor, " Geschichte d. Papste," iv. 375; M. Guazzo, 371.

morency, who wrote himself to tell the Cardinal how well Madama had borne the journey.

" I cannot tell you," he adds, " how splendidly Monsignor Reverendissimo has received the Duchess, and how sumptuously he has feasted us. Here we mean to rest all to-day, and to-morrow we will pursue our journey with the utmost diligence."

But so pressing was the Cardinal, and so luxurious were the quarters provided for them, that the travellers remained at Trent several days, and only resumed their journey on the 27th of October.

The most arduous part of the way now lay before them, and Benedetto describes how they harnessed the mules to the chariot in order that the Duchess and her ladies might drive across the Brenner Pass, at least as far as Innsbruck. Montmorency was in some doubt as to the route which the Duchess had better take through Germany, but, much to his satisfaction, he found the long-expected letter from the Emperor awaiting him at Innsbruck. It was written from Monzone on the last day of October, a fortnight after Christina had left Pavia. Charles put the blame of his delay on the Queen of Hungary's shoulders, and, since it was too late to wait for her directions, bade him consult the Cardinal of Trent as to their future journey.

" If you have already left Trent, you had better go on either by road or else by the Rhine. If you are at Innsbruck, you can take advice from the King our brother or from Dr. Matthias Held "—one of Ferdinand's most trusted German Councillors—" and choose whichever route they consider the safest. If you have received no letters from the Queen, you had better send a messenger to Flanders, and we will inform you as soon as we know her pleasure regarding our niece's future plans."

10

In conclusion the Emperor tells Montmorency that
he is sending the letters patent for which he asked,
although they are hardly necessary, and has already
told the Queen to refund all the expenses which he
has incurred, and to be mindful of his great and long
services.[1]

The travellers spent some time at Innsbruck in
the ancient castle which is still adorned with the
Sforza arms, and Christina saw the superb monument
erected by her great-grandfather Maximilian in the
church hard by. Ferdinand and his wife and daughters
were in Vienna, but the route which Montmorency
chose was that followed by most travellers, along the
Lake of Constance and down the Rhine to Spires.
From the first Christina had been very anxious to visit
her sister Dorothea on her journey north, and she
succeeded in obtaining her uncle's consent to this
arrangement. The two Princesses had not met since
Christina left Brussels in the spring of 1534, and
Dorothea was no less impatient to see her sister.
Even before the travellers reached Trent, they met
two Genoese merchants, who told Montmorency that
on their way through Germany they had seen the
Count Palatine Frederic and Madama la Principessa,
his wife, with a great company, on their way to
Heidelberg to await the Duchess's coming. When,
in November, the travellers at length reached Heidelberg, they found themselves impatiently expected,
and Christina received the warmest welcome from the
Elector Palatine and his family.

Festivities such as Frederic and Dorothea took
delight in—jousting, banquets, and dances—followed
each other in rapid succession, and the castle blazed

---

[1] Papiers d'État, 82, 13, Archives du Royaume, Bruxelles.

with innumerable torches through the winter nights. It was a great change from the funereal blackness of the Castello of Milan and the desolate halls of Pavia, and the young Duchess enjoyed it to the full. The days sped by all too quickly, and so happy were the sisters in each other's company that the Elector invited Christina to stay over Christmas. The young Duchess accepted the proposal gleefully, and all were preparing to spend a joyous festival, when Montmorency received peremptory orders from the Queen-Regent to bring her niece forthwith to Flanders, After this no delays were possible. The sisters parted sadly from each other, and the travellers once more took boat and sailed down the Rhine to Cologne.

From here it was an easy journey to Aix-la-Chapelle, and through the friendly State of Cleves to Maestricht, and thence to Louvain and Brussels. On the 8th of December Christina set foot once more in the ancient palace of the Dukes of Brabant, and was clasped in her aunt's arms. Ten days afterwards she wrote a letter to inform the Emperor of her safe arrival, and of " the good and loving welcome " which she had received from " Madame my aunt." She begged His Majesty to keep her still in his remembrance, and signed herself, " Your humble niece, Chrétienne." [1]

She was at home once more among her own people, and all the strange sights and scenes, all the wonderful experiences which she had known, in these four eventful years, seemed to fade away like a dream. But she had left Flanders a child, and she came back a woman.

[1] Papiers d'État, 82, 19 ; State Papers, Record Office, viii. 6; Calendar of State Papers, xii. 2, 415, 419.

IV.

Christina's return was impatiently awaited at Brussels. The courtiers who remembered her mother, and had known her as a child, were eager to see the young Duchess, whose courage and wisdom had been shown in such trying circumstances. All through the summer her coming had been expected, and the Regent was seriously annoyed at the prolonged delays which had hindered her niece's departure from Milan. Her heart yearned over the child from whom she had parted with so much reluctance. More than this, she had in her mind's eye a second husband ready for the young Duchess. This was William, the only son and heir of the reigning Duke of Cleves. A handsome and well-educated young man of twenty-two, the young Duke had not yet developed that fatal weakness of purpose which proved his bane, and was to all appearances an excellent match for the Emperor's niece. The political advantages of the union were obvious. Duke John had married the heiress of Jülich and Bergh, and reigned over three rich and peaceful provinces on the Lower Rhine. He had always been on friendly terms with the Emperor, and when, a few months after the Duke of Milan's death, he asked for the young widow's hand on behalf of his son, Mary welcomed these advances gladly, and hastened to communicate them to the Emperor.[1] At first Charles replied coolly that, if the marriage with Angoulême could not be arranged, the proposals made by the King of Scotland or Cleves might be entertained. In October, 1536, Mary sent a confidential messenger, La Tiloye, to Genoa to learn the Emperor's

[1] Lanz, ii. 657.

pleasure in the matter, but nothing further was done. After the fresh outbreak of war in 1537, and the invasion of Artois by the French, Charles became more alive to the importance of the question, and wrote to his sister from Spain, saying that he had ordered the Widow of Milan to go to the Low Countries, and hoped she would proceed at once to the conclusion of the marriage with Cleves.[1]

At that moment all Mary's energies were absorbed in the struggle with France. She herself went to Lille to superintend military operations, and appeared on horseback in the trenches before Thérouenne, where her courage excited the admiration of John Hutton, the English Ambassador. " Let the King but tarry fifteen days," she exclaimed, " and I will show him what God may strengthen a woman to do !" But, in spite of these brave words, Mary, as Hutton soon discovered, was sincerely desirous to end the war. " The Queen's anxiety for peace, he wrote home, " is as great as her ardour in war."[2] She knew the straits to which the Emperor was reduced and the exhaustion of the Treasury. " The poverty of this country is so great," she wrote to Charles on the 9th of June, " that it is impossible to provide necessary funds for the war. We must have peace, or we are lost."[3] Under these circumstances she lent a willing ear to her sister Queen Eleanor's advances, and the two sisters had the satisfaction of arranging a truce at Bomy, a village near Thérouenne. The siege of this city was raised, the French evacuated the towns which they held, and on the 10th of September peace was ratified by the Emperor at Monzone.

[1] Lanz, iii. 667, 677.
[2] State Papers, Record Office, vii. 695.   [3] Lanz, ii. 675.

Mary felt that she could once more breathe freely. She lost no time in renewing negotiations with the Duke of Cleves, and the proposed marriage became the talk of the Court. " The Queen," wrote Hutton, on the 2nd of September, from Bruges, where Mary was hunting after her wont and spending all day in the saddle, " looketh daily for the Duchess of Milan, who shall be married to the Duke of Cleves's son and heir." [1] A month later the Cleves Envoys arrived at Brussels, and, after repeated interviews with the Queen and her Council, returned, well satisfied, to obtain their master's consent to the terms of the contract. The news spread rapidly, and was reported by Ambassadors from Spain and Germany, from Rome and Paris, with the same unanimity. Suddenly an unexpected event altered the face of affairs. Charles of Egmont, the fiery old Duke of Guelders, who had for many years been the Emperor's bitter enemy, fell ill, and, feeling his end to be near, summoned the Estates of his realm to choose a successor. Since he had no issue, his own wish was to leave his States to the French King; but his subjects positively refused to be handed over to a foreign Power, and chose the young Duke William of Cleves, who hastened to visit Nimeguen, where he was acclaimed by his future subjects. This was a clear breach of faith, since, by the treaty concluded a year before with the Emperor, Guelders was to pass into his hands at Charles of Egmont's death, and the ancient rights to the duchy which the House of Cleves formerly claimed had been already sold to the Dukes of Burgundy.[2] Mary's indignation was great. She wrote angrily to tell

[1] Calendar of State Papers, Henry VIII., xii. 2, 231.
[2] Henne, vii. 263, 267.

William of Cleves that Guelders was the property of the Emperor, and that if he persevered in his pretensions all idea of his marriage to her niece must be abandoned. The young Duke returned a courteous answer, saying that nothing could be farther from his thoughts than a breach of loyalty to the Emperor, and professing the utmost anxiety for the marriage. At the same time the old Duke's action excited great annoyance in Lorraine, where his nephew, the reigning Duke Anthony, claimed to be heir to Guelders, through his mother, Philippa of Egmont. An attempt to pacify him by reviving a former marriage contract between his son Francis and the Duke of Cleves's daughter Anne met with no encouragement, and Ambassadors were sent to Guelders to enter a protest on the Duke of Lorraine's behalf.[1] But Charles of Egmont turned a deaf ear to all remonstrances, and on the 27th of January, 1538, William of Cleves received the homage of the States of Guelders, and was publicly recognized as the old Duke's successor.

Such was the state of affairs when Christina reached Brussels on the 8th of December, 1537. Her faithful guardian, Montmorency, alludes to the Cleves marriage in the following letter, which he addressed to Cardinal Caracciolo on the 5th of January, 1538:

" I wrote last from Trent on the 26th of October, and since then have received several letters from you, and have duly informed the Duchess of their contents. She is very grateful for your kindness regarding her affairs, and begs you not to relax your efforts. . . . As to Madama's marriage with Cleves, as far as I can learn, it will not take place, because the Duke has quarrelled with Lorraine, and Guelders is interfering. Negotiations, however, are not yet broken off.'

[1] Calendar of State Papers, Henry VIII., xiii. 1, 35.

Three months later he referred to the matter again in another letter, and this time expressed his conviction that the marriage would never take place.[1]

Montmorency's own claims had not been forgotten. Soon after his return he married a lady of the Lannoy family, and was appointed Bailiff of Alost. Both Charles and Mary treated him with marked favour, and employed him on important diplomatic missions. But he still held an honorary post in the Duchess's household, and never ceased to be her devoted servant.

During the winter Hutton alluded repeatedly to the affair of Cleves in his letters to Cromwell, saying that the Duke had been recognized by the Communes of Guelders as their liege lord, and that the Queen quite refused to let him wed the Duchess, although he was still eager for the alliance. All sorts of wild rumours were flying about, and an Italian merchant at Antwerp wrote to London that young Cleves was about to marry the daughter of Lorraine, with Guelders as her dowry. But on the 25th of January Hutton reported that the Queen had sent Nassau and De Praet to Duke William, to break off marriage negotiations and clear her of all former promises.[2]

Christina herself was the person least concerned in these rumours. Princes and Ministers might wrangle as they chose; they could not destroy the happiness of being in her old home, surrounded by familiar faces. The sound of the French tongue and the carillon in the towers were music in her ears. Three things above all impressed Italian travellers, like Guicciardini and Beatis, who came to the Low Countries for

---

[1] Carteggio Diplomatico, 1537-38, Archivio di Stato, Milan.
[2] State Papers, xiii. 1, 8; Record Office, viii. 27, 29.

the first time—the cleanliness of the streets and houses, the green pastures with their herds of black and white cows, and the beautiful church bells. These were all delightful to the young Duchess, who had been so long absent from her old home. The city of Brussels, with its fine houses and noble churches, its famous hôtel-de-ville, and 350 fountains, was a pleasant town to live in. And the Palace of Brabant itself was a wonderful place. There was the great hall, with its lofty pointed arches, and priceless Burgundian tapestries, and the golden suns and silver moons recently brought back from the New World by Cortes, the conqueror of Mexico.

The Queen gave Christina a suite of rooms close to her own, looking out on the glossy leaves and interwoven boughs of the labyrinth, and the gardens beyond, which Albert Dürer had called an earthly paradise, and which the Cardinal of Aragon's secretary pronounced to be as beautiful as any in Italy.[1] Here the young Duchess lived with her ladies and household, presided over by Benedetto da Corte and Niccolò Belloni. Every morning she attended Mass in the Court chapel, and dined and spent the evenings with the Queen. On fine days, when Mary could spare time from public affairs, they rode out together and hunted the deer in the park, or took longer expeditions in the Forest of Soignies. As fearless and almost as untiring a rider as her aunt, Christina was quite at home in the saddle, and followed the Queen's example of riding with her foot in the stirrup, an accomplishment which was new in those days, and excited Brantôme's admiration.[2]

[1] L. Pastor, " Reise des Kardinal Luigi d'Aragona," 116. L. Guicciardini, "Paesi-Bassi," 74.   [2] "Œuvres," xii. 107.

The following Christmas was celebrated with great festivity at Brussels. The war was over, and the presence of a youthful Princess gave new charm to Court functions. Wherever Christina went she made herself beloved. Her quick wit and frank enjoyment of simple pleasures charmed everyone. Although in public she still wore heavy mourning robes after the Italian fashion, and hid away her bright chestnut locks under a black hood, in the evening, by her aunt's desire, she laid aside her weeds, and appeared clad in rich brocades and glittering jewels. Then she conversed freely with her aunt's ladies and with the foreign Ambassadors, or played cards with the few great nobles who were admitted to the Queen's private circle—Henry, Count of Nassau, the proudest and richest lord in Flanders; the Duke of Aerschot and his wife, Anne de Croy, the heiress of the Princes of Chimay; his sister, Madame de Berghen; Count Büren; and a few others.

Among them was one whom the young Duchess regarded with especial interest. This was the hero of S. Pol, René, Prince of Orange. The only son and heir of the great House of Nassau, René had inherited the principality of Orange, in the South of France, from his uncle Philibert of Châlons, the Imperialist leader who fell at the siege of Florence, and whose sister Claude was Henry of Nassau's first wife. As a child René had been Prince John of Denmark's favourite playmate, and Christina had not forgotten her brother's old friend. Now he had grown up a handsome and chivalrous Prince, skilled in all knightly exercises. He had won his first laurels in the recent campaign, and was the foremost of the valiant band which surprised the citadel of S. Pol. The Queen

honoured him with her especial favour, and, as the
Nassau house stood close to the palace, the young
Prince was often in her company. When, on Shrove
Sunday, a grand tournament was held at Court, one
troop, clad in blue, was led by Count Büren's eldest
son, Floris d'Egmont; and the other by René, wearing
the orange colours of his house, with the proud motto,
Je maintiendrai. Christina looked down from her
place at the Queen's side on the lists where the
gallant Prince challenged all comers, and it was from
her hand that the victor received the prize. Neither
of them ever forgot that carnival.[1]

[1] State Papers, Henry VIII., Record Office, viii. 16.

BOOK VI

THE COURTSHIP OF HENRY VIII.

1537—1539

I.

THE Widow of Milan's fate still hung in the balance. While Mary of Hungary had not yet lost all hope of marrying her to the Duke of Cleves, and Queen Eleanor was no less anxious to see her the wife of a French Prince, fresh proposals reached Brussels from an unexpected quarter. This new suitor was none other than the Emperor's *bel oncle*, King Henry of England. This monarch, who had openly defied the laws of the Church, and after divorcing Charles's aunt, had pronounced Queen Katherine's daughter to be illegitimate, could hardly expect to find favour in the eyes of the Regent. Mary's own opinion of Henry's character is frankly given in a very interesting letter which she wrote to her brother Ferdinand in May, 1536, when the King of England had sent Anne Boleyn to the block and made Jane Seymour his third wife.

" I hope," she wrote, " that the English will not do us much harm now we are rid of the King's mistress, who was a good Frenchwoman, and whom, as you have no doubt heard, he has beheaded; and since no one skilful enough to do the deed could be found among his own subjects, he sent for the executioner of S. Omer, in order that a Frenchman should be

the minister of his vengeance. I hear that he has
married another lady, who is said to be a good Imperialist, although I do not know if she will remain
so much longer. He is said to have taken a fancy
to her before the last one's death, which, coupled
with the fact that neither the poor woman nor any
of those who were beheaded with her, saving one
miserable musician, could be brought to acknowledge
her guilt, naturally makes people suspect that he
invented this pretext in order to get rid of her. . . .
It is to be hoped—if one can hope anything from such
a man—that when he is tired of this wife he will
find some better way of getting rid of her. Women,
I think, would hardly be pleased if such customs
became general, and with good reason; and although
I have no wish to expose myself to similar risks, yet,
as I belong to the feminine sex, I, too, will pray that
God may preserve us from such perils."[1]

But whatever Mary's private opinions were, political
reasons compelled her to preserve a friendly de-
meanour towards King Henry. The English alliance
was of the utmost importance to the trade of the
Netherlands, and the enmity of France made it essen-
tial to secure Henry's neutrality, if not his active
help. The death of Queen Katherine, as Cromwell
wrote, had removed " the onelie matter of unkindness " between the two monarchs, and was soon followed by more friendly communications. When the
news of Prince Edward's birth reached Spain, the
Emperor held a long conversation with Sir Thomas
Wyatt, the poet and scholar, who had been sent to
the Imperial Court early in 1537. He expressed
great pleasure at the news, laughing and talking
pleasantly, inquiring after the size and goodliness of
the child, and ended by saying frankly that he
approved of the King's recent marriage as much as

[1] Papiers d'État, 1178, Archives du Royaume, Bruxelles.

he had always disliked his union with Anne Boleyn.[1]
These last remarks must have fallen strangely on the
ears of Wyatt, whose old intimacy with the hapless
Queen had nearly cost him his life, and whose death
he lamented in some of his sweetest verse.   But he
was too good a courtier not to repeat them in his letters
to Cromwell and the King.   The news of the Prince's
birth was shortly followed by that of the Queen's
death, which took place at Hampton Court on the
24th of October.

" Divine Providence," said the royal widower,
" has mingled my joy for the son which it has pleased
God to give me with the bitterness of the death of
her who brought me this happiness."

Cromwell wrote to inform Lord William Howard,
the special Envoy who had taken the news of the
Prince's birth to France, of Her Grace's death, and
in the same letter desired him to bring back particulars of two French ladies who had been recommended as suitable successors to the late Queen,
since His Majesty, " moved by tender zeal for his
subjects," had already resolved to marry again.   One
of these was King Francis's plain but accomplished
daughter Margaret, who eventually married the Duke
of Savoy, although Cromwell, knowing his master's
tastes, remarked that, from what he heard, he
" did not think she would be the meetest."[2]   The
other was Mary, Duchess of Longueville, the eldest
daughter of Claude de Guise, brother of the Duke of
Lorraine.   The charms of this young widow were
renowned at the French Court, and the English
Ambassador's reports of her modesty and beauty

---

[1] Calendar of State Papers, xii. 2, 367.
[2] State Papers, Henry VIII., Record Office, viii. 2.

inspired Henry with an ardent wish to make her his wife. Even before Jane Seymour was in her grave, he attacked the French Ambassador, Castillon, on the subject, and suggested that both these Princesses, and any other ladies whom the King of France could recommend, might be sent to meet him at Calais.[1] Francis, who was more gallant in his relations with women than his brother of England, laughed long and loudly when this message reached him, and sent Castillon word that royal Princesses could not be trotted out like hackney horses for hire ! He quite declined to allow his daughter to enter the lists; and as for Madame de Longueville, whom the King was pleased to honour with his suit, she was already promised to his son-in-law, the King of Scots. This fickle monarch, who had courted Dorothea and Christina by turn, and finally married Madeleine de Valois, had lost his young wife at the end of six months, and was already in search of another. At the same time Francis sent his royal brother word that he should count it a great honour if he could find a bride in his realm, and that any other lady in France was at his command.[2] But Henry was not accustomed to have his wishes thwarted, and in December, 1537, he sent a gentleman of his chamber, Sir Peter Mewtas, on a secret mission to Joinville, the Duke of Guise's castle on the borders of Lorraine, to wait on Madame de Longueville, and find out if her word was already pledged. Both Madame de Longueville and her clever mother, Antoinette de Bourbon, re-

[1] J. Kaulek, " Correspondance Politique de M. de Castillon," 4, 5 ; Calendar of State Papers, xii. 2, 394.
[2] Calendar of State Papers, xii. 2, 392 ; G. Pimodan, " La Mère des Guises, 72.

turned evasive answers, saying that the Duke of
Guise had agreed to the marriage with King James,
but that his daughter's consent had never been given.
This reply encouraged Henry to persevere with his
suit, while Mewtas's description of the Duchess's
beauty, in Castillon's words, " set the tow on fire." He
complained that his brother had behaved shamefully
in preferring the beggarly King of Scots to him, and
was forcing the lady to marry James against her will.
In vain Castillon told him that Madame de Longueville
had been promised to the King of Scots before Queen
Jane's death, and that Francis could not break his
word without mortally offending his old ally and son-
in-law. Nothing daunted, Henry sent Mewtas again
to Joinville in February, 1538, to obtain Madame de
Longueville's portrait, and ask if she were still free.
This time his errand proved fruitless. The marriage
with the King of Scots was already concluded, and
the contract signed. Nevertheless, Henry still harped
on the same string. " Il revient toujours à ses
moutons," wrote Castillon, " et ne peut pas oublier
sa bergère." " Truly he is a marvellous man!"[1]

Meanwhile Cromwell, who had no personal inclination for the French alliance, was making inquiries in
other directions. Early in December, while Mewtas
was on his way to Joinville, the Lord Privy Seal wrote
privately to Hutton, desiring him to send him a list
of ladies in Flanders who would be suitable consorts
for the King. In a letter written on the 4th of December, the Ambassador replied that he had little
knowledge of ladies, and feared he knew no one at
the Regent's Court " meet to be Queen of England."

[1] Kaulek, 12, 15; Calendar of State Papers, xiii. 1, 54.

" The widow of Count Egmont," he wrote, " was a fair woman of good report, and the Duke of Cleves had a marriageable daughter, but he heard no great praise of her person or beauty. There is," he added, " the Duchess of Milan, whom I have not seen, but who is reported to be a goodly personage of excellent beauty."[1]

Five days later Hutton wrote again, to announce the arrival of the Duchess, who entered Brussels on the 8th, and was received by a great company of honourable gentlemen.

" She is, I am informed, of the age of sixteen years, very high in stature for that age—higher, in fact, than the Regent—and a goodly personage of competent beauty, of favour excellent, soft of speech, and very gentle in countenance. She weareth mourning apparel, after the manner of Italy. The common saying here is that she is both widow and maid. She resembleth much one Mistress Skelton,[2] that sometime waited in Court upon Queen Anne. She useth most to speak French, albeit it is reported that she can speak both Italian and High German."

The same evening Hutton added these further details in a postscript addressed to Cromwell's secretary, Thomas Wriothesley:

" If it were God's pleasure and the King's, I would there were some good alliance made betwixt His Highness and the Emperor, and there is none in these parts of personage, beauty, and birth, like unto the Duchess of Milan. She is not so pure white as was the late Queen, whose soul God pardon, but she hath a singular good countenance, and when she chanceth to smile, there appeareth two pits in her cheeks and one in her chin, the which becometh her right excellently well."[3]

[1] State Papers, Record Office, viii. 5.

[2] Anne Boleyn's cousin Mary Skelton, who had been a great favourite with the King (see Calendar of State Papers, xiii. 1, 24).

[3] State Papers, Record Office, viii. 7.

The honest Englishman's first impressions of Christina were evidently very favourable. During the next week he watched her carefully, and was much struck by " the great majesty of her bearing and charm of her manners." At the same time he expressed his earnest conviction that, now peace was concluded between the Emperor and the French King, a close alliance between his own master and the Emperor was the more necessary, and suggested that a marriage between Henry and the Duchess, and another between the Princess Mary and the Duke of Cleves, would be very advantageous to both monarchs, who would then have all Germany at their command.

Cromwell lost no time in placing these letters in his master's hands. Hutton's account of the Duchess's beauty and virtues made a profound impression on the King, and, since Madame de Longueville was beyond his reach, he determined to pay his addresses to the Emperor's niece. With characteristic impetuosity, he wrote to Wyatt on the 22nd of January, saying that, as the Duchess of Milan's match with the Duke of Cleves was broken off, he thought of honouring her with an offer of marriage. This he desired Wyatt to suggest as of himself, in conversation with the Emperor and his Ministers, Granvelle and Covos, giving them a friendly hint to make overtures on behalf of the said Duchess.[1]

Strangely enough, two years before Charles had himself proposed this alliance between his niece and the King of England. In May, 1536, when he was hurrying northwards to defend Savoy against the French, the news of Anne Boleyn's fall reached him at Vercelli. Without a moment's delay he wrote to

[1] Calendar of State Papers, xiii. 1, 42.

Chapuys, his Ambassador in London, saying that, since Henry, being of so amorous a complexion, was sure to take another wife, and it was most important that he should not marry in France, Chapuys might propose his union with one of the Emperor's nieces, either Queen Eleanor's daughter, the Infanta Maria of Portugal, or the widowed Duchess of Milan, " a beautiful young lady, very well brought up, and with a rich dower." And then, as if a qualm had seized him at the thought of sacrificing Christina to a man of Henry's character, he added a postscript desiring the Ambassador not to mention the Duchess unless His Majesty should appear averse to the other.[1]

By the time, however, that these letters reached London, it was plain that the fickle monarch's affections were already fixed on Jane Seymour, and nothing more came of the Emperor's proposal until, in January, 1538, Henry himself wrote to Wyatt. Sir Thomas, who knew his royal master intimately, hastened to approach the Emperor, and on the 2nd of February Charles wrote from Barcelona to Chapuys, saying that, although royal ladies ought by right to be *sought*, not *offered*, in marriage, the King's language was so frank and sincere that he was willing to waive ceremony, and lend a favourable ear to his brother's proposal. Before these letters reached the Imperial Ambassador, he received a message from Henry, saying that he wished to treat of his own marriage with the Duchess of Milan, being convinced that a Princess born and bred in Northern climes would suit him far better than the Portuguese Infanta. The next day Cromwell paid a visit to

[1] Calendar of Spanish State Papers, v. 2, 572.

Chapuys, and confirmed every word of the royal message.[1]

On the eve of Valentine's Day Henry saw Castillon, and told him in bitter tones that, if his master did not choose to give him Madame de Longueville, he could find plenty of better matches, and meant to marry the Duchess of Milan and conclude a close alliance with the Emperor.[2]

On the same day the German reformer Melanchthon, writing from Jena to a Lutheran friend, summed up the situation neatly in the following words:

" The Widow of Milan, daughter of Christian, the captive King of Denmark, was brought to Germany to wed the young Duke of Juliers. This is now changed, for Juliers becomes heir to Guelders, against the Emperor's will, and the girl is offered to the Englishman, whom the Spaniards, aiming at universal empire, would join to themselves against the Frenchmen and us. There is grave matter for your consideration."[3]

II.

The ball was now set rolling, but, as Chapuys foretold, there were many difficulties in the way. For the moment, however, all went well. Henry sent Hutton orders to watch the Duchess closely, and report on all her words, deeds, and looks. In obedience to these commands, the Ambassador hung about the palace from early morning till late at night, was present at supper and card parties, attended the Queen out riding and hunting, and lost no opportunity of entering into conversation with Christina herself.

[1] Calendar of Spanish State Papers, v. 2, 429.
[2] Kaulek, 24; Calendar of State Papers, xiii. 1, 82.
[3] Calendar of State Papers, xiii. 1, 93.

One evening towards the end of February a page
brought him some letters from the Duchess's servant,
Gian Battista Ferrari, who had friends among the
Italian merchants in London, with a request that
the Ambassador would forward them by his courier.
The next morning, after Mass, when the Queen passed
into the Council-chamber, Hutton took advantage of
this opportunity to thank the Duchess most humbly
for allowing him to do her this small service. Christina
replied, with a gracious smile, that she would not have
ventured to give him this trouble, had she not been
as ready herself to do him any pleasure that lay in
her power.

It was stormy weather. For three days and nights
it had rained without ceasing, and courtiers and
ladies alike found the time hang heavy on their hands.
" This weather liketh not the Queen," remarked
Christina, who was standing by an open window
looking out on the park. " She is thereby penned up,
and cannot ride abroad to hunt." As she spoke, the
wind drove the rain with such violence into her face
that she was obliged to draw back farther into the
room, and Hutton, growing bolder, asked if it were
true that the Duchess herself loved hunting.
" Nothing better," replied Christina, laughing; and
she seemed as if she would gladly have prolonged the
conversation. But then two ancient gentlemen drew
near—" Master Bernadotte Court, her Grand Master,
who, next to Monsieur de Courrières, is chief about
her and another "—and, with a parting bow, the
Duchess retired to her own rooms.

" She speaketh French," adds Hutton in reporting
this interview to Cromwell, " and seemeth to be of
few words. And in her speaking she lispeth, which

doth nothing misbecome her.   I cannot in anything
perceive but she should be of much soberness, very
wise, and no less gentle."[1]

Among the ladies who came to Court for the
Carnival fêtes, Hutton found a friend in the
Duke of Aerschot's sister, Madame de Berghen, a
lively lady whom he had known in the town of
Berghen-op-Zoom, where he had spent much time as
Governor of the Merchant Adventurers. The Dutch
merchants in this city had presented him with a
house, an honour which the Ambassador appreciated
highly, although he complained that it led him into
great extravagance, and that the furniture, tapestries,
and pictures, necessary for its adornment, " plucked
the lining out of his purse, and left him as rich as a
newly-shorn sheep."[2]

One day Madame de Berghen saw Hutton in the
act of delivering a packet of letters which Wyatt had
forwarded from Barcelona to the Queen, and her
curiosity was excited by the warmth of Mary's thanks.
That evening she invited the English Ambassador to
dinner to meet her kinsman the Bishop of Liége, " a
goodly personage," remarks Hutton, " but a man of
little learning and less discretion, and, like most
Bishops in these parts, very unfit for his office."
When this secular ecclesiastic retired, the Lady
Marchioness, " whose tongue always wagged freely,"
asked Hutton if the letters which he had delivered to
the Queen came from England, and confessed that
she hoped they contained good news regarding the
Duchess of Milan, whose beauty, wisdom, and great
gentleness, she could not praise too highly. She told
him that he would have been amazed had he seen

[1] State Papers, Record Office, viii. 16.   [2] Ibid., viii. 30.

Christina gorgeously apparelled as she was the day
before, and confided to him that the Duchess was
having her portrait taken by the Court painter,
Bernard van Orley, and had promised to give it to
her. Hutton begged to be allowed to borrow the picture in order to show it to his wife, and told Cromwell
that as soon as he could secure the portrait he would
send it to England. Accordingly, on the 9th of
March the Ambassador received the picture, which
Madame de Berghen begged him to accept as her gift,
and sent a servant to bear it without delay to the
Lord Privy Seal's house in St. James's. Late on the
following evening, much to the Ambassador's surprise, a young Shropshire gentleman, named Mr.
Philip Hoby, who had lately entered Cromwell's service, appeared at his lodgings, accompanied by the
King's painter, Master Hans Holbein. At this time
the German master was at the height of his reputation.
Since 1536, when he entered Henry's service as Court
painter, he had executed some of his finest portraits,
including the famous picture of the King in Whitehall
Palace, the superb portrait of Queen Jane, and that
of Cromwell himself, which is so marvellous a revela-
tion of character. Now the Lord Privy Seal sent him
across the Channel to take a sketch of the Duchess
of Milan, and bring it back with all possible despatch.

Hutton's first idea was to send a messenger to stop
the bearer of the Flemish portrait, fearing it might
give a wrong impression of the lady, " since it was
not so perfect as the cause required, and as the said
Mr. Haunce could make it." But his servant had
already sailed, and the Ambassador could only beg
Cromwell to await Master Hans's return before he
formed any opinion of the Duchess. The next morn-

ing he waited on the Queen, and informed her how
the Lord Privy Seal, having received secret overtures from the Imperial Ambassador for a marriage
between the King's Majesty and Her Grace of Milan,
thought the best way to approach the King was to
show him a portrait of the Duchess.

" And forasmuch as his lordship heard great
commendation of the form, beauty, wisdom, and
other virtuous qualities, with which God had endowed the Duchess, he could perceive no means more
meet for the advancement of the same than to procure her perfect picture, for which he had sent a
man very excellent in the making of physiognomies."

After long and elaborate explanation, Hutton asked
humbly if his lordship's servant might salute the
Duchess, and beg her to appoint a time and place for
the painter to accomplish his task.

Mary was evidently greatly surprised to hear of
the Ambassador's errand. She started from her
chair in amazement, but, quickly recovering com-
posure, she sat down again, and listened atten-
tively till Hutton had done speaking. Then she
thanked him and Lord Cromwell for their good-will
to the Emperor, and said that she had no objection
to grant his request, and that he should see the
Duchess herself. With these few words she rose
and passed into the Council-chamber. Presently
Christina entered the room, attended by two ladies.
She listened graciously to Hutton's message, expressed her gratitude to Lord Cromwell for his kind
intentions, and sent Benedetto da Corte back with
him to meet the English gentleman. Fortunately,
Philip Hoby was a pleasant and cultivated young
man who could speak Italian fluently. He conversed for some time with Messer Benedetto, much

to Hutton's envy and admiration, and at two o'clock that afternoon was conducted by him into the presence of the Duchess. Cromwell had given Hoby minute instructions as to his behaviour on this occasion, and had composed a long and elaborate speech which he was to deliver to Christina herself.

" The said Philip shall, as of himself, express a wish that it might please the King, now a widower, to advance Her Grace to the honour of Queen of England, considering her virtuous qualities were a great deal more than ever was notified, and for a great confirmation of amity and love to continue between the Emperor's Majesty and the King's Highness."

Hoby was charged to take careful note of the Duchess's answers, gestures, and expression, and was especially to note if she seemed favourably inclined to these proposals, in order that he might be able to satisfy Henry's anxiety on the subject.[1]

Philip Hoby was too accomplished a courtier not to discharge his errand with tact and courtesy. The Duchess was graciously pleased to accede to his request, and at one o'clock the next day Holbein was ushered by Messer Benedetto into his mistress's presence. The time allowed for the sitting was short, but Master Hans was an adept at his art, and had already taken drawings in this swift and masterly fashion of all the chief personages at the English Court.

" Having but three hours' space," wrote Hutton, " he showed himself to be master of that science. For his picture is very perfect; the other is but slobbered in comparison to it, as by the sight of both your lordship shall well perceive."[2]

[1] British Museum, Additional Manuscripts, 5,498, f. 2 ; Calendar of State Papers, xiii. 1, 130.

[2] State Papers, Record Office, viii. 17-19.

An hour afterwards Hoby and the painter both took leave of the Duchess and started for England.   In order to avoid suspicion and observe the strict secrecy enjoined by Cromwell, Hoby did not even seek a farewell audience ˏfrom the Regent, who contented herself with sending friendly greetings to the Lord Privy Seal, saying that he should hear from her more at large through the Imperial Ambassadors.

The precious sketch, from which Holbein afterwards made " the great table "[1] which hung in the Palace of

[1] Holbein's portrait is described in the Catalogues of the King's pictures at Westminster in 1542 and 1547 as " No. 12. A greate Table with the picture of the Duchess of Myllane, being her whole stature."   After Henry's death it passed into the hands of Fitzalan, Earl of Arundel, the King's Lord Chamberlain and godson, who married Lady Katherine Grey, and acquired the Palace of Nonsuch, with most of its contents.   When he died, in 1580, it became the property, first of his elder daughter Jane, wife of Lord Lumley, and then of her great-nephew, Thomas Howard, Earl of Arundel.   This great collector took the Duchess of Milan's portrait with him abroad during the Civil Wars, and after his death, in 1645, it hung, with many other Holbeins, in the house of his widow at Amsterdam.   Lady Arundel left the whole collection to her son, Henry Howard, who became the sixth Duke of Norfolk, and Holbein's portrait remained in the family until, in 1909, it was acquired by the National Gallery for the sum of £72,000.   A second portrait of the Duchess of Milan, a half-length, is mentioned in Henry VIII.'s Catalogues ("No. 138. A Table with a picture of the Duchess of Myllane"), and was discovered by Sir George Scharf in a waiting-room near the private chapel at Windsor.   This is probably the portrait by Van Orley which Hutton sent to England before Holbein's arrival at Brussels. The attitude of the sitter, her dress and features, are the same as in Holbein's picture, but the face is less finely modelled and lacks charm and expression.   The hands are in a slightly different position, and instead of one big ruby ring she wears three rings —a cameo and a gold ring on the right hand, and a black ring, the badge of widowhood, on the third finger of the left hand.   This curious and interesting portrait is plainly the work of an inferior

Westminster until Henry's death, was safely delivered into Cromwell's hands, and shown by him to
the King on the 18th of March. Henry was singularly pleased with the portrait, and, as his courtiers
noticed, seemed to be in better humour than for
months past. For the first time since Queen Jane's
death he sent for his musicians, and made them play
to him all the afternoon and evening. Two days
afterwards he went to Hampton Court, and " gave
orders for new and sumptuous buildings " at this
riverside palace. After that he returned to Whitehall by water, accompanied by his whole troop of
musicians, paid a visit to his brother-in-law's wife,
Katherine, Duchess of Suffolk, and resumed his old
habit of going about with a few of his favourites in
masks—" a sure sign," remarked Chapuys, " that he
is going to marry again."

The Imperial Ambassadors, Chapuys and his
colleague Don Diego Mendoza, were now treated with
extraordinary civility. They were invited to Hampton Court, where Henry entertained them at a
splendid banquet, and showed them his " fine new
lodgings " and the priceless tapestries and works of
art with which Cardinal Wolsey had adorned this
magnificent house. The next day they were taken
to the royal manor of Nonsuch to see the little Prince,
" one of the prettiest children you ever saw, and his
sister, Madam Elizabeth, who is also a sweet little
girl." Then they went on to Richmond to visit Prin-

---

artist, and, as the Ambassador justly remarked, bears no comparison with Holbein's Duchess—" surely," in the words of his
biographer, " one of the most precious pictures in the world "
(Wornum's " Life of Holbein," p. 322; L. Cust in the *Burlington
Magazine*, August, 1911, p. 278; and Sir G. Scharf in " Archæologia," xl. 205).

cess Mary, who played to them with rare skill on both spinet and lute, and spoke of her cousin the Emperor in terms of the deepest gratitude. The French Ambassadors, Castillon and the Bishop of Tarbes, who arrived at Hampton Court just as the Imperial Envoys were leaving, were received with marked coolness, a treatment, as Chapuys shrewdly remarks, "no doubt artfully designed to excite their jealousy."[1]

The sight of Holbein's portrait revived Henry's wish to see Christina, and he pressed Chapuys earnestly to induce his good sister the Queen of Hungary to bring her niece to meet him at Calais. But on this point Mary was obdurate. She told the Ambassador that this was out of the question, and although she wrote civilly to the Lord Privy Seal, thanking him for his good offices, she complained bitterly to Chapuys of Cromwell's extraordinary proceeding in sending the painter to Brussels, and laid great stress on her condescension in allowing him to take her niece's portrait. So far Charles himself had never written fully to his sister on the subject, and Mary asked Chapuys repeatedly if these proposals really came from the Emperor, and if the King and Cromwell were sincere. As for her part, she believed these flattering words were merely intended to deceive her. Chapuys could only assure her that both Henry and his Minister were very much in earnest. When the courier arrived from Spain, the King was bitterly disappointed because there was no letter from Charles, and sent Cromwell twice to implore the Ambassadors, for God's sake, to tell him if they had any good news to impart. On Lady Day the Minister came to Chapuys's lodgings, and, after two hours' earnest con-

[1] Calendar of Spanish State Papers, v. 2, 523.

versation, went away " somewhat consoled." The next day Henry sent for the Ambassadors, and discussed the subject in the frankest, most familiar manner, ending by saying with a merry laugh: " You think it a good joke, I trow, to see me in love at my age !"

In his impatience, Henry complained that Hutton was remiss in his duties, and did not say enough about the Duchess in his despatches. Yet the excellent Ambassador was unremitting in his attendance on Her Grace, and spent many hours daily at Court, watching her closely when she danced or played at cards, and telling the King that he " felt satisfied that her great modesty and gentleness proceeded from no want of wit, but that she was rather to be esteemed wisest among the wise."[1]

From the day of Hoby's visit Christina treated Hutton with marked friendliness, and threw aside much of her reserve in talking with him. On the bright spring days, when the Queen and her niece hunted daily in the forest, the Englishman seldom failed to accompany them. He admired the Duchess's bold horsemanship, and was much struck by the evident delight which she and her aunt took in this favourite sport. By way of ingratiating himself with Mary, he presented her with four couple of English hounds, " the fairest that he had ever seen," and a fine gelding, which made Christina remark that he had done the Queen a great pleasure, and that she had never seen her aunt so well mounted. Hutton hastened to reply that, since Her Grace was good enough to admire the horse, he would do his utmost to secure another as good for her own use,

[1] State Papers, Record Office, viii. 21.

which offer she accepted graciously.[1] All these incidents naturally provoked attention, and, in spite of the secrecy with which the negotiations were carried on, the King's marriage with the Duchess of Milan was freely discussed both in Flanders and in England.

" Few Englishmen," wrote the Duke of Norfolk to Cromwell on the 6th of April, " will regret the King of Scots' marriage to Madame de Longueville, hoping that one of Burgundian blood may have the place she might have had."[2]

And the report that after Easter the King was going to meet his future bride at Calais became so persistent that even Castillon believed it, and complained to his royal master of the strange alteration in Henry's behaviour, and of the marvellous haughtiness and coldness with which he was now treated.[3]

III.

On the 27th of March the Imperial Ambassadors dined at the Lord Privy Seal's house, to meet Archbishop Cranmer, Chancellor Audley, Thomas Brandon, Duke of Suffolk, the Lord High Admiral Southampton, and two other Bishops, who were the Commissioners appointed to treat of two royal marriages. One of these was the long-planned union of Princess Mary with the Infant Don Louis of Portugal, brother of the reigning King, which was the ostensible object of Don Diego's mission to England. The other was the King's own marriage with the Duchess, which Henry sent word must be arranged at once, since

---

[1] State Papers, Record Office, viii. 30.
[2] Calendar of State Papers, xiii. 1, 263.
[3] Kaulek, 29, 33, 35.

until this was concluded he absolutely refused to treat of his daughter's alliance with the Infant. As they sat down at table, by way of *Benedicite*, remarks Chapuys, the King's deputies began by rejoicing to think they had not to deal with Frenchmen, and pouring scorn on their mendacious habits. But before the end of the meeting many difficulties had arisen. First of all the English Commissioners demanded that the Count Palatine should renounce all his wife's rights to the crown of Denmark without compensation. Then the question of the Papal dispensation, which was necessary owing to Christina's relationship to Katherine of Aragon, was mooted, and, as Chapuys soon realized, was likely to prove an insuperable difficulty, since nothing would induce Henry to recognize the Pope's authority.[1]

During the next few weeks several meetings between the Commissioners took place, and the Ambassadors were repeatedly admitted to confer with the King and his Privy Council; but little progress was made, and Chapuys informed the Regent that there was even less hope of agreement than there had been at first. Henry on his part complained loudly of the coldness of the Imperial Envoys, and of their evident desire to push forward the Portuguese marriage and drop his own, which was the one thing for which he really cared.[2] An attempt to effect some mode of reconciliation between him and the Pope only incensed Henry, who sent two Doctors of Law, Bonner and Haynes, to Madrid, to protest against the meeting of a General Council, and to point out how the Bishops of Rome wrested Scripture

[1] Calendar of Spanish State Papers, v. 2, 524.
[2] Calendar of State Papers, xiii. 1, 258.

to the maintenance of their lusts and worldly advantage. And he told Don Diego angrily that the meeting of a Council would do him the worst injury in the world, since if he refused to attend it he would be cut off from the rest of Christendom.[1] To add to the King's ill-temper, he was suffering from a return of the ulcers in the leg from which he had formerly suffered, and for some days his condition excited serious alarm.

On his recovery, Castillon, who had been looking on with some amusement while the Emperor's folk were " busy brewing marriages," approached His Majesty with flattering words, and tried to instil suspicions of Cromwell into his mind. Henry swallowed the bait greedily, and the French Ambassador's remarks on his favourite's " great Spanish passion " rankled in his mind to so great an extent that he sent for Cromwell and rated him soundly, telling him that he was quite unfit to meddle in the affairs of Kings. The wily Frenchman, satisfied that the only way of managing this wayward monarch was to make him fall in love, took advantage of his present mood to speak to him of the Queen of Scotland's sister, Louise de Guise, whom he described as being quite as beautiful as herself, with the additional advantage of being a maid, and not a widow. Henry, who was on his way to Mass when Castillon made this suggestion, slapped him familiarly on the back, and laughed, saying he must hear more of this young lady. The next day the Comptroller of the King's Household was sent to ask the Ambassador for particulars about Mademoiselle de Guise, and was told that she was so like Madame de Longueville that you

[1] Calendar of Spanish State Papers, v. 2, 526, 558.

would hardly know the sisters apart, and that a
Scotchman who had seen both, wondered how King
James could prefer Mary to so lovely a creature as
Louise. The French Ambassador now found himself overwhelmed with attentions. The King sent
him presents of venison and artichokes from his
gardens, invited him to spend Sunday at Greenwich, and, when the plague broke out in London,
lent him the beautiful old house in Chelsea which
had belonged to Sir Thomas More, as a country
residence.[1]

The wedding of King James was finally celebrated
at Châteaudun on the 9th of May, and, hearing that
the Duke of Guise and his fair daughter Louise had
accompanied the new Queen to Havre, Henry sent
Philip Hoby across the Channel to see Mademoiselle de
Guise and have her picture painted. These orders
were duly executed, and Louise's portrait, probably
painted by Holbein, was placed in the King's hands.
But, although Henry " did not find the portrait ugly,"
he was now anxious to see Louise's younger sister,
Renée, who was said to be still more beautiful, and
would not be put off when Castillon told him that
she was about to take the veil in a convent at Reims.

" No doubt," remarked Montmorency, the Constable of France, " as King Henry has made himself
Pope in his own country, he would prefer a nun to
any other Princess."[2]

Nothing would now satisfy Henry but that the
French King or Queen should meet him at Calais
with the Duke of Guise's daughters, Mademoiselle de
Lorraine, and Mademoiselle de Vendôme, who had
all been recommended to his notice. When the

[1] Kaulek, 48, 50, 53, 58, 70.   [2] Ibid., 58, 73; Pimodan, 73.

English Envoy, Brian, proposed this to Queen Eleanor, she replied indignantly that she was not a keeper of harlots, and the Constable told Castillon once more that French Princesses were not to be trotted out like hackneys at a fair. At last the Ambassador, tired of repeating that this plan was impossible, asked Henry if the Knights of King Arthur's Round Table had ever treated ladies in such a fashion. This brought the King to his senses. He reddened and hesitated, and, after rubbing his nose for some moments, said that his proposal might have sounded a little uncivil, but he had been so often deceived in these matters that he could trust no one but himself.[1]

Still Henry would not give up all hope of winning the fair Louise, and towards the end of August he sent Philip Hoby on a fresh errand to Joinville. As before, he was to take Holbein with him, and, after viewing well the younger sister, ask the Duchess of Guise for leave to take the portraits of both her daughters, Louise and Renée, " in one faire table." Hoby was to explain that he had business in these parts, and that, since he had already made acquaintance with Mademoiselle de Guise at Havre, he could not pass Joinville without saluting her. On leaving Joinville he was to proceed to the Duke of Lorraine's Court, and inform him that the Lord Privy Seal, having heard that His Excellency had a daughter of excellent quality, begged that the King's painter might be allowed to take her portrait. On the 30th of August the travellers reached Joinville, as we learn from the following letter addressed by the Duchess of Guise to her eldest daughter in Scotland:

[1] Kaulek, 76, 79, 81; Spanish State Papers, vi. 1, 9.

" It is but two days since the King of England's gentleman who was at Havre, and the painter, were here.   The gentleman came to see me, pretending that he was on his way to find the Emperor, and, having heard that Louise was ill, would not pass by without inquiring after her, that he might take back news of her health to the King his master.   He begged to be allowed to see her, which he did, although it was a day when the fever was on her, and repeated the same words which he had already said to me. He then told me that, as he was so near Lorraine, he meant to go on to Nancy to see the country.   I have no doubt that he was going there to draw Mademoiselle's portrait, in the same way that he has drawn the others, and so I sent down to the gentleman's lodgings, and found that the said painter was there.   Since then they have been at Nancy, where they spent a day and were well feasted and entertained, and at every meal the *maître d'hôtel* ate with them, and many presents were made them. That is all I know yet, but you see that, at the worst, if you do not have your sister for a neighbour, you may yet have your cousin."[1]

This time Hoby's journey was evidently unsuccessful.   Louise was ill of intermittent fever, and Renée had already been sent to the convent at Reims, where she was afterwards professed; and it is clear from Antoinette's letters that she had no wish to marry either of her daughters to Henry.   A month before, on the 3rd of August, she wrote to the Queen of Scotland: " I have heard nothing more of the proposals which you know of "; and again on the 18th: " I have begged your father to speak of these affairs to the King, that we may be rid of them if possible, for no one could ever be happy with such a man."[2]

As for Anne de Lorraine, in spite of many excellent qualities, she lacked the beauty and charm

---

[1] Balcarres Manuscripts, ii. 20.   [2] *Ibid.*, ii. 10.

of her cousins, and, as her aunt Antoinette said,
" elle est bien honnête, mais pas si belle que je
voudrais."[1]

The result of these disappointments was to revive
Henry's wish to marry Christina. Several times in
the course of the summer Castillon remarked that
this monarch was still hankering after the Duchess of
Milan, and had repeatedly tried to induce the Regent
to bring her niece to meet him at Brussels. " The
King my master," said Cromwell to Chapuys, " will
never marry one, who is to be his companion for life,
without he has first seen and known her."[2] In a
long and careful paper of instructions which Henry

[1] There has been some confusion as to the date of Holbein's visit to Joinville, owing to a mistake in the Calendar
of State Papers (xiii. 1, 130), where Cromwell's instructions
to Hoby for his journeys to Brussels and France are entered
under the date of February, 1538. But the Duchess of Guise's
letter (see Appendix), as well as the payment of £10 made by
Sir Brian Tuke, Treasurer of the Household, to Hans Holbein on
the 30th of December, 1538, " for going to the parts of High
Burgony about certain of the King's business," make it clear
that this journey took place at the end of August (G. Scharf,
" Archæologia," xxxix. 7). From Lorraine the painter went on
to Bâle, where he spent some months, and returned to England
at Christmas. The original documents in the British Museum
(Additional Manuscripts, 5,498, f. 1) bear no date, and are on
separate sheets, and the heading of the instructions regarding
the journey to Brussels was added by a later hand, and is thus
worded : " Instructions given by the L. Cromwell to Philip Hoby,
sent over by him to the Duchess of Lorraine, then Duchess of
Milan "—i.e., Christina, Duchess of Lorraine, at that time Duchess
of Milan. But the editor of the Calendars inserted the words
" to the " between " then " and " Duchess of Milan," thus making
it appear that Hoby went first to Lorraine, and then to the Duchess
of Milan, whereas the journey to Brussels took place in March,
and that to Lorraine in August. Since this chapter was written,
the subject has been fully dealt with by Mr. A. B. Chamberlain
in the Burlington Magazine, April, 1912.

[2] Calendar of Spanish State Papers, v. 2, 531.

drew up for the Ambassador Wyatt, he lays great
stress on this point.

" His Grace, prudently considering how that marriage is a bargain of such nature as may endure for
the whole life of man, and a thing whereof the
pleasure and quiet, or the displeasure and torment,
doth much depend, thinketh it to be most necessary,
both for himself and the party with whom it shall
please God to join him in marriage, that the one
might see the other before the time that they should
be so affianced, which point His Highness hath
largely set forth heretofore to the Emperor's Ambassador."[1]

But on her side Mary was equally inflexible.
Nothing would induce her to take a step forward
in this direction, and even Hutton began to realize
how coldly the marriage overtures were received at
Brussels. The Queen never failed to ask after the
King's health or to express her anxiety for the
strengthening of the ancient friendship between the
realm of England and the House of Burgundy; but
when the Ambassador ventured to allude to the
subject of her niece's preferment, she invariably
gave an evasive reply. Since both the Queen and
the Duchess spent much of the summer hunting
in the Forest of Soignies, or in more distant parts,
Hutton seldom had an opportunity of seeing Christina. Her servants were still very friendly, especially the Lord Benedick Court, as Hutton calls the
Italian master of her household. One evening in
June, when Hutton had been at Court, Benedetto
came back to supper with him, whether of his own
accord or at his mistress's command the Englishman could not tell. As they walked along the street,

[1] Nott's " Life of Wyatt," ii. 488.

Benedetto asked the Ambassador if he had brought the Queen any good news about the Duchess. Hutton replied that the first good news must come from the Emperor, and, to his mind, was a long time upon the road. The old man looked up to heaven, and said devoutly: " I pray God that I may live to see her given to your master, even if I die the next day. But," he added significantly, " there is one doubt in the matter." Hutton asked eagerly what this might be, upon which Benedetto explained that, as the King's first wife, the Lady Katherine, was near of kin to the Duchess, the marriage could not be solemnized without the Pope's dispensation, and this he feared His Majesty would never accept. The Ambassador replied warmly that he did not know what might be against the Bishop of Rome's laws, but that he was quite sure his master would do nothing against God's laws. Then they sat down to supper with other guests, and nothing further was said on the subject. But the old Italian knew what he was talking about, and the Papal dispensation proved to be the one insuperable obstacle which stood in the way of a settlement.[1]

Another of Christina's servants, Gian Battista Ferrari, paid a visit to England this summer, and brought back glowing accounts of the beauties of London and the splendours of King Henry's Court. He had an Italian friend named Panizone, who was one of the royal equerries, and had been sent over to England with some Barbary horses from the Gonzaga stables. Panizone introduced him to Cromwell, who entertained him hospitably, and sent him back to tell his mistress all that he had seen and

[1] State Papers, Record Office, viii. 33.

done at the Court of Whitehall. Christina was exceedingly curious to hear Battista's account of his visit, and was surprised when he told her that England was as beautiful as Italy. When she proceeded to inquire if he had seen the King, Battista replied that he had been fortunate enough to be received by His Majesty, and broke into ecstatic praises of Henry's comeliness, gracious manners, and liberality. The Duchess said that she had often heard praises of His Grace, and was glad to know from Battista's lips that they were true. After supper she sent for him again, and he informed her that Chapuys had told him the marriage would shortly be concluded. " At this it seemeth she did much rejoice." So at least Battista assured Hutton.[1] Ferrari himself was evidently very anxious to see his mistress Queen of England, and in a letter which he addressed on the 7th of September to his friend, " Guglielmo Panizone scudier del Invictissimo Rè d'Inghilterrà a Londra, alla Corte di sua Maestà," he wrote, "Madama the Duchess, my mistress, loves the King truly," and proceeded to send commendations to the Lord Privy Seal, Signor Filippo (Hoby), Portinari, and others. This letter contained one sad piece of news. " The Ambassador here is said to be dying; I am grieved because of the friendship between us and his excellent qualities. The next one we have will, I hope, be yourself."[2] Battista's news was true. Honest John Hutton, the popular Governor of the Merchant Adventurers, fell ill at Antwerp, and died there on the 5th of September. His genial nature had made him a general favourite,

[1] State Papers, Record Office, viii. 40.
[2] Calendar of State Papers, xiii. 2, 119,

and he was lamented by everyone at Court. " It is a great loss," wrote Don Diego to Cromwell, " because he was so good a servant and so merry and honest a soul." To his own master, the Emperor, he remarked that the English Ambassador who had just died was a jovial, good-natured man, but more fit for courtly functions and social intercourse than grave political business, for which he had neither taste nor capacity.[1]

IV.

The meeting of the Emperor and King of France at Aigues-Mortes in July, 1538, produced a marked change in the political situation. This interview, which the Pope had failed to bring about at Nice, was finally effected by Queen Eleanor, and the two monarchs, who had not met since Francis was a prisoner at Madrid, embraced each other, dined together, and ended by swearing an inviolable friendship. The truce was converted into a lasting peace, and several marriages between the two families were discussed in a friendly and informal manner.

" Never," wrote the Constable to Castillon, " were there two faster friends than the King and Emperor, and I do not for a moment imagine that His Imperial Majesty will ever allow the Widow of Milan to marry King Henry ! So do not believe a single word that you hear in England !"[2]

This unexpected reconciliation was a bitter pill to Henry and Cromwell. The French and Imperial Ambassadors at Whitehall exchanged the warmest congratulations, and did not fail to indulge in a hearty laugh at King Henry's expense. On the 21st of August Chapuys and Don Diego followed the

[1] Calendar of Spanish State Papers, vi. 1, 42.   [2] Kaulek, 77.

Court to Ampthill, where the King was hunting, and were entertained by Cromwell at one of his own manors. As they sat down to dinner, the Lord Privy Seal asked brusquely if it were true that the King and Emperor had made peace, to which the Ambassadors replied in the affirmative. He then proceeded to start a variety of disagreeable topics. First he remarked that he heard the Turk was already in Belgrade; next he said that the young Duke of Cleves had taken possession of Guelderland, upon which Chapuys retaliated by expatiating on the perfect friendship and understanding between Charles and Francis. After dinner they were admitted into the King's presence, and informed him that the Queen of Hungary had received the powers necessary for the conclusion of the Duchess's marriage, and wished to recall Don Diego in order that he might draw up the contract. Henry expressed great sorrow at parting from the Spaniard, and, drawing him apart, begged him to induce the Queen to treat directly with him, repeating two or three times that he was growing old, and could not put off taking a wife any longer. Meanwhile Cromwell was telling Chapuys, in another corner of the hall, how much annoyed the King had been to hear that the Emperor was treating of his niece's marriage with the Duke of Cleves, which would make people say either that she had refused the King or else had only accepted Henry after refusing Cleves. Chapuys stoutly denied the truth of this report, and Cromwell confessed that the King was very eager for the marriage, and, if there were any difficulty about the Duchess's dowry, he would gladly give her 20,000 crowns out of his own purse.[1]

[1] Calendar of Spanish State Papers, vi. 15-31.

As the Ambassadors were putting on their riding-boots, Cromwell ran after Don Diego with a present from his master of £400, after which they returned to London and dined in Chelsea with Castillon, to meet Madame de Montreuil, the lady-in-waiting of the late Queen Madeleine of Scotland, who was returning to France. They all spent a merry evening, laughing over King Henry's matrimonial plans, and Castillon declared that the King and Lord Privy Seal were so much perturbed at his master's alliance with the Emperor that they hardly knew if they were in heaven or on earth.[1]

Don Diego arrived in Flanders to find general rejoicings—" gun-shots and melody and jousting were the order of the day "—and an English merchant declared that the proud Spaniards were ready to challenge all the world. Queen Mary marked the occasion by honouring her favourite, Count Henry of Nassau, with a visit at his Castle of Breda in Holland. The beautiful gardens and vast orchards planted in squares, after the fashion of Italy, which excited the Cardinal of Aragon's admiration, were in their summer beauty, and a series of magnificent fêtes were given in honour of the Queen and her companion, the Duchess of Milan. The Count was assisted in doing the honours by his third wife, the Marchioness of Zeneta, a rich Spanish heiress, whom the Emperor had given him in marriage, and his son René, Prince of Orange. The presence of Christina at Breda on this occasion, and the attentions that were paid her by her hosts, naturally gave rise to a report that she was about to wed the Prince, and Cromwell told Don Diego before he left Dover that this rumour had

[1] Calendar of Spanish State Papers, vi. 41.

caused the King great annoyance.[1] But the festivities at Breda met with a tragic close. On the
day after the royal ladies left the castle, Henry of
Nassau died very suddenly, and Don Diego heard
the sad news when he reached the castle gates, on
his way to salute his kinswoman, the Marchioness.

The Ambassador now hastened to Court, and craved
an audience of the Queen to deliver King Henry's
letters; but he found her little inclined to attend to
business, and engaged in preparations to pay a visit
to King Francis, who had gallantly invited her to
a hunting-party at Compiègne. At first there had
been some doubt if the Duchess should be of the
party, but Queen Eleanor was eager to see her niece,
and Christina was nothing loth to take part in these
brilliant festivities. Meanwhile Henry's renewed impatience to conclude his marriage was shown by the
promptitude with which another Ambassador was
sent to take Hutton's place.

On the 27th of September the new Envoy, Stephen
Vaughan, was admitted into the Queen's presence,
and begged for an answer to the letters delivered by
Don Diego. Mary told him that he might inform
His Majesty that there was no truth in the reports
of her niece's marriage, and that, if any coolness had
arisen between them, it was the King's own fault
for seeking a wife in other places. Hoby's mission
to Joinville and Nancy was, it is plain, well known
at Brussels. But the Queen kept her counsel, and
told Vaughan that, if his master was still in the same
mind, she would urge the Emperor to hasten the
conclusion of the treaty. Only she must beg the
Ambassador to have a little patience, as her time

---

[1] Calendar of Spanish State Papers, vi. 46.

was fully occupied at this moment. But the next day he was again put off, and told the Queen would see him when she reached Mons. Accordingly, Vaughan and his colleague, Thomas Wriothesley, Cromwell's confidential secretary, arrived at this town on the 8th, only to be told by Don Diego that they must await the Queen's pleasure at Valenciennes. The Spanish Ambassador did his best to atone for their disappointment by giving them an excellent dinner, and lending them two of his own horses with velvet saddles and rich trappings for the journey.[1]

At length, at eight on Sunday morning, the 6th of October, they were conducted into the Queen's presence by the Grand Falconer, Molembais, and Vaughan, who spoke French fluently, explained Henry's reasons for arranging the marriage treaty without delay. Mary replied briefly that she had already written to accede to the King's request, and that no further steps could be taken until after her meeting with the French King. Dinner was being served while she spoke these words, and, as the meat was actually coming in, the Ambassadors were compelled to retire. Before they left the room, however, they saluted the Duchess, who was standing near her aunt, and ventured to tell her how much my Lord Privy Seal remained her humble servant, although, as she no doubt knew, his overtures had been so coldly received. Christina smiled and thanked them for their good-will with a gentle grace, which went far to mollify their ruffled feelings, and made Wriothesley write home that all Hutton had

[1] State Papers, Record Office, viii. 53, 56; Calendar of State Papers, xiii. 2, 214.

said of the Duchess's charms was true. " She is as
goodly personage, of stature higher than either of us,
and hath a very good woman's face, competently
fair and well favoured, but a little brown."[1]

As if to make amends for these delays, the great
lords in attendance overwhelmed the Ambassadors
with civilities. Aerschot invited them to dinner;
Count Büren embraced them warmly and asked affectionately after the King; De Praet, Molembais, and
Iselstein, escorted them to the door, and Don Diego
made them a present of wine. When Wriothesley
fell ill of fever at Cambray, the Queen sent her own
physician to attend him, and begged him either to
remain there or return to Brussels. This he refused
to do, and travelled on by slow stages to Compiègne,
hoping to obtain another audience there. But the
roads were bad, and two leagues from Cambray one
of the carts broke down, leaving the English without
household stuff or plate when Don Diego came to
supper.[2]

On Tuesday news reached Cambray that King
Francis was on his way to salute the Queen, and
Mary rode out to meet him, leaving the Duchess of
Milan at home with others, who like herself, remarks
Wriothesley, had no great liking for Frenchmen.[3] But
the King's greeting was most cordial, and when, on
the following day, Queen Eleanor arrived with a great
train of lords and ladies, there was much feasting
and merriment, until on the 10th the whole party
started for Compiègne.

It was a brilliant company that met in the ancient

---

[1] State Papers, Record Office, viii. 56-60.
[2] Calendar of State Papers, xiii. 2, 245, 247.
[3] State Papers, Record Office, viii. 67.

castle of the French Kings, in the forest on the banks of the Oise, near the bridge where, a hundred years before, Jeanne d'Arc had made her last heroic stand. King Francis had summoned all the Princes and Princesses of the blood to do honour to the Queen of Hungary, and the neighbouring villages were filled to overflowing with Court officials and servants. There was the King himself, a fine figure in cloth of gold and nodding plumes, gallant as ever in spite of ill-health and advancing years, with a glance and smile to spare for every fair lady; and there was his consort, Queen Eleanor, too often neglected by her fickle lord, but now radiant with happiness, and in her beautiful robes and priceless pearls, as winning and almost as fair as when she fascinated the young Palatine twenty years ago. The sense of family affection was as strong in Eleanor as in all the Habsburgs, and she was overjoyed to meet her sister and embrace the daughter of the beloved and lamented Isabella. With her came the King's daughter Margaret, the homely-featured but pleasing and accomplished Princess for whom a royal husband was still to be found, and who, the courtiers whispered, might now wed the Prince of Spain.

Her brothers were there too—the dull and morose Henry, who had succeeded his elder brother as Dauphin two years before, but had never recovered from the effects of his long captivity in Spain; and the more lively but weak and vicious Charles of Angoulême, now Duke of Orleans, whom Eleanor was so anxious to see married to the Duchess of Milan. With them was the Dauphin's Italian wife, Catherine de' Medici, whose wit and grace atoned in her father-in-law's eyes for her lack of beauty, although her husband's heart was given to Diane de Poitiers, and a childless marriage made her unpopular in the eyes of the nation. But a galaxy of fair ladies surrounded the King and Queen. Chief among them was Madame d'Étampes, whose dazzling charms had captivated the fickle King, and who now reigned supreme both in Court and Council. Of the youthful ladies whose charms had aroused King Henry's interest, only Mademoiselle de Vendôme was here. The fair Louise had not yet recovered from her illness, and the Duchess of Guise was nursing her at Joinville. But both her father, Claude of Guise, the Governor of Burgundy, and his brother, the Cardinal of Lorraine, were present, and held a high place in the King's favour. Claude's elder brother, the Duke of Lorraine, had lately been to meet the Emperor at Aigues-Mortes and plead his claims to Guelders, but on his return he fell ill with a severe attack of gout, and was unable to obey the King's summons. In his stead he sent Duchess Renée his wife, another Bourbon Princess, a daughter of Gilbert de Montpensier and sister of the famous Constable. Her daughter Anne remained at home to nurse the Duke, but her eldest son, Francis, came with his mother to Compiègne. This cultured and polished Prince, who bore the King's name, had been brought up at the French Court, and could ride and joust as well as any of his peers; but he was quite thrown into the shade by his cousin, Antoine de Bourbon, Duke of Vendôme, the darling of the people and the idol of all the ladies. A head and shoulders taller than the Dauphin and his brother, Antoine was the cynosure of all eyes at Court festivals. The elegance of his attire, the inimitable grace with which he raised his hat, his wit and gaiety,

fascinated every woman, while the gilded youth of
the day copied the fashion of his clothes and the
precise angle at which he wore the feather in his cap.
Frivolous, volatile, and recklessly extravagant, Vendôme wore his heart on his sleeve, and was ready to
enter the lists for the sake of any fair lady. He fell
desperately in love with the Duchess of Milan at first
sight, and devoted himself to her service. As premier
Prince of the blood, he rode at Christina's side, and led
her out to dance in the eyes of the Court. Together they
joined in the hunting-parties that were organized on
a vast scale in the Forest of Compiègne, and while all
the French were lost in admiration at the fine horsemanship of the royal ladies, Antoine de Bourbon
threw himself at the Duchess's feet, and declared
himself her slave for life. But whether this gay
cavalier was too wild and thoughtless for her taste,
or whether her heart was already given to another,
Christina paid little heed to this new suitor, and
remained cold to his impassioned appeals. " The
Duke of Vendôme," wrote Wriothesley to Cromwell,
" is a great wooer to the Duchess, but we cannot hear
that he receiveth much comfort."[1]

On the 17th of October the Constable de Montmorency prevailed on the royal party to accompany
him to his sumptuous home at Chantilly, nine leagues
farther on the road to Paris. This brave soldier and
able Minister had grown up in the closest intimacy
with the Royal Family, and was habitually addressed
as " bon père " by the King's children, but had, unfortunately, excited the hatred of the reigning
favourite, the Duchess of Étampes, who called him

[1] State Papers, Record Office, viii. 78; Calendar of State
Papers, xiii. 2, 255.

openly " un grand coquin," and declared that he tried
to make himself a second monarch. On the other hand,
his constant loyalty to Queen Eleanor gratified Mary
of Hungary, who now gladly accepted his invitation
to Chantilly.

Anne de Montmorency was as great a patron of
art as his royal master, and during the last fifteen
years he had transformed his ancestral home into a
superb Renaissance palace. The halls were decorated
with frescoes by Primaticcio; the gardens were adorned
with precious marbles and bronzes, with busts of the
Cæsars and statues of Mars and Hercules, with fountains of the finest Urbino and Palissy ware. Portraits by Clouet, priceless manuscripts illuminated by
French and Burgundian masters, and enamels by
Léonard Limousin, were to be seen in the galleries.
But what interested Mary and Christina most of all
were the tapestries woven at Brussels from Raphael
of Urbino's cartoons, which the Constable had rescued
after the sack of Rome, and which he restored some
years later to Pope Julius III.[1]

After entertaining his guests magnificently during
two days, the Constable accompanied them on a
hunting-party in the forest, and finally brought
them back to Compiègne on the 19th of October.
Here the Queen of Hungary's return was impatiently awaited by the English Ambassadors, who
found themselves in a miserable plight. The town
was so crowded that they had to be content with the
meanest lodgings; the hire of post-horses cost forty
pounds, and provisions were so scarce that a partridge
or woodcock sold for tenpence, and an orange for
more than a groat. The King's Ambassadors at the

---

[1] F. Decrue, "Anne de Montmorency," 415, 418, 491.

French Court—Sir Anthony Browne, and Bonner, the Bishop-elect of Hereford—who joined them at Compiègne on the 14th, were in still worse case ; for they could get no horses for love or money, and spent six days without receiving a visit from the Court officials. These outraged personages stood at the window, and saw the French Councillors, and even the Constable, go by, without giving them the smallest sign of recognition. At least, Vaughan and Wriothesley were treated with the utmost civility by the Flemish nobles, and their audience was only deferred on account of the Queen's visit to Chantilly. Don Diego was courtesy itself, and, before he started for Spain, wrote a letter to Cromwell, assuring him that Queen Mary was the truest friend and sister his master could have, but that it had been impossible for her to attend to business when her days were spent in festivities and family meetings.[1] At length, on Sunday, the 20th, the Ambassadors were received by the Queen, and introduced Browne and Bonner, as well as Dr. Edward Carne, a learned lawyer whom Henry had sent to assist in drawing up the marriage treaty. Mary informed them that Francis was bent on taking her to the Duke of Vendôme's house at La Fère on the way home, but begged Wriothesley, who was still unwell, to go straight to Brussels. The next day Browne started for England, saying that it was impossible to follow a King who " goes out of all highways," and on the 22nd Wriothesley and his companions set out on their return to Brussels.[2]

---

[1] State Papers, xiii. 2, 238.
[2] Ibid., xiii. 2, 247, 248.

V.

By the end of October the English Envoys were back at Brussels, rejoicing to be once more in comfortable quarters. Here they found great fear and distrust of France prevailing, and much alarm was expressed lest the Queen should have been induced to give the Duchess of Milan in marriage to a French Prince. This, however, was not the case, and the English Ambassadors were satisfied that beyond feasting and merrymaking nothing had been done. A friendly gentleman, Monsieur de Brederode, told them that there had been some attempt at marriage-making among the women. Queen Eleanor still pressed her sister earnestly to further the marriage of Christina with the Duke of Orleans, as the best way of insuring a lasting peace, and had revived her old dream of marrying her daughter, Maria of Portugal, to the Prince of Spain. But Mary turned a deaf ear to all these proposals, saying that she could not consider them without Charles's approval. At La Fère, in the valley of the Oise, Francis entertained his guests at a splendid banquet, after which he presented Mary with a very fine diamond, and Christina with a beautiful jewel, besides lavishing rings, bracelets, brooches, caps, and pretty trinkets from Paris and Milan, Lisbon and Nuremberg, on the ladies of their suite. Here he took leave of his guests, but the Duke of Vendôme insisted on escorting the Queen and her niece as far as Valenciennes.[1]

On Monday, the 4th of November, Mary and Christina reached Brussels, and were received with warm demonstrations of affection. Now, " after all these

[1] Calendar of State Papers, xiii. 2, 261.

gay and glorious words," the English Ambassadors
confidently hoped to see some end to their toil.   But
they soon realized that their hopes were doomed to
disappointment.   First the Queen was too tired to
receive them; then nothing could be done until the
return of the Duke of Aerschot, who was her chief
adviser.   At length, on the 16th, the first conference
took place at the Duke's house.   The Captain of the
Archers, Christina's old friend De Courrières, conducted the Ambassadors to the room where the Commissioners were awaiting them—Aerschot, Hoog-
straaten, Lalaing, and the Chancellor of Brabant, Dr.
Schoren, " a very wise father."   After a lengthy
preamble, setting forth the powers committed to the
Regent, the terms of the contract were discussed.
The chief points on which Wriothesley insisted were
that Henry should be allowed to see his bride, that
the payment of her dowry should be assigned to
Flanders instead of Milan, and that Christina's title
to Denmark should be recognized, although, remarked the Ambassador, " for my little wit I care not
if this last condition were scraped out of the book."[1]
The Duchess's claim to the throne of Denmark, as
Wriothesley realized, was so remote that it seemed
hardly worth discussing.   The dowry and the question of the Papal dispensation were the two real
stumbling-blocks, and he advised Cromwell, if the
King was really anxious to secure this desirable wife,
not to press the former point, money being so scarce
in Spain and the Netherlands that the Emperor
would rather leave his niece unwed, than part with
so large a sum.   At the close of the sitting the Duke
of Aerschot begged Wriothesley to stay to dinner,

[1] Calendar of State Papers, xiii. 2, 255.

and gave him the chief place at table and pre-eminence
in all things. The fare was abundant; four courses
of ten dishes were served in silver, with " covers of a
marvellous clean and honourable sort," and carvers
and waiters stood around, and attended as diligently
to the Ambassador's wants as if he were a Prince.
Later in the evening the Duke's brother-in-law, the
Marquis of Berghen, who was always well disposed
to the English, came to supper, and chatted pleasantly
for some time, but shocked Wriothesley by asking him
if it were true that all religion was extinct in England, that Mass was abolished, and that the bones
of saints were publicly burned. Cromwell's Com-
missioner, who had himself plundered the shrines of
St. Swithun at Winchester and of St. Thomas at
Canterbury, could hardly deny this latter charge,
although he declared stoutly that only such money-
making devices and tricks of the friars as the Rood
of Boxley and the tomb of Becket had been unmasked. But, in spite of the outward civility with
which the Ambassador was treated, he realized that
all good Catholics in Flanders looked on him with
horror and disgust.

All through the summer abbeys and shrines had
been going down fast. " Dagon is everywhere falling," wrote a Kentish fanatic, and, as Castillon said,
by the end of the year hardly a single abbey was left
standing. The recent trend of political events had
served to excite the King's worst passions, and when
the French Ambassador went to see him early in
November, he found him in a towering rage. The
French had treated his Ambassadors abominably;
the Emperor and King were plotting together to take
the Duchess of Milan away from him and give her to

Monsieur de Vendôme, which, " if it be done, would finish the picture."[1] Late on this same evening, Lord Exeter, a grandson of Edward IV. and head of the noble house of Courtenay, and his cousin, Lord Montague, the son of Lady Salisbury and brother of Cardinal Pole, were thrown into the Tower on the charge of high-treason. All that the most prolonged cross-examination of their servants and friends could bring out to prove their guilt, was that in my Lord of Exeter's garden at Horsley Place, in Surrey, Sir Edward Nevill had been heard singing merry songs against the knaves that ruled about the King, and, clenching his fist, had cried: " I trust to give them a buffet and see honest men reign in England one day." But the King had long ago told the French Ambassador that he was determined to exterminate the White Rose, and, as Castillon remarked, no pretext was too flimsy to bring men to the block. On the 9th of December, Exeter, Montague, and Nevill, all died on the scaffold, and Castillon wrote to King Francis: " No one knows who will be the next to go." Terror reigned throughout the land, and no one of noble birth was safe.[2] Mary of Hungary might well shudder at the thought of giving her niece to such a man. But every day her position became more difficult. Soon after her return from Compiègne she wrote to Charles, urgently begging for instructions as to how she was to proceed with the English Ambassadors. If the King persists in treating of the Duchess's marriage, is she to consent or to refuse altogether ? And if so, on what pretext ? Is she to discuss the question of the Papal dispensation, which Henry will never

---

[1] Calendar of State Papers, xiii. 2, 289.
[2] *Ibid.*, xiii. 2, 291, 296.

consent to receive from the Pope, but without which
the Emperor cannot possibly allow the union.[1]   In
reply to this letter, Charles wrote from Toledo, on the
5th of December, telling her to temporize with the
English, and to consult her Council on the best
method of procedure.[2]

A carefully-worded paper, in Mary's own handwriting, setting forth the results of the deliberation
with the Council in clear and concise language, was
forwarded to the Emperor early in January:

" If the King of England would seriously mend his
ways and proceed to conclude the marriage in earnest,
not merely to sow dissension between His Majesty
and the King of France, this would no doubt be the
most honourable alliance for the Duchess and the
most advantageous for the Low Countries; but there
is no evidence of this—rather the reverse, as your
Ambassador in France tells us, from what he hears of
the conversations held by King Henry with the French
Envoy in London.   The Queen considers this point to
be entirely settled, and it remains only to know Your
Majesty's wishes.   Are we to dissemble with the
English as we have done till now, which, however,
is very difficult, or are we to break off negotiations
altogether ?   This can best be done by putting forward quite reasonable terms, but which are not agreeable to the King.   The Queen begs His Majesty to tell
her exactly what she is to do, remembering that the
King of England, when he cannot ally himself with
the Emperor or in France, may seek an alliance with
Cleves, and will be further alienated from religion, and
may do much harm by putting himself at the head of
the German Princes—all of which she prays Your
Majesty to consider."[3]

But no reply to this appeal came for many weeks.
In vain Mary implored Charles to put an end to this

[1] Calendar of Spanish State Papers, vi. 1, 96.
[2] Lanz, ii. 686.
[3] Papiers d'État, 82, 20, Archives du Royaume, Bruxelles.

interminable procrastination, and relieve her from the necessity of dissembling with the English Ambassadors, who never left her in peace.

" Once more, Monseigneur," she wrote at the end of January, " I implore you tell me if I am to allow these conferences to drag on, for it is impossible to do this any longer without the most shameless dissimulation."[1]

Still no answer came from Spain, and the solemn farce was prolonged. During the next two months frequent meetings between the Commissioners were held at Brussels, and the Queen herself was often present. " Indeed," wrote Wriothesley, " she is one and principal in it, and how unmeet we be to match with her ourselves do well acknowledge."[2] But little progress was made, although Henry, in his anxiety for the marriage, offered to give the Duchess as large a dowry as any Queen of England had ever enjoyed. On St. Thomas's Day he informed the French Ambassador in the gallery at Whitehall that his marriage was almost concluded.

" All the same," wrote Castillon to the Constable, " I know that he would gladly marry Madame de Guise had he the chance. If you think the King and Emperor would enjoy the sport of seeing him thus *virolin-virolant*, I can easily get it up, provided you show his Ambassador a little civility, and make the Cardinal and Monsieur de Guise caress him a little."[3]

But two days after this interview Henry addressed a pathetic appeal to the Regent on his behalf, saying that " old age was fast creeping on, and time was slipping and flying marvellously away." Already the whole year had been wasted in vain parleyings, and, since

[1] Lanz, ii. 296.   [2] State Papers, Record Office, viii. 72.
[3] Calendar of State Papers, xiii. 2, 467, 468.

MARY, QUEEN OF HUNGARY
By Bernard van Orley (Cardon Collection)

To face p. 188

neither money nor prayers could redeem this precious
time, he could wait the Emperor's pleasure no longer,
but must seek another bride.   If this appeal produced
no effect, he told Wriothesley to take leave of the
Duchess, and declare to her the great affection which
the King bore her, and how earnestly he had desired
to make her his wife, but, since this was plainly impossible, he must " beg her not to marvel if he joined
with another."[1]   When this letter reached Brussels,
Mary and Christina were absent on a hunting expedition, but on New Year's Eve they returned.
The Queen received Wriothesley the next morning,
and, after listening patiently to the long discourse
in which he delivered his master's message, said that
she was still awaiting the Emperor's final instructions,
remarking that perhaps the King hardly realized the
distance between Spain and Flanders.   There was
nothing for it but to await the coming of the courier
from Spain.   But even Wriothesley began to realize
that, " for all this gentle entertainment and fair words
and feastings," the deputies meant to effect nothing.

Like Hutton, the Ambassador felt the spell of
Christina's charms, and certain expressions which her
servants Benedetto and Ferrari had dropped, led him
to suppose that the Duchess was favourably inclined
towards his master.   But he was convinced that
attempts had been made to poison her mind against
the King, and to prefer the suit of William of Cleves
or of Francis of Lorraine, who was also said to be
seeking her hand.

" I know," he wrote to Cromwell, " that some of
these folks labour to avert the Duchess's mind from
the King's Majesty, and to rest herself either upon

[1] State Papers, Record Office, viii. 110, 118, 123.

Lorraine or Cleves; but as far as I can learn she is wiser than they, and will in no wise hearken to them, offering rather to live a widow than to fall from the likelihood of being Queen, and to light so low as from a mistress to become an underling, as she must if she marry either of them, their fathers and mothers being yet both alive. What for the virtue that I think I see in her, the good nature that every man must note her to be of, as well as her good inclination to the King's Majesty, I have privily wished myself sometimes that the King might take her with nothing, as she hath somewhat, rather than His Highness should, by these cankered tongues, be tromped and deceived of his good purpose, and so want such a wife as I think she would be to His Grace. For I shall ever pray God to send His Majesty such a mate, humble, loving, and of such sort as may be for His Grace's quiet and content, with the increase of the offspring of his most noble person."[1]

VI.

At length the eagerly - expected courier reached Brussels, but, as usual, the Queen and Duchess were away hunting, and it was only on the 1st of February that the Ambassadors obtained their desired audience. Mary received them in her bedroom between seven and eight in the morning, and told them that the Emperor had decided to await the arrival of the Count Palatine,. who with his wife, the Duchess's elder sister, was shortly expected at Toledo, in order that he might discuss the subject fully with them; but, since she knew Henry to be impatient for an answer, she had despatched a trusty messenger, Cornelius Scepperus, to Spain to beg her brother for an immediate decision.[2]

Wriothesley now ventured on a bold step. As the

---

[1] Calendar of State Papers, xiv. 1, 37.
[2] State Papers, Record Office, viii. 139.

Queen rose to leave the room, he begged, in order to satisfy his own peace of mind, to be allowed to ask her one question, hoping that she would give him a frank answer. At these words Mary blushed deeply, conscious of the double part that she was playing, and bade him speak, assuring him that she would take whatever he said in good part. " Madame," returned Wriothesley, " I beseech Your Grace to tell me plainly how you find the Duchess herself affected towards this marriage with the King my master." If, as was commonly reported, the Duchess had really said that she minded not to fix her heart that way, all his efforts were but lost labour. And he made bold to ask this question because he knew that of late " divers malicious tongues, servants of the Bishop of Rome, had dared to speak lewdly in hugger - mugger of the King's Majesty." The question was an awkward one, but Mary proved equal to the occasion. She thanked the Ambassador for his frankness, and replied with some warmth that she was quite sure her niece had never spoken such words, and that, if evil men spoke lewdly of the King, she would know how to deal with them. " Touching my niece's affection," she added, " I dare say unto you, that if the Emperor and your master the King agree upon this marriage, she will be at the Emperor's command."

Wriothesley could only express his gratitude for this gracious answer, even if it were not so plain as he could have wished. Seeing that nothing else would satisfy him, the Queen referred him to the Duchess herself, and at two o'clock the same afternoon the Ambassador was conducted to Christina's lodgings. He found her standing under a canopy in a hall hung with black velvet and damask, with five or

six ladies near her, and a dozen gentlemen and pages
at the other end of the room. Christina received him
with a graceful salute, bade him heartily welcome,
and asked the purpose of his errand. Wriothesley
proceeded to explain the object of his visit at great
length, saying that he was quite sure that a lady of
her gravity and discretion would never allow such
unseemly words to pass her lips; yet, since untrue
and wicked reports might have reached her ears and
cooled her inclination towards the King, he felt it
would be his bounden duty, were this true, to inform
His Majesty, in order that he might withdraw his
suit without further waste of time and dishonour.

Christina listened to this long harangue without
moving a muscle. When the Ambassador had ended,
she desired him to put on his cap, saying it was a
cold day, and that she regretted not to have noticed
that he was uncovered before. Wriothesley replied
that this was his duty, and that he hoped often to
have the honour of talking with her bareheaded in
the future. Without paying any heed to this last
remark, Christina replied in the following words:

" Monsieur l'Ambassadeur, I do heartily thank you
for your good opinion of me, wherein I can assure you,
you have not been deceived. I thank God He hath
given me a better stay of myself, than to be of so
light a sort as, by all likelihood, some men would
note me. And I assure you that neither these words
that you have spoken, nor any like to them, have
passed at any time from my mouth, and so I pray
you report for me."

But grateful as Wriothesley expressed himself for
this frank answer, he was not yet satisfied. " It is
an evil wind, as we say in England, that bloweth

no man good," and at least the Duchess would see by this, how little faith was to be placed in idle tales. " There are those," he said mysteriously, " who play on both hands; they tell Your Excellency many things, and us somewhat." But would she go farther, and tell him if he might assure the King his master of her own good inclination towards the marriage ? At these words Christina blushed exceedingly, and said with some hesitation: " As for my inclination, what should I say ?   You know I am at the Emperor's commandment."   And when the Ambassador pressed her to be a little plainer, she smiled and repeated: " You know I am the Emperor's poor servant, and must follow his pleasure !"

" Marry !" exclaimed Wriothesley; " why, then I may hope to be one of the first Englishmen to be acquainted with my new mistress. Oh, madame, how happy shall you be if you are matched with my master—the most gentle gentleman that liveth, his nature so benign and pleasant that I think no man hath heard many angry words pass his mouth. As God shall help me, if he were no King, instead of one of the most puissant Princes of Christendom, I think, if you saw him, you would say that for his virtues, gentleness, wisdom, experience, goodliness of person, and all other gifts and qualities, he were worthy to be made a King. I know Your Grace to be of goodly parentage, and to have many great Princesses in your family, but if God send this to a good conclusion, you shall be of all the rest the most happy !"

This fulsome panegyric was too much for Christina's gravity. She listened for some time, like one that was tickled, then smiled, and almost burst out laughing, but restrained her merriment with much diffi-

culty, and, quickly recovering herself, said gravely
that she knew His Majesty was a good and noble
Prince. " Yes, madame," replied the Ambassador,
with enthusiasm, " and you shall know this better
hereafter. And for my part, I would be content, if
only I may live to see the day of your coronation, to
say with Simeon, " Nunc dimittis servum tuum,
Domine." And he dwelt with fervour on the wish
of the English to have her for their Queen, and on
the admiration and love which the fame of her beauty
and goodness had excited in the King. Christina
bowed her thanks, saying that she was much bounden to
His Majesty for his good opinion, and then, calling her
Grand Master, bade him escort the Ambassador home.

" Your Majesty," wrote Wriothesley to the King
that evening, " shall easily judge from this of what
inclination the women be, and especially the Duchess,
whose honest countenance, with the few words that
she wisely spoke, make me to think there can be no
doubt in her. A blind man should judge no colours,
but surely, Sir, after my poor understanding and the
little experience that I have, she is marvellous wise,
very gentle, and as shamefaced as ever I saw so witty
a woman. I think her wisdom is no less than the
Queen's, which, in my poor opinion, is notable for
a woman, and I am deceived if she prove not a good
wife. And somewhat the better I like her for that
I have been informed that, of all the whole stock of
them, her mother was of the best opinion in religion,
and showed it so far that both the Emperor and all the
pack of them were sore grieved with her, and seemed in
the end to hold her in contempt. I would hope no less
of the daughter, if she might be so happy as to nestle in
England. Very pure, fair of colour she is not, but a
marvellous good brownish face she hath, with fair red
lips and ruddy cheeks. And unless I be deceived in
my judgment, she was never so well painted but her
living visage doth much excel her picture."[1]

[1] State Papers, Record Office, viii. 140-148.

Two things, Wriothesley told Cromwell, in a letter
which he wrote to him the next day, were plain:
the Queen would be very loth to let them go with
nothing settled, and the Duchess was well inclined,
considering that nothing had as yet been said to her
on the King's behalf. And he suggested that he might
be allowed to show her a portrait of Henry, the sight of
which, he felt sure, would make her die a maid rather
than marry anyone else. " The woman is certainly
worthy to be a Queen," he adds, " and in my
judgment is worth more than all the friendship and
alliances in the world."[1]

Unfortunately, these letters, which the writer
hoped would give the King so much pleasure, found
Henry in a furious temper. In January, 1539, Pope
Paul III. issued the long-delayed Bull of excommu-
nication, and called on the Emperor and the French
King to declare war on the heretic monarch, and forbid all intercourse between their subjects and the
misguided English. Cardinal Pole, whose kinsmen
Henry had beheaded, and whose own life had been
attempted by his emissaries, was sent to Spain to
induce Charles to take up arms against " this abom-
inable tyrant and cruel persecutor of the Church of
God."[2] At the same moment a treaty was signed
between Charles and Francis at Toledo, by which
the two monarchs pledged themselves to conclude
no agreements with Henry excepting by mutual
consent.[3]

Henry now became seriously alarmed. He complained bitterly to Castillon of the way in which he

---

[1] Calendar of State Papers, xiv. 1, 93, 121.
[2] Ibid., xiv. 1, 14; Calendar of Spanish State Papers, vi. 1, 97.
[3] Ibid., xiv. 1, 26.

was reviled in France, not only by the vulgar, but by the Cardinal of Paris and members of the Council. And he sent Cromwell to Chapuys with an imperative summons to come to Court without delay. The Imperial Ambassador obeyed, and came to Whitehall on the Feast of the Three Kings. Henry was on his way to Mass, but he stopped to greet Chapuys, and complained once more of the Queen of Hungary's interminable delays and of the scandalous treatment of his Ambassadors. Chapuys made the best excuses which came into his mind, and assured the King that Mary was only awaiting the Emperor's instructions as to the Papal dispensation, and that he would hear from Spain as soon as the Palatine had reached Toledo. To this Henry vouchsafed no answer, but walked straight on, to the door of the chapel.

During Mass Cromwell entered into conversation with Chapuys, and told him that the Pope had thrown off the hypocrite's mask, and was doing his best to kindle a flame in Italy. Before the Ambassador could reply he changed the subject, and said he saw clearly that the Emperor intended to marry his niece to Cleves or Lorraine. Chapuys laughed, and remarked that the Duchess could hardly be given to both Princes, but added in all seriousness that his master knew the difference between the King of England and these suitors. After dinner Henry seemed in a better temper, but told Chapuys in confidential tones that he was growing old, and that his subjects pressed him to hasten his marriage, and that these vexatious delays were all due to the French, who boasted that the Emperor could do nothing without their consent.

" He seemed in great trouble," reported Chapuys, " and it is plain, as everyone about him tells me, that he is very much in love with the Duchess of Milan. He told one of his most intimate friends the other day that he would gladly take her without a penny. . . . And just now the French Ambassador asked me if it were true that he had sent her a diamond worth 16,000 ducats."[1]

At the same time Chapuys heard that Henry was negotiating with the German Princes, and offering his daughter Mary to the young Duke of Cleves, in order to prevent him from marrying the Duchess. " He is so much in love," wrote Castillon, " that for one gracious word from her I believe he would go to war to recover Denmark."[2]

The same week Henry wrote to Wyatt, complaining bitterly of the treatment which he had received from his imperial brother, as being wholly unworthy of a Prince who professed to be his zealous friend. " After so hot a summer we saw never so cold a winter; after all these professions of love and friendship, in the end nothing but a cold frost." He ended by declaring he would no longer be kept " hanging in the balance," and must have an immediate answer, even if it were a flat denial.[3]   At length even Charles could procrastinate no longer, and on the 15th of February he told Wyatt that it was impossible for the marriage to take place without the Pope's dispensation, as the King's dispensation would never satisfy the Duchess herself, or any of her relations, and might cause endless inconvenience if children were born of the union. " All the stay," wrote Cromwell to Wriothesley, " is upon the dispensation,

[1] Calendar of State Papers, xiv. 1, 16-19.
[2] Ibid., xiv. 1, 52; Lanz, ii. 297-306.   [3] Nott, ii. 306.

to which they object now, but whereof they never spake before."[1]

Even before the courier from Spain arrived, Henry's face was so black that Castillon wrote home begging to be recalled, and declaring that this King was the most cruel and dangerous man in the world. He was in such a rage that he had neither reason nor understanding left, and once he found out that Francis could do nothing for him, Castillon was convinced that his own life would not be worth a straw. A few days later the Ambassador left London, and rejoiced to find himself safely back in France.[2]

VII.

While London was full of alarms, Wriothesley and his colleagues were spending a gay Shrovetide at Brussels, all unconscious of the clouds that were darkening the horizon. During the last few weeks nobles and courtiers had vied with each other in paying them attentions. Visitors of the highest rank honoured their humble lodgings. Madame de Berghen, Aerschot's lively sister—" a dame of stomach that hath a jolly tongue "—dined with them. The Queen herself was expected to pay them a visit, and great preparations in the way of plate and furniture were made for her reception. Count Büren, a very great man in Holland, was particularly friendly, and impressed Wriothesley so much by his honesty and loyalty that he gave him the best horse in his stables. Another day he entertained the Captain of Gravelines, who railed against the abominations of

[1] Calendar of Spanish State Papers, vi. 1, 145.
[2] Kaulek, 84.

Rome to his heart's content, and told him it would be
the Pope's fault if the King's marriage were not concluded. Carnival week brought a round of festivities.
On Monday, the 17th of February, the Ambassadors
were invited to meet the Queen at supper at the Duke
of Aerschot's house, and were received at half-past five
by the Duchess and her sister-in-law, Madame de
Berghen. The Duchess sent for her young daughter
and her two sons—boys of ten and twelve—and
presently they were joined by Monsieur de Vély, the
new French Ambassador. Wriothesley expressed great
pleasure at meeting him, saying that, since their
masters were good friends, they ought not to be
strangers, and received a cordial reply. The rest of
the company looked on with some surprise at these
friendly fashions, a rumour being abroad that the
French King was about to attack England and force
Henry to submit to the Pope. Then a flourish of
trumpets, sackbuts, and fifes, was heard at the gates,
and the guests rose as the Queen and Duchess entered
the hall. At supper the French Ambassador sat on
the Queen's right, and Wriothesley on her left, while
Christina was between him and Vaughan. Madame
d'Egmont sat next to Dr. Carne, and the Prince of
Orange was on the Duchess of Aerschot's right hand.
Mary made herself very agreeable to both her neighbours, and when, after supper, her chapel choir
sang roundelays and merry drinking-songs, she asked
Wriothesley if he were fond of music, and invited
him to sup with her on the morrow and hear her
minstrels. The Ambassador confessed that he was
very fond of music, and often had some at his poor
home to cheer his dull spirits. " Well, it is an honest
pastime," said the Queen, " and maketh good diges-

tion, for it driveth thoughts away." Here Wriothesley ventured to remark that he would feel merrier if he had not wasted so much time here, and asked if there was still no news from Spain. "None," replied the Queen; and Wriothesley observed that reports reached him from Germany that the Emperor was merely trying to gain time, and meant to do the Bishop of Rome's bidding. " Jesus !" exclaimed the Queen, " I dare say the Emperor never meant such a thing;" upon which Wriothesley hastened to say that he felt sure the Emperor was too wise and honourable a Prince to deceive the King, but now that he had made friends with his old enemy, he hoped he would not make a new enemy of his old friend. After supper the Duke and several ladies came in, wearing masks and rich costumes, and threw dice with the Queen and her niece for some fine diamonds, which the Princesses won. Then the Prince of Orange led out Christina to dance, and the other youthful guests followed suit, while Wriothesley sat at the Queen's side on the daïs and watched the princely pair.

The next evening (Shrove Tuesday) Wriothesley and his colleagues dined at the palace, and this time the English Ambassador sat in the post of honour, on the Queen's right, with the Duchess on his left. Mary was in high spirits, toasted her guests and drank with each of them in turn. After supper Wriothesley approached Christina, and ventured to tell her that she would be happy if her best friends did not put hindrances in her way, and begged her not to lend ear to malicious reports of his master. The Duchess shook her head, saying she would listen to no calumnies, and always hold the King to be a

noble Prince.   But he felt sure that she was afraid
of the Queen, and told her he hoped to converse more
freely with her another time.   Never had he seen
her look so beautiful as she did that night; never did
he wish more ardently to see her his master's bride.
" For indeed it were pity," he wrote home, " if she
were bestowed on a husband she did not like, only to
serve others."

There was one Prince at table for whom, it was easy
to see, Christina had no dislike.   This was René of
Orange, who had an opportunity of distinguishing
himself in his lady's eyes that evening.   The Queen
led the way into the great hall, where first Aerschot
and three other nobles challenged all comers to fight,
and then the Prince of Orange and Floris d'Egmont
took their places at the barriers, and broke lances
and received prizes for their valour, while the Queen's
band of lutes, viols, and rebecks, played the finest
music that Wriothesley had ever heard.   When the
jousting was ended, Mary led her guests to the royal
gallery, where another banquet was served, and there
was much lively discourse, and more talking than
eating.   So that gay Carnival came to a close, and
with it the last hope of winning the fair Duchess's
hand.[1]

An unpleasant surprise was in store for Wriothesley the next morning.   Certain disquieting rumours
having reached Brussels, Vaughan went to Antwerp on Ash Wednesday, and found great consternation among the English merchants.   A proclamation
had been issued forbidding any ships to leave the
port, and several English vessels laden with merchan-
dise had been detained.   The wildest rumours were

[1] Calendar of State Papers, xiv. 1, 125, 126

current on the Exchange.   It was commonly said
that the Emperor, with the Kings of France and
Scotland, had declared war on King Henry, and that
a large Dutch and Spanish fleet was about to sail
for England.   Already in Brussels gallants and pike-
men were taking bets on the issue of the war, and
Wriothesley wrote to Cromwell that he and his
colleagues " might peradventure broil on a faggot."
He was unable to obtain an audience until Friday,
when the Queen told him that, by the Emperor's
orders, she was recalling Chapuys to conduct the
marriage negotiations.   This unexpected intimation,
coming as it did after the startling news from Antwerp, disconcerted him considerably.   He sent an
express to London, and received orders to take his
departure at once.   Castillon was already on his way
to France, but Henry quite refused to let Chapuys
go until Wriothesley and Vaughan had left Brussels.
A long wrangle between the two Courts followed.
The Ambassadors were detained on both sides.   The
Spanish and Dutch ships in English harbours were
stopped, all ports were closed, and active preparations were made for war along the shores of the
Channel.

" After fair weather," wrote Cromwell to Wriothesley, " there is succeeded a weather very cloudy.
Good words, good countenance, be turned, we perceive, to a wonderful strangeness.   But let that pass.
They can do us no harm but to their own detriment."[1]

The situation of the Ambassadors was by no means
pleasant.   A marked change was visible in the behaviour of the Court.   They were " treated as very
strangers " by those nobles who had been their best

[1] State Papers, Record Office, viii. 155.

friends. No one called at their house or came to dine with them. The Duchess's servants, who used to go to and fro constantly, now dared not come except at dusk—" in the owl-flight "—and would not allow Wriothesley to send them home by torchlight. Wherever they went, the English heard their King slandered, and met with cold looks and scornful words. Worse than all, they were forced to pay excise duties—" eighteen pence on every barrel of beer above the price asked by the brewer "—an indignity to which no Ambassador before had ever been exposed. " I write in haste and live in misery," wrote Wriothesley to Cromwell on the 7th of March.[1]

The Emperor, however, was still friendly. His heart was set on a Crusade against the Turk, and he had no wish to embark on war with England. Pole met with a cold reception at Toledo, and, finding Charles averse to executing the Pope's sentence, retired to his friend Sadoleto's house at Carpentras. This was a relief to Henry, and he bade Wyatt thank his imperial brother, but could not forbear pointing out that these friendly words agreed ill with the doings of his officers in the Low Countries. A despatch addressed to Wyatt on the 10th of March contains a long recital of the extraordinary treatment which his Ambassadors at Brussels had met with:

" Since Lent began, as for a penance, their entertainment hath been marvellous strange—yea, and stranger than we will rehearse: strangeness in having audience with long delay, strangeness in answer and fashion. Also they have been constrained to pay Excise, which no Ambassador of England paid in any man's remembrance. They have complained to the Queen, but nevertheless must pay or lack drink. . . .

[1] State Papers, Record Office, viii. 166, 175.

These rumours and hints of war, the arrest of our ships, this strangeness shown to our Ministers, this navy and army in readiness, the recall of Chapuys, ran abroad this realm and everywhere. We do not write to you the rumours half so spiteful, and the entertainment half so strange, as it hath been. I think never such a thing was heard, and especially after a treaty of marriage such a banquet !"[1]

Henry concluded this letter by saying that, since the Emperor insisted on the need of Papal dispensation, there could be no further question of any marriage between him and the Duchess, and he would be now at liberty to seek another wife. On the same day he wrote to Carne, who had been secretly corresponding with the Duke of Cleves, telling him to open negotiations for a marriage with that Prince's sister, the Lady Anne.[2]

Twelve days after this despatch was sent to Spain Wriothesley left Brussels. At Calais he met Chapuys, who had just crossed the Channel, and Mary's almoner, the Dean of Cambray, who was being sent to take the Ambassador's place, and was awaiting a fair wind to embark for Dover. All three Ambassadors dined in a friendly manner with Lord Lisle, the Deputy Governor of Calais, and continued their respective journeys without hindrance. But the much-discussed marriage treaty was at an end. The long - drawn comedy had reached its last act. " All hope of the Duchess," wrote Wriothesley to Cromwell, " is utterly past."

The rupture was loudly lamented by the English merchants in Antwerp, and keen disappointment was felt throughout England, where the marriage had

---

[1] Nott, " Life of Wyatt," ii. 511.
[2] Calendar of State Papers, xiv. 1, 189, 191.

always been popular.   Among many scattered notices
of the feeling which prevailed on the subject, the
following incident is of especial interest, because of
the sidelight which it throws on Christina's personal
reluctance to the marriage.

On a summer evening in August, 1539, five months
after Wriothesley left Brussels, a married priest
named George Constantyne, of Llan Hawaden in
South Wales, rode from Chepstow to Abergavenny
with John Barlow, Dean of Westbury.   The priest
had got into trouble in Wolsey's time, for buying
copies of Tyndale's New Testament, and was forced
to fly the country and practise as a physician for
several years in the Netherlands.   Now he had returned to England, and was on his way to his old
home in Wales.   He walked from Bristol to Westbury,
where he supped with Dean Barlow, a brother of his
friend the Bishop of St. Davids, who made him heartily
welcome, and invited him to be his travelling companion the next day to Pembrokeshire.   As the
two ecclesiastics rode through the green valleys on
the way to Abergavenny, the Dean asked Constantyne
if he could tell him why the King's marriage had
been so long delayed.   The priest replied that he,
for his part, was very sorry the King should still be
without a wife, when he might by this time have been
the father of fair children.   As the Dean knew, both
the Duchess of Milan and she of Cleves were spoken of,
and now the little doctor, Nicholas Wotton, had been
sent to Cleves with Mr. Beard, of the Privy Chamber,
and the King's painter; so there was good hope of a
marriage being concluded with the Duke of Cleves,
who favoured God's word, and was a mighty Prince
now, holding Guelderland against the Emperor's will

But why, asked the Dean, was the marriage with the
Duchess of Milan broken off ? Constantyne, who
was familiar with all the gossip of the Regent's Court,
replied that the Duchess quite refused to marry the
King, unless he would accept the Bishop of Rome's
dispensation, and give pledges that her life would be
safe and her honour respected. " Why pledges ?"
asked the Dean innocently. " Marry !" returned
Constantyne, " she sayeth that, since the King's
Majesty was in so little space rid of three Queens, she
dare not trust his Council, even if she dare trust His
Majesty. For in Flanders the nobles suspect that
her great-aunt, Queen Catherine, was poisoned,
that Anne Boleyn was innocent of the crimes for
which she was put to death, and that the third wife,
Queen Jane, was lost for lack of attention in child-
bed." Such, at least, were the mutterings which
he heard at Court before Whitsuntide. The Dean
remarked that he was afraid the affair of Milan must
be dashed, as Dr. Petre, who was to have gone to
fetch the royal bride from Calais, was at the Court of
St. James's last Sunday ; upon which Constantyne gave
it as his opinion that there could be no amity between
the King and the Emperor, whose god was the Pope.

So the two men talked as they rode over the
Welsh hills on the pleasant summer evening. But
the poor priest had good reason to regret that he had
ever taken this ride; for his false friend the Dean
reported him as a Sacramentary to the Lord Privy
Seal, and a few days after he reached Llan Hawaden
he was arrested and thrown into the Tower, where he
spent several months in prison as a penalty for his
freedom of speech.[1]

[1] " Archæologia Cambrensis," xxiii. 139-141.

BOOK VII

CLEVES, ORANGE, AND LORRAINE

1539—1541

I.

THE negotiations for the King of England's marriage
with the Duchess of Milan were broken off. But
there was no lack of suitors for Christina's hand.
During the winter and spring of 1539 the Emperor's
niece received offers of marriage from three princely
bridegrooms. The first of these was Antoine, Duke
of Vendôme, whose courtship of the Duchess on the
journey to Compiègne had aroused King Henry's
jealousy. The second was William of Cleves, who
since the old Duke Charles's death had taken possession of Guelders, and was now seeking to obtain the
investiture of the duchy, together with Christina's
hand. The third was Francis, the Marquis of Pont-
à-Mousson, and heir of Lorraine. From the day that
this Prince first met the Duchess at Compiègne, he
sought her for his bride with a constancy and stead-
fastness that were eventually to be crowned with
success. But for the moment the Duke of Cleves
seemed to have the best chance of winning the coveted
prize. From the first Mary of Hungary had regarded
this alliance with favour, and when, in January, 1539,
she consulted her Councillors on the Duchess's mar-

riage, it was this union which met with their highest approval.

" Duke William," wrote the Queen in her reply to the Emperor, " has greatly offended Your Majesty, both as a private individual and sovereign lord, by taking possession of Guelders. Still, as he renews his suit and professes to be your loyal friend and servant, it would be well to treat with him and offer him the Duchess's hand, on condition that he will give up Guelderland."[1]

The alternative proposal, she proceeded to say, deserved consideration, seeing the great anxiety which the Duke of Lorraine's son showed for the marriage. No doubt the Emperor's niece, with her large dowry, would be a very honourable match for him, and well worth the surrender of his rights on Guelders; but, since it was most desirable to recover this duchy without delay, it might be well to secure the help of Lorraine by this means.

The situation was a difficult one, and from the moment of the old Duke's death in June, 1538, Mary had never ceased to entreat Charles to come to Flanders and take active measures for the recovery of Guelders before it was too late. Throughout the winter Duke William went from town to town, endearing himself to his new subjects; and when the deputies of Lorraine asserted their master's superior claims, he told them that he would never give up Guelders to any mortal man. By the death of his father on the 6th of February, 1539, he succeeded to the rich provinces of Cleves and Jülich, and became the wealthiest and most powerful Prince in North Germany.[2]

---

[1] Papiers d'État, 82, 20, Archives du Royaume, Bruxelles.
[2] Lanz, ii. 297; Calendar of State Papers, xiii. 2, 16.

Still Charles put off his coming, and told his sister that he was bent on undertaking a second Crusade against the Turks, and could not spare the time for a journey to Flanders. This was too much for Mary's equanimity, and she protested in the strongest language against the Emperor's folly in exposing his person to such risks, declaring that this Crusade would not only prove the utter ruin of the Netherlands, but of all Christendom.[1] Fortunately, Mary's remonstrances were supported by the Emperor's wisest Councillors, and, in deference to their representations, he decided to abandon his Crusade for the present and come to Flanders. This decision was confirmed by the discontent which the Duke of Cleves's intrigues helped to foment in Ghent—always a turbulent city—as well as by the news that the King of England had entered into a close alliance with Cleves, and was about to marry his sister.

Cromwell, with his habitual duplicity, had been in correspondence with the German Princes while he professed to be zealous for the Emperor's alliance; and in March Christopher Mont, his Envoy to Frankfort, was desired to make diligent inquiries as to the shape, stature, and complexion, of the Duke of Cleves's sister Anne. If these were satisfactory, he was to suggest that proposals of marriage should be made by that Prince and his brother-in-law, the Elector John Frederick of Saxony. Mont sent glowing descriptions of the lady's beauty, and was bold enough to declare that she excelled the Duchess of Milan as much as the golden sun excels the silver moon.[2]

[1] Lanz, ii. 289, 683.
[2] State Papers, Record Office, Henry VIII., i. 605; Calendar of State Papers, xiv. 1, 192.

Henry was now all on fire to see the Lady Anne, although he had not yet lost all interest in Christina, whose name still figures constantly in letters from Brussels. On the 6th of April we hear that the Duchess of Milan is sick of fever, and ten days later Cromwell writes to the King that Her Grace is no longer sick, and that " at Antwerp the people still cherish a hope that Your Highness will yet marry her."[1] If he could not make her his wife, the King was determined to prevent another suitor from succeeding where he had failed, and renewed his offer of his daughter Mary with a large dowry to the Duke of Cleves. William, however, showed no alacrity to avail himself of this offer, and sent Envoys both to Brussels and Toledo to press his suit for Christina's hand.

The sudden death of the Empress at Toledo on the 1st of May altered all Charles's plans. A few weeks before this Isabella had given birth to a son, who only lived a few hours, and Charles had written to inform his sister of the infant's death. On the 2nd of May he wrote a few touching lines with his own hand to tell Mary the grievous news. The doctors had pronounced her to be out of danger, but catarrh attacked the lungs, and proved fatal in a few hours.

" I am overwhelmed with sorrow and distress, and nothing can comfort me but the thought of her good and holy life and the devout end which she made. I leave you to tell my subjects over yonder, of this pitiful event, and ask them to pray for her soul. I will do my best to bow to the will of God, whom I implore to receive her in His blessed paradise, where I feel certain that she is. And may God keep you, my dear sister, and grant you all your desires."[2]

[1] Calendar of State Papers, xiv. 1, 348, 374.
[2] See Appendix; Papiers d'État, 82, 26, Archives du Royaume, Bruxelles.

When this sad event took place, Christina's sister Dorothea and her husband, Count Frederic, were staying at the Imperial Court. These adventurous travellers had come to Spain in the vain hope of inducing the Emperor to support their claims on Denmark, and, after crossing the Pyrenees in rain and snow, had at length reached Toledo, where they were hospitably entertained. The Empress treated Dorothea with great affection, but Frederic's German servants, who consumed five meals a day and ate meat on Ash Wednesday, shocked the Spanish courtiers, and drew down the censures of the Inquisition upon them. Even the Emperor asked his cousin why he brought so numerous a suite on his travels; but, although he would make no promises of further help, he good-naturedly paid Frederic's expenses at Toledo, and gave him a present of 7,000 crowns. The death of the Empress, Dorothea's best friend, put an end to all hope of further assistance. The Emperor shut himself up in a Carthusian convent, and the Palatine and his wife started for the Low Countries.[1] On their way through France they were royally entertained by the King and Queen in the splendid Palais des Tournelles, and Francis took so great a fancy to his wife's niece that Eleanor felt it wise to keep Dorothea continually at her side. Here they were detained some time by Frederic's illness, and after his recovery spent several days at Chantilly with the Constable, and at the King's fine new villa of Cotterets, on their way to the Netherlands.[2]

Here the travellers were eagerly awaited by Chris-

---

[1] Hubert Thomas, 376-390; Cust, " Gentlemen Errant," 377-379.

[2] " Zimmerische Chronik," ii. 547.

tina and her aunt. After the funeral services for the repose of the Empress's soul had been duly celebrated, and the last requiem sung in S. Gudule, the Queen set out on a progress through Holland and Friesland, and spent some time at Bois-le-Duc, on the frontiers of Guelders, trying to arrange matters with the Duke of Cleves. But, although friendly letters and messages were exchanged, nothing could be settled until the Emperor's arrival, which was now delayed till the autumn, and the Court moved to the Hague for August. Here the Queen received news that the Count Palatine and his wife had reached Dordrecht and were coming by sea to Holland. Christina at once travelled to Rotterdam, intending to go by boat to meet the travellers. But the weather was rough and stormy, and the sailors were reluctant to set out. The Duchess, however, would hear of no delay, and, embarking in a small boat, bade the sailors put out to sea. Hardly had they left the shore before a terrific gale sprang up, and from the deck of their ship the Palatine and his wife saw a barque tossed on the raging seas, sending up signals of distress. Altering their course, they hastened to the rescue, and found, to their great surprise, that the Duchess of Milan was on board. Count Frederic scolded his sister-in-law soundly for her rashness, but Dorothea was enchanted to see Christina, and laughed and cried by turn as she embraced her.[1] The Queen awaited the travellers no less eagerly, in her anxiety to hear the latest news from Spain, and agreed readily to Frederic's proposal that his wife should remain at the Hague while he returned to Germany. Early in September the Palatine took leave of his relatives and

---

[1] H. Thomas, 396.

went to Antwerp, saying that he must raise money for
his journey to Heidelberg. But he kept his true desti-
nation a secret. During his illness in Paris, Bishop
Bonner had brought Frederic a letter from Cromwell,
begging him to come to England, since he was only
divided from this country by a narrow arm of the
sea, and His Majesty was very anxious to see him
again. All immediate alarm of war had died away,
and the irascible monarch's anger was allayed by the
arrival of a new French Ambassador in the person of
Marillac, and by the permission which Mary gave him
to buy ammunition in the Low Countries. In return,
he ordered an imposing requiem to be held in St.
Paul's for the late Empress, and desired Cromwell
and the Dukes of Norfolk and Suffolk, with twenty
Bishops, to attend the service.[1] He resumed his old
habit of spending the summer evenings on the river,
enjoying the music of flutes and harps, and sent to
France and Italy for excellent painters and musicians
—a sure sign, Marillac was told, that he was about
to marry again. Another fête, at which the Ambassador declined to be present, was a mock-fight on the
Thames between two galleys, one of which bore the
King's arms, while the other was decorated with an
effigy of the Pope with the triple tiara and keys,
attended by the Cardinals. The show ended in the
triumph of the English sailors, who threw the Pope
and Cardinals into the river—" the whole thing,"
according to Marillac, " being as badly represented
as it was poorly conceived."[2]

Now the King was anxious to hear the Emperor's
intention from the Palatine's own lips, while Frederic
on his part was flattered by this powerful monarch's

[1] Kaulek, 104.   [2] *Ibid.*, 105.

invitation, and felt that his assistance might prove of use in his visionary schemes for the recovery of Denmark. But, knowing that of late relations between Henry and the Queen had been strained, he kept his counsel, and told no one but his wife that he was bound for Calais.

Here he was courteously entertained by Lord Lisle, an illegitimate son of Edward IV., and escorted by him to Canterbury and London. Frederic was lost in admiration at the rows of stately palaces along the Thames, and the fine Castle of Richmond, but was disappointed, when he visited Westminster Abbey, not to see the famous antlers of the stag which King Dagobert caught, and which wore a golden collar inscribed with the words, " Julius Cæsar let me go free." Afterwards he learnt that these legendary trophies had lately been removed by the King's orders, for fear the monks, whom he was about to expel, might conceal them.

In the absence of the King at Ampthill, Cromwell, who had been told to " grope out the reason of Frederic's coming, entertained the Count splendidly at his own house, and showed him the Tower of London and the Temple Church. But the Deputy's wife, Lady Lisle, who looked on Cromwell with deep distrust, begged her husband to beware of the Lord Privy Seal's fair words, and was none too well pleased to hear that he had partaken of the partridge pasty and baked cranes which she had sent from Calais, together with her own toothpick for the Palsgrave's use, having noticed that her noble guest " used a quill to pick his teeth with."[1]

Meanwhile the Palatine's visit to England was

---

[1] Calendar of State Papers, xiv. 2, 61; H. Thomas, 393-398.

exciting much curiosity, and not a little alarm, in some quarters. The Pope and the French King feared it might lead to a secret covenant between Henry and Charles, while in London it was commonly reported that Frederic came to renew negotiations for his union with the Duchess of Milan, and the Duke of Cleves hastily sent Ambassadors to conclude his sister's marriage. These Envoys reached Windsor on the same day as the Count Palatine, whom Henry invited to a banquet there on the 24th of September. When he bade the Lord High Admiral escort the Palsgrave to Windsor, Southampton, eager to curry favour with the King, expressed his opinion that the Cleves alliance was preferable to a marriage with a French Princess or one of the Emperor's family, " albeit the Duchess of Milan was a fair woman and well spoken of," and told the King of the resentment which his union with the Lady Anne had aroused at the Court of Brussels. Henry remained plunged in thought for some moments; then a smile broke over his face, and he exclaimed: " Have they remembered themselves now ? They that would not when they might, when they would they shall have nay !"[1]

Nothing was lacking, however, to the splendour of the Palatine's reception at Windsor. The Duke of Suffolk rode out to meet him beyond Eton Bridge with 100 horsemen clad in velvet, and the banquet was served on golden dishes in a hall carpeted with cloth of gold, to the strains of delicious music from the King's famous band. The Cleves Envoys were at table, but after dinner the King took the Count apart, and conversed with him for over two hours on

[1] State Papers, Record Office, Henry VIII., i. 616; Calendar of State Papers, xiv. 2, 54.

his travels.   Frederic took this opportunity of begging
the King to help him in driving out the usurper of
Denmark, and releasing his unhappy father-in-law,
Christian II.[1]   Henry listened kindly, and promised
to consider the matter, but no mention was made of
Christina.   The next day a great hunting-party was
given in the Palsgrave's honour.   A pavilion of green
laurel boughs was set up in a meadow on the banks
of the river, and while the King and his guests were
at dinner the merry note of hunting-horns rang
through the air, and a stag bounded across the turf,
followed by the hounds at full cry.   Immediately the
whole party sprang to horse and joined in the chase,
which lasted for three hours, and ended in the
slaughter of thirty-four stags.   From Windsor
Frederic went to Hampton Court, and on the 3rd of
October finally took leave of the King, who gave him
2,000 crowns as a parting gift.   Hubert also received
a silver cup from the Lord Privy Seal, who begged
him and his lord to return at Christmas, and surprised
him by asking if the Palsgrave had any castle to let
or sell, as it might be convenient for him to secure a
retreat abroad.   The Minister evidently realized the
precarious nature of his position, and Hubert remembered his request when he heard of the doom which
soon afterwards overtook the King's favourite.[2]

In his last interview Henry told the Count that he
feared it would be impossible for him to join in any
enterprise against Denmark, as his new allies the
German Princes were in league with the present King.
At the same time he informed his good cousin of his
intended marriage to the Lady Anne of Cleves, a

[1] Calendar of State Papers, xiv. 2, **66, 69,** 94, **368.**
[2] H. Thomas, 399-401; Kaulek, 136.

Princess of suitable age and elegant stature, and begged him to obtain a safe-conduct from the Regent for his bride's passage through the Low Countries.[1] The next day Frederic crossed the Channel and joined his wife at Brussels. Here, as Dorothea had already told him, he found the Queen much displeased at the trick which he had played her, and Hubert came in for his share of blame. They soon left Brabant for Heidelberg, and the Palatine sent Lady Lisle—or, as he called her, " Madame ma bonne mère "—a barrel of fine red and white Rhine wine in remembrance " of her loving son."[2]

II.

King Henry's marriage to Anne of Cleves, as Southampton told his master, was exceedingly unpopular in the Netherlands. The alliance of so powerful a monarch with Duke William was fraught with danger, and the people bitterly resented the insult which, in their eyes, had been offered to the Duchess of Milan. The merchants of Antwerp said openly that, if King Henry chose to break faith with their Princess, he should not enjoy the company of another wife, and declared they would not allow the Lady Anne to pass through their city. The Cleves Envoys in England were so much alarmed by these reports that they travelled back to Düren in disguise, and advised the bride to take the sea-route from Germany. But Mary of Hungary was too wise to show her annoyance, and sent a gracious message to Henry, saying that she would send Count Büren to wait on the Lady Anne, on her journey through the

[1] Kaulek, 135.
[2] Calendar of State Papers, xiv. 2, 215; H. Thomas, 401.

Emperor's dominions. The King wrote back in high
glee to thank " his dearest sister," and on the 27th of
December his new bride landed safely at Dover.[1]
The loyal citizens of Flanders consoled themselves with
the thought that, if their Duchess was not to be Queen
of England, they would keep her among them, and
the old rumour was persistently repeated : " She shall
marry the Prince of Orange." All through the past
year René had devoted himself to Christina's service,
had worn her favours and broken lances in her honour.
Her Italian servants called him openly the Duchess's
cavaliere sirvente.[2] But it was plain to Italians and
Flemings alike that the affection was not at all on
one side, and that this gallant Prince had won Christina's heart. Old courtiers smiled kindly on the
young couple, and ladies drew aside discreetly to
leave them together. They were eminently fitted
for each other by age, race and character. If the
succession to the principality of Orange, which had
been lately restored by the French King, hardly entitled René to a place among the reigning Princes of
Europe, at least he could offer her splendid homes
at Brussels and Breda, and a position which many
ladies of royal birth might envy. The Countess
Palatine Dorothea privately encouraged the Prince,
and her husband warmly approved of the match, and
said openly that, since his sister-in-law could not be
King Henry's wife, she had better marry the man of
her choice, and not waste the best years of her life,
as he himself had done.[3]

[1] Calendar of State Papers, xiv. 2, 127, 232; Calendar of
Spanish State Papers, vi. 1, 200; Kaulek, 138, 139.
[2] Calendar of State Papers, xiv. 2, 127; Nott, ii. 399.
[3] Calendar of State Papers, xvi. 61; Henne, vi. 301-396.

Queen Mary was, clearly, not averse to the Prince's suit, and had a strong liking for René; but reasons of State prevented her from giving the union her public sanction, and all parties were agreed that nothing could be arranged until the Emperor's arrival. The date of his journey was now definitely fixed, and in November Mary told the English Ambassador Vaughan that her brother would be at Brussels by the New Year. Charles at length realized the critical situation of affairs, and saw that if he wished to keep his provinces *de par-deça* he must no longer delay his coming.[1] In September, 1539, the citizens of Ghent, who had long been discontented, broke into open revolt. After refusing to pay their share of the subsidy voted by the States, the leading citizens put to death their chief magistrate, Lieven Pyl, because he declined to bear their insolent message to the Regent, and proceeded to tear up the famous " Calf-vel," a parchment deed containing an agreement which they had made with Charles V. twenty-four years before. Worse than all, they sent deputies to King Francis, asking him to defend their liberties against the Emperor. At the first tidings of these disorders Mary hastened to Malines and took energetic measures to suppress the insurrection, which had already spread to several of the neighbouring towns.[2] For some weeks the alarm was great, and watchers were posted on the tower of S. Rombaut night and day; but the Queen's presence of mind, and the support of her able lieutenants, Aerschot and De Courrières, who was now Bailiff of Alost, succeeded in confining the mutiny to the walls of Ghent. A

[1] State Papers, Record Office, viii. 205.
[2] Bulletin de la Commission d'Histoire, série ii., 3, 490.

simultaneous rising at Maestricht was put down by
the Prince of Orange, who raised 300 horse and
hastened to restore order in that city. But the
citizens of Ghent still openly defied the Regent,
although Francis, to do him credit, refused to help
the rebels. More than this, he addressed a letter
with his own royal hand to Charles, saying that, if the
Emperor was coming to chastise his revolted subjects,
he hoped that he would do him the honour of passing
through France, assuring him, on the faith of a
Prince, that every possible honour and hospitality
would be shown him.[1]

So critical was the situation, both with regard to
Ghent and Guelders, that Charles decided to accept
the offer and take the shortest route to Flanders.

" My good brother the Emperor," wrote Francis
to his Ambassador in England, " is coming to visit
me on his way to the Low Countries, a thing which
not only does me the greatest honour, content, and
pleasure, but is a proof of the good and perfect friendship between us."

He expressed the same feelings in still stronger
terms to Wyatt, whom Cromwell sent to Blois in
December to be present at the meeting of the two
monarchs.

" The Emperor," he added, " is doing me the greatest honour that can be, by coming to visit me, and
showing thereby that he taketh me for an honest
man."[2]

On the 23rd of November Charles left Burgos, and
four days later he entered Bayonne, attended by the

---

[1] Granvelle, "Papiers d'État," ii. 540; Calendar of State Papers,
xiv. 1, 437, 2, 193; Gachard, "Relation des Troubles de Gand,"
258.

[2] Kaulek, 142; Nott, ii. 353.

Dauphin and the Constable Montmorency, whom
the King had sent to meet him on the frontier. He
had begged Francis to dispense with ceremonies, as
his great object was to reach Flanders as quickly as
possible, and to excuse him from entering on political
matters, since he could not decide anything of importance until he had seen the Queen-Regent.[1] But,
in spite of this request, he was everywhere received
with the utmost pomp and festivity. Triumphal
arches were erected at the city gates, and the prison
doors were thrown open at his entrance. Bordeaux
presented him with 300 barrels of wine, Poitiers gave
him a golden eagle, Orleans a dinner-service of richly
chased plate. The meeting of the two monarchs
took place at Loches on the 10th of December.
Charles, clad in deep mourning, walked under a
canopy of cloth of gold, adorned with the imperial
eagles, across the picturesque court to the gates of the
castle, where King Francis met him, surrounded by a
brilliant company. Three times over he embraced
his guest, and led him to the hall, where Eleanor, in
robes of purple satin glittering with pearls, welcomed
her brother with transports of joy. Banquets and
hunting-parties now followed each other, as the Court
journeyed by slow stages along the banks of the Loire,
from one fair château to another. At Amboise a heap
of tow caught fire as Charles rode up the famous spiral
staircase in the dusk, and he narrowly escaped being
suffocated. But, mercifully, no one was injured, and
Francis escorted his imperial brother by way of Blois
and Orleans to Fontainebleau, where Christmas was
spent and the Emperor was allowed to enjoy a week's
rest. On New Year's Day the Emperor entered Paris,

[1] Gachard, 252.

where the Parliament and University received him
" as if he were a god from heaven," and the following
motto was inscribed on the gates in golden letters:

" Ouvre, Paris, ouvre tes hautes portes,
Entrer y veut le plus grand des Chrétiens."[1]

Queen Eleanor, who scarcely left her brother's
side, took him to see the *Sainte Chapelle* which St.
Louis had built to receive the Crown of Thorns, and
escorted him to the Louvre, where sumptuous rooms
had been prepared for his reception. On Sunday
a grand tournament was held on the Place des Tournelles, in front of the palace which then occupied the
Place des Vosges, and the Duke of Vendôme and
the Count of Aumale opened the joust, while it was
closed by Francis of Lorraine, the Marquis of Pont-
à-Mousson. Charles left Paris on the 7th of January,
and was presented by the city with a silver model
of the Column of Hercules, seven feet high, bearing
his motto, *Plus oultre*.[2] The King took his guest to
dine at his new pleasure-house, the Château de
Madrid, accompanied him to St. Denis, where he
visited the Tomb of the Kings, and went on to the
Constable's house at Chantilly. Finally, on the 20th,
the Emperor took his leave of the King and Queen
at St. Quentin, and with tears in his eyes thanked
his host for this truly brotherly reception.[3]

In spite of the sinister warnings which Charles had
received before he set out on his journey, in
spite of Mary of Hungary's fears and of Madame
d'Étampes's thinly-veiled hostility, the experiment

[1] Gachard, 49.
[2] Henne, vii. 4; A. de Ruble, " Le Mariage de Jeanne d'Albret,"
46; R. de Bouillé, " Histoire des Ducs de Guise," i. 123.
[3] Gachard, 305.

had proved a brilliant success. Spanish and French poets celebrated the triumph of Peace over War, and the return of the golden age. And Charles himself laughed heartily when the King's jester, Triboulet, told him that he had inscribed His Imperial Majesty's name on his Calendar of Fools, because he had been so rash as to venture into his enemy's country, but now that he had reached the end of his journey without mishap, he should rub out Charles's name, and write that of Francis in its place.[1]

The French King went home in high delight, and wrote to Marillac saying that now all his differences with the Emperor would be easily arranged. During those five weeks the King had respected his guest's wishes and avoided politics, but the Constable, who enjoyed the Emperor's confidence in a high degree, had made good use of this opportunity, and flattered himself that he had been entirely successful. He was above all anxious to effect a marriage between the widowed Emperor and the King's daughter, and told Granvelle that Madame Marguerite was a rose among thorns, an angel among devils, and that, if His Imperial Majesty thought of making a second marriage, he could not do better. But Charles was firmly resolved never to take another wife, and, when the Constable pressed the point after he had left France, wrote that he must beg the King to give up all idea of such a union, as he did not intend to marry again, and was too old for Madame Marguerite.[2]

In spite of the splendour and cordiality of his reception, Charles was sad and tired, and longed more

---

[1] M. du Bellay, iv. 413.

[2] Granvelle, "Papiers d'État," ii. 562; Kaulek, 153.

than all else to find himself among his kindred and
people. It was with heartfelt relief that he reached
Cambray, and found the Prince of Orange, the Duke
of Aerschot, and his faithful De Courrières, with the
Archers' Guard, awaiting him. The next day he
went on to Valenciennes, where his loyal subjects
welcomed his return with passionate joy. Triumphal
arches adorned the streets, and the houses were
hung with tapestries. Now it was his turn to act as
host, and do honour to the Dauphin and Duke of
Orleans, who, with Vendôme, the Constable, and
Aumale, the Duke of Guise's eldest son, had insisted
on escorting him across the frontier.[1] The keys of
the city were presented to the Dauphin at the Cambray gate, torches blazed all along the streets, and
the bells rang merry peals as Charles led the way to
the ancient hôtel-de-ville, known as La Salle, where
the Queen of Hungary and the Duchess of Milan
received him with open arms. The next two days
were given up to mirth and festivity. Charles showed
the French Princes the sights of the town, while the
Constable was invited to dine alone with the Queen
and her niece, and sat down to table between the
two royal ladies. A splendid banquet was followed
by a ball, which lasted far on into the morning.
All the ladies appeared in magnificent costumes—
French, Italian, Flemish, or Spanish, as they chose—
and wore the richest jewels. The Emperor moved
through the vast hall, blithe and debonair beyond his
wont, jesting with his old friends and rejoicing to be
once more in his native land. Mary and Christina,
both of whom, remarks the chronicler, although
widows, were still young and beautiful, danced with

[1] Gachard, 531.

the French Princes all the evening, and were in high spirits.[1] There was much gay talk, and the Pope's Legate, the young Cardinal Farnese, amused the guests with stories of the latest gossip from the Court of England, which Queen Eleanor had heard from Marillac. According to him, the new Queen, Anne of Cleves, was too old and ugly for King Henry's taste, while her dresses and those of her German " Fraus " were so monstrous that the King would not allow them to appear at Court, and told his wife to adopt French fashions.[2]

The next morning the French Princes appeared early to bid the Queen farewell, and were very gracious in their manner of leave - taking. The Dauphin received a superb diamond jewel in the shape of a griffin, and a very fine emerald was bestowed on the Constable. There was some talk of a marriage between the Duke of Orleans and a daughter of King Ferdinand, while the King of Navarre and his wife, Margaret of Angoulême, were eager for a match between their only daughter, Jeanne, and the Prince of Spain. Vendôme probably realized that he had little chance of winning the Duchess of Milan, but he shrugged his shoulders and went his way gaily, saying he would wed the Pope's granddaughter, Vittoria Farnese, the sister of the boy Cardinal. And they all rode off in high spirits to join the King at La Fère and show him the Emperor's costly gifts. They met him on his way back from hunting, riding at the side of the Queen's litter, clad in a scarlet cloak, which made the English Ambassador remark how much better Eleanor was treated since her

[1] Gachard, 664-666.
[2] Calendar of State Papers, xv. 65.

brother's visit. And the whole Court, in Bishop Bonner's words, "made much demonstration of gladness, thinking they have God by the foot."[1]

III.

Among all his political anxieties and preoccupations, the Emperor had not forgotten his niece. Before he left Spain on this perilous journey through his old enemy's country, he drew up a paper of instructions to be given to his son Philip in case of his own death. A large part of this advice was devoted to the choice of a wife for the Prince himself, the heiress of Navarre being on the whole, in Charles's opinion, the most eligible bride for his son. After suggesting various alliances for his little daughters, Maria and Juana, the Emperor proceeded to urge on his successor the importance of finding a husband for his niece, the Widow of Milan, saying that he counted her as one of his own children. Three Princes, he said, were all eager to marry her—the Duke of Cleves, the heir of Lorraine, and the Duke of Vendôme—but it would be necessary to defer his decision until he had ascertained the best measures for recovering Denmark and settling the question of Guelders. "And if God," he added, "should call to Himself the Palatine Frederic, who is old and broken, one of these Princes might marry his widow."[2] Christina's marriage, it is easy to see, was closely bound up with the settlement of Guelders, an object which lay very near to her uncle's heart.

The English Ambassador Wyatt, who had been

---

[1] State Papers, Record Office, viii. 236, 237.
[2] Granvelle, "Papiers d'État," ii. 542.

posting after the Emperor across France, " through
deep and foul roads," was convinced that Charles
in his heart of hearts cared more for Guelders than he
did for all Italy. This earnest desire to recover
Guelders was, he felt sure, the true reason why the
Emperor had undertaken this long journey in the
depth of winter, and exposed his person to such great
risks in passing through France. When, contrary to
the Constable's express orders, Wyatt obtained an
audience from the Emperor at Châtelhérault, as he
came in from hunting with the Dauphin, and informed him of His Majesty's marriage and alliance
with Cleves, Charles turned angrily on him, saying:

" What hath Monsieur de Cleves to do with
Guelders ? I mean to show him that he has played
the young man. I hope the King will give him good
advice, for, I can tell you, Monsieur de Cleves shall
give me reason. I say he shall—he shall ! If he
does," he continued, laying his hand on his heart,
" he shall find in me a Sovereign, a cousin, and a
neighbour. Otherwise he will lose all three."[1]

When, two months later in Brussels, Wyatt craved
another interview of the Emperor, and begged him
in Henry's name to look favourably on his brother-
in-law's petition, Charles said he must desire the
King not to meddle between him and his subjects,
repeating the same words, " Je ne ferai rien," two
or three times over. An Envoy from the Duke of
Cleves came to meet him at Brussels, but was told
that the Emperor could not attend to his master's
business until the affairs of Ghent were settled. These,
as Wyatt remarked, had already quieted down in a
singular manner from the moment that the Emperor

[1] Nott, ii. 358.

started on his journey, and deputies from the revolted city had been sent to meet him at Valenciennes.
But he refused sternly to see them, saying that they
would learn his pleasure when he came to Ghent.[1]

It was Charles's intention to overawe the turbulent
city by an imposing display of armed force. On the
14th of February, 1540, he entered Ghent—"that great,
rich, and beautiful city," writes the city chronicler,
" with its broad streets, fair rivers, noble churches,
houses, and hospitals, the finest in the Netherlands "
—at the head of a stately procession. The Queen
rode on his right hand, the Duchess of Milan on his
left, followed by the Princess of Macedonia and other
ladies in litters, the officers of the household, and a
long train of foreign Ambassadors, Princes, and
Knights of the Golden Fleece. Cardinal Farnese,
Don Ferrante Gonzaga, Viceroy of Sicily, the Prince
of Orange, the Dukes of Alva and Aerschot, Count
Egmont, Büren, De Praet, Lalaing, and Granvelle,
were all present. In their rear came the troops—
4,000 horse, 1,000 crossbowmen, 5,000 *Landsknechten*,
and a strong body of artillery, numbering in all
60,000 persons and 15,000 horses. Their entry lasted
six hours, and it was dusk before the last guns and
baggage defiled through the streets. Charles, with his
sister and niece, alighted at the Prinzenhof, the house
where he had been born just forty years before, and
the Archers' Guard took up their station at the gates.[2]
A strong body of infantry was encamped in the neighbouring market-place, pickets of cavalry occupied
the chief squares, and the rest of the troops were
quartered in other parts of the city. But there was

---

[1] Nott, ii. 380, 391.
[2] Gachard, " Relation des Troubles de Gand," 65.

not the least show of resistance on the part of the citizens. Absolute tranquillity reigned everywhere while the stricken city awaited the Emperor's sentence. It was, as might be expected, a severe one. Twenty-three of the ringleaders were arrested, and after a prolonged trial were found guilty. On the 17th of March, nine of these were put to death in the market-place, while the others were banished and heavily fined. On the 29th of April the Emperor convened the chief officers of State and magistrates in the great hall of the Prinzenhof, and, in the presence of the Queen and her Court, delivered his sentence on the guilty city. The charters and privileges of Ghent were annulled, the property of the Corporation was confiscated, and heavy additional fines were imposed, beside the payment of the 400,000 florins which had been the cause of the quarrel. In their consternation, the burghers turned to Mary and implored her to intercede on their behalf; but she could only advise them to throw themselves on the Emperor's mercy. On the 3rd of May a memorable and historic scene took place in the court of the Prinzenhof. Here the Emperor, seated on a tribunal, with his crown on his head and sceptre in his hand, and surrounded by the Archers' Guard, received the senators and chief burghers, as, robed in black, with bare heads and feet, and halters round their necks, they knelt in the dust at his feet. The sentence of condemnation was read aloud in the presence of a brilliant assembly of nobles and courtiers, and of a vast crowd who looked on from the windows and roofs of the neighbouring houses. Then Mary, who occupied a chair at her brother's side, rose, and, turning to the Emperor, in eloquent words implored him to have pity on his poor city of Ghent, and to remember that he had been born there. The Emperor gave a gracious answer, saying that out of brotherly love for her and pity for his poor subjects he would pardon the citizens and restore their property. But he decided to build a citadel to keep the city in subjection, and, after taking his brother Ferdinand to the top of the belfry tower to choose a site, he eventually fixed on the high ground above the River Scheldt, where St. Bavon's Abbey stood. The demolition of the ancient monastery was at once begun, and before the Emperor left Ghent the first stone of the new fortress was laid.[1]

While these tragic events were taking place, a succession of illustrious guests arrived at Court. First of all, at the end of February, came Ferdinand, King of the Romans, a simple and honest Prince, the best of husbands and fathers, and as fondly attached to his sister Mary as she was to him. At the same time the Palatine Frederic sent his wife to join the family party and plead her unfortunate father's cause with the all-powerful Emperor. Although his journey to England had failed to secure Henry's support, he still cherished designs against Denmark, and was anxious to prevent a renewal of the truce between the Low Countries and King Christian III. After consulting Archbishop Carondelet, the President of the Council, and Granvelle, the two sisters, Dorothea and Christina, drew up a petition to the Emperor, imploring him to have pity on the poor prisoner, who had already languished seven years in solitary confinement, and reminding him gently of the pledges given to the Palatine at his marriage.

[1] Henne, vii. 40-90; Gachard, 67-70, 389.

" My sister and I "—so ran the words of Dorothea's prayer—" your humble and loving children, entreat you, as the fountain of all justice, to have compassion on us. Open the prison doors, which you alone are able to do, release my father, and give me advice as to how I may best obtain the kingdom which belongs to me by the laws of God and man."[1]

But although the sisters' touching appeal on behalf of their captive father moved many hearts, and both Henry VIII. and James V. of Scotland wrote to assure the Palatine of their sympathy, no one was inclined to embark on so desperate an enterprise, and Dorothea went back to her lord at Heidelberg without having obtained any satisfaction. On the 14th of April a truce was concluded with the Danish Envoys, who had followed the Emperor to Ghent, and the illusory hopes of the three crowns which had been so long dangled before the Palatine's eyes melted into thin air.[2]

There was still one important question awaiting settlement. William of Cleves had sent three successive Ambassadors to congratulate Charles on his return and to seek the investiture of Guelders at his hand. Now, at King Ferdinand's instance, he arrived at Ghent one day in person, to the surprise of the whole Court.

" The Duke of Cleves," wrote an eyewitness of his entry, " has come to Ghent with a fine suite, to claim Guelders and marry the Duchess of Milan. This is not to be wondered at, for she is a young and very beautiful widow as well as a Princess of the noblest birth. He who wins her for his bride will be a fortunate man."[3]

---

[1] Lanz, ii. 308.   [2] Henne, vii. 282; Nott, ii. 418.
[3] Gachard, 65, 71.

The English Ambassador at Düren, Nicholas
Wotton, had done his utmost to prevent the Duke
from accepting Ferdinand's invitation; and Wyatt
was charged by Cromwell to neglect no means of
preventing an alliance which would defeat all his
schemes. The wily Ambassador laid his snares
cleverly. When the Cleves Ambassador, Olisleger,
told him that the Duke was about to wed the Duchess,
he whispered that his master had better be careful
and take counsel of King Henry before he took any
further pledges.

" I told him," wrote Wyatt to King Henry, " to
advise his master, in case of marriage, to use his
friend's counsel, and herein, if I shall be plain with
Your Majesty, I cannot but rejoice in a manner of the
escape that you made there; for although I suppose
nothing but honour in the Lady, yet methinketh
Your Highness's mate should be without mote or
suspicion; and yet there is thought affection between
the Prince of Orange and her, and hath been of long;
which, for her bringing-up in Italy, may be noted but
service which she cannot let, but I have heard it to
proceed partly from her own occasion.   Of this Your
Majesty will judge, and do with your friend as ye
shall think. meet."[1]

René's courtship of the Duchess was no secret,
and Christina's preference for the popular Prince was
plain to everyone at the Imperial Court; but the unworthy insinuations by which the Ambassador strove
to blacken her character were altogether his invention.
Since this was the surest way to win both Henry's
and Cromwell's favour, Wyatt made unscrupulous
use of these slanders to poison William of Cleves's
mind against the Duchess whose hand he sought.

---

[1] Nott, ii. 398.

On the 13th of April the Duke arrived at Ghent, and
was met by the Prince of Orange, who brought him
to King Ferdinand's rooms. Late the same evening
the English Ambassador had a secret interview with
him, and did his utmost to dissuade him from entering into any treaty with the Emperor. The Duke's
irresolution was now greater than ever. The next
day Ferdinand himself conducted him into the
Emperor's presence, where he received the most
friendly greeting, and was invited to join the imperial
family at dinner. The gracious welcome which he
received from Mary, and the sight of Christina, went
far to remove his doubts, and during the next few
days the harmony that prevailed among the Princes
excited Wyatt's worst misgivings. The Venetian
Ambassador, Francesco Contarini, met the Countess
Palatine returning from Ghent, and heard from her
servants that a marriage was arranged between her
sister and the Duke of Cleves. Monsieur de Vély, the
French Envoy, sent this report to Paris, and it was
confidently asserted at the French and English Courts
that Cleves had settled his quarrel with the Emperor,
and was to wed the Duchess.[1]

But these reports were premature. The Duke
told Wotton and Wyatt that nothing would induce
him to give up Guelders, and at their suggestion he
placed a statement of his claims in the hands of
Ferdinand, who promised to submit the document
to the Emperor. During the next fortnight the
question was discussed in all its bearings by Charles
and his Councillors. The Duke pressed his suit for
the Duchess's hand, and the Emperor went so far as
to offer him the reversion of Denmark if he would

[1] Nott, ii. 417; State Papers, Record Office. viii. 329.

renounce Guelders. But William was as obstinate as
the Emperor, and, when Ferdinand induced Charles
to offer Cleves his niece and the duchy of Guelders for
his lifetime, he quite refused to accept this proposal.
All Ferdinand could persuade him to do, was to
consent that the question of Guelders should be
referred to the Imperial Chamber, a compromise
which satisfied neither party. Still friendly relations were maintained outwardly. On Sunday, the
27th of April, the imperial family attended Mass in
state, the Emperor riding to the Church of St. John
with the King of the Romans and the boy Legate,
Cardinal Farnese, on his left, followed by the Dukes
of Brunswick, Cleves, Savoy, and the Marquis of
Brandenburg. In the afternoon Ferdinand sent for
the Duke again, and made one more attempt to
arrange matters, without success. Some insolent
words spoken by Cleves's servants aroused the Emperor's anger, upon which the Duke became alarmed,
and sent Wotton word that, seeing no hope of agreement, he intended to return home. Early the next
morning, without taking leave of anyone, he rode
out of the town secretly, and never halted until he
was safe in his own dominions. His royal brother-in-
law, King Henry, sent him a long letter, congratulating him on his safe return, and advising him
solemnly not to marry the Duchess of Milan without
finding out the true state of her affections towards
the Prince of Orange, lest he should be deceived.
Wotton told the King, in reply, that the Duke's affection for Christina was now cooled, partly because she
had refused him, and partly because of the information
which Henry had given him. All idea of the marriage
was certainly abandoned, and on the 22nd of June

Cleves himself wrote to tell Henry that he had received friendly overtures from the French King, and was sending Ambassadors to make proposals for his niece, the Princess of Navarre.[1]

Meanwhile the Duke's strange conduct had excited much surprise at Ghent. The Emperor, who had spent the anniversary of his wife's death in retirement at a Carthusian convent in the neighbourhood, returned to find Cleves gone. Henry of Brunswick rode with his friend to the outskirts of the town, and hurried back to be present at the imperial table, where he tried to explain the Duke's abrupt departure by saying that he was afraid of treachery. But Ferdinand and Mary were both seriously annoyed, and the only member of the family to rejoice was Christina, who felt that she could once more breathe freely.

The pacification of Ghent was now complete, and the bulk of the forces were disbanded. On Ascension Day—the 6th of May—the imperial family attended Mass at St. John's, the Queen " walking lovingly up the church, hand in hand with the King of the Romans." The Ambassadors were all present, as well as Cardinal Farnese—in Wotton's opinion " a very calf, and a greater boy in manners and condition than in years."

On the 12th the King of the Romans took leave of his family, but the Council at which he assisted lasted so late in the evening that he did not actually set out on his journey till two o'clock on the following day. About six in the cool hours of the May morning, the Emperor, with his sister and niece, rode out to see the foundations of the new citadel laid, and

[1] Calendar of State Papers, xv. 349, 367.

then continued their journey towards Antwerp, where " great gun-shot " and bonfires welcomed their arrival.[1]

IV.

The Court spent the next three weeks at Bruges, the beautiful old city which was always a favourite with Charles and his sisters, in the ancient Prinzenhof where their mother had died.   During these summer days many important events took place, and startling news came from England.   On the 10th of June Cromwell was suddenly arrested and sent to the Tower on a charge of high-treason.   A fortnight later the new Queen, Anne of Cleves, left Whitehall for Richmond, and on the 9th of July her marriage was pronounced null and void by a decree of Convocation. The ostensible reason for the divorce was a pre-contract between Anne and Francis of Lorraine.   It was true that as children they had been affianced by their respective parents, but, as was common in such cases, all idea of the marriage had been afterwards abandoned, and Henry had professed himself entirely satisfied with the explanations given by Anne's relatives on the subject.   But from the first moment that he met his bride at Rochester, on New Year's Day, 1540, he was profoundly disappointed.   When Cromwell asked him how he liked her, he replied, " Nothing so well as she was spoken of," adding that, had he known as much of her before as he did now, she should never have set foot in his realm.   However, he felt constrained to marry her, for fear of " making a ruffle in the world," and driving her brother

---

[1] State Papers, Record Office, viii. 336, 340, 354; Calendar of State Papers, xv. 318.

into the Emperor's arms. At Whitsuntide he told Cromwell that from the day of his marriage he had become weary of life, and took a solemn oath that before God Anne had never been his lawful wife.

From that moment Cromwell knew that his own fate was sealed. " The King loves not the Queen," he said to Wriothesley. " What a triumph for the Emperor and the Pope !" A week afterwards he was committed to the Tower, and on the 28th of July he was beheaded.[1]

The news of his fall was received with general satisfaction abroad. King Francis gave vent to boisterous joy, and sent his brother word how sincerely he rejoiced to hear that this false and wicked traitor, who had brought the noblest heads in England to the block, was at length unmasked. The Emperor, on the contrary, showed no surprise or emotion when he heard the news from Archdeacon Pate, the new Envoy who had succeeded Wyatt, but merely said : " What ! is he in the Tower of London, and by the King's counsel ?" And when, on the 6th of July, Pate informed him that the King had repudiated his wife, he cast his eye steadfastly on the speaker, and asked what scruples His Majesty entertained regarding his marriage with the daughter of Cleves. The Ambassador explained, as best he could, what he took to be the motives of the King's action, upon which the Emperor said that he was convinced Cromwell was the true cause of all the terrible crimes which had of late years been committed against religion and order in England. So friendly was the Emperor that Pate wrote to the Duke of Norfolk: " If His Majesty hath thereby lost the hearts of the Electors, he hath in

---

[1] Calendar of State Papers, xv. 363, 390, 391.

their places gained those of the Emperor and the French King."[1]

Both at Bruges and Antwerp the news aroused much excitement among the merchants, who were unanimous in the opinion that the King now intended to take the Duchess of Milan " for the true heart which she bore him." But nothing was further from Christina's mind. She had rejoiced at the failure of the King's suit, and saw the Duke of Cleves leave Ghent without regret. Now all seemed ripe for the fulfilment of her long-cherished hopes. The Prince of Orange had been unremitting in his attendance on the Emperor since his arrival, and, as all men knew, was honoured by His Majesty's confidence and affection. His popularity with the army was unbounded, and it was a common saying that wherever the Prince's little pony went, every Dutchman would follow. The Queen looked kindly on his suit, and Christina's heart was already his own. But when, in these bright June days at Bruges, he modestly laid his suit before the Emperor, an unexpected difficulty arose. Three years before a marriage with the Duke of Lorraine's only daughter had been proposed for the young Prince of Orange by his uncle, William of Nassau-Dillenburg, the head of the German branch of the house. The idea met with Henry of Nassau's cordial approval, and at his request the Emperor sent his servant Montbardon to obtain Duke Antoine's consent. This was granted without any difficulty, and the contract was drawn up before the Count of Nassau's death.[2] Now the Duke urged the Prince to keep this long-standing

[1] Kaulek, 191; State Papers, Record Office, viii. 386, 397, 412.
[2] L. Hugo, " Traité sur l'Origine de la Maison de Lorraine," 212.

engagement and marry his daughter Anne—the plain but excellent lady whose portrait Holbein had taken for King Henry. The Prince had never seen his destined bride, and was very reluctant to carry out the contract, but the Emperor was resolute. Antoine already had a serious grievance in the matter of Guelders, and it was of the highest importance to secure his alliance. Accordingly, Charles told René that he must prove himself a loyal knight, and with his own hand drew up the articles of the marriage treaty, and sent them to Nancy by the Archdeacon of Arras. Christina's name is never mentioned in the whole transaction. It was the old story of the Count Palatine and the Archduchess Eleanor. She was a daughter of the House of Habsburg, and knew that the Emperor's will must be obeyed. So she could only bow her head in silence and submit to his decrees. If she wept bitter tears, it was in secret, in her quiet chamber in the ancient Cour des Princes at Bruges, looking down on the green waters of the canal.[1]

There was great rejoicing throughout Lorraine when the Emperor's messenger reached Nancy and the marriage was proclaimed. Anne was very popular throughout the duchy, and since her mother's death, a year before, had taken a prominent place at the ducal Court, where her tact and kindness made her universally beloved. The wedding took place in the last week of August at Bar.[2] All the members of the ducal house were present, including the Duke and Duchess of Guise, with their sons and daughters, and the Cardinal of Lorraine, who came from the French Court to pronounce the nuptial blessing.

[1] State Papers, Record Office, viii. 398.
[2] Pfister, " Histoire de Nancy," ii. 188.

The Prince of Orange's martial appearance and his splendid suite made a favourable impression on his new relatives, as Antoinette de Bourbon wrote to her daughter in Scotland:

"I have delayed longer than I intended before writing to you, but we have been so well amused by the wedding of Mademoiselle de Lorraine that until this moment I have not had leisure to begin this letter. Yesterday we left the assembled company. There was a very large gathering, and the wedding took place last Tuesday. Monsieur le Prince arrived honourably attended, and is, I can assure you, a very charming and handsome Prince. He is much pleased with his bride, and she is devoted to him. They are to go home in a fortnight. The fête was at Bar, but there were very few strangers present—only a few nobles and ladies of the neighbourhood."[1]

On the 27th of September the Prince of Orange brought his bride to Brussels, where the States were assembled. The whole Court rode out to welcome the happy pair, and escorted them to the Nassau palace, where the Prince changed his travelling dress for a Court mantle, and hastened to pay his respects to the Emperor. A succession of fêtes was given in their honour, and dances, masques, and banquets, were the order of the day. The Princess charmed everyone by her gracious manners, and her fine figure and splendid clothes and jewels became the object of general admiration.

On the 2nd of October a grand tournament was given in the Prince's house, which the Emperor, Queen Mary, and Christina, honoured with their presence. René himself challenged all comers at the barriers, and his wife was the most charming

---

[1] Balcarres Manuscripts, ii. 15, Advocates' Library, Edinburgh.

hostess. Before Charles left, he presented Anne with a costly ring, and appointed the Prince to succeed Antoine de Lalaing as Stadtholder of Holland and Friesland. Three days afterwards the newly-married pair left Court for their own home at Breda, and the Emperor set out on a progress through Artois and Hainault, leaving his sister and niece at Brussels.

René's wife soon became a great favourite with the Queen, and Christina danced as gaily as the rest at the wedding fêtes. But it is significant that the only mention made of her in contemporary records is in the despatches of the English Ambassador, Richard Pate, who tells us that the Duchess of Milan spent much of her time in the company of her brother-in-law, the Palatine.[1] Frederic had come to Brussels to confer with the Emperor on German affairs, and, if possible, to raise a loan of 600,000 ducats for his intended campaign against Denmark. But although Charles professed himself ready and anxious to oblige his good cousin, the Regent would give him no answer, and ended by telling him to get the money from the Imperial Treasury. Richard Pate held long and confidential conversations with the Palatine, who recalled his visit to Windsor with delight, and spoke with warm admiration of the beauty of the singing in St. George's Chapel. He was curious to know if his old friend the King had grown as fat as he was represented in recent portraits, and rejoiced to hear that His Majesty was lusty and merry. As for the Duchess of Milan, he could only feel sorry that so charming a lady should still lack a husband, and frankly regretted that she had not married King Henry, or, failing

[1] State Papers, Record Office, viii. 444.

him, the Prince of Orange.[1] After his return to
Germany, Frederic made another attempt to bring
about his sister-in-law's marriage to the Duke of
Cleves, who still hesitated between his old love for
Christina and his reluctance to give up Guelders.
But negotiations were already in progress with another
suitor, who had bided his time patiently, and who
was now at length to obtain his reward.

The Prince of Orange's union with Anne of Lorraine had strengthened the ties that bound her father
to the Emperor, and a second marriage, which took
place this autumn, united the two houses still more
closely. Among the young nobles who accompanied
René to Bar for his wedding was Charles, Prince of
Chimay, the eldest son of the Duke of Aerschot, the
wealthy and powerful Governor of Brabant, who was
foremost among the Regent's confidential advisers,
and whom she affectionately called by the pet name
of " Moriceau."   On the death of his mother in 1539,
the young Prince had succeeded to her vast estates,
and lived at the fine castle of Beaumont, near the
French frontier.   At Bar he saw and fell in love with
Louise de Guise, the lovely girl whom Henry VIII.
would gladly have made his wife. But there were
difficulties in the young suitor's way.   His own family
began by opposing the marriage, and it was some time
before Charles's consent could be obtained.   The
Duke of Guise had long been the Emperor's most
bitter enemy, and was known to have strongly opposed his journey through France. Fortunately,
Duchess Antoinette was from the first on the lovers'
side, and succeeded in gaining her husband's consent. For some time past King Francis had been

---

[1] Calendar of State Papers, Henry VIII., xvi. 1, 60.

trying to arrange a marriage between her eldest son, the Count of Aumale, and the Pope's granddaughter, " *Vyquetorya* Farnese," as Louise calls her in one of her letters. But the Pope haggled over the dowry, and insisted on asking the Emperor's consent; so that Antoinette had a troublesome task in her lord's absence, and complained sorely to the Queen of Scotland of these vexatious delays.

" By way of consolation, however," she writes on the 30th of November, " we have an offer for your sister. Monsieur le Duc d'Aerschot has sent to ask for her, on behalf of his eldest son, the Prince of Chimay, a youth about twenty, handsome and well brought up, we hear. He will give him a portion of 50,000 crowns a year, and he will have some fine estates, such as the duchy of Aerschot, the principality of Chimay, the counties of Beaumont and Porcien, most of them near Guise. I have told your father, who is at Court, and he approves, and has spoken to the King and to our brothers, who all advise us to accept the proposal. So do my brother-in-law [the Duke of Lorraine] and my mother [Madame de Vendôme]. It has been arranged that we should all meet at Bar on the Conception of Our Lady, as my lord the Duke wishes the matter to be settled at his house. I hope your father will be there, but if not he will give me the necessary powers. If things can be arranged, she will be well married, for the Prince has great possessions and beautiful houses, and plate and furniture in abundance. But it is a great anxiety to be treating of two marriages at once."[1]

Happily for the good Duchess, the young Prince had his way, and the contract between him and Louise was duly signed at Bar on the 22nd of December. On the same day the Emperor, accompanied by the Regent and Duchess of Milan, paid a visit to the Duke of Aerschot at Beaumont, and offered him

[1] Balcarres Manuscripts, ii. 22.

their warmest congratulations on his son's marriage.[1]
The wedding took place at Joinville in the following
March, by which time Christina's own marriage to
Louise's cousin was arranged, and all Lorraine rang
with the sound of wedding-bells.

V.

The vaunted alliance between Charles and Francis
did not last long, and less than a year after the
Emperor and King had parted at St. Quentin,
vowing eternal friendship, a renewal of war seemed
already imminent. Francis was bitterly disappointed
to find that none of the great results which he
expected from Charles's visit had come to pass.
The Emperor firmly declined to marry his daughter,
and gave no signs of surrendering Milan to the Duke
of Orleans. All he would offer was the reversion of
the Low Countries as his daughter's portion if she
married Orleans. This failed to satisfy Francis, who
declared that he would have Milan and nothing else.
In order to prevent his niece, Jeanne of Navarre,
marrying the Prince of Spain, the King offered her to
the Duke of Cleves, who signed a treaty with France
this summer, but was not actually affianced to the
little Princess until the Duchess of Milan was finally
betrothed to Francis of Lorraine. Upon hearing of
the alliance between France and Cleves, Charles
retaliated by solemnly investing his son Philip with
the duchy of Milan. This ceremony took place at
Brussels on the 11th of October, and was regarded
by Francis as an open act of defiance. He vented his

[1] W. Bradford, " Itinerary of Charles V.," 517; State Papers,
Record Office, viii. 508.

anger on the Constable, who asked leave to retire; while Madame d'Étampes did her best to obtain her rival's disgrace and induce the King to declare war against the Emperor. But Francis was loth to let his old servant go, and said to Montmorency, with tears in his eyes: "How can you ask me to let you leave me? I have only one fault to find with you, that you do not love what I love."[1] The Constable consented to remain, and for the moment the crisis was delayed.

After visiting the forts along the frontier and leaving garrisons in every town, the Emperor came to Namur for Christmas, and prepared for his final departure. Forty chariots were needed for his own use, and all the horses and carts in the neighbouring provinces were requisitioned to provide for the conveyance of his immense suite. On Innocents' Day the Court moved to Luxembourg, and all the gentlemen of the countryside rode out to meet the Emperor. With him came the Queen and the Duchess of Milan, and on the same evening they were joined by the Duke of Lorraine and his son Francis, the Marquis of Pont-à-Mousson. On the Feast of the Three Kings the imperial party attended Mass in the cathedral, and the Emperor, after his usual custom, presented golden cups to three abbeys in the town. And on the same day the marriage of the Marquis to the Duchess of Milan was finally concluded, to the great delight of the old Duke, who was as much pleased as the bridegroom. Two days afterwards Charles took an affectionate farewell of his sister and niece, and went on to Regensburg, leaving them to return to Brussels, while the Duke of Lorraine hastened to

[1] F. Decrue, "Montmorency à la Cour de François I.," i. 392.

Nancy to summon the States and inform his loyal
subjects of his son's marriage.[1]

On the 1st of March the contract drawn up by
the Imperial Ministers, Granvelle and De Praet,
was signed by the Duke of Lorraine at Bar, and on the
20th by the Emperor. The ducal manors of Blamont
and Denœuvre were settled upon the Duchess, and, in
order that she might not lose any rank by her marriage, the Marquis received the title of Duke of Bar.[2]
On the 12th of March the Queen and Duchess both
went to the Castle of Beaumont in Hainault, to be
present at the splendid reception which the Duke of
Aerschot gave his daughter-in-law. The Duchess of
Guise herself accompanied the beloved Louise to her
future home, and wrote the following account of the
festivities to Queen Mary of Scotland from her husband's château at Guise:

" Madame,
    " I have been so confidently assured that the
safest way for letters is to send them by Antwerp
merchants that I am sending mine by this means,
and your sister will be my postmistress in future.
I wrote to tell you of the conclusion of her marriage,
and sent the articles of the treaty and the account of
her wedding by your messenger. I have just taken
her to her new home, a fine and noble house, as well
furnished as possible, called Beaumont. Her father-
in-law, the Duke, received her very honourably,
attended by as large and illustrious a company as you
could wish to see. Among others, the Queen of
Hungary was present, and the Duchess of Milan,
and both the Prince and Princess of Orange, who, by
the way, is said to be with child, although this is
not quite certain as yet, and I confess I have my
doubts on the subject. I think your sister is very

---

[1] Gachard, " Voyages de Charles V.," ii. 167.
[2] A. Calmet, " Histoire de Lorraine," iii. 387.

well married. She has received beautiful presents,
and her husband has made her a very rich wedding-
gift. He is young, but full of good-will and excellent
intentions. It did not seem at all like Lent, for the
sound of trumpets and the clash of arms never ceased,
and there was some fine jousting. At the end we
had to part—not without tears. I am now back at
Guise, but only for one night, and go on to-morrow
to La Fère. My brother the Cardinal, and my
brother and sister of St. Pol, will be there on Wednesday. For love of them I will stay at La Fère over
Thursday, and set out again on Friday, to reach
Joinville as soon as may be, in the hope of finding
your father still there, as well as our children—that
is to say, the little ones and the priests."[1]

Ten days later Louise herself wrote a long and
happy letter to her sister from Beaumont, full of the
delights of her new home and of the kindness with
which she had been received by her husband's family.

" MADAME,
    " Since God gave me this great blessing of a
good husband, I have never found time to write to
you. But I can assure you that I count myself
indeed fortunate to be in this house, for, besides all
the grandeur of the place, I have a lord and father-
in-law whom I may well call good. It would take
three sheets of paper if I were to tell you all the
kindness with which he treats me. You may therefore be quite satisfied of your sister's happiness, and
she is further commanded to offer you the very humble
service of the masters and lords of this house, who
beg that you will employ them on any occasion that
may arise, since they will always be very glad to
obey your wishes. We also have a very wise and
virtuous Queen, who has done me the greatest honour
by coming here to our house, expressly, as she con-
descended to say, to receive me. She told me herself that she meant to take me for her very humble

---

[1] Balcarres Manuscripts, ii. 5 (see Appendix). The priests were
Antoinette's two sons, Charles, Archbishop of Reims, and Louis,
both of whom afterwards became Cardinals.

daughter and servant, and that in future she hoped
I should be often in her company, which, considering
how little she has seen of me, was exceedingly kind.
The Duchess of Milan said the same, and was the
best and kindest of all. We may soon hope to see
her in Lorraine, for her marriage to the Marquis is
in very good train. Since my mother went home,
she has sent a letter asking me to find out if this
route to Scotland will be shorter than the other.
If this is the case, and you like to send me your
letters for her, I shall be delighted. Only, Madame,
you must be sure to address your packets to the Duke
of Aerschot, which will be easy for you, as then the
merchants who come from Scotland will leave them
at Antwerp or Bruges, or any other town, and they
will not fail to reach me, since my father-in-law is
greatly loved and honoured throughout the Netherlands. And I pray that God will give you a long and
happy life.

" Your very humble and obedient sister,
" LOUISE OF LORRAINE.

" From Beaumont, the 25th day of March."[1]

The keenest interest in these marriages was shown
at the Court of Scotland. King James wrote cordial
letters from Edinburgh to his sister-in-law and to
the Duke of Aerschot, and congratulated the Princess
of Orange on her happy expectations, begging her
to write to him and his wife more frequently.[2] Anne
had always been on affectionate terms with her
aunt and cousins at Joinville, and the presence of
Louise at Brussels this summer was another bond
between them.

Meanwhile King Francis was greatly annoyed to
hear of the Duchess of Milan's marriage. He complained bitterly to the Duke of Guise and the Cardinal of their brother's desertion, and vowed that

---

[1] Balcarres Manuscripts, ii. 153 (see Appendix).
[2] *Ibid.*, ii. 157.

Antoine and his son should feel the full weight of his displeasure.   He was as good as his word, and, when the Prince assumed the title of Duke of Bar, disputed his rights to this duchy on the ground that it was a fief of the Crown.   In order to satisfy these new claims, the Duke was compelled to sign an agreement on the 22nd of April, by which he and his son consented to do homage to the King for the duchy of Bar, and to grant free passage of French troops through this province.[1]

At the same time Francis invited the Duke of Cleves to come to Blois, as he wished his marriage to the Princess of Navarre to be celebrated without delay.   On the 11th of April the States assembled at Düsseldorf were amazed to hear from Chancellor Olisleger that their Duke, being unable to obtain the Duchess of Milan's hand without the surrender of Guelders, was about to contract another marriage with the Princess of Navarre, and had actually started on his wedding journey.[2]   The King and Queen of Navarre had always been averse to their daughter's union with the Duke of Cleves, but Margaret's resistance was overcome by the royal brother whom she adored, and her husband gave a reluctant consent to the marriage; but the little Princess Jeanne, a delicate child of twelve, refused in the most determined manner to marry this foreign Prince.   In vain she was scolded and whipped, and threatened by her uncle the King with worse punishments.   For many weeks the child persisted in her refusal, and, when compelled to yield, signed a pro-

[1] State Papers, Record Office, viii. 609.

[2] State Papers, Record Office, viii. 550; Calendar of State Papers, xv. 344, 362; A. de Ruble, " Mariage de Jeanne d'Albret," 83.

test on the eve of her marriage, which with the secret
connivance of her parents was duly witnessed and
preserved.   On the 14th of June, 1540, the strange
wedding was finally solemnized at Châtelhérault, on
the Garonne.   A series of Arcadian fêtes in beautiful
summer weather were given by King Francis, who
never lost an opportunity for indulging his love of
romance. Arbours and colonnades of verdure were
reared on the river-banks.   King Arthur and the
Knights of the Round Table were seen riding forth
in quest of adventure; highborn ladies, clad as
nymphs and dryads, danced on the greensward by
torchlight.[1] The bridegroom gave his bride magnificent jewels, although Jeanne was never seen in
public, and did not even appear at the ball on the
night before the wedding.   Finally, when all were
assembled in the royal chapel, and the King came to
lead his niece to the altar, the little Princess, weighed
down by her costly jewels and gold and silver brocades,
was unable to walk. " Take her by the neck !"
cried the impatient monarch to Montmorency, and
the Constable of France, not venturing to disobey the
royal command, lifted up the frightened child in
his arms and bore her to the altar before the eyes of
the whole Court.   As he did so he was heard to
mutter, " C'en est fini, de ma faveur, adieu lui dis !"
and, surely enough, the day after the wedding he
received his dismissal, and left Court, never to
return during the lifetime of Francis.[2]

The Duke had agreed, in order to satisfy the King
and Queen of Navarre, that the marriage should be

---

[1] M. du Bellay, " Mémoires," iv. 415.

[2] A. de Ruble, 118; F. Decrue, " Anne de Montmorency à la
Cour de François I.," 403.

merely formal, and consented to leave his unwilling bride with her parents for another year. Accordingly, three days later he bade them farewell, and rode, attended by a strong French escort, through the Ardennes, and travelled down the Moselle and Rhine to Cologne. As he passed through Luxembourg he saw the trained bands gathering in force on the frontier, and heard that they were assembling under Count Büren to meet his successful rival, Francis of Lorraine, and bring him to Brussels for his wedding.[1]

Here great preparations had been made to do honour to the Emperor's niece, and the guests came from far and wide. Christina's trousseau was worthy of her exalted rank, and the Queen presented her with a wonderful carcanet of rubies, diamonds, and emeralds, with pendants of large pear-shaped pearls. The marriage was solemnized on Sunday, the 10th of July, in the great hall where, twenty-six years before, Isabella of Austria, had been married to the King of Denmark. Only two of the foreign Ambassadors were absent from the wedding banquet—the Englishmen Vaughan and Carne—a fact which naturally excited much comment. King Henry changed colour when Chapuys told him of Christina's marriage, and was at no pains to conceal his surprise and vexation. He said repeatedly that he wondered how the Emperor could allow so noble and renowned a Princess to marry the Marquis, when there could be no doubt that Anne of Cleves was his lawful wife, and insisted that this had been the chief reason of his own separation from this lady. After the wedding he again referred to the incident, and told Chapuys in con-

[1] State Papers, Record Office, viii. 585.

fidence that the Duke of Lorraine had secretly made over his rights on Guelders to the French King, and would never help the Emperor against France, since Monseiur de Guise and the Cardinal of Lorraine were entirely on the French side. Chapuys listened with polite attention, and reported most of the King's conversation for the amusement of the Court at Brussels.[1]

Here a series of fêtes took place after the wedding. A grand tournament was held in front of the hôtel-de-ville, followed by the mock siege of a fortress in the park, and a hunting-party in the Forest of Soignies.[2]

On the 14th, the Duke and Duchess of Bar left Brussels to pay a round of visits in the neighbourhood and " see the country," and on the 27th the Queen went to meet them at the Duke of Aerschot's hunting-palace at Heverlé, near Louvain, and spent several days there with the two other newly-married couples, the Prince and Princess of Orange and the Prince and Princess of Chimay.[3]

Finally, on the 1st of August, the bride and bridegroom set out on their journey, attended by a brilliant company, which included the Prince and Princess of Orange, the Duke of Aerschot, the Prince and Princess of Chimay, the Counts of Berghen, Büren, and Brederode. They travelled by slow stages, resting at Namur, Luxembourg, Thionville, and Metz. Triumphal arches were erected over the gates of each city, and the burghers came out in procession to greet the bride. At Metz Christina was presented with an illuminated book on " Marriage," by the

---

[1] Calendar of Spanish State Papers, vi. 1, 332, 349.
[2] Henne, vii. 282; Calendar of State Papers, xvi. 1, 470.
[3] Calendar of State Papers, xvi. 1, 508.

Regent of the University, Édmond du Boullay, and the Chapter of Toul offered her a gold cup, filled with 300 crowns, while the city gave her 200 crowns and ten barrels of choice wine.[1]

On the 8th the wedding-party reached Pont-à-Mousson, and found a large family gathering waiting to receive them. A few days before the Cardinal of Lorraine had joined the Duke and Duchess of Guise at Joinville, and had accompanied them to Pont-à-Mousson, as Antoinette wrote,

" in order to give our new Lady her first greeting and conduct her to Nancy. Great preparations have been made to welcome her, and there is to be some fine jousting. I will tell you if there is anything worth writing, and must confess I am very curious to see if the Marquis makes a good husband. At least the country rejoices greatly at the coming of so noble and excellent a lady."[2]

The Duchess of Guise had collected most of her family for the occasion, and brought four of her sons —Aumale, Mayenne, Charles, Archbishop of Reims, and Louis, Bishop of Troyes—to Pont-à-Mousson, as well as her little grandson, the Duke of Longueville, the Queen of Scotland's son by her first marriage. Duke Antoine and his younger son, Nicholas de Vaudemont, Bishop of Metz, were also present, together with all the chief nobles of Lorraine.

It was a strange meeting. Guise and his sons had often crossed swords with the Prince of Orange and Aerschot, and the Duke had refused to meet the Emperor on his memorable visit to Chantilly. Now he was engaged in repairing the forts along the

[1] J. B. Ravold, " Histoire de Lorraine," iii. 743; Hugo, 217; C. Pfister, " Histoire de Nancy," ii. 192.

[2] Balcarres Manuscripts, ii. 4 (see Appendix).

frontier in view of another war, an occupation which
had at least one merit in his wife's eyes, and kept
him longer at home than he had been for many years.
All alike, however, friends and foes, joined in giving
the new Duchess a hearty welcome, and drank
joyously to the health and prosperity of the illustrious
pair.

At Pont-à-Mousson Francis took his bride to the
convent of Poor Clares, to see his grandmother,
Philippa of Guelders, who had taken the veil twenty
years before, but still retained all her faculties, and
was the object of her sons' devoted affection. The
Duke of Guise and his wife constantly visited the
good old lady, whose name appears so often in
Antoinette's letters, and who now embraced her new
granddaughter tenderly and gave the bridal pair her
blessing. The next day Christina entered Nancy,
where immense crowds assembled to receive her, and
choirs of white-robed maidens welcomed her coming
at the ancient gateway of La Craffe. One quaint
medieval practice which had lasted until this century
was dispensed with. It was the custom for a band
of peasants from the neighbouring village of Laxou,
to beat the pools in the marshes under the palace
walls all through the night when the Princes of
Lorraine brought their brides home, to drive away
the frogs, whose croaking might disturb the ducal
slumbers. But instead of this, the peasant women
of Laxou stood at the palace gates as the Duchess
alighted, and presented her with baskets of flowers and
ripe strawberries and cherries.[1]

A grand tournament was held the following morning, on the Place des Dames in front of the ducal

---

[1] Pfister, ii. 63, 188; Ravold, iii. 703.

palace, in which many of the Flemish nobles took part, and was followed by a state banquet and ball—" all very sumptuously done," wrote Lord William Howard, the English Ambassador.[1]   Then the wedding festivities came to an end, the gay party broke up, and the old city which was henceforth to be Christina's home resumed its wonted air of sleepy tranquillity.

[1] State Papers, Record Office, viii. 609.

BOOK VIII

CHRISTINA, DUCHESS OF LORRAINE

1541—1545

I.

THE ducal house of Lorraine, into which Christina had now married, was one of the oldest and proudest in Europe. The duchy took its name of Lotharingia from Lothair, a great-grandson of Charlemagne, who reigned over a vast kingdom stretching from the banks of the Scheldt and Rhine to the Mediterranean. After this monarch's death, his territories became the object of perpetual contention between the German Empire and France, and were eventually divided among a number of Counts and Barons who owned the Emperor or the French King as their suzerain. Godfrey of Bouillon, the leader of the first Crusade, was one of many illustrious Princes who reigned over Lorraine; but Gerard d'Alsace, who died in 1046, was the ancestor of the ducal house to which Christina's husband belonged.[1] From him descended a long line of hereditary Princes, who were loyal vassals of France and took an active part in the wars against England. Raoul, the founder of the collegiate church and Chapter of St. Georges at

[1] Abbé Calmet, " Histoire Ecclésiastique et Civile de Lorraine," i. 190.

Nancy, was killed fighting valiantly at Crécy, and his
son John was taken prisoner with the French King by
the Black Prince at Poitiers. Duke John's second son,
Ferry, Count of Vaudemont and Joinville, fell at Agincourt. In 1444 this Prince's grandson, Ferry II., the
representative of the younger branch of the House
of Lorraine, married Yolande, daughter of René of
Anjou, King of Provence, Jerusalem, and Sicily, and
Duke of Lorraine in right of his wife, Isabella, the
heiress of Duke Charles II. Yolande, whose sister,
Margaret of Anjou, married Henry VI., became
Duchess of Lorraine after the death of her nephew
in 1473, and united the two branches of the family
in her person. But she renounced the sovereignty in
favour of her son, René II., who still bore the proud
title of King of Sicily and Jerusalem, although, as the
English Ambassador, Wotton, remarked, he had never
seen either the one or the other. René had a fierce
struggle for the possession of Lorraine with Charles
of Burgundy, who defeated him completely in 1475,
and entered Nancy in triumph. But in January,
1477, King René recovered his duchy with the help
of the Swiss, and Charles was defeated and slain in a
desperate battle under the walls of Nancy.[1]

Ten years later René married Philippa of Egmont,
sister of Charles, Duke of Guelders, and, together with
his admirable wife, devoted the rest of his life to the
welfare of his subjects and the improvement of the
capital. During his reign the ducal palace, founded
by his ancestors in the fourteenth century, was en-
larged and beautified, and the neighbouring church
and convent of the Cordeliers were built. Here
René was buried after his early death in 1508, and his

---

[1] Hugo, 196, 200.

sorrowing wife reared a noble monument in which he
is represented kneeling under a pinnacled canopy
crowned by a statue of the Virgin and Child.[1]

Six stalwart sons grew up under Philippa's watchful
eye, to bear their father's name and maintain the
honour of his house. The eldest, Antoine, succeeded
René as Duke of Lorraine and Bar, and the second,
Claude, became a naturalized French subject, and
inherited the family estates in France, including
Joinville, Guise, and Aumale. Both Princes were
educated at the French Court, where Claude became
the friend and companion of the future King Francis,
and in 1513 married Antoinette de Bourbon, the
Count of Vendôme's daughter. This lovely maiden
was brought up with her cousins, Louis XII.'s
daughters, the elder of whom married Francis of
Angoulême, the heir to the Crown. When, in 1515,
this Prince succeeded his father-in-law on the throne,
he promised the young Duke of Lorraine the hand of
Louis XII.'s widow, Mary of England; but the fair
Dowager had already plighted her troth to Brandon,
Duke of Suffolk, and Antoine consoled himself with
another Princess of the blood royal, Renée de Bourbon,
daughter of Gilbert de Montpensier and Chiara Gonzaga. The wedding was celebrated at Amboise on
the 26th of June, 1515, and Antoine and Claude both
left their brides in Lorraine with Queen Philippa
while they followed Francis to Italy. There they
fought gallantly by the King's side at Marignano.
Antoine was knighted on the field of battle, while
Claude received a dangerous wound, and a third
brother was slain in the mêlée. Two of Philippa's
younger sons lost their lives in the French King's

---

[1] Calmet, iii. 325; A. Hallays, " Nancy " (" Villes Célèbres "), 31.

later campaigns.   One was killed at Pavia, and Louis,
the handsomest of all his handsome race, died of the
plague in Lautrec's army before Naples.   A sixth
son, Jean, Bishop of Metz, was made a Cardinal at
twenty, and, like his brother, Claude of Guise, became
a prominent figure at the French Court.

During Antoine's absence his duchy was governed
wisely and well by his mother, Philippa; but when he
no longer needed her help, the good Queen retired
from the world, and on the 8th of December, 1519,
entered the Order of the Poor Clares at Pont-à-
Mousson.   Here she spent the remaining twenty-
seven years of her life in works of devotion, and
edified her family and subjects by the zeal with which
she performed the humblest duties, going barefoot
and wearing rough serge.   But she still retained great
influence over her sons, who were all deeply attached
to her and often came to visit her in the convent.
By a will which she made when she forsook the world,
she left her furniture, jewels, and most of her property,
to her second son, Claude, " pour aider ce jeune
ménage,"[1] and the Duke and Duchess of Guise went
to live at her dower-house of Joinville, the *beau
châtel* on the heights above the River Marne, which
had once belonged to St. Louis's follower, le Sieur
de Joinville.   Here that remarkable woman, Duchess
Antoinette, the mother of the Guises, reared her large
family, the six sons who became famous as soldiers
or prelates, and the four beautiful daughters who
were courted by Kings and Princes.   Antoine's wife,
Renée, had not the ability and force of character
which made her cousin a power at the French Court,
as well as in her own family, but she was greatly

[1] Calmet, i. 176; Hugo, 244; " Inventaire de Joinville," i. 378.

beloved in Lorraine, and inherited the cultivated tastes of her Gonzaga mother—the sister of Elizabeth, Duchess of Urbino, and sister-in-law of the famous Isabella d'Este. Renée brought the graces and refinement of the Mantuan Court to her husband's home, and the blossoming of art which took place at Nancy during Antoine's reign was largely due to her influence.

A whole school of local architects and painters were employed to adorn the ducal palace, which under his rule and that of his immediate successors became, in the words of a contemporary, " as fine a dwelling-place for a great Prince as could possibly be desired."[1] King René had rebuilt the older portions of the house; his son now added the noble gateway known as " La Grande Porterie," with his own equestrian statue carved by Mansuy Gauvain, and the magnificent upper gallery called " La Galerie des Cerfs," from the antlers and other trophies of the chase which hung upon its walls.[2] A wealth of delicate sculpture was lavished on the façade. Flowers and foliage, heraldic beasts and armorial bearings, adorned the portal; " le bœuf qui prêche "—an ox's head in a pulpit—appeared in one corner, and on the topmost pinnacle, above the busts of René and Antoine, a monkey was seen clad in a friar's habit. Within, the vaulted halls were decorated with stately mantelpieces and richly carved friezes. Without, the roofs glittered with gilded copper fretwork and a tall bronze *flèche*, bearing the cross of Lorraine and the thistle of Nancy, crowned the " Tour du Paradis," which enclosed the

[1] H. Lepage, " Le Palais Ducal de Nancy," 10; C. Pfister, ii. 29; " La Ville de Nancy," 65.
[2] Pfister, ii. 26; A. Hallays, " Nancy," 37-39.

GRANDE PORTERIE, PALAIS DUCAL, NANCY

To face p. 260

fine spiral staircase leading to the Galerie des Cerfs.
Another round tower, containing an inclined way
broad enough for a horse and chariot, stood in the
older part of the palace, and led up to the Treasury,
where the Crown jewels were kept. Here, too, were
the apartments occupied by the ducal family. On
one side they opened on to the " Cour d'Honneur,"
where tournaments and pageants were held. On the
other the windows looked down on the gardens, with
their cut yews and box hedges, their arbours and
bosquets, and in the centre a superb fountain
adorned with *putti* by Mansuy Gauvain; while beyond
the eye ranged across the sleepy waters of the moat to
green meadows and distant woods.[1] The grand portal
and state-rooms at the new end of the palace looked
down on the Grande Rue, and were only divided by a
narrow street from the shops and stalls of the market-
place. The fact that the Duke's house stood in the
heart of the city naturally fostered the affection with
which he was regarded by the people of Nancy. The
citizens were familiar with every detail of the ducal
family's private life, and took the deepest interest in
their comings and goings, their weddings and funerals,
in the guests who arrived at the palace gates, and in
the children who grew up within its walls.

Duke Antoine was especially beloved by his subjects. Early in life he had learnt by experience the
horrors of war, and all through his reign he tried
manfully to preserve a strict neutrality between the
rival powers on either side, with the result that
Lorraine enjoyed an unbroken period of peace and
prosperity. The burden of taxation was lightened,
trade and agriculture flourished, and the arts were

[1] Lepage, " Palais Ducal," 3; Pfister, ii. 188.

encouraged by this good Prince, who was justly called the " father of his people." When his beloved wife Renée died, in June, 1539, his sorrow was shared by the whole nation.

" Since I sent my last letter," wrote the Duchess of Guise to her daughter in Scotland, " you will have heard of the death of your aunt—whom God pardon —a fortnight ago. The attack—a *flux de ventre*— which carried her off only lasted nine days, but she was enfeebled by long illness. Nature could no longer offer any resistance, and God in His good pleasure took her to Himself. She died as a good Christian, doing her duty by all and asking forgiveness of everyone, and remained conscious to the end. After Friday morning she would not see her children, or even her husband, but, as this distressed him greatly, she sent for him again after she had received God. On Sunday she was anointed with holy oil, and died at ten o'clock the next evening. It was the tenth of June. It is a heavy loss for all our family, but your uncle bears up bravely. He sent for us, and I set out for Nancy at once, but only arrived there after her death. Your father, with whom I have been in Picardy, followed on Saturday. I have just returned to Pont-à-Mousson, where I came to see my mother-in-law, the good old Queen. The funeral will be on St. John's Day, and your aunt will be buried in the Cordeliers, opposite the tomb of the late King " (René II.).[1]

Four days after his wife's death, Antoine himself sent these touching lines to his niece, the Queen of Scotland:

" I was glad to hear from you the other day, Madame, and must tell you the great sorrow which it has pleased God to send me, in calling my wife to Himself. She died on the morrow of Pentecost. God be praised, Madame, for the beautiful end which she made, like the good Christian that she was. Com-

[1] Balcarres Manuscripts, ii. 17.

mend me to the King your lord; and if there is any
service which I can render you or him, let me know,
and I will do it gladly.
          " Your humble and loving uncle,
                              " ANTOINE."[1]

Renée bore the Duke a large family, but only
three of her children lived to grow up: Francis,
Marquis of Pont-à-Mousson, born in 1517; Anne, the
Princess of Orange, who was five years younger; and
Nicolas, Count of Vaudemont, born in 1524, who
took Deacon's Orders, and became Bishop of Metz
when the Cardinal of Lorraine resigned this see.
Francis had the French King for his godfather, and
was sent, as a matter of course, to be educated at
the Court of France with the Dauphin. This Prince
inherited the tall stature and regular features of his
father's family, together with his mother's love of
art and letters. His studious tastes and quick intelligence made him the delight of all his teachers,
and King Francis was heard to say that the Marquis
du Pont was the wisest Prince of his age. But
although he could ride and tilt as well as any of his
peers, he was never robust, and the strain of melancholy in his nature increased as years went by. In
1538 the young Marquis accompanied his father to
meet the Emperor at Aigues-Mortes, and made a very
favourable impression on Charles, who proposed that
he should marry one of King Ferdinand's daughters.
Several other alliances had been already suggested
for this promising Prince.[2] In 1527, while he was
still a boy, the fateful marriage between him and Anne
of Cleves had been arranged; and when this was
abandoned, King Francis first offered him one of his
own daughters, and then his cousin, Mary of Vendôme,

---

[1] Balcarres Manuscripts, ii. 84.   [2] Ibid., ii. 20.

whom the King of Scotland had deserted for the fair
Duchess of Longueville. At the same time
Henry VIII. asked Castillon to arrange a marriage
between his daughter Mary and the heir of Lorraine.[1]
But from the moment that Francis of Lorraine saw
the Duchess of Milan at Compiègne his choice never
wavered, and his constancy triumphed in the end
over all difficulties.

The lamented death of Duchess Renée, and the
marriage of her only daughter, Anne, in the following
year, had left the palace at Nancy without a mistress,
and rendered Christina's presence there the more
welcome. The old Duke was as proud of his daughter-
in-law as his subjects were of their young Duchess,
and Christina's frank manners and open-handed
generosity soon made her very popular in Lorraine.
She received a cordial welcome from Antoinette and
the Guise Princes at Joinville, and was on the best
of terms with her young brother-in-law, Monsieur de
Metz. Above all, she was adored by her spouse, whose
devotion to Christina quickly dispelled the Duchess of
Guise's fears lest this grave and thoughtful Prince
should not prove a good husband. His love satisfied
every longing of her heart, and filled her soul with
deep content. After all the storms of her early
youth, after the lonely months at Milan and Pavia,
after the disappointment of her cherished hopes, the
young Duchess had found a happiness beyond her
highest dreams. As she wrote to her old friend
Granvelle a few months later: " My husband treats
me so kindly, and has such great affection for me,
that I am the happiest woman in the whole world."[2]

[1] Kaulek, 54.
[2] F. v. Bucholtz, " Geschichte d. Kaiser Ferdinand I.," ix. 141.

II.

The King of France's ill-temper was the one draw-back to the general satisfaction with which Christina's marriage had been received. The coldness with which he treated the Duke of Lorraine and his son, the sacrifice of their rights on Bar, rankled in the old man's heart. His surprise was the greater when he received a courteous invitation to bring his son and daughter-in-law on a visit to the French Court. His brother the Cardinal wrote saying that Queen Eleanor was anxious to see her niece, and that the King wished to confer the Order of St. Michel on her lord, and begged Duke Antoine to accompany the young couple to Fontainebleau.

Christina and her husband, who since his mar-riage had become a strong Imperialist, were reluctant to accept the invitation, lest an attempt should be made to draw Lorraine into an alliance against the Emperor. But the Cardinal's bland promises and Antoine's anxiety to keep on good terms with the King prevailed over their hesitation, and early in November the two Dukes and the young Duchess spent three days at Fontainebleau. Hunting-parties and banquets occupied the first two days. Eleanor took the greatest delight in her niece's company, and the King, who could never resist a woman's charms, was assiduous in his attention to Christina. The Queen of Navarre's presence afforded the Duchess additional pleasure, and this accomplished Princess showed her Leonardo and Raphael's paintings, and did the honours of the superb palace which had excited the Emperor's admiration two years before. On the third evening the King expressed his wish

to confer the Order of St. Michel on the young Duke
in so pressing a manner that it was impossible to refuse
this offer. But an unpleasant surprise was in store
for him and his father. The next morning the
Cardinal informed them that the King demanded
the cession of the town and fortress of Stenay, in
return for the privilege of holding the duchy of Bar.
This unexpected demand aroused an indignant
protest from Antoine and Francis. Stenay was one
of the bulwarks of Lorraine, and its position on the
frontiers of Luxembourg made it of great importance
to the defence of the empire. But nothing that the
Duke and his son could say was of the slightest avail.
They were told that if Stenay was not surrendered
peaceably the King would declare war and reduce
their country to subjection. These threats alarmed
the old Duke to such a pitch that before leaving
Fontainebleau he was induced to sign a treaty by
which Stenay was given up in perpetuity to the
French Crown. It was a grievous blow to the prestige
of Lorraine, and filled Christina and her husband
with grave fears for the future. The following letter
which the Duchess wrote to Granvelle a few weeks
afterwards shows how bitterly she resented the
wrong :

" You have no doubt heard of the voyage which
the Lord Duke my father-in-law, my husband, and I,
took to the French Court, where we made a very
short stay, but one which turned out very badly for
our house. For the King used violent threats to my
father and husband, and sent my uncle the Cardinal
to tell them that, if they did not satisfy his demands,
he would prove their worst enemy, and make them
the smallest people in the world. So they were compelled to give him the town of Stenay, which is a
great loss to this house, and has vexed my husband

and me sorely, showing us how much we are despised on that side, and to what risk of destruction we should be exposed if it were not for the good help of the Emperor, in whom I place my whole trust."[1]

Unfortunately for the Duchess and her husband, Charles was at this moment engaged in his disastrous expedition to Algiers. The news of the tempest which wrecked his fleet on the coast of Africa had reached the French Court, and it was confidently asserted that the Emperor himself had perished, or was a prisoner in Barbarossa's camp. These disquieting rumours were set at rest early in December by his safe return to Cartagena with the remnants of his army. But his enemies had been active in his absence. On the 15th of November the Duke of Lorraine set his seal to the deed of cession, and a week later a French garrison took possession of Stenay. General indignation was excited throughout Europe by this arbitrary act. Mary of Hungary entered a vigorous protest in her brother's name against this surrender of an imperial fief, and no sooner did the news reach Charles than he told his Ambassador to require the French King to do homage for the town. The new English Ambassador, Paget, who arrived at Fontainebleau a few days after the Lorraine Princes left Court, noticed that the King " looked very black, as if the Imperial Envoy had spoken of matters not all the pleasantest "; while he informed his royal master that the entertainment of the Duke of Lorraine had been but cold, and that he had lost all credit with the French.[2] When Chapuys told King Henry at Christmas how King Francis had snatched

---

[1] Granvelle, " Papiers d'État," ii. 618; Bucholtz, ix. 141.

[2] State Papers, Record Office, viii. 639, 644, 655.

Stenay from the Duke of Lorraine, the English
monarch only shrugged his shoulders, saying he had
always known no good would come out of that
marriage.[1]

Meanwhile Christina and her husband found some
consolation for their wounded feelings in the friendly
reception which they met with at Joinville, on their
return from France. The Duke and Duchess of Guise
came to meet them at Annonville, and were eager to
do honour to their nephew's bride and show her the
beauties of their stately home. They had lately decorated the halls and chapel with paintings and statues,
and Antoinette had laid out terraced gardens along the
wooded slopes on the River Marne, adorned with
pavilions and fountains. Nothing escaped the eye
of this excellent lady, who watched over the education
of her children and the welfare of her servants, and
managed her kitchen, stables, and kennels, with the
same indefatigable care. Her household was a model
of economy and prudence, and her works of mercy
extended far beyond the limits of Joinville. The
active correspondence which she kept up with her
eldest daughter, the Queen of Scotland, abounds in
details regarding every member of her family, and
above all her little grandson, the Duke of Longueville.
The Duchess's letters are naturally full of this precious
boy, who was the pet and plaything of the whole
household, and on whose perfections she is never
tired of dwelling. For his mother's benefit, she sends
minute records of his height and appearance, of the
progress which he is making at lessons, the walks
which he takes with his nurse.

[1] Calendar of Spanish State Papers. vi. i, 436; Calendar of
State Papers, xvi. i, 690.

" We have here now," she wrote to Mary of Guise, on the 18th of November, " not only your uncle, but the Duke and Duchess of Bar, on their way back from Court. They are all making good cheer with us, and your father is so busy entertaining them that you will hardly have a letter from him this time. Your eldest brother [Aumale] is here too, but goes to join the King at Fontainebleau next week. I shall go to my mother [the old Countess of Vendôme], who is quite well, and so also is the good old Queen, your grandmother. I have kept as a *bonne bouche* for you a word about our grandson, who will soon be a man, and is the finest child that you ever saw. I am trying to find a painter who can show you how tall, healthy, and handsome, he is."

Sad news had lately come from Scotland, where the Queen's two children, a boy of a year old and a new-born babe, had died in the same week. Antoinette's motherly heart yearned over her absent daughter in this sudden bereavement.

" Your father and I are sorely grieved at the loss you have suffered," she wrote to Mary; " but you are both young, and I can only hope that God, who took away those dear little ones, will send you others. . . . If I were good enough for my prayers to be of any avail with God, I would pray for this, but I can at least have prayers offered up by others who are better than I am, especially by the good Queen in her convent and her holy nuns. We are glad to hear the King bears his loss with resignation, and trust God will give you patience to live for Him in this world and in the next, to which tribulation is the surest way."

And in a postscript she adds a word of practical advice, saying that she did not like to hear of the poor babes having so many different nurses, and fears this may have been one cause of the mischief.[1]

In return for this affectionate sympathy, King

[1] Balcarres Manuscripts, ii. 3, 6.

James sent his mother-in-law a fine diamond and a portrait of himself, which arrived during Christina's visit, and excited much interest at Joinville. All the Duchess of Guise's daughters were absent from home, the youngest, Antoinette, having joined her sister, Abbess Renée, in the convent at Reims, where she afterwards took the veil. But her eldest son, as we have seen, was at Joinville on this occasion. A tall, dark-haired, olive-skinned youth, recklessly brave and adventurous, Aumale was a great favourite both in Court and camp, and his mother had been sadly disappointed at the failure of the marriage negotiations, which had cost her so much time and trouble. The Pope's daughter, Vittoria Farnese, who was to have been his wife, had since then been offered in turn to the Prince of Piedmont and the Duke of Vendôme, and was eventually married to the Duke of Urbino. Aumale himself cared little for the loss of the Italian bride, whom he had never seen, and had hitherto shown no eagerness for matrimony, but the sight of Christina made a deep impression upon him, and he never forgot his fair cousin's visit to Joinville. The most friendly relations prevailed between the two families, and frequent visits were interchanged during the winter. Christmas was celebrated with prolonged festivities at Nancy, and on the 6th of February the old Duke wrote from Joinville to his niece, the Queen of Scotland:

" Your father and I have spent the last week together, and have made great cheer with all our family. Your son, De Longueville, is very well, and has grown a fine boy.

" Your very humble and affectionate uncle,
" Antoine." [1]

[1] Balcarres Manuscripts, ii. 85.

In spite of these distractions, Christina found it difficult to make her husband forget the loss of Stenay. The injustice which had been done to the House of Lorraine still rankled in his mind, and he feared that the Emperor would hold him responsible for the surrender of the town, and regard it as an act of disloyalty. Christina accordingly addressed a long letter to Granvelle, explaining that her husband had been very reluctant to accept the French Order of St. Michel, and had only done this at his father's express command, before there had been any mention of surrendering Stenay. Now she feared that the King might make some fresh demand, which would complete the destruction of the ducal house, and could only beg the Emperor to help them with his advice and support.

" For you may rest assured," she goes on, " that, whatever His Majesty is pleased to command, my husband and I will obey, although, as you know, my father-in-law is somewhat difficult to please, and we must do his will for the present. So I beg you earnestly to point this out to His Majesty, and ask him to give us his advice; for since our return to Nancy my husband has been so sad and melancholy, and so full of regret for the great wrong which his house has suffered, that I am quite afraid it will injure his health. Once more I beg you, Monsieur de Granvelle, to be a good friend to us in the present, as you have been in the past . . . for we have received so much kindness from you that I hope you will not hesitate to give us whatever advice seems best in your eyes. As for me, I am so much indebted to you for having helped to place me where I am, that you and yours will always find me ready to do you service. For I can never forget that it is to you I owe my present great happiness."[1]

[1] Bucholtz, ix. 142.

Charles, however, wrote kindly to his niece, and refused to listen to the unkind tongues who tried to poison his mind against her husband. By degrees the young Duke recovered his equanimity, and devoted his attention to beautifying the ducal palace of Nancy. In the last years of Renée's life a Lorraine artist, Hugues de la Faye, had been employed to paint subjects from the life of Christ at one end of the " Galerie des Cerfs," and hunting-scenes at the other. Christina's presence gave new impulse to the work, and the large quantity of gold-leaf and azure supplied to the painters in the Duke's service, show how actively the internal decoration of the palace was carried on. In one particular instance Christina's influence is clearly to be traced. By Duke Antoine's orders, a fresco of the Last Supper was begun by Hugues de la Faye in the refectory of the Cordeliers, but was only completed after this painter's death in 1542, by Crock and Chappin. These two Lorraine artists were sent to Italy by Duke Francis soon after his accession, and visited Milan amongst other places. Here they saw Leonardo's famous " Cenacolo " in the refectory of S. Maria le Grazie, which was closely connected with the Sforza Princes, and must have been very familiar to Christina when she lived in Milan. The fresco which they executed at Nancy is said to have been a replica of Leonardo's great work, and kneeling figures of Antoine and Renée were introduced on the same wall, in imitation of the portraits of Lodovico Sforza and Beatrice d' Este which are still to be seen in the Dominican refectory at Milan. Unfortunately, the Lorraine masters' painting suffered a still worse fate than Leonardo's immortal work, and, after being partly spoilt by damp, was finally destroyed thirty years ago and replaced by a modern copy.[1]

During this winter, when Christina was happily settled in her new home and surrounded by loyal friends and subjects, news came from England of the trial and execution of Henry VIII.'s fifth Queen, Catherine Howard. When the Duke and Duchess were at Fontainebleau, rumours reached the Court that this unhappy lady, of whom Henry was deeply enamoured but a short time before, had been suddenly banished from his presence, and taken into custody. " Par ma foi de gentil homme !" exclaimed King Francis when he heard the account of the Queen's misdeeds. " She has done wondrous naughtily !"[2]   But in England, as Chapuys reported, much compassion was felt for the King's latest victim, who had dragged down the noble house of Howard in her fall. Lord William Howard, the late Ambassador, was hastily recalled from France, and sent to the Tower with his mother, the old Duchess of Norfolk. The King himself, wrote Chapuys, felt the case more than that of any of his other wives, just as the woman who had lost ten husbands grieved more for the tenth when he died than for any of the other nine ! But when the luckless Queen was beheaded, Henry recovered his spirits, and spent Carnival in feasting and entertaining ladies with a gaiety which made people think that he meant to marry again. " But few, if any, ladies of the Court," remarked Chapuys, " now aspire to the honour of becoming one of the King's wives."[3]

[1] H. Lepage, " Le Palais Ducal de Nancy," 9; Pfister, ii. 256.

[2] State Papers, Record Office, viii. 636.

[3] Calendar of Spanish State Papers, vi. 1, 473; Calendar of State Papers, xvi. 2, 51.

It was an honour to which Christina herself had never aspired. One day at the Court of Nancy, conversation turned on the King of England, and some indiscreet lady asked the Duchess why she had rejected this monarch's suit. A smile broke over Christina's face, and the old dimples rose to her cheeks as she replied that, unfortunately, she only had one head, but that if she had possessed two, one might have been at His Majesty's disposal. It was a characteristic speech, and has passed into history.[1]

III.

All through the winter of 1541-42 preparations for war were actively carried on in France, and intrigue was rife among the Courts of Europe. Francis was determined to profit by his rival's misfortunes, in spite of the remonstrances of the Pope and of the deputies who were sent by the Imperial Diet to adjure him not to trouble the peace of Christendom while the Emperor was fighting against the Turks. By the end of the year he succeeded in forming a strong coalition, which included Scotland, Denmark, Sweden, and Cleves. The Palatine Frederic had once more pressed his wife's claims to the three kingdoms, with the result that Christian III. lent a willing ear to the

[1] The authenticity of this well-known saying has been often disputed, and was certainly never addressed by the Duchess to either of Henry VIII.'s Ambassadors. But Christina's words were recorded by Joachim Sandrart, who wrote in the seventeenth century, as having been spoken by a Princess of Lorraine, whom the English King had wooed in vain, and were afterwards quoted by Horace Walpole "as the witty answer of that Duchess of Milan whose portrait Holbein painted for Henry VIII." (see Wornum's "Life of Holbein," 311; J. Sandrart, "Deutsche Akademie"; and Walpole's "Anecdotes of Painting").

French King's advances, and sent Envoys to Fontainebleau, where a secret treaty between France and Denmark was signed a few days after the Duke and Duchess of Lorraine had left Court. Francis was now exceedingly anxious to draw Lorraine into the league and induce Duke Antoine to take up arms against the Emperor. In May he set out on a progress through Burgundy and Champagne, taking the Queen and all the Court with him, to inspect the fortifications of the eastern frontier and enjoy some hunting on the way. " Tell the Pope," he said merrily to the Legate Ardinghelli, " that I do nothing but make good cheer and amuse myself, whether I·entertain fair ladies or go a-hunting the deer." Paget and the other Ambassadors complained bitterly of the bad quarters " in peevish villages " which they had to put up with as they followed the King from place to place, wherever " great harts were to be heard of."[1] Fortunately, he found excellent sport at the Duke of Guise's château of Esclaron, where he spent three weeks, and declared that he had never been so happy in his life.

" The King," wrote Duchess Antoinette to Mary of Scotland, " has found so many big stags here that he says he was never in a place which pleased him better, and that in spite of torrents of rain and God knows what mud ! And you cannot think how fond he is of your father."[2]

She herself went to Esclaron to receive her royal guest, taking the eight-year-old Duke of Longueville with her, to make his bow to the King and be petted by Queen Eleanor and her ladies. But the life of

---

[1] State Papers, Record Office, viii. 641; Calendar of State Papers, xvii. 711.
[2] Balcarres Manuscripts, ii. 12.

a Court lady, as she told her daughter, was little to her taste, and she returned to Joinville early in June, to keep the Fête-Dieu and prepare her husband's and sons' equipment for the war which was expected to begin immediately. Two days later, on the 10th of June, the Duke and Duchess of Bar paid the French King a visit at Esclaron, and were present at the reception of the Swedish Ambassadors, whom Gustavus Wasa had sent to sign the new treaty. The ceremony took place in a large barn hung with tapestries and wreathed with green boughs. The King and his guests sat on a raised daïs, draped with cloth of gold, under a canopy, while the Princes of the blood and the other courtiers, among whom were no less than six Cardinals, stood below. Here Francis listened patiently to a long Latin harangue from the Swedish Ambassador, and then, coming down from his seat, he mingled freely in the crowd of Cardinals and Princes, gentlemen and yeomen, who stood " all in a heap " at the doors of the barn, and showed himself very affable, although, in Paget's opinion, " his manner lacked the majesty which he had noticed in his own master on similar occasions."[1]

Christina looked with curiosity at these Envoys from the Northern kingdom over which her father had once ruled, many of whom had known the captive monarch in old days. This time she and her husband had no cause to complain of the King's treatment. He was all courtesy and smiles, and assured them in the most cordial terms of the singular affection which he bore to all their house. But he soon saw that there was no prospect of inducing Antoine and his son to join him against Christina's uncle, and

[1] Calendar of State Papers, xvii. 232.

on the 12th of June he consented to sign an agreement by which he promised to respect the neutrality of Lorraine and the properties of the Duke's subjects.[1] After spending another week at Joinville, enjoying the splendid hospitality of the Guises, he left Eleanor with the Duchess, and went on to Ligny, a strong fortress on the borders of Luxembourg, where he gave orders for the opening of the campaign.

By the middle of July four separate armies had invaded the Emperor's dominions. Guise and Orléans fell upon Luxembourg, Vendôme entered Flanders, the Dauphin attacked Roussillon, and the forces of Cleves, under the redoubtable Guelders captain, Martin van Rossem, laid Brabant waste with fire and sword. But they met with determined opposition in every quarter, and the heroism of the Regent and her captains saved the Netherlands from ruin.

" The attack," wrote De Praet to Charles on September 21, 1542, " was so secretly planned and so well carried out that it is a miracle Your Majesty did not lose your Pays-Bas. We must thank God first of all, and next to Him the Queen, to whose extreme care, toil, and diligence, this is owing."[2]

Fortunately for the Imperialists, Francis's extravagance had emptied his treasury. All his money, as Paget reported, was spent in building new palaces and buying jewels for himself and his favourites. Stenay and other places had been fortified at vast expense, and by the end of the year most of the French forces were disbanded for lack of funds.

It was a sad autumn at Joinville, where the good

---

[1] Granvelle, "Papiers d'État," ii. 628; Calendar of State Papers, xvii. 273. [2] Lanz, ii. 364.

Duchess wept and prayed for her absent lord and sons, and sighed to think they were fighting against her daughter Louise's husband and father-in-law. In September Guise was invalided home, and he was hardly fit to mount his horse again when the parents received the news of Louise's death, which took place at Brussels on the 18th of October. The charming Princess had always been a delicate girl, and now she died without leaving a child to comfort the husband and father who had loved her so well. This sad event was followed by tidings of the disaster which had befallen the King of Scotland's army in Solway Moss, and of his death on the 18th of December. Antoinette's heart bled for her widowed daughter, who had just given birth to an infant Princess at Linlithgow. " It came with a lass, and it will go with a lass," were the words of the King when he was told of the child's birth, a few days before he died at Falkland Palace. Both Guise and Aumale would gladly have hastened to Mary's help, but it was impossible for them to leave the camp at this critical moment, and Antoinette could only beg her daughter to keep up her courage and trust in God, " the Almighty, who would defend her and the poor little Queen, who although so young is already exposed to the insults of her enemies."[1]

It was a no less anxious time for Christina in her home at Nancy. From the palace roof the smoke of burning villages was to be seen in all directions, and the people of Lorraine were exposed to frequent raids from the hordes of irregular soldiers in both armies, and were compelled to raise trained bands for the defence of the frontiers. It was only by the

---

[1] Balcarres Manuscripts, ii. 13.

strictest observance of the laws of neutrality that an outbreak of actual hostilities could be avoided. When Aumale was badly wounded by a shot from a crossbow in the siege of Luxembourg, his uncle the Duke sternly refused to have him carried into his neighbouring castle of Longwy; and when Mary of Hungary proposed to garrison this fortress to protect his subjects from French aggression, he declined her offer firmly at the risk of incurring the imperial displeasure.[1] Christina herself spent Christmas at Fontainebleau with her aunt, Queen Eleanor. This poor lady was distracted with grief at the war between her husband and brother, and spent much time in making futile attempts to induce her sister, the Regent, to listen to peace negotiations. Early in December, while the King was hunting at Cognac, she sent a gorgeous litter to Bar to bring the Duchess to Court, and kept her there till the middle of January.[2] A month afterwards—on the 13th of February— Christina gave birth to her first child, a son, who received the name of Charles, after her imperial uncle. There was great rejoicing in Nancy, where the happy event took place, and the old Duke himself went to Pont-à-Mousson to bear the good news to the venerable Queen Philippa, who thanked God that she had lived to see her great-grandson. The little Prince's christening was celebrated with as much festivity as the troubled state of the country would allow, and Christina's faithful friend, the Princess of Macedonia, who had followed her to Lorraine, held the child at the font and was appointed his governess.[3]

[1] Pimodan, 81; Bouillé, i. 142.

[2] Calendar of Spanish State Papers, vi. 2, 262.

[3] Calmet, i. 265; Pfister, ii. 200.

Two days before the Prince's birth a secret treaty between the Emperor and King Henry was concluded at Whitehall. Chapuys had at length attained the object of his untiring efforts, and De Courrières was sent from Spain on a confidential mission to induce Henry to declare war against France. The defeat of the Duke of Aerschot at Sittard excited general alarm in Flanders, and Mary was at her wits' end for money and men. But the Emperor himself was hastening across the Alps to the help of his loyal provinces. The marriage of his son Philip with the Infanta of Portugal had been finally settled, and with the help of this Princess's large dowry and another half-million of Mexican gold, Charles was able to raise a large army of German and Italian troops. On the 22nd of August he appeared in person before Düren, the capital of Cleves, which surrendered within a week. The Duke threw himself on the victor's mercy, and was pardoned and invested anew with his hereditary duchies, while Guelders was annexed to the Netherlands and the Prince of Orange became its first Governor. William of Cleves on his part renounced the French alliance, and agreed to marry one of King Ferdinand's daughters. His previous marriage with Jeanne d'Albret was annulled by the Pope, and this resolute young Princess had the satisfaction of carrying her protest into effect. Encouraged by these successes, Charles now laid siege to Landrécy, the capital of Hainault, which had been captured and fortified by the French, and was joined by a gallant company of English under Lord Surrey and Sir John Wallop. "Par ma foi!" exclaimed the Emperor, as he rode down their ranks, "this is a fine body of gentlemen! If the French King comes, I will live and die with the English."[1]   But Francis refused to be drawn into a battle, and the approach of winter made both armies retire from the field.

The Duke of Lorraine took advantage of this temporary lull to mediate between the two monarchs. Old as he was, and suffering severely with gout, Antoine came to the Prince of Chimay's house with his son Francis, and begged for an audience with the Emperor and Regent, who were spending a few days at Valenciennes, on their way to Brussels.   Charles sent him word not to come into his presence if he brought offers from the French King; but in spite of these peremptory orders the two Dukes arrived in the town on Sunday, the 17th of November, and were received by the Emperor after dinner.   Antoine delivered a long oration begging His Imperial Majesty to make peace for the sake of Christendom, and, laying his hand on his breast, swore that he had taken this step of his own free will, without communicating with any other person.   The old man's earnestness touched Charles, who answered kindly, saying that he was always welcome as a cousin and a neighbour, and that this was doubly the case now that his son had married the Emperor's dearly loved niece.   But he told him frankly that he had been too often deluded by false promises to listen to French proposals for peace, and that in any case he could do nothing without the consent of his ally, the King of England.   Nothing daunted, the old Duke went on to visit the Regent, and was found by Lord Surrey and the English Ambassador Brian sitting at a table before a fire in the Queen's room, playing at cards.   Antoine greeted Brian as an old friend, and asked him to

[1] Calendar of State Papers, Record Office, ix. 522.

drink with him.   But Mary sternly refused to listen
to the Duke's errand, being convinced that he came
from the King, and declaring that all the gentlemen
in his suite were good Frenchmen.   When he and his
son were gone, she called Brian to her, and said:
" Monsieur l'Ambassadeur, heard you ever so lean a
message ?"   " Madame," replied   the   Englishman,
" if the broth be no fatter, it is not worth the supping,"
a sentiment which provoked a hearty laugh from the
Queen.[1]

Neither Queen Eleanor, who sent an entreating
letter with a present of falcons to her sister, nor
Cardinal Farnese, who brought fresh proposals of
peace from the Pope, fared any better.   The young
Duchess Christina now determined to make an attempt
herself, and came to meet her uncle at Spires when
he attended the Diet.   The ostensible reason of this
journey was to visit her sister Dorothea, but Charles,
divining her intention, sent the Countess Palatine
word that if the Duchess of Bar brought proposals
of peace she might as well stay at home.   Christina,
however, arrived at Spires on the 8th of February,
with a train of fourteen ladies and fifteen horse, and
spent a week with the Count and Countess Palatine.
The sisters saw the Emperor and King Ferdinand every
day, and were to all appearance on the most affectionate
terms with them.   But nothing transpired as to what
passed between Christina and her uncle in private.
On the day that she left Spires to return to Nancy,
Frederic heard of the death of his brother, the Elector
Palatine, and hastened to Heidelberg with Dorothea
to attend his funeral and take possession of the rich

[1] Calendar of State Papers, xviii. 2, 216; State Papers, Record
Office, ix. 557; Bucholtz, ix. 263.

Rhineland, to which he now succeeded. Six weeks later he returned to do homage for the Palatinate, and assist at the wedding of his cousin Sabina with Lamoral d'Egmont, the hero of so many hard-fought fields. The Emperor gave a sumptuous banquet in honour of his gallant brother-at-arms, Dorothea led the bride to church, and Frederic, in a fit of generosity, settled 14,000 florins on his young kinswoman.[1]

In this same month Ambassadors arrived at Spires from Christian III. of Denmark, who had quarrelled with the French King and was anxious to make peace with the Emperor. In spite of a protest from the Palatine, a treaty was concluded on the 23rd of May, by which Charles recognized the reigning monarch's title to the crown. So the long war, which had lasted twenty-one years, was at length ended, and the Emperor finally abandoned the cause of Christian II. But a clause was added by which his daughters' rights were reserved, and a promise given that the severity of his captivity should be relaxed and that he should be allowed to hunt and fish in the park at Sonderburg. Christian III. gladly agreed to these more humane conditions, and even offered to give Dorothea and Christina a substantial dowry, but the Palatine refused to accept any terms, and persisted in asserting his wife's claims.[2]

IV.

Soon after her return from Spires, on the 20th of April, 1544, Christina gave birth, at Nancy, to a daughter, who was named Renée, after the late Duchess. But her happiness was clouded by the ill-

[1] Altmeyer, " Relations," etc., 476; Gachard, " Voyages de Charles V.," ii. 285.

[2] Schäfer, iv. 462; Calendar of State Papers, xix. 1, 349.

ness of her husband, whose health had become a
cause of grave anxiety. Fighting was renewed with
fresh vigour in the spring, and unexpected success
attended the imperial arms. Luxembourg was recovered by Ferrante Gonzaga, and the French invaders were expelled from most of the strongholds
which they held in this province. The war raged
fiercely on the borders of Lorraine, and the annoyance
to which his subjects were exposed, induced Duke
Antoine to make another effort at mediation. Since
the Emperor turned a deaf ear to all appeals, he decided to apply to King Francis in person, and on the
8th of May he set out in a litter for the French Court;
but when he reached Bar he was too ill to go any
farther, and took to his bed in this ancient castle of
his ancestors. His sons hastened to join him, and
Christina followed them as soon as she was able to
travel, and arrived in time to be present at her father-
in-law's death-bed. The fine old man made his will,
appointed his brothers, the Duke of Guise and the
Cardinal, to be his executors, and with his last breath
begged his son to rule Lorraine wisely and raise as
few extraordinary taxes as possible. Above all, he
adjured him to preserve his people from the scourge
of war, and use every endeavour to obtain the restoration of peace. With these words on his lips, he
passed away on the 19th of June, 1544.[1] The new
Duke was as anxious for peace as his father, but the
moment was unpropitious for any efforts in this direction. King Henry had at length taken the field and
invaded Picardy with a large army, and the Emperor
was bent on carrying the war into the heart of
France, and urged his ally to meet him under the

[1] Calmet, ii. 1196; Pfister, ii. 192.

walls of Paris.   On the 17th of June Charles himself
came to Metz with Maurice of Saxony and the young
Marquis Albert of Brandenburg, the boldest warrior
in Germany, and prepared plans for the extension
of the campaign which Ferrante Gonzaga and the
Prince of Orange were carrying on in Champagne.
Here Francis of Lorraine joined him as soon as he
was able to mount a horse, and, after spending some
days at Metz, induced the Emperor to accompany
him to Nassau-le-Grand, where Christina was awaiting
him.[1]   On his way Charles stopped at Pont-à-
Mousson, and paid a visit to Queen Philippa, the
sister of his old enemy Charles of Guelders, for whom
he had always entertained a genuine regard, and who
was proud to welcome the great Emperor under her
convent roof.   Since the death of the Empress, five
years before, Charles had formed a fixed resolution
to end his days in some cloistered retreat, and he
looked with admiration, not unmixed with envy, on
the aged Queen's peaceful home, and the garden
where she hoed and raked the borders and planted
flowers with her own hands.   It was a memorable
day in the convent annals, and one which left pleasant
recollections in the Emperor's breast.[2]

   But although Charles was full of affection for
Christina and her husband, he declined to receive
the Cardinal of Lorraine, who begged for an interview, and during his brief visit not a word was
spoken with regard to overtures of peace.[3]   On the
12th of July he took leave of the Duke and Duchess,

[1] Gachard, " Voyages," ii. 289; Calendar of State Papers,
Record Office, ix. 724.
[2] Calendar of State Papers, xix. 1, 564.
[3] Calendar of State Papers, Record Office, x. 43.

and joined the Prince of Orange's camp before St. Dizier. This town was strongly fortified, but René had taken up his position near a bridge across the Marne, and opened fire from a battery of guns placed in the dry bed of the castle moat. Charles himself visited the trenches on the day of his arrival, and early the next morning the Prince of Orange walked round to inspect the artillery with Ferrante Gonzaga. The Marquis of Marignano was sitting in a chair, which had been brought there for the Emperor's use the day before, and, seeing the Prince, sprang to his feet and offered him his seat. Compliments were exchanged on both sides, and the Prince finally sat down in the empty chair. He had hardly taken his seat before he was struck by a shell which, passing between the Viceroy and the Marquis, broke one of his ribs, and shattered his shoulder to pieces. They bore his unconscious form to the Emperor's tent, where he lay between life and death for the next forty-eight hours. The whole camp was filled with consternation.

" I doubt yet what will become of him," wrote Wotton, who had followed Charles to the camp. " If he should die of it, it were an inestimable loss to the Emperor, so toward a gentleman he is, so well beloved, and of such authority among men of war."

Before the writer had finished his letter, a servant came in to tell him that the Prince was gone.[1]

A Spanish officer on the spot wrote a touching account of the Prince's last moments. From the first the doctors gave little hope, and when the Emperor heard of René's critical state he hastened to the wounded hero's bedside, and knelt down, holding

---

[1] State Papers, Record Office, ix. 733.

his hand in his own. The Prince knew him, and begged him as a last favour to confirm the will which he had made a month before, and take his young cousin and heir, William of Nassau, under his protection. Charles promised to do all in his power for the boy, and, with tears streaming down his face, kissed the Prince's cheek before he passed away.

" His Majesty the Emperor," continued the same writer, " saw him die, and after that retired to his chamber, where he remained some time alone without seeing anyone, and showed how much he loved him. The grief of the whole army and of the Court are so great that no words of mine can describe it."[1]

From all sides the same bitter wail was heard. There was sorrow in the ancient home at Bar, where René's marriage had been celebrated with great rejoicing four years before. The Duke and Duchess wept for their gallant brother-in-law, and Christina thought, with tender regret, of the hero who in youthful days had seemed to her a very perfect knight. The sad news was sent to De Courrières at the English camp before Boulogne, by his Lieutenant of Archers, and the veteran shed tears over the gallant Prince whom he had often followed to victory. Great was the lamentation at Brussels when the truth became known. Nothing but weeping was heard in the streets, and Queen Mary retired to the Abbey of Groenendal to mourn for the loss which the Netherlands had sustained by René's untimely death.[2] In his own city of Breda the sorrow was deeper still. There his faithful wife, Anne of Lorraine, was waiting anxiously for news from the battle-field. Her father

---

[1] Calendar of Spanish State Papers, vii. 267.

[2] Calendar of State Papers, xix. 1, 608; Calendar of Spanish State Papers, vii. 280.

had died a few weeks before, and now her lord was torn from her in the flower of his age, and she was left a childless widow. Early in the year she had given birth to a daughter, who was christened on the 25th of February, and called Mary, after her godmother, the Queen of Hungary, but who died before she was a month old. Now report said that she was about to become a mother for the second time, but her hopes were once more doomed to disappointment. By René's last will, his titles and the greater part of his vast estates passed to his cousin William of Nassau, a boy of eleven, while a large jointure and the rich lands of Diest were left to Anne for her life.[1] The Prince's corpse, clad in the robes of a knight of the Golden Fleece, was borne to Breda, and buried with his forefathers; but his heart was enshrined in the Collegiate Church of Bar, among the tombs which held the ashes of his wife's ancestors. On his death-bed René had expressed a wish that a representation of his face and form, not as he was in life, but as they would appear two years after death, should be carved on his tomb. This strange wish was faithfully carried out by Anne of Lorraine, who employed Ligier-Richier, the gifted Lorraine sculptor, to carve a skeleton with upraised hand clasping the golden casket which contained the dead hero's heart. The figure, carved in fine stone of ivory whiteness, was, as it were, a literal rendering of the words, " Though after my skin worms destroy this body, yet in my flesh shall I see God." At the Revolution, the Collegiate Church of Bar, with the chapel of the Lorraine Princes, which Montaigne called the most

1 Calendar of State Papers, xix. 1, 71; Groen v. Prinsterer, " Archives de la Maison d'Orange," i. 1.

sumptuous in France, was entirely destroyed; but René's monument was saved and placed in the Church of St. Étienne, where it is commonly known as " La Squelette de Bar."[1]

The memory of this popular Prince lingered long in the land of his birth, and his fame lived in the songs of Flanders and Holland for many generations. One of the best known begins with the lines:

> " C'est le Prince d'Orange,
> Trop matin s'est levé,
> Il appela son page,
> Mon Maure, est-il bridé ?
> Que maudit soit la guerre—
> Mon Maure, est-il bridé ?"[2]

And so the story goes on through many stanzas, which tell how, in spite of his wife's dark forebodings, the hero rode out to the wars to fight against the French, how he met with his fatal wound, and never came home again.

V.

The Prince's death threw a gloom over the imperial camp, but did not diminish the warlike ardour of his battalions, who swore with one voice that they would avenge their leader. On the 17th of August St. Dizier at length surrendered. " A right dear-bought town," wrote Wotton, " considering the number of men lost in the assault, and chiefly the inestimable loss of that noble Prince." Ferrante immediately sent a troop of light horse, with Francesco d' Este at their head, against Joinville, the splendid home of the Guises, although, as Wotton remarked, this was rather a house of pleasure than a

[1] C. Cournault, " Ligier-Richier," 28.
[2] R. Putnam, " William the Silent, Prince of Orange," ii. 435.

stronghold. The castle was spared by order of the Emperor for the sake of his niece Christina, who begged him not to add to the Princess of Orange's grief by destroying her uncle's house; but the town and churches were sacked and set on fire, and the beautiful gardens, with their fine water-shows and temples, were destroyed.[1] The news was received with consternation in Paris, where Antoinette and her grandson had taken refuge, and the Duchess's brother, Cardinal Bourbon, wrote to the Scottish Queen telling her of the report that the enemy had burnt down Joinville, which had fortunately proved to be false. " The destruction of such a beautiful house," he adds, " would indeed have been sad."[2] This calamity had been averted by Christina, but, in their anger at the damage done by the imperial troops, the Guise Princes hardly remembered the debt that they owed her. The King was furious, and in the first burst of his indignation sent the Duke of Lorraine a message, threatening to destroy him and all his house. The Duke now determined to go to the French Court to defend himself from these charges and see if it were possible to make proposals of peace in this quarter. The Emperor's rapid advance had excited great alarm in Paris. Even the King awoke to a sense of danger, and said to Margaret of Navarre, the sister to whom he turned in all his worst troubles, " *Ma mignonne*, pray God to spare me the disgrace of seeing the Emperor encamped before my city of Paris." Queen Eleanor, in her distress, sent a Dominican friar in whom she had great confidence—

[1] Bouillé, ii. 148; Pimodan, 183; Oudin, " Histoire des Guises," Bib. Nat., f. 118; Calendar of State Papers, Record Office, x. 6, 43.
[2] Calendar of State Papers, xix. 2, 63.

Don Gabriel de Guzman—to implore her brother to hear her prayers. But Charles was still obdurate. He received Francis of Lorraine in the camp after the Prince of Orange's death, but when he heard that his nephew was going to the French Court, he sent Montbardon to beg the Duchess, " as she loved him," not to let her husband go to France so soon after he had seen him, lest people should think that he was sent by the Emperor to treat of peace.

Christina replied in a letter written, as Wotton remarked, in her own hand, telling her uncle that she had sent a servant post-haste to overtake her husband, but that he was already at Châlons, and had gone too far to retrace his steps. In spite of this manful attempt, the Duke never reached Paris; he fell from his horse in a fainting fit at Épernay, and was brought back in a litter to Bar, where Christina nursed him for several weeks.[1] His efforts, however, proved more effectual than he had expected. The Emperor's precautions were necessary owing to the jealousy with which the English King regarded every proposal of peace on the part of his ally, but in reality Charles was almost as eager as Francis to put an end to the war. His resources were exhausted, the plague was raging in Luxembourg and Flanders, and he realized the danger of advancing into the enemy's country with the Dauphin's army in his rear, while his hopes of the English march on Paris had been disappointed by Henry's delays before Montreuil and Boulogne. Under these circumstances he felt that he could no longer refuse to treat with his foes. On the 29th of August, a week after the Duke had started on his unfortunate journey, Admiral l'Annebaut and the

---

[1] Calendar of Spanish State Papers, vii. 296-298.

French Chancellor were admitted into the Emperor's presence, in the camp near Châlons, and conferences were opened between them and Granvelle, with the happy result that on the 19th of September peace was signed at Crépy-en-Laonnois.

By this treaty the Duke of Orleans was to be given either the Emperor's daughter in marriage, with the reversion of the Netherlands as her dower, or else one of his Austrian nieces with the immediate possession of Milan. In return Francis was to renounce his claims on Naples and Artois, restore the Duke of Savoy's dominions, and endow his son with large estates and revenues. All the towns and fortresses which had been captured during the recent war were to be restored, including Stenay, which, as Charles pointed out, the King of France " had seized in the strangest manner, and held by force without paying homage, although it is notoriously a fief of the empire."[1] As soon as peace was signed, Granvelle's son, the young Bishop of Arras, was sent to ask the English King to become a party to the treaty; but Henry, who had just taken Boulogne after a long siege, quite refused, and professed great surprise to hear that the Emperor had agreed to terms which seemed to him more befitting the vanquished than the victor. On the other hand, a strong party at the French Court complained that the rights of the Crown were sacrificed to the personal aggrandisement of Orleans, and on the 12th of December the Dauphin signed a secret protest against the treaty, which was witnessed by Vendôme and Aumale.[2] But in the provinces where war had been

[1] Calendar of Spanish State Papers, vii. 305.
[2] Ibid., vii. 1, 350, 355.

waging, peace was welcomed with thankfulness, and the ruler and people of Lorraine could once more breathe freely.

The Duke of Lorraine was now able to convey his father's body from the Castle of Bar, where he had died, to Nancy. On the 15th of September he and his brother set out at the head of the funeral procession, along roads lined with crowds of people weeping for the good Duke who had ruled the land so well. But since it was impossible for the Duke of Guise and his family to come to Nancy at present, the last rites were put off till the following year, and the old Duke's remains were left to repose for the time in the Church of St. Georges.[1] Little dreamt these loyal subjects that before the year was over the young Duke, on whom their hopes were fixed, would himself be numbered with the dead, and lie buried in his father's grave. But for the moment all was well. The return of peace was hailed with rejoicing, and the restitution of Stenay removed a blot from the scutcheon of Lorraine, while the independence of the duchy was confirmed by a decree of the Diet of Nuremberg, to which the Emperor gave his sanction.[2]

The Duke and Duchess received a pressing invitation to join in the festivities that were held at Brussels to celebrate the peace. Charles and Mary arrived there on the 1st of October, and were shortly followed by Queen Eleanor, bringing in her train the Duke of Orleans and the Duchess of Étampes, who had used all her influence with the King to bring about peace, chiefly from jealousy of the Dauphin and his mistress, Diane de Poitiers. The burghers of Brussels gave

[1] Calmet, ii. 1196; Pfister, ii. 192.

[2] Calmet, ii. 1281; Ravold, 744; Pfister, ii. 188; Calendar of Spanish State Papers, vi. 2, 262.

the imperial family a magnificent entertainment at the hôtel-de-ville, and presented Eleanor with a golden fountain of exquisite shape and workmanship; while the Emperor lavished costly presents on his guests, and gave the Queen of Hungary the fine domains of Binche and Turnhout in gratitude for her services. Unfortunately, Christina was detained at Nancy by a return of her husband's illness, and did not reach Brussels till the 4th of November. By this time Eleanor had set out on her return, and Christina, eager to see her aunt, followed her to Mons, and spent two days in her company. On the 7th the Duchess came back to Brussels with her brother-in-law, Nicolas de Vaudemont, and remained with her uncle and aunt during a fortnight. It was her first visit to Brussels since her wedding, more than three years before, and old friends and faces welcomed her on all sides. But one familiar figure was missing, and she found a melancholy pleasure in the company of her sister-in-law, the widowed Princess of Orange, whom she saw for the first time since her gallant husband's death. Charles treated his niece with marked kindness, and gave her a superb necklace of pearls and diamonds as a parting present.[1]

The winter was spent happily at Nancy, where the new Duke and Duchess made themselves popular with all classes. Francis gave free rein to his love of art and letters, and encouraged scholars and artists by his enlightened patronage. He took passionate delight in music, and was never happier than when he could surround himself with the best singers and players on the lute and viol. Christina shared his

---

[1] Henne, viii. 212-215; T. Juste, "Marie de Hongrie," 120; Calendar of State Papers, xix. 2, 340.

artistic tastes, and was greatly interested in the improvements of the ducal palace. Together they made plans for the decoration of its halls and gardens, and for the construction of new buildings and churches in different parts of Lorraine, while the Court painters, Crock and Chappin, were sent to Italy to collect antiques and study the best examples of art and architecture.[1] At the same time Christina took deep interest in the condition of her humbler subjects, and tried to relieve distress by founding charitable institutions on the pattern of those in Flanders. A new period of peace and prosperity seemed to have dawned on Lorraine, and everything promised a long and happy reign.

By the end of the year the Duke and Duchess of Guise returned to Joinville, and were actively engaged throughout the winter in rebuilding the ruined town and repairing the damage done by the imperial soldiery. Old quarrels between the two houses were forgotten, and friendly intercourse was renewed. In February the Duke and Duchess of Lorraine were present in the chapel of Joinville, at the consecration of Guise's son Charles, as Archbishop of Reims, and in March the Cardinal of Lorraine came to Nancy to discharge the duties of executor to the late Duke. Antoine had provided liberally for all his children. Nicolas de Vaudemont, his younger son, received a sum of 15,000 crowns, and Christina gave her brother-in-law a handsome present of furniture, to help him in setting up house. Some lordships near Joinville were left to the Duke of Guise, and everything was amicably arranged.[2]

---

[1] Pfister, ii. 256; H. Lepage, " La Ville de Nancy," 65.
[2] Calendar of Spanish State Papers, viii. 102; Bouillé, i. 244.

Suddenly the Duke fell ill for the third time, and during several days his life was in danger. Wotton was convinced that he had been poisoned by his French enemies, and so alarming were the reports which reached Brussels, that the Emperor wrote privately to his new Ambassador in Paris, Granvelle's brother-in-law, St. Mauris, begging him to keep a watchful eye on the affairs of Lorraine, lest Guise and the Cardinal should take advantage of their nephew's condition to seize his domains. But this time Francis recovered once more, and was able to make his solemn entry into Nancy on the 16th of April. At the Porte St. Nicolas he was met by the three orders—the nobles, clergy, and people—and walked on foot, with Nicolas de Vaudemont at his side, followed by his Ministers, to the Church of St. Georges. Here, kneeling at the high-altar, he kissed the relic of the True Cross, and took a solemn oath to respect the privileges of the people of Lorraine and the liberties of the city of Nancy. After this a *Te Deum* was chanted and a banquet held in the ducal palace.[1] The next week, by the advice of his doctors, Antoine Champier and Nicolas le Pois, he went to Blamont, in the hope that the invigorating air of the hills might complete his cure; but he grew weaker every day, and was subject to frequent fainting fits of an alarming nature. In her anxiety, Christina sent to Strasburg and Fribourg for well-known physicians, and Mary of Hungary despatched her own doctor to Nancy, and consulted eminent doctors in London and Paris on the patient's symptoms.[2] But all

[1] Calendar of Spanish State Papers, viii. 195; Pfister, ii. 192; Granvelle, "Papiers d'État," iii. 110.
[2] Ravold, iii. 764; Calmet, ii. 1276.

was of no avail, and as a last resource the Duke was carried in a litter to Remiremont, his favourite shooting-lodge in the heart of the Vosges. It was the end of May, and the beautiful woods along the mountain slopes were in the first glory of their spring foliage. For a moment it seemed as if his delight in the beauty of the place and the life-giving influence of sunshine and mountain air would restore him to health. But already the hand of Death was upon him. On the Fête-Dieu he became much worse, and his end was evidently near; but he was perfectly conscious, and, sending for a notary, he made his last will, appointing his wife Regent of the State and guardian of her little son and daughter, and commending her and his children to the Emperor's care. After this he received the last Sacraments, and passed quietly away on Friday, the 12th of June. He was not yet twenty-eight, and had reigned exactly one year.[1] Death had once more severed the marriage tie, and Christina, who but lately called herself the happiest woman in the world, was left stricken and desolate, a widow for the second time, at the age of twenty-three.

[1] Pfister, ii. 192.

BOOK IX

CHRISTINA, REGENT OF LORRAINE

1545—1552

I.

THE premature death of her husband left Christina
in a position of exceptional difficulty. Everything
combined to add to her distress. She herself was in
delicate health, expecting the birth of another child
in a few weeks, her only son was an infant of two
years and a half, and she had not a single near relative
or tried Minister to give her the help of his counsel
and experience. The Duke had appointed her Regent
of Lorraine during his son's minority, but even before
he breathed his last, her claims to this office were disputed. Although Christina herself was popular with
all classes of her son's subjects, there was a strong
party in Lorraine which dreaded the influence of her
powerful uncle. At the head of this party was the
Rhinegrave, Jean de Salm, an able nobleman who
had always been French in his sympathies, and who
now seized the opportunity of the Duke's last illness
to advance the claims of Monsieur de Metz, seeing that
this young Prince would be an easy tool in his hands.
At ten o'clock on the Fête-Dieu, when the Duke
had received the last Sacraments, the Count de Salm
entered his room with Nicolas de Vaudemont, and

thus addressed him : " Monseigneur, if it please God
to call you to himself, do you wish that Monsieur de
Metz, your brother, should have a share in the
administration of your State and the care of your
children, without prejudice to the arrangements
which you have already made, by word and in writing,
with your august wife the Duchess ?" The dying
Prince, who was hardly conscious, murmured a faint
" Yes," upon which the Count summoned a notary
to write down the Duke's last wishes, and proceeded
to read the document to the Duchess in the presence
of her servants.[1]   Christina, in her bitter distress,
paid little heed to this interruption, and was only
anxious to return to her dying husband's bedside;
but immediately after his death she found herself
compelled to face the question.   Owing to her
delicate state of health, she decided to put off the
Duke's funeral, as well as that of his father, until
the following year.   A week after his death she joined
her young children at her dower-house of Denœuvre,
and at the same time the Duke's body was removed
by Count de Salm, as Marshal of Lorraine, to the
collegiate church of this place, and buried in a temporary grave, after lying in state during three days.

The Emperor was at Worms with the Elector
Palatine and his wife when the news of the Duke of
Lorraine's death reached him, and sent Montbardon
at once to his niece with letters of condolence.
Christina availed herself of this opportunity to ask
her uncle's advice regarding the deed drawn up by
Jean de Salm.   Charles, realizing the critical nature
of the situation, immediately sent one of his most
trusted servants, François Bonvalot, Abbot of Luxeuil,

---

[1] Calmet, ii. 1276, iii. 47; Granvelle, " Papiers d'État," iii. 152.

to Nancy, with orders to assure the Duchess of his protection, and if possible secure her the Regency and sole charge of her children. Bonvalot was the brother of Granvelle's wife, the excellent Madame Nicole, and had only lately resigned the office of Ambassador at Paris, and retired to Besançon to administer the affairs of this diocese as coadjutor of the Bishop. No one was better fitted to help the widowed Duchess than this statesman, who was intimately acquainted with the intrigues of the Guise Princes and the French Court. He hastened to Denœuvre without delay, and, as soon as he had seen Christina, wrote the following letter to his brother-in-law, St. Mauris, giving a clear and graphic account of the situation:

"My Brother,
        " The Emperor, having been informed of Monsieur de Lorraine's death, has sent me here to help his niece the Duchess, and to secure her the administration of the State and the guardianship of her children, which belongs to her by right and reason, but which Monsieur de Metz is trying to claim, by virtue of the custom of this country, as well as of certain acts somewhat suspiciously passed by the Count de Salm and other of the nobles when the late Lord Duke was *in extremis*. . . . His Majesty, being anxious to comfort the said lady in her great affliction, and act the part not only of a good uncle, but of a true father, has sent me here to give her advice and help, and begs you to tell the Most Christian King the wrong which has been done her in this strange fashion, and which His Imperial Majesty will never allow, because of the close relation in which this lady stands to him. He hopes that the King will join with him in this, for the sake of the friendship which he has ever borne to this house and to this widowed lady and her orphan children, whose fathers and protectors their two Majesties ought to be. His Imperial Majesty begs the King most earnestly not to allow the said lady to be

deprived of this Regency to which Monsieur de Metz
pretends, in spite of common right and the ancient
custom of Lorraine, as the Count of Salm's deed
abundantly shows, since this would have been super-
fluous if the custom were such as he pretends it to
be. You will lay these same reasons before the
Cardinal and Monsieur de Guise. If you are told that
Queen Yolande resigned the government of Lorraine
in favour of her son, you will reply that this was done
of her own free choice; and if any person objects
that the mother of the late Duke Antoine and the
Cardinal and Sieur de Guise did not retain the administration after her husband's death, you will point
out that the said Duke was of full age, and that the
said lady was content to lay down the government
on this account. . . . And, further, you will inquire
what the King intends to do in the matter, and if
he means to support Monsieur de Metz or take any
steps prejudicial to the said lady and the tranquillity of
these lands, and will inform His Imperial Majesty
and myself of these things without delay."[1]

When Bonvalot wrote this letter from Denœuvre,
on the 27th of June, the young Archbishop of Reims
had already arrived there, with an agreement drawn
up by his uncle the Cardinal, which he submitted
to the Duchess for approval. He informed the Abbot
that King Francis trusted the said lady would avoid
all occasion of strife, which, as Bonvalot remarked,
was exactly what the Emperor wished, and Monsieur de
Metz, by his singular action, had done his best to prevent. In this difficult situation Christina showed remarkable good sense and tact. She told Bonvalot
frankly that she would gladly avail herself of her
brother-in-law's help in the administration of public
affairs, and wished to treat him with perfect friendliness
as long as she retained the sole charge of her children
and the chief authority in the State. Accordingly,

[1] Granvelle, iii. 159-163.

the agreement proposed by the Cardinal was adopted,
with some modifications, and signed at Denœuvre, on
the 6th of August, by Christina, Nicolas, the Count
de Salm, and other chief officials of Lorraine. The
Duchess and her brother-in-law were appointed joint
Regents, and were to affix their seal to all public
deeds. Vaudemont was given a key of the Treasury,
and was allowed the patronage of one out of every
three vacant offices; but the real authority, as well
as the care of her children, was vested in the Duchess.
Bonvalot told the Emperor that, under the circumstances, this was the best arrangement that could be
made, and Charles of Lorraine and his family had
nothing but praise for the Duchess's good-will and
moderation.[1]

A fortnight later, Christina gave birth to her second
daughter, who was named Dorothea, after the Countess
Palatine. But the severe mental strain which the
mother had undergone affected the child, who was a
cripple from her birth. On the 5th of November the
Treaty of Denœuvre was ratified by the States assembled at Neufchâteau, not, however, without considerable discussion. Some of the nobles tried to limit the
Regents' powers, and managed to insert a provision
that none but Lorrains should hold offices of State,
a measure clearly aimed at the Flemings and Burgundians in the Duchess's service. Nicolas de
Vaudemont, being young and inexperienced, agreed
readily to these demands, which drew forth a strong
protest from the Emperor and Mary of Hungary. To
add to Bonvalot's dissatisfaction, Monsieur de Metz
accompanied the Archbishop on his return to France,

---

[1] Calendar of Spanish State Papers, viii. 195; Granvelle,
iii. 226.

without even informing Christina of his intention. In spite of these provocations, she maintained the same conciliatory attitude, and her prudence and modesty excited the Abbot's sincere admiration. The Emperor addressed an affectionate letter to his niece, assuring her of his fatherly love and protection, and saying that he would never cease to regard her interests as his own. " And it will be a great pleasure to me," he adds, " if you will often write to me, and I on my part will let you hear from me in the same manner."[1]

Christina now returned to spend Christmas at Nancy, and settled in the ducal palace with her children. Monsieur de Metz gave up his bishopric, and renouncing the ecclesiastical profession adopted the style of Count of Vaudemont. But he showed no further disposition to make himself disagreeable to his sister-in-law, and their mutual relations were rendered easier by the presence of the Princess of Orange, who spent most of the year at Nancy. The two widowed Princesses were drawn together by that tenderest of ties, the memory of those whom they had loved and lost. Henceforth they became the dearest and closest of friends. During all the troubles and sorrows of the next twenty years Anne's loyalty to her sister-in-law remained unshaken. Her strong common-sense and practical qualities, her coolness and courage in emergencies, were a great support to Christina, while the confidence that Mary of Hungary reposed in her proved no less valuable. The harmony of the family circle continued unbroken, and the internal administration of Lorraine was carried on as peaceably as before. The conduct of

[1] Lanz, ii. 478-484.

foreign affairs presented far greater difficulties, and all Christina's prudence was needed to steer the way safely through the rocks that lay in her course.

In spite of his friendly professions, the French King, it soon became evident, was likely to prove a troublesome neighbour. As Wotton wrote when Francis of Lorraine died, " If the sweet, vain hope of the delivery of Milan did not let him, I think the Duke's death might easily provoke the French King to attempt somewhat on Bar and Lorraine."[1] Even before her husband's death, Christina had been involved in a long correspondence regarding Stenay, which the French refused to give up until Duke Antoine's letters surrendering the town could be produced. The missing papers were at length discovered in possession of the French Governor, De Longueval, who had maliciously concealed them, and the town was evacuated at the end of August, 1545. Ten days afterwards the Duke of Orleans died of the plague at Abbeville, in his twenty-fifth year. The loss of this favourite son was a heavy blow to Francis. " God grant," he wrote to the Emperor, in an outburst of deep emotion, " that you may never know what it is to lose a son !" The event, as it happened, proved most opportune for Charles, who was released from the unpleasant necessity of giving his daughter or niece to a worthless Prince, with Milan or the Netherlands as her dower. But it naturally provoked Francis to demand fresh concessions and revive his old claim to Milan.

The effect of this new quarrel was to increase Christina's difficulties. When the French at length abandoned Stenay, it was found that not only the

---

[1] State Papers, Record Office, Henry VIII., x. 490.

recent fortifications had been destroyed, as agreed upon in the Treaty of Crépy, but that the old walls of the town had been pulled down. Mary of Hungary justly complained that the defenceless state of Stenay was a grave cause of danger to Luxembourg, and urged her brother to garrison the town, declaring, if war broke out, the Duchess would be unable to maintain the neutrality of Lorraine. Charles, who had already left the Netherlands to attend the Diet of Regensburg, now invited his niece to meet him at Waldrevange, on the frontiers of Luxembourg, and discuss the matter. Christina obeyed her uncle's summons gladly, and assured him that she was quite alive to the importance of Stenay, and had already asked her subjects' help in rebuilding the town walls. But since the presence of an imperial force might excite suspicion, she proposed to place a young Luxembourg Captain named Schauwenbourg in command of the garrison. The plan met with Charles's approval; but Mary was by no means satisfied, and begged the Emperor to insist on an oath of allegiance to himself being taken by the garrison and burghers. Charles replied that no doubt the best plan would be to keep Stenay altogether, but that this would be a direct violation of the Treaty of Crépy, as well as a wrong to the little Duke, and might stir up the French " to make a great broil."[1]

The invaluable Bonvalot was now called in, and accepted Christina's invitation to attend the funeral of the two Dukes on the 14th of June. But when the Abbot reached Nancy, he found that only Duke Antoine's obsequies were about to be solemnized, and that the Duchess had deferred those of her hus-

[1] Granvelle, iii. 206-225.

band in compliance with a request from the Guise
Princes. On the day after the old Duke's funeral,
Bonvalot had a long interview with Christina, who
expressed her anxiety to meet her aunt's wishes,
and explained that Vaudemont was only afraid of
arousing the suspicions of the French. While she
was speaking, Nicolas himself came in and told the
Abbé how grateful he felt to the Emperor for the
affection which he showed to his little nephew, and how
fully he realized the importance of defending Stenay,
but that he dared not risk exciting the displeasure
of Francis, who was already advancing a thousand
new claims on Bar. The members of the Ducal
Council, to whom the matter was referred, expressed
the same opinion, telling Bonvalot that they looked
to the Emperor as their father and protector, and
would guard Stenay as the apple of their eye. The
Abbot was satisfied with these assurances, and
advised the Emperor to leave the matter in his
niece's hands. Charles had empowered him to offer
Nicolas the restitution of the Abbey of Gorzes, which
he had formerly held, and which the Imperialists
had recovered from the French and rebuilt at considerable expense. But Christina would not hear
of this, saying that her brother-in-law cared more
for the good of the State than for his private advantage, and Nicolas himself told Bonvalot that he would
not endanger his nephew's realm for ten wealthy
abbeys.

"As for madame your niece, Sire," wrote the
Abbot, "I have always found her most anxious to
please Your Majesty, at whatever cost. But as a
mother she naturally fears to run any risks which
might injure her children, and would, if possible,
avoid these perils. She begged me, with tears in her

eyes, to make Your Majesty understand this, and
have pity upon her, trusting that you will be content
with the promises of the Council, or else find another
and less dangerous way of defending Stenay. Sire,
I could not refuse to give you this message, in obedience to Her Highness's express commands, and beg
you very humbly to take them in good part."[1]

So the incident closed, and for the time being
nothing more was heard of Stenay.

II.

The Duke of Guise and his family now stood higher
than ever in the King's favour. His eldest son,
Aumale, was dangerously wounded in the siege of
Boulogne by an English spear, which penetrated so
deeply into his forehead that the surgeon could only
extract the steel by planting his foot on the patient's
head. After this ordeal the Count lay between life
and death for several weeks, and owed his recovery
to the tender nursing of his mother, who preserved
as a trophy at Joinville the English spearhead which
so nearly ended her son's career.[2] As soon as he
was able to move, the King sent for Antoinette, and
insisted on taking her to hunt at St. Germain, and
consulting her as to his latest improvements in this
palace. Her grandson, the young Duke of Longueville, was also a great favourite at Court, and when
peace was at length concluded, the King gave him a
copy of the new treaty with England to send to the
Queen of Scotland. The boy enclosed it in a merry
letter, sending his love to the little Queen his sister,
and telling his mother that if she would not come to

[1] Granvelle, iii. 235, 236.   [2] Bouillé, i. 155; Pimodan, 88.

France he meant to come and see her, and was old and strong enough to face the roughest sea-voyage.[1]

The Cardinal now announced his intention of taking the whole family back to Joinville, to attend the ducal funeral; but once more the King interfered, and kept them at Court for the christening of the Dauphin's daughter, which was celebrated with great pomp at Fontainebleau. Henry VIII. stood godfather, and the little Princess was named Elizabeth, after the King's mother, " as good and virtuous a woman as ever lived," said the English Ambassador, Sir Thomas Cheyney; while the Imperialists declared that the name was chosen because of its popularity in Spain and of the hopes of the French that the child might one day wed Don Carlos.[2]

Meanwhile the arrival of the Guises was anxiously awaited at Nancy. On the 17th of July Christina wrote to inform Abbot Bonvalot that she had at length been able to fix the date of her husband's funeral:

" Monsieur de Luxeuil,
    " I must inform you that I have heard from the Cardinal and the Duke of Guise, who hope to be here by the end of the month, so the service will be held on the 6th of August, all being well. I beg you will not fail to be present. As for my news, all I have to tell you is that the King is giving me great trouble in Bar, and is trying to raise a tax in the town, which has never been done or thought of before. I fear that in the end I, too, shall have to go to Court, but shall wait until I hear from the Emperor. Can you give me any information as to his movements? All I can hear is that His Majesty is collecting a large

---

[1] Balcarres Manuscripts, ii. 53, 60, iii. 102.
[2] Calendar of State Papers, xxi. 592, 642; Calendar of Spanish State Papers, viii. 431.

army to make war on the Princes of the Empire,
who have rebelled against him. I pray God to help
him, and send him success and prosperity, and have
good hope that my prayers will be heard, as this will
be for the good of Christendom. Here I will end,
Monsieur de Luxeuil, praying God to have you in His
holy keeping.

" La bien votre,
" CHRESTIENNE."[1]

The coming of the Guises, however, was again
delayed, and the funeral did not take place until the
17th of August. On the previous day the Duke's
corpse was brought from Denœuvre to Nancy by the
great officers of State, and laid on a bier in the
Church of St. George's, surrounded by lighted torches
and a guard of armed men, who kept watch all night.
The funerals of the Dukes of Lorraine had always been
famous for their magnificence, and there was an old
proverb which said: " Fortunate is the man who has
seen the coronation of an Emperor, the sacring of
a King of France, and the funeral of a Duke of
Lorraine."[2] On this occasion nothing that could
heighten the imposing nature of the ceremony was
neglected. All the Princes of the blood, Nicolas
of Vaudemont, the Duke of Guise with his five sons
and grandson, rode out from the ducal palace to the
Church of St. Georges, and took their places, as chief
mourners, at the head of the long procession that
wound through the streets to the Cordeliers' shrine.
In their train came a multitude of clergy, nobles, and
Ambassadors from all the crowned heads in Europe,
followed by a motley crowd of burghers and humble
folk, all in deep mourning, with torches in their hands.
The chariot bearing the coffin was drawn by twelve

---

[1] Granvelle, iii. 237.   [2] A. Hallays, 40.

horses, draped with black velvet adorned with the cross of Lorraine in white satin. The Duke's war-horse, in full armour, was led by two pages, while the servants of his household walked bareheaded on either side, with folded arms, in token that their master needed their services no more. On the hearse lay an image of the dead Prince, with the ducal baton in his hand, clad in crimson robes and a mantle of gold brocade fastened with a diamond clasp. This effigy was placed on a huge catafalque erected in the centre of the church, lighted with a hundred torches, and hung with banners emblazoned with the arms of Lorraine, Bar, Provence, Jerusalem, and the Sicilies.

In the tribune above the choir knelt the Princess of Orange, the Duchess of Guise, and her newly-wedded daughter-in-law, Diane of Poitiers's daughter Louise, Marchioness of Mayenne, all clad in the same long black mantles lined with ermine. The Countess Palatine, Dorothea, had arrived at Nancy on the 17th of June, to attend her brother-in-law's funeral, but as the Guises failed to appear, she returned to Heidelberg at the end of a fortnight.

Christina herself was unable to be present, " owing to her excessive sorrow," writes the chronicler, and remained on her knees in prayer, with the Princess of Macedonia and her young children, in her own room, hung with black, while the requiem was chanted and the last rites were performed.[1] When all was over, and the " two Princes of peace," as De Boullay called Francis and his father, were laid side by side in the vault of the Friars' Church, the vast assembly dispersed and the mourners went their

[1] Calmet, ii. 1276, 1281; Pfister, ii. 203.

ways. Only Anne of Lorraine remained at Nancy with her sister-in-law, who could not bear to part from her. A letter which this Princess wrote to her cousin, the Queen of Scotland, this summer is of interest for the glimpse which it gives of the widowed Duchess and the boy round whom all her hopes centred:

"Your Majesty's last letters reached me on the day when I arrived here from home, and I regret extremely that I have been unable to answer them before. I am very glad to hear you are in good health and kind enough to remember me. On my part, I can assure you that there is no one in your family who thinks of you with greater affection or is more anxious to do you service than myself. I did not fail to give your kind message, to Madame de Lorraine, my sister, and Her Highness returns her most humble thanks. You will be glad to hear that her son is well and thriving. I pray God that he may live to fulfil the promise of his early years. Everyone who sees him speaks well of him, and his nature is so good that I hope he will grow up to satisfy our highest expectations. May God grant you long life!
"Your humble cousin,
"ANNE DE LORRAINE."[1]

The Princess of Orange was still in Lorraine when King Francis came to visit the Duchess. This monarch was as active as ever, in spite of frequent attacks of illness, and spent the autumn in making a progress through Burgundy and Champagne, hunting and travelling seven or eight leagues a day in the most inclement weather.

In October he came to Joinville, and Christina, glad to be relieved of the necessity of going to Court herself, invited him to pay her a visit at Bar. In

[1] Balcarres Manuscripts, ii. 156.

this once stately Romanesque castle, of which little now remains, the Duchess and the Princess of Orange, " dowagers both," as Wotton remarks, entertained Francis magnificently, and provided a series of hunting-parties and banquets for his amusement.

The true object of the King's visit was to arrange a marriage between the Duchess and the Count of Aumale. The young soldier made no secret of his love for his cousin's beautiful widow, Antoinette was anxious to see her son settled, and both the King and the Guises were fully alive to the political advantages of the alliance. On the 26th of October Wotton wrote from Bar, " The fame continues of a marriage between the Dowager of Lorraine and the Count of Aumale," although, as he had already remarked in a previous letter, it was hard to believe the Duchess's uncles would consent to the union. Aumale's own hopes were high, and he sent a messenger to Scotland to tell his sister of the good cheer which they were enjoying in Madame de Lorraine's house at Bar.[1]

But these hopes were doomed to disappointment. Christina was determined never to marry again. Like her aunt, Mary of Hungary, having once tasted perfect happiness, she was unwilling to repeat the experiment. Her beauty was in its prime, her charms attracted lovers of every age and rank. During the next ten or twelve years she was courted by several of the most illustrious personages and bravest captains of the age. She smiled on all her suitors in turn, and gave them freely of her friendship, but remained true to her resolve to live for her children alone, and took for her device a solitary

[1] Calendar of State Papers, xxi. 2, 121 ; Balcarres Manuscripts, ii. 87.

tower with doves fluttering round its barred windows, and the motto *Accipio nullas sordida turris aves* (A ruined tower, I give shelter to no birds), as a symbol of perpetual widowhood.[1] Aumale consoled himself by winning fresh laurels in the next war, and before long married another bride of high degree; but Brantôme, who was intimate with the Guises, tells us that he never forgave Madame de Lorraine for rejecting his suit, and remained her bitter enemy to the end of his life.[2] The King took Christina's refusal more lightly. He never treated women's fancies seriously, and when he found that Aumale's suit was not acceptable, he sought the Duchess's help in a scheme that lay nearer his heart. This was the marriage of his own daughter Margaret with Philip of Spain, whose young wife had died, in June, 1545, a few days after giving birth to the Infant Don Carlos. The old scheme of marrying this Princess to the Emperor's only son was now revived at the French Court, and Christina, who had always appreciated Madame Marguerite's excellent qualities, entered readily into the King's wishes. But, as she soon discovered, her aunt, Queen Eleanor, was greatly opposed to the idea, and still ardently wished to see Philip married to her own daughter, the Infanta Maria of Portugal.[3]

From Bar Francis returned to spend All Hallows at Joinville, where he enjoyed fresh revels, and delighted the Duke of Longueville by telling him to make haste and grow tall, that he might enter his service.

[1] N. Ratti, " La Famiglia Sforza," ii. 86.
[2] Brantôme, " Œuvres," xii. 114.
[3] Calendar of Spanish State Papers, viii. 501.

" Now he goes," wrote the boy's tutor, Jean de
la Brousse, " to keep Christmas at Compiègne, and
will spend the winter in Paris, watching how matters
go with the Emperor and the Protestants, whose
armies have been three months face to face, and yet
do not know how to kill each other."[1]

In the same letter the writer describes how, on his
journey to Plessis, to bring the Princess of Navarre
to Court, he met the Queen of Scotland's sister,
Madame Renée, with a number of old monks and
nuns, on her way from Fontévrault to Joinville. On
the 16th of December Madame Renée took possession
of the Convent of St. Pierre at Reims, of which she
was Abbess, and the Duchess of Lorraine and the
Princess of Orange were among the guests present
at this ceremony, at the entry of her brother the
Archbishop into his episcopal city on the following
day.

Meanwhile the news of Christina's supposed marriage
travelled far and wide. It reached Venice, where the
fate of the Duchess who had once reigned over
Milan always excited interest, and was reported to
King Henry of England by one of his Italian agents.
His curiosity was aroused, and when the French
Ambassador, Odet de Selve, came to Windsor, he
asked him if his master had concluded the marriage
which he had in hand. " What marriage ?" asked
De Selve innocently. " That of Madame de Lorraine," replied Henry testily. " With whom ?" asked
the Ambassador. But Henry would say no more,
and relapsed into sullen silence.[2] He had come back
from Boulogne seriously ill, and grew heavier and
more unwieldy every day. A week afterwards he

---

[1] Balcarres Manuscripts, ii. 65 ; iii. 105, 114.
[2] Calendar of State Papers, xxi. 2, 172, 187.

had a severe attack of fever, and on his return to London sent Norfolk and Surrey to the Tower.

Mary of Hungary was so much alarmed at this fresh outbreak of violence that she sent to Chapuys, who was living in retirement at Louvain, for advice. The veteran diplomatist, who for sixteen years had toiled to avoid a rupture between the two monarchs, wrote back, on the 29th of January, 1547, advising the Queen to take no action. " Physicians say," he added, " that the best and quickest cure for certain maladies is to leave the evil untouched and avoid further irritation." When the old statesman wrote these words, the King, whose varying moods he knew so well, had already ceased from troubling. He died at Whitehall on the 28th of January, 1547.

The news of his royal brother's death moved the King of France deeply. " We were both of the same age," he said, " and now he is gone it is time for me to go hence, too."[1] In spite of the painful ailments from which he suffered, Francis still moved restlessly from place to place. Towards the end of Lent he left Loches to spend Easter at St. Germain, but fell ill on the way, and died at Rambouillet on the 31st of March.

The death of these two monarchs, who filled so large a place in the history of the times, produced a profound sensation throughout Europe. No one felt the shock more than the Duchess, who had been courted by one Prince, and had lately received the other under her roof. But a third death this spring touched her still more closely. On the 28th of February the good old Queen Philippa passed away in her humble cell at Pont-à-Mousson. As she lay

[1] Brantôme, iii. 164.

dying she asked what was the day of the week, and, being told it was Saturday, remarked: " All the best things of my life came to me on this day. I was born and married to my dear husband on a Saturday, I entered Nancy amid the rejoicings of my people, and I forsook the world to take the veil, on this day, and now on Saturday I am going to God." Her children and grandchildren knelt at the bedside, but Guise, her best-loved son, only arrived from Paris at the last moment. She opened her eyes at the sound of his voice. " Adieu, mon ami," she said, " and do not forget to keep God before your eyes." These were her last words, and as the pure spirit passed out of this life the sound of weeping was broken by the joyous songs of her pet lark.[1]

She was buried, as she desired, in the convent cloister, and the people, who venerated her as a saint, flocked to the funeral. Christina employed Ligier-Richier, the sculptor of the Prince of Orange's monument, to carve a recumbent effigy of the dead Queen in coloured marbles on her tomb. The black cloak and grey habit were faithfully reproduced, the finely-modelled features were rendered in all their ivory whiteness, and a tiny figure of a kneeling nun was represented in the act of laying the crown at her feet. When the convent church was pillaged by rioters in 1793, this monument was buried by the nuns in the garden. Here it was discovered in 1822, and brought to Nancy, where it now stands in the Church of the Cordeliers, near the stately tomb which Philippa herself had reared to her husband, King René.[2]

[1] Pimodan, 95; Bouillé, i. 160.

[2] Hallays, " La Ville de Nancy," 22 ; C. Cournault, " Ligier-Richier," 34.

III.

Of the three great monarchs whose fame had filled the world during the last forty years, only one remained alive, and he was engaged in a desperate struggle. Throughout the autumn and winter of 1546-47, Charles V. carried on a vigorous campaign against the coalition of Princes known as the League of Schmalkalde. Christina watched the progress of the war with keen anxiety, and saw with distress that her brother-in-law, the Palatine, had joined the rebel ranks. Frederic had never forgiven the Emperor for sacrificing his wife's rights by the Treaty of Spires, and showed his displeasure by refusing to attend the Chapter of the Golden Fleece at Utrecht in January, 1546. He further annoyed Charles by introducing Lutheran rites at Heidelberg, and on Christmas Day he and Dorothea received Communion in both kinds at the hands of a Protestant pastor in the Church of the Holy Ghost. But he still hesitated to take up arms against the friend of his youth. At length, in August, he declared himself on the Protestant side, and for the first time the red flag of the Palatinate was seen in the camp of the Emperor's foes. Before long, however, his courage failed him, and when Charles recovered the imperial city of Halle, in Suabia, Frederic hastened thither to make his peace. Tears rose to the veteran's eyes when the Emperor said how much it had grieved him to see so old a friend in the ranks of his foes, but hastened to add that he forgave him freely and would only remember his past services. From this time the Palatine's loyalty never again wavered, but he

was obliged to restore Catholic rites in Heidelberg
and to give up his fortress of Hoh-Königsberg in
Franconia to Albert of Brandenburg.[1]

The Duke of Würtemberg and the cities of Ulm
and Augsburg soon followed the Palatine's example,
and Charles's triumph was complete by the decisive
victory of Mühlberg. " God be thanked, who never
forsakes his own," wrote Granvelle to Mary of
Hungary from the battle-field, at midnight on the
24th of April.[2] The Elector John Frederick of
Saxony and the Landgrave of Hesse were made
prisoners, the League of Schmalkalde was dis-
solved, and Titian commemorated the Emperor's
heroic deeds in a famous equestrian portrait.

The peace of Lorraine was insured by the victory
of Mühlberg, and Christina shared in the general
sense of relief with which the close of the war was
hailed. When, in the following autumn, the Regent
and the Princess of Orange rode to meet the Emperor
at the Diet of Augsburg, the Duchess joined them
on the frontiers of Lorraine. These three august
ladies reached Augsburg on the 21st of November,
and were received by King Ferdinand, his son Archduke Maximilian, and the Prince of Piedmont, who
met them outside the gates, and escorted them to
the Emperor's lodgings in the fine house of the
Fuggers. Here the Countess Palatine and Ferdinand's
daughter, the Duchess of Bavaria, were awaiting
them at the doors of the courtyard, and conducted
them into Charles's presence. During the next three
months Christina lived in the great banker's house,
with the other members of the imperial family, as

---

[1] Gachard, ii. 338; L. Haüsser, i. 603; G. Voigt, " Albert von
Brandenburg," i. 164.   [2] Granvelle, iii. 265.

her uncle's guest. Augsburg itself was a noble city. The wealth of her merchants, the splendour of their houses and gardens, amazed every stranger who entered her gates. " The Fuggers' house," wrote Ascham, " would overbrag all Cheapside." The copper roofs glittered in the sun, the carved and painted decorations of the interior were of the most costly and elaborate description.[1] And this winter the streets of Augsburg were thronged with Princes and ladies. It was the gayest and most splendid Diet ever seen. Never before had so many Archduchesses and Duchesses been present, never was there so much dancing and jousting and feasting. On St. Andrew's Day the whole imperial family attended a solemn Mass in honour of the Knights of the Fleece, and were entertained by the Emperor at a banquet, after which the Queen of Hungary received the Companions of the Order in her apartments. On Christmas Day all the Princes and Princesses were present at High Mass in the Cathedral, and on the Feast of the Three Kings they attended service in the Court chapel, when Granvelle's son, the young Bishop of Arras, officiated, and the Palatine, the Marquis of Brandenburg, and the Archduke, presented the customary offerings of gold, frankincense, and myrrh, in the Emperor's name. Except on these state occasions, Charles dined alone and never spoke at meals, but generally sat by the window for an hour or two afterwards, talking to his brother and sister or nephews and nieces.

King Ferdinand's rooms, on the contrary, were never empty. He had lost his faithful wife, Anna of

[1] Gachard, " Voyages de Charles V.," ii. 350-355; R. Ascham, " Works," ii. 267; " Travail and Life of Sir T. Hoby," 7.

Bohemia, in January, but his son and daughter were lavish in dispensing their father's hospitality. Like his sister Mary, Ferdinand was very fond of music, and enjoyed listening to his fine Kapelle, while one of his favourite jesters was always present to amuse the Electors and Princesses at his table.[1] His son, the Archduke Max, as Ascham calls him, was a gay and pleasant gentleman, " of goodly person and stature," speaking eight languages, and very popular with all classes, especially the Lutherans, whose opinions he was supposed to affect. Charles's other nephew, Emanuel Philibert, the Prince of Piedmont, was another gallant squire of dames, as ready to take part in masque and dance as he was foremost in active warfare. Every evening there was music and dancing in the King's rooms, and the old halls of the merchants rang to the sound of laughter and melody. In that joyous throng the Countess Palatine was the gayest of the gay, and Christina forgot her sorrows to become young once more.

There was one man among the Princes assembled at Augsburg who gazed with frank admiration at the handsome Duchess; this was the Marquis Albert of Brandenburg, Lord of Culmbach and Burgrave of Nuremberg. While still a boy he succeeded to his father's principality in Franconia, and was educated by his uncle, the Duke of Prussia and Grand-Master of the Teutonic Order. Although brought up a Lutheran, he entered the Emperor's service before he was twenty, and fought gallantly in the wars of Cleves and Champagne. A wild and reckless spirit, who rode hard, drank deep, and knew no fear, Albert was adored by his soldiers, whose toils and hardships

Bucholtz, vi. 298, 300.

he shared with cheerful courage, while his name was the terror of all peaceful citizens. " Thunder and lightning, devouring fire," wrote a contemporary, " are not more terrible than the Marquis Albert on the battle-field."[1] But there was a fascination about this ruthless dare-devil which no woman could resist. His sisters were passionately devoted to him, and Bona, the Queen of Poland, tried in vain to marry him to one of her daughters. Roger Ascham describes him as

" another Achilles, his face fair and beautiful, but stern and manly, with flowing locks and great rolling eyes, yet with a sad, restless look, as if he was ever seeking what he could not find. A man of few words withal, but with a deep, strong voice, ever more ready to hear than to speak."[2]

There seemed no heights to which this soldier of fortune could not aspire. The Emperor treated him with fatherly affection, and the Queen and the Duchess of Lorraine honoured the sumptuous banquets, in which he displayed his usual prodigality, careless of the debts with which he was already loaded.

Once more rumour was busy with Christina's name. The Marquis Albert proclaimed himself her devoted servant, and her marriage with the young King Sigismund of Poland was seriously discussed at Augsburg. This monarch's wife, the Archduchess Elizabeth, had died before his accession, and his sister, the Electress Hedwig of Brandenburg, was eager to bring about a union between him and the Duchess of Lorraine;[3] but, as usual, these rumours ended in smoke, and the

---

[1] Voigt, ii. 7.   [2] Ascham, iii. 32; Voigt, i. 197.
[3] Bulletins de la Commission d'Histoire, xii. 156; Calendar of State Papers, Edward VI., 17.

only marriage announced at Augsburg was that of the Archduke Max and his cousin the Infanta Maria of Spain, an alliance which had long been privately arranged.

Early in the New Year another distinguished person arrived at Augsburg, in the person of the great Venetian master, Titian. He came in obedience to an urgent summons from the Emperor, and during the next few months painted a magnificent series of portraits, including those of Charles and Ferdinand, the captive Elector of Saxony, Chancellor Gran-velle, his wife, and his son, the Bishop of Arras, who was a great admirer of Titian's art. Fourteen years before, this same master had taken Christina's portrait, when she came to Milan as the youthful bride of Francesco Sforza; now he saw her again in the flower of her womanhood, and, had opportunity offered, would doubtless have painted her again. But disquieting rumours of unrest on the frontiers of Lorraine reached Augsburg, and on the 16th of February the Duchess set out on her return to Nancy. The Emperor gave his niece a costly ring as a parting present, and Archduke Max, the Marquis Albert, the Prince of Piedmont, together with the Countess Pala-tine and the Princess of Orange, escorted her some leagues on her way. When, a month later, the Queen of Hungary left Augsburg, she paid Christina a visit at Nancy, bringing with her Anne of Lorraine and William, the young Prince of Orange, a promising boy of fifteen, who was being educated at Court, and met with a kindly welcome from the Duchess and her subjects for the sake of the lamented Prince whose name he bore.[1] By Mary's advice, the Regents took active measures

[1] Gachard, ii. 357.

CHARLES V. (1548)

By Titian (Munich)

To face p. 322

for the defence of the frontier and the fortification of Nancy. An arsenal was founded, and two bastions, which became known as those of Denmark and Vaudemont, were built near the palace. Other improvements were carried out at the same time: the marshy ground under the walls was thoroughly drained, and converted into a spacious square called La Place de la Carrière; many of the streets were paved and widened; and the Count of Salm, Bassompierre, and several of the nobles, built fine new houses along the Grande Rue, opposite the Galerie des Cerfs.[1]

The Emperor remained at Augsburg throughout the summer, endeavouring to effect a lasting settlement of the religious question. On the 30th of June the so-called " Interim " was proclaimed, a compromise which satisfied no one, and was described by Thomas Hoby, a young Englishman who came to Augsburg this summer on his way to Italy, as an attempt to set up the old Babylon again in Germany.[2] A fortnight later the Diet was prorogued, and Charles started for the Netherlands, where he arrived on the 8th of September, after more than two years' absence.

A few weeks before his arrival a marriage had taken place, greatly to Mary's satisfaction, between the widowed Princess of Orange and the Duke of Aerschot.[3] This nobleman, the premier peer of the realm and doyen of the Golden Fleece, had lost his second wife in 1544, but was still in the prime of life, and, as his daughter-in-law, Louise de Guise, told her sister, was honoured and beloved throughout the Netherlands Christina could not herself be present at the wedding,

---

[1] H. Lepage, " La Ville de Nancy," 44; Calendar of State Papers, Foreign, Edward VI., i. 16.

[2] T. Hoby, " Memoirs," 6.

[3] Calendar of State Papers, Edward VI., i. 25.

but her brother-in-law Nicolas went to Brussels to give his sister away. Here he fell in love with Count Egmont's sister Margaret, and asked her hand in marriage. This alliance met with the warm approval of the Emperor and the Regent, but caused Christina many searchings of heart. Already more than one attempt had been made by the Guises to marry Vaudemont to a French bride, and she feared that this union would excite great displeasure in some quarters. In her alarm she wrote to the Emperor, begging him to forbid the marriage as dangerous to the welfare of her State. Charles, however, declined to interfere, and sent Granvelle's brother, Chantonnay, to advise his niece politely to mind her own business.

" Since the Count of Vaudemont is bent on marrying," he wrote to his Envoy, " it is far better that he should come here for a wife than go to France; and the Duchess need not feel in any way responsible for the alliance, which is entirely his own doing. . . . And, indeed, I do not see how he could honourably break his word, since we ourselves urged our cousins of Egmont to agree to his proposals. But tell him to come here as soon as he can, to prevent the French from making any more mischief !"[1]

There was nothing more to be said, and the wedding was celebrated in the Court chapel at Brussels, after vespers, on the 23rd of January, 1549. The bride, richly clad in cloth of gold and decked with priceless gems, was led to the altar by the Queen, while Charles brought in the bridegroom. A banquet and masque were afterwards held in the palace, at the close of which Mary once more took the bride by the hand and conducted her into the nuptial chamber, hung with crimson brocade and costly tapestries. The next morning the newly-wedded Countess ap-

---

[1] Granvelle, iii. 335.

peared at Mass, in another costume of green velvet embroidered in silver, and jousts and dances succeeded each other during the following three days, ending with a magnificent banquet given by the Duchess of Aerschot.[1]

Among the company present on this occasion was the Dowager Queen Eleanor, who came to Brussels on the 5th of December, to make her home with her beloved brother and sister. On his death-bed Francis I. was seized with remorse for the way in which he had neglected his wife, and begged his daughter Margaret to atone for his shortcomings. But although Margaret carried out her father's last instructions faithfully, and asked his widow to remain at Court, the new King showed his stepmother scanty kindness, and Eleanor left France with few regrets. Another guest at Margaret of Egmont's wedding was Christina's cousin, Duke Adolf of Holstein, the King of Denmark's youngest brother. Most of his life had been spent in Germany, and he had taken part in the campaign of Mühlberg with his friend Albert of Brandenburg. Now, following the wild Marquis's example, he came to Brussels in October, 1548, and entered the Emperor's service. This new recruit was cordially welcomed, and gave a signal proof of his valour by carrying off the first prize in the tournament held at the palace.

Christina herself maintained the prudent attitude which she had adopted with regard to Vaudemont's marriage, and refused to countenance by her presence a union which excited much unfriendly criticism in France. Two other weddings in which she was also keenly interested took place about the same time. On the 20th of October her old suitor, the brilliant

[1] Gachard, ii. 377.

22

and volatile Duke of Vendôme, was married at
Moulins to Jeanne d'Albret, the heiress of Navarre.
This strong-minded Princess, who refused to wed
the Duke of Cleves, and took objection to Aumale
because his brother was the husband of Diane de
Poitiers's daughter, fell suddenly in love with
Vendôme, and insisted on marrying him in spite of
her mother's opposition. So radiant was Jeanne on
her wedding-day that King Henry declared her to
be the most joyous bride whom he had ever seen.
Six weeks later Aumale himself was married at
St. Germain to Anna d' Este, daughter of Duke Ercole II. of Ferrara and Renée of France. Ronsard
sang the praises of this Italian Venus who had taken
the Mars of France for her lord, and Vendôme, gay
and inconsequent as ever, sent his old rival in war
and love a merry letter, bidding him follow his good
example, and stay at home to play the good husband.[1]
This union with the King's first cousin satisfied the
highest ambitions of the Guises, while Anna's charm
and goodness were a source of lasting content to
Duchess Antoinette. Christina was one of the first
to greet the bride on her arrival at Joinville. At
first the two Princesses, Brantôme tells us, looked at
each other shyly, but with evident curiosity. The
tale of Aumale's courtship was well known, and
Christina naturally felt keen interest in the Este
Princess who came from Beatrice's home and was the
cousin of Francesco Sforza. " Anna," writes the
chronicler, " was tall and beautiful, but very gentle
and amiable. The two ladies met and conversed
together, and were soon the best of friends."[2]

[1] A. de Ruble, " Le Mariage de Jeanne d'Albret," 243-246;
Bouillé, 204.
[2] Brantôme, " Œuvres," xii. 115.

IV.

Christina's absence from her brother - in - law's wedding had been a great disappointment to her aunts, and she received a pressing invitation to come to Brussels for the fêtes in honour of the Prince of Spain, whose arrival was expected early in the spring of 1549. Accordingly, on the 28th of March the Duchess reached Brussels, attended by the Princess of Macedonia, and was received by the Grand-Écuyer Boussu and a brilliant escort of gentlemen. One of these was the Marquis Albert, whose name of late had been frequently coupled with her own, the other his friend Duke Adolf of Holstein. Christina naturally hailed this meeting with her cousin, especially now that his brother, King Christian, had alleviated the rigour of her father's captivity. Since the Palatine had abandoned all attempts to maintain his wife's claims, the reigning monarch had agreed to release his unfortunate kinsman from the dungeons of Sonderburg. On the 17th of February the two Kings met and dined together in a friendly manner, after which the deposed monarch was removed to Kallundborg, a pleasantly-situated castle on a promontory of Zeeland, where he spent the remaining ten years of his life in comparative freedom.[1] This, indeed, was all that the Emperor desired. In a secret paper of instructions which he drew up for Philip in case of his own death, he enjoined his son to cultivate peaceable relations with the King of Denmark, and do his utmost to keep the Princesses Dorothea and Christina in his good graces, and insure their father's good treatment, " without allowing him

[1] Schäfer, iv. 472; Bucholtz, vii. 572.

such a measure of liberty as might enable him to assert his old claims and injure our State of Flanders as he did before."[1] Unfortunately, the interest with which Christina regarded the Danish Prince proved fatal to Adolf's friendship with the Marquis. Before the outbreak of the Schmalkalde War, Adolf had become affianced to Albert's sister, Fräulein Kunigunde. The wedding-day was fixed, and the citizens of Nuremberg had prepared gold rings and jewels for the bride, but the disturbed state of Denmark compelled the Duke to postpone his marriage for a time. Then, as ill-luck would have it, he met the Duchess of Lorraine at the New Year festivities at Augsburg, and fell desperately in love with her. From this moment he forgot Fräulein Kunigunde, and took the first excuse he could find to break off his engagement. Albert never forgave the wrong, and, although the two Princes met at Brussels and walked side by side in the Court chapel on Candlemas Day, the old friendship between them was turned to bitter enmity.[2]

But now private grievances had to be put aside, and friends and foes alike joined in the public rejoicings which welcomed the Prince of Spain's arrival. Charles was anxious to present his son to his future subjects in the most favourable light, and no pains were spared to produce a good impression both on Philip himself and on the loyal people of Brabant. On the 1st of April, Mary of Hungary, Christina, and Anne of Aerschot, accompanied by the whole Court, received the Prince at Ter Vueren, where they

[1] Granvelle, iii. 207.
[2] Lodge, " Illustrations," i. 183; Calendar of the Manuscripts of the Marquis of Salisbury, i. 110; Voigt, i. 197.

entertained him at dinner and witnessed a military parade and sham-fight on the plains outside the town. In the evening Philip made his state entry into Brussels, clad in crimson velvet and riding on a superb war-horse, attended by Albert of Brandenburg, Adolf of Holstein, the Princes of Piedmont, Orange, and Chimay, Alva, Egmont, Pescara, and many other illustrious personages. The chief burghers and city guilds met the Prince at Ter Vueren, and escorted him to the palace gates, where the two Queens and Christina conducted him into the Emperor's presence. Philip fell on his knees, and his father embraced him with tears in his eyes, and conversed with him for over an hour. At nightfall the whole city was illuminated, and bonfires blazed from all the neighbouring heights. The next day a tournament was held on the Grande Place, and a splendid gold cup was presented to the Prince by the city, while the States of Brabant voted him a gift of 100,000 florins and hailed him with acclamation as the Emperor's successor. But in the evening these rejoicings were interrupted by the news of the Duke of Aerschot's sudden death. He had gone to Spires to meet the Prince, but had over-exerted himself, and died very suddenly at his castle of Quievrain. It was a grievous blow to Anne of Lorraine, who was once more left a widow, before she had been married quite nine months. The deepest sympathy was felt for her at Court, and Mary lamented the loss of her wisest Councillor. All festivities were put off till Easter. Philip spent Holy Week in devotional exercises, and rode to S. Gudule on Palm Sunday, at the head of a solemn procession of knights bearing palms.

Charles took advantage of this quiet season to

initiate his son into the administration of public
affairs and make him acquainted with the leading
nobles of the Netherlands. But the impression produced by Philip was far from being a favourable one.
Short in stature and blond in complexion, with his
father's wide forehead and projecting jaw, he was
Flemish in appearance, but Spanish by nature. His
taciturn air and haughty and reserved manners
formed a striking contrast to the frank and genial
ways which endeared Charles V. to all classes of
his subjects. Thomas Hoby, who saw Philip at
Mantua, noticed what " small countenance " he
made to the crowd who greeted his entry, and heard
that he had already " acquired a name for insolency."
Wherever he went it was the same. " His severe
and morose appearance," wrote the Venetian Suriano,
" has made him disagreeable to the Italians, hated by
the Flemings, and odious to the Germans." His
marked preference for all that was Spanish gave
deadly offence to the Emperor's old servants, and
people in Brussels said openly that when Philip came
to the throne no one but Spaniards would be employed
at Court. In vain his father and aunt warned him
that this exclusive temper was ill-suited to a Prince
who was called to rule over subjects of many nations.
He spoke little in public and rarely smiled. During
the year which he spent at Brussels people said that
he was never seen to laugh except on one occasion,
when all the Court witnessed the famous national
fête of the Ommegang from the hôtel-de-ville, on
the Fête-Dieu. Among the varied groups in the
procession was a bear playing on an organ, while
children dressed up as monkeys danced to the music,
and unhappy cats tied by the tail in cages filled the

air with discordant cries. At the sight of these grotesque figures even Philip's gravity gave way, and he laughed till the tears ran down his cheeks.[1]

This cold and haughty Prince, who took no pains to commend himself to his future subjects, showed a marked preference from the first for his cousin Christina. He sought her company on every possible occasion, gave her rich presents, and devoted himself to her service with an ardour which became a cause of serious annoyance to his aunts.

" Queen Eleanor," wrote the French Ambassador Marillac, " is always trying to treat of her daughter's marriage with the Prince, but with very little success, and the great attentions which he pays the Duchess of Lorraine, the evident delight which he takes in her society, and the gifts which he bestows upon her, have excited great jealousy."[2]

Before long Christina herself found Philip's attentions embarrassing, and felt that it would be the path of wisdom to leave Court. She was present, however, at a second tournament given on the Grande Place, on the 6th of May. That day Count d'Aremberg (the husband of Christina's intimate friend Margaret la Marck), Mansfeldt, Horn, and Floris de Montmorency, held the lists against all assailants, while Alva and Francesco d'Este were the judges. Philip, who inherited little of his father's taste for knightly exercises, but had been practising riding and jousting diligently during the last few weeks, entered the lists, and was awarded a fine ruby as a prize, Egmont and the Prince of Piedmont being the other victors. Albert of Brandenburg was present,

[1] Henne, viii. 373.
[2] Gachard, " Retraite de Charles V.," i. 72; Manuscript 8,625, f. 235, Bibliothèque Nationale, Paris.

but declined to take part in the tournament. He had seldom been seen at Court since Philip's arrival and spent most of his time in his own quarters, compiling an account of his grievances against the Emperor. One day Charles, fearing to lose his services, sent Granvelle to offer him an honourable and lucrative office in the Imperial Mint. Albert replied loftily that, since he was born a Brandenburg, no office which the Emperor had to bestow, could exalt his station, and that as he never managed to keep a sixpence in his own pocket, he would rather not attempt to meddle with other people's money. A few days after this he asked leave to retire to his own domains. The last time that he appeared in public was at the banquet which followed the tournament, in the hôtel-de-ville; here he sat at the Emperor's table, opposite the Duchess of Lorraine, who was placed between Philip and Emanuel Philibert of Piedmont, while Adolf of Holstein sat next to the Princess of Macedonia. All these illustrious guests joined in the ball which closed the day's festivities, and dancing was kept up with great spirit until after midnight.[1]

Early the next morning Christina left Brussels, accompanied by Vaudemont's wife, Margaret of Egmont, and escorted for several miles on her journey by the Prince of Spain. Three weeks later the Marquis Albert also left Court, without taking leave of the Emperor or the Queens. His abrupt departure excited general surprise, and no one knew whether it was due to his quarrel with the Duke of Holstein, or to some imaginary affront from the Prince or the Duchess of Lorraine; but when he was at some distance from the town he sent back a warrant for a

[1] Gachard, ii. 389.

S. GUDULE, BRUSSELS

HÔTEL-DE-VILLE, BRUSSELS

To face p. 332

pension of 4,000 crowns a year, which he had received
from the Emperor, as a sign that he was no longer
in his service.

During the course of the summer Philip made his
" joyeuse entrée " into the different cities of the
Low Countries, and a memorable series of fêtes was
given in his honour by Mary of Hungary at her
beautiful summer palace of Binche. At the end of
August the Duchess of Aerschot gave birth to a
posthumous son, who was christened by the Bishop
of Arras in the Court chapel, and named Charles
Philip, after his godfathers, the Emperor and the
Prince. But while Anne's second marriage and her
brother's union with Egmont's sister strengthened
the ties between Lorraine and Flanders, the close
connection of the younger branch of the ducal house
with France increased daily. After the marriage of
Guise's third son, Mayenne, with Diane de Poitiers's
daughter, his brothers were loaded with favours of
every description. Aumale was created a Duke
and appointed Governor of Savoy, and Charles was
made a Cardinal at the King's request, and loaded
with rich benefices. Their mother stood sponsor to
Henry II.'s daughter Claude, who was one day to be
the wife of Christina's only son, and had the deputies
of the thirteen Swiss cantons for her godfathers. A
new link was forged by the coming of the little Queen
of Scots to France in the autumn of 1548, as the
future bride of the Dauphin. Antoinette met her
granddaughter at Brest, and brought her to St. Germain, where the charms of the little Queen soon won
all hearts. " I can assure you," wrote the proud
grandmother to her eldest son, " she is the best and
prettiest child of her age that was ever seen !" And

her uncle the Cardinal added: " She already governs
both the King and Queen." At the Court ball in honour
of Aumale's wedding, all the guests stood still to
watch the lovely little Queen and the Dauphin
dancing hand in hand, and the King smiled maliciously
when the English Ambassador remarked that it was
the most charming thing in the world to see the two
children together.[1]

When Christina returned to Lorraine in May, 1549,
all the Guises were at Paris for the King and Queen's
state entry, and the young Duke of Longueville led
his grandmother's white horse in the procession.
After this Antoinette brought her daughter-in-law
to spend the autumn quietly at Joinville, and great
was the rejoicing when, on the last day of the year,
Anna gave birth to her first son, the Prince who was
to become famous as " Henri le Balafré." Christina
was careful to remain on good terms with the family at
Joinville, and the presence of the Duchess of Aerschot,
who spent the winter in Lorraine, increased the friendly
intercourse between the two houses. Anne's letters
to her aunt and cousins abound in playful allusions to
early recollections, and she always addressed Aumale
as " Monsieur mon serviteur" and signed herself
" Votre bonne maîtresse." When, in January, 1550,
the Duke of Guise fell ill, Christina sent her steward
Grammont repeatedly to make inquiries at Joinville.

" We cannot rest satisfied," wrote the Duchess of
Aerschot from Nancy, " without hearing the latest
accounts of my uncle, and trust the bearer will bring
us good news, please God ! My sister, Madame de
Lorraine, is so anxious about him that she feels she

---

[1] Maitland, " Miscellany," i. 219; A. de Ruble, " La Jeunesse
de Marie Stuart," 104.

must send over again. I cannot tell you, my dear aunt, how much she thinks of you, and how anxious she is to do you any service in her power. As for myself, if there is anything that I can do, you have only to speak, and you will be obeyed."[1]

After a long illness, Claude of Guise breathed his last on the 12th of April, and was followed to the grave within a month by his brother, Cardinal Jean, who died at Nogent-sur-Seine, on his return from Rome. The Duke's funeral was solemnized in the Church of St. Laurent at Joinville, with all the elaborate ceremonial common on these occasions. Antoinette made a great point of Christina's attendance, and Anne promised to do her best to gratify her aunt's wish in the matter.

" I shall be very glad," she wrote, " if it is possible for Madame my sister to be present at the obsequies of my uncle—to whom God grant peace !—and will do my utmost to effect this, not only because of my own anxiety to see you and my cousins, but because I would gladly give you pleasure."[2]

Accordingly, the two Duchesses, accompanied by the Count and Countess of Vaudemont and several nobles, arrived at Joinville on Saturday, the 29th of June, to condole with the widow and attend the funeral rites that were protracted during the next three days. Never was there a more attached family than this of the Guises.

" I cannot tell you the grief I feel," wrote the Queen of Scotland to her bereaved mother. " You know as well as I do that I have lost the best father that ever child had, and am left both orphaned and widowed."

[1] Pimodan, 367; Bouillé, 349; Bibliothèque Nationale, F.F. 20,467, f. 39; Gaignières Manuscripts, 349, f. 7.

[2] Pimodan, 375; Bibliothèque Nationale, F F. 20, 468, f. 9.

An imposing monument, adorned with rich marbles and bas-reliefs of the dead Prince's battles, was raised by Antoinette to her husband's memory in the church at Joinville. In the centre the Duke and Duchess were both represented clad in robes of state, kneeling with hands clasped together, and a long Latin epitaph relating the hero's great deeds was inscribed below, ending with the words:

" Antoinette de Bourbon, his wife, and her six sons, have erected this tomb, in token of undying sorrow and love for an incomparable husband and the best of fathers."[1]

V.

Charles V. had long cherished a wish to remove the bones of his ancestor Charles the Bold from the church of St. Georges at Nancy, where they had been buried after his defeat, and bring them to rest in his daughter Mary's tomb at Bruges. At first Christina hesitated to give her consent, fearing to arouse the resentment of her subjects, who were proud of possessing this trophy of King René's victory, but the urgent entreaties of her aunts at length induced her to yield, and, after ascertaining that neither Vaudemont nor the States of Lorraine had any objection to offer, she consented to her uncle's request, on condition that the removal of the remains should be effected as quietly as possible. Late in the evening of the 22nd of September, 1550, three imperial deputies, the Bishop of Cambray, the Chief Justice of Luxembourg, and the herald Toison d'Or, met the Provost and Canons of St. Georges in the crypt

[1] Bouillé, i. 227.

of the collegiate church.   A solemn requiem was chanted, after which the tomb was opened and the bones, wrapt in a white linen shroud, were reverently laid in a wooden casket and committed to the charge of two friars.   A gift of 100 gold crowns was made to the church in the Emperor's name, and the precious casket was placed on a chariot drawn by four black horses, escorted by a troop of twenty men-at-arms. The little procession travelled the same night to Metz, and thence across the frontier to Luxembourg.   Bells were tolled in all the towns and villages on their way, and the *De Profundis* was chanted wherever a halt was made, until on the 24th the casket was safely deposited in the choir of the Cordeliers' church at Luxembourg.   Here Charles of Burgundy's bones were placed in the grave of John of Luxembourg, the blind King of Bohemia, who fell at Crécy, until, nine years later, they were finally laid to rest by his daughter's side in the shrine of Our Lady at Bruges.[1]

When this pious act was safely accomplished, Christina set out with Anne of Lorraine and the Count and Countess of Vaudemont to join the imperial party at Augsburg.   Charles, Philip, and Ferdinand, had been attending the Diet in this city since July, and were joined there by Mary of Hungary, who, however, was obliged to return to the Netherlands on the 26th of September, owing to troubles on the French frontier.   Christina's presence was the more welcome. On the 30th of the same month Philip and his uncle Ferdinand were riding in the fields near Augsburg, when they noticed a cloud of dust on the highroad, and, galloping off in this direction, met the Duchess

[1] Calmet, ii. 1296, iii. 423; Granvelle, iii. 430.

of Lorraine and her companions, with a large train of followers. Philip gallantly escorted his cousin to the Emperor's lodgings, where she spent the next three weeks. Her coming was the signal for a round of festivities. While Charles and Ferdinand rode together in earnest converse, or sat with closed doors debating public matters, Philip and a few chosen friends—the Prince of Piedmont, Duke Adolf, Pescara, and Ruy Gomez—spent the days with the Duchess and her ladies. Sometimes they went hunting on the Bavarian plains, sometimes they danced or played cards, and every evening they met at supper in Christina's rooms.[1]

On the 16th of October a joust was held in the court of the Fuggers' house, and the Emperor, with his niece and Duchess Anne, looked on from the windows. Egmont and Vaudemont were judges, and Count Lalaing and Floris de Montmorency won the prizes. The Cardinal of Trent entertained the company at supper, and left the next day for Genoa to receive Maximilian, the King of Bohemia, who had been sent for from Spain to take part in the family conference. Three days later Philip gave a tournament on a grander scale, in honour of the Duchess, and entered the lists clad in ruby velvet and white satin, as he figures in the portrait which Titian painted. This time Christina's presence seems to have inspired him with unwonted prowess. He broke many lances, and won a fine gold chain, which he presented to his cousin. She on her part entertained the King of the Romans and all the knights who rode in the jousts at a sumptuous banquet and ball, which ended in

[1] Gachard, ii. 424; Bulletins de la Commission d'Histoire, série 2, xii. 189.

the Prince presenting rings to all the ladies and receiving a kiss from each in turn.

This festive evening marked the close of Christina's
visit to Augsburg. The next morning she set out
for Nancy, " leaving the Court sad and widowed,"
writes an Italian chronicler, " bereft of her presence,
and without a lady to amuse the Princes or entertain
the Emperor's guests." Philip escorted her for some
miles on her journey, and took an affectionate farewell of his favourite cousin, whom he never saw again
until he was the husband of Mary Tudor.[1]

Christina's route lay through the duchy of Würtemberg and along the valley of the Neckar. At Esslingen, the free imperial city on the banks of this river
she met the new English Ambassador, Sir Richard
Morosyne, on his way to Augsburg. In his train
was a young secretary called Roger Ascham. He had
been Lady Jane Grey's tutor, and had left his Greek
studies and pleasant college life at Cambridge with
some reluctance, but was keenly enjoying his first
sight of foreign parts. The journey up the Rhine in
a fair barge with goodly glass windows afforded him
great pleasure. He gazed in admiration at the
castles and abbeys perched on the crags, and the
vines laden with purple grapes that grew in terraces
along the banks, while the river at Spires—" broader
a great deal than the Thames at Greenwich "—made
him realize for the first time why the Greeks wor-
shipped river-gods. In the Court chapel at Brussels
he caught a glimpse of Queen Eleanor,

" looking as fair and white as a dove in her embroidered linen robe, with her ladies clad in black
velvet with gold chains, and white plumes in their
caps, like boys rather than maidens."

[1] Guazzo, 730; Gachard, ii. 424.

Then, as he rode through Tongres, he met the
Queen of Hungary posting back from Augsburg, with
only thirty courtiers in her train, " having outridden
and wearied all the rest, and taken thirteen days to
do a journey that men can scarce do in seventeen !"
" She is a virago," the young Englishman remarked,
" never so well as when she is flinging on horseback or
hunting all day."[1] Now, at Esslingen, Ascham fell in
with another noble lady, " the Duchess of Milan and
Lorraine, daughter to the King of Denmark." Unlike
Mary of Hungary, who posted so fast that no ladies
could keep pace with her, Christina was always attended
with a large retinue. Brantôme tells us that at Court
she assumed a state which rivalled that of the Queen
of France herself. On this journey she rode a white
palfrey, and was followed by sixteen maids of honour
on horseback and four chariots filled with ladies,
escorted by a troop of 300 horse. Thirty-six mules
and a dozen waggons, laden with chamber-stuff,
brought up the rear, and a great crowd of " rascals
belonging to her kitchen and stables came drabbling
in the dirt on foot." Roger looked with admiration
at the fine horses with their rich trappings, and was
profoundly impressed by the tall stature and stately
bearing of the Duchess. " I have never seen a lady of
her port in all my life !" he exclaimed. His interest was
heightened when he heard " that she should once have
married King Henry VIII., before my Lady Anne of
Cleves," and was told that she had now been with the
Emperor at Augsburg, " where she was thought by
some to have been a-wooing to the Prince of Spain."[2]

From Esslingen, Christina had intended to go to
Heidelberg, on a visit to her sister, but the unsettled

[1] Ascham, ii. 245-257.   [2] *Ibid.*, ii. 260.

state of affairs made her presence necessary at home, and she hurried on to Nancy. The French were once more busy with preparations for war, and grew every day more insolent in their language. Even the Emperor's old ally, the Constable Montmorency, who had been recalled to Court by Henry II., joined the war party, and seemed to be as violent as the Guises. At the same time fresh trouble was brewing in Germany. The Interim had proved very unpopular. Magdeburg refused to accept the new edict, and Maurice of Saxony, who was sent against the city, carried on the siege in so half-hearted a manner that doubts of his loyalty were felt, while the Marquis Albert kept away from Court and sulked, like Achilles of old, in his tent. But the worst of all the Emperor's troubles were those which had arisen in his own family.

Granvelle confessed to Paget at Brussels that it had not been easy for Charles to obtain the recognition of his son as his successor in Flanders, and that he foresaw this would be a far harder matter in Germany. From the first, Philip's haughty manners and Spanish reserve were bitterly resented by the Princes of the Empire, and Charles realized with dismay how difficult it would be to obtain their consent to the adoption of his son as coadjutor of the King of the Romans, and his ultimate successor on the imperial throne. He had first of all to reckon with Ferdinand. This monarch had always been on the most affectionate terms with his brother, but was naturally indignant when rumours reached him, through the Marquis Albert's servants, that the Emperor intended to make Philip King of the Romans in his place. In vain his sister Mary assured him that

23

this idea had never been entertained. His resentment
was kindled, and he and King Maximilian were prepared to resist stoutly any infringement of their rights.[1]
Everyone noticed how grave and pensive Charles
appeared when he entered Augsburg, and, although
the prolonged family conferences which took place
were conducted in strict secrecy, rumour was busy
with conjecture, and the latest gossip from Augsburg
was greedily devoured at the French Court. At
this critical moment Chancellor Granvelle, who for
twenty-five years had been Charles's most trusted
Councillor, died after a few days' illness at Augsburg.
Friends and foes alike expressed their grief in the
warmest terms. The Constable wrote letters of condolence to his widow, and Charles and Ferdinand came in
person to visit Madame Nicole, but found this excellent
woman too much overcome with grief to be able to
speak. It was an irreparable loss to the Emperor,
and no one was better aware of this than himself.
" My son," he wrote to Philip, " you and I have lost
a good bed of down."[2] Granvelle's son, Antoine
Perrenot, the Bishop of Arras, succeeded him as
imperial Chancellor, but had neither his father's
wisdom nor experience, and was little fitted to cope
with the gravity of the situation.

Charles now sent for the Queen of Hungary, who
hastened to Augsburg in September; but even she
could effect little.

" Queen Mary," wrote Stroppiana, the Duke of
Savoy's Ambassador, " is here to persuade the King
of the Romans to accept the Prince of Spain as coadjutor, but finds the ground very hard, and by what
I hear can obtain nothing."[3]

[1] Bucholtz, vi. 458.   [2] Granvelle, i. 2-6, iii. 448, 451.
[3] Bulletins, etc., série 2, xii. 188.

After Mary's departure, Charles's difficulties increased every day, and Christina tried in vain to pour oil on the troubled waters. She amused Philip, and did her best to console the Emperor in his fits of profound dejection. When she was gone he turned once more to Mary, and begged her earnestly to come to his help.

" I had some hope," he wrote on the 6th of December, " that the King our nephew might be persuaded to consent to the only plan by which the greatness and stability of our house can be maintained. But, as you will see by this letter, which my brother gave me the day before yesterday, I begin to feel that my hope was vain. And I think that in this he does me great wrong, when I have done so much for him. My patience is almost at an end, and I wish with all my heart that you were here, as you can help me more than anyone else. So I beg you to hasten your coming as soon as possible, and shall await your arrival with the utmost anxiety."

To this letter, which had been dictated to his secretary, Charles added the following postscript, written with his own gouty hand:

" I can assure you, my dear sister, that I can bear no more unless I am to burst. Certainly I never felt all that the dead King of France did against me, nor all that the present one is trying to do, nor yet the affronts which the Constable puts upon us now, half as keenly as I have felt and am feeling the treatment which I have received from the King my brother. I can only pray God to grant him good-will and understanding, and give me strength and patience, in order that we may arrive at some agreement, and that, if your coming does not serve to convert him, it may at least give me some consolation.
" Your loving brother,
" CHARLES."[1]

[1] Lanz, iii. 11.

On receiving this letter, Mary started for Augsburg
without a moment's delay. Attended only by the
Bishop of Cambray and three ladies, the brave Queen
rode all the way from Binche to Augsburg in twelve
days, and arrived at five o'clock on the evening of
New Year's Day, 1551.

All through November and December the Emperor
hardly left his room. When he dined with the
Knights of the Fleece on St. Andrew's Day, the hall
was heated like a furnace, and Marillac, the French
Ambassador, remarked that he looked so old and
feeble he could not be long for this world.[1] But on
the Feast of the Three Kings he dined in public, with
his brother and sister, and his two nephews, Maximilian, who had arrived from Spain on the 10th of
December, and the young Archduke Ferdinand.
They were, to all appearances, a happy and united
family, and Stroppiana noted an evident improvement in the Emperor's spirits. Roger Ascham
watched these illustrious personages with keen interest. He describes how Charles and Ferdinand sat
under the cloth of state and ate together very hand-
somely, " his Chapel singing wonderful cunningly all
dinner-time." " The Emperor," he remarked, " hath
a good face, constant air, and looked somewhat like the
parson of Epurstone. He wore a black taffety gown,
and furred nightcap on his head, and fed well of a capon
—I have had a better from mine hostess Barnes many
times." Ferdinand he describes as " a very homely
man, gentle to be spoken to of any man," the Prince of
Spain as " not in all so wise as his father." But King
Max was Roger's favourite—" a Prince peerless " in
his eyes. He is never tired of extolling this " worthy

[1] P. de Vaissière, " Vie de Charles de Marillac," 174, 178.

gentleman, learned, wise, liberal, gentle, loved and praised of all."[1]

During the next few weeks prolonged conferences were held in the Emperor's rooms. King Max from the first flatly refused to consent to Philip's appointment as coadjutor with the King of the Romans, and the quarrel waxed hot between them. Night and day Arras went secretly to and fro with letters between Charles and Ferdinand. If the Queen of Hungary was seen leaving the King of the Romans with flushed face and flashing eyes, it was a sure sign that things were going badly for the Emperor. If Ferdinand and his sons wore a joyous air, and there were tokens of affection between them and Mary, Stroppiana and Marillac were satisfied that all was going well.[2] As for Philip and Max, it was easy to see that there was no love lost between them. They met occasionally at night in Charles's rooms and exchanged formal greetings, but never paid each other visits or attended Mass and took meals together. The rivalry between the two Princes became every day more marked.

" The King of Bohemia," writes Marillac, " is frank, gay, and fearless, and is as much beloved by the Germans as Don Philip is disliked. His Spanish education, haughty bearing, and suspicious nature, all help to make him unpopular, although to please his father he wears German clothes and tries to adopt German customs, even with regard to drink, so that two or three times he is said to have taken more than he could well carry."[3]

Nor was Philip more fortunate in his attempts to distinguish himself in the tilting. In the jousts held

[1] Ascham, ii. 268.   [2] Bulletins, série 2. xii. 188
            [3] Vaissière, 186-188.

at Candlemas, Marillac reports that all jousted badly,
but Philip worst of all, for he never broke a single
lance; and Ascham remarks that the Prince of Spain
" jousted genteelly, for he neither hurt himself, nor
his horse and spear, nor him that he ran with." He
redeemed his character to some extent, however, in
a tournament given a week later in the Queen's
honour, and succeeded in winning one prize; while the
Prince of Orange and Archduke Ferdinand were the
heroes of the day. " And as for noble Max, he ran not
at all."[1]

A few days afterwards the Diet was prorogued,
and Stroppiana told Marillac that owing to Mary's
influence a secret agreement had been framed, by
which Philip was to have a share in the administration of imperial affairs, and that, when he succeeded
his uncle as Emperor, Maximilian should become
King of the Romans. On the 10th of March an
agreement to this effect was drawn up by the Bishop
of Arras, and signed by all four Princes. On the same
day Mary gave a farewell banquet, after which Ferdinand took an affectionate farewell of his brother,
and went to Vienna with his sons.

" Noble Max," wrote Ascham, " goes to meet the
Turk. I pray God he may give him an overthrow.
He taketh with him the hearts, good-will, and prayers,
of rich and poor."[2]

On the 7th of April Mary left for Brussels, after
giving an audience to Morosyne, who saw that " she
was in the dumps," although she smiled two or three
times and tried to hide her feelings.[3] By this time
she had probably realized how fruitless all attempts

---

[1] Ascham, ii. 280; Gachard, ii. 853.   [2] Ascham, ii. 278.
[3] Calendar of State Papers, Foreign, Edward VI., i. 85.

to conciliate the German Princes would prove. The Electors unanimously declined to sanction the agreement which had been the cause of so many heart-burnings, and it remained a dead letter. The Archbishop of Treves declared that there could only be one Emperor in Germany and one sun in heaven. The Palatine, says Morosyne, like the wise old fox that he was, replied that so important a question needed time for consideration, and Joachim of Brandenburg vowed that he would never consent to a scheme which would be odious to all Germany.[1] Philip returned to Spain at the end of May, and the Emperor was reluctantly compelled to accept the inevitable, and surrender the long-cherished hope that his son would succeed to his vast empire.

VI.

While the eyes of all Europe were fixed on the imperial family at Augsburg, Christina waited anxiously for news in her palace at Nancy. She had sent two of her Italian secretaries, Innocenzo Gadio and Massimo del Pero, to wait on the Queen of Hungary, with strict orders to keep her informed of all that was happening. Gadio's cipher letters have unluckily disappeared, but some of those addressed to him by Niccolò Belloni have recently been discovered in a private library near Pavia.[2] Belloni belonged to a good Milanese family, and had, at his parents' entreaty, been retained by the Duchess in her service

[1] Bucholtz, vi. 467.

[2] These extracts from manuscripts preserved in the Biblioteca of Zelada, near Pavia, are published by the kind permission of their owner, Count Antonio Cavagna-Sangiuliani.

when she left Italy. He had succeeded Benedetto da Corte as master of her household, and followed Christina to Lorraine. Niccolò enjoyed his mistress's complete confidence, and his letters to Messer Innocenzo reveal all that was passing in her mind at this critical moment. On the 2nd of January, 1551, he writes:

" HONOURED FRIEND,
   " Madame's page arrived a few days ago with your letters, which were most anxiously expected and gratefully read by Her Excellency. The next morning she received those which came by Heidelberg, and yesterday those which you sent by the Flemish servant, which gave Her Excellency still greater pleasure. She deciphered them herself, and read them over several times. You will continue to write as before, and I will tell you all I hear from other quarters. Do not fail to report every detail of the difficulties which are delaying the negotiations, using Madame's ordinary cipher for this purpose. . . . I send this messenger by the post to seek for news, so do not keep him at Augsburg more than a day, even if Monsignore d'Arras's letter is not ready, as another courier will be sent in four or five days. I have received Don Ferrante's letters, and should be glad to know if my letters for Fanzoni and Trissino are gone to Milan. Tell Signor Badoër [the Venetian Ambassador] that I will not fail to satisfy his curiosity, but it will take some time to obtain the desired information and will require great caution. . . . Send me some fine writing-paper, please —very fine, I repeat, because it is for Madame."

Christina's Milanese servants evidently carried on a correspondence with their friends at home through the imperial messengers who were sent from Augsburg to the Viceroy, and the Princess of Macedonia constantly despatched packets to Milan and Mantua by the same channel, while the Duchess herself often wrote to Don Ferrante regarding the payment of her

dowry and questions affecting the city of Tortona.
A week later Christina sent a Lorraine gentleman,
Monsieur de Saint-Hilaire, to convey her salutations
to the King of Bohemia, on his arrival at Augsburg,
and Belloni took this opportunity to beg Gadio to be
diligent in reporting everything he heard, for Madame's
benefit, assuring him that Her Excellency read his
letters again and again, and believed implicitly in
their contents. On the 12th of February he repeated
the same orders:

" It would be well if you would write fuller particulars of the great matter in hand, above all whatever you hear of the angry disputes and quarrels which
have arisen between the Prince and the King of
Bohemia, including all the bad language which they
use—in fact, everything that is said on the subject.
It will all be treated as strictly confidential, and I for
my part know that the King will not be governed by
the Prince, and will use rude and contemptuous words,
as you may imagine ! These are the things that Her
Highness wishes to learn from your letters. . . . I may
possibly take a flight to the Court of France, so, if you
wish to write to me privately, address your letters to
the Princess of Macedonia, who will keep them safely
for me, especially if they come from Italy. Your
letters of the 29th of January and 3rd of this month
have arrived, and are, as usual, most welcome, and
Her Excellency agrees with you that nothing has
really been arranged. Once the business for which
you were sent to Augsburg is settled, Her Excellency
thinks you may as well return, and be sure that you
bring plenty of letters for Her Excellency from all the
world, and a whole waggon-load of news ! I am sorry
to hear that your horse has hurt his foot and you
have had to sell him cheap. You must procure
another, and Madame will pay for it all. Only let us
have the truth about these negotiations !"

But the Duchess changed her mind again, and Innocenzo was desired to stay at Augsburg as long as the

Queen was there, even if the King and his sons had left, in order that she might hear all that her aunt had to tell of these important matters. Niccolò's last letter to Augsburg is dated the 13th of March, and contains a reminder to Gadio to bring the writing-paper for Madame, and to make inquiries about a new method of coining money at the Imperial Court, which had excited the Princess of Macedonia's curiosity.[1] The flight to the French Court which Niccolò meditated in March, 1551, was taken in the company of the Count of Vaudemont, who went to Blois to pay his respects to the King and Queen, and discover if there were any truth in the sinister report that Henry II. was planning the conquest of Lorraine. But he only met with civil speeches, and found the Court on the eve of a journey to Brittany, to meet the Dowager Queen of Scotland, who was coming over to see her child and visit her aged mother at Joinville. So the Count was able to allay his sister-in-law's alarms, and, instead of the dreaded threats of invasion, brought back a proposal from the King that her son should be affianced to one of his little daughters. The offer excited some surprise, considering the strained relations that existed between Henry II. and Charles V., but Christina returned a courteous reply, and promised to lay the matter before the States of Lorraine.[2] For the present she felt that she could breathe freely and give herself up unreservedly to the enjoyment of a visit which she was expecting from her sister Dorothea.

Since the restoration of peace in Germany, the Elector Palatine had devoted his time and money to the im-

[1] Manuscript vii., Biblioteca di Zelada.
[2] Calendar of State Papers, Foreign, Edward VI., i. 79; Granvelle, iii. 522.

provement of his ancestral castle at Heidelberg. His
natural love of building found expression in the noble
Renaissance court, with the lovely oriel and grand
Hall of Mirrors, where we may still read " Frau
Dorothea's " name, and the arms of the Three Kingdoms by the side of the Palatine's lion and the badge
of the Golden Fleece. But the passion for travel and
adventure was still strong in the old Palsgrave's
breast, and when the last stone had been placed on the
lofty bell-tower he and his wife set out, with a great
company of courtiers and ladies, for Lorraine. They
sailed down the Rhine to Coblenz, and, taking horse,
rode through Treves and Metz, where Christina met
them, and the whole party proceeded to Pont-à-
Mousson and the Count of Vaudemont's castle at
Noményy. Here they attended the christening of the
Countess's daughter, and Frederic stood sponsor, while
his wife was proxy for the French Queen, after whom
the child was named. After a week of festivities, the
party went on to a hunt at Condé, the Duke's fair
château in the forest on the banks of the Moselle, and
killed five stags. Hubert, who accompanied his
master and gives every detail of the journey, relates
how the Palatine, tired with the day's sport, accepted
a seat in the Duchess's chariot, and how his companion, Count Jacob von Busch, being a big man,
weighed down the carriage on one side, much to the
amusement of Dorothea, who laughed till the tears
ran down her cheeks. But heavy rains had made
the roads almost impassable, and presently the wheels
caught in a rut and the chariot was upset. The ladies
were covered with mud, and Dorothea's face was
badly scratched; but she made light of the accident,
and only laughed the more as, leaving the lumbering

coach in the ditch, they mounted horses to ride to
Nancy. At the gates of the city they were met by the
young Duke Charles, a handsome boy of eight, who
lifted his cap with charming grace, and, springing to the
ground, embraced his uncle and aunt, and rode at their
side, conversing in a way that amazed the Germans.

" We all wondered," writes Hubert, " at the beauty
and wisdom of the boy, who is indeed remarkably
intelligent, and has been trained by his lady mother
in all knowledge and courtesy."[1]

His sisters, Renée and Dorothea, received the guests
at the palace gates, " both lovely little maidens," says
Hubert, " only that the youngest is lame and cannot
walk, for which cause her uncle and aunt embraced
her the more tenderly." All the fatigues of the journey
were forgotten in the delights of the week which the
travellers spent at Nancy. The Duchess prepared a
new pastime for each day, and masques, jousts, and
dances, followed each other in gay succession. On the
last day Christina took her guests to the beautiful
grassy vale known as the Ochsenthal. It was a lovely
May morning, and a banquet was served in a green
bower on the banks of the stream. Suddenly a merry
blast of bugles rang out, and, while huntsmen and dogs
chased the deer, two parties of horse galloped up, and,
charging each other, crossed swords and fired guns. " It
might have been an invasion of the Moors !" exclaims
Hubert, who enjoyed the surprise as much as anyone.
At sunset the warriors returned to the palace, where
the fairest maidens of the Duchess's Court crowned
the victors with roses, and danced with them till
morning. The next day Frederic and Dorothea made
the Duchess and her children and servants handsome

[1] Hubertus Thomas, 464.

presents of gold chains and rings and brooches, and
Christina, not to be outdone, gave Hubert a massive
silver tankard, begging him to keep it in remembrance
of her, and continue to serve the Palatine and her
sister as well in the future as he had done in the past.
After this we need not wonder at the glowing pages in
which the honest secretary praises the delicacy of the
viands, the choice flavour of the wines set before the
guests, and the polished manners of the Court of Nancy.

" Indeed," he adds, " some of our Germans complained that there was too little beer, because people
here do not sit up drinking all night, and go to bed
like pigs, as we do at Heidelberg."[1]

The young Duke and his sisters accompanied the
guests to Lunéville, where they spent Whitsuntide
together and took their leave, the little ladies shedding
many tears at parting from their aunt. Even then
Christina could not tear herself from her sister, and the
next day, as the Palatine and his wife were dining at
one of the Duke's country-houses on their route, the
Duchess suddenly appeared, riding up the hill. Hubert
and his comrades ran out to welcome her, waving
green boughs in their hands, and greeted her with
ringing cheers, and they all sat down to a merry meal.
Dorothea begged her sister to accompany her to
Alsace; but the Duchess could not leave home, and
the travellers pushed on that night to Strasburg, and
on the 1st of June reached Heidelberg, where they
were greeted by a gay peal of bells from the new-built
tower. It was the last visit that either Frederic or his
wife ever paid to Lorraine. When the sisters met again,
Christina was an exile and a fugitive, and had lost son
and home, together with all that she loved best on earth.

[1] Hubertus Thomas, 467; L. Haüsser, i. 625.

BOOK X

THE FRENCH INVASION

1551—1553

I.

MICHAELMAS DAY, 1551, was memorable, both in France and Germany, for a snowstorm of extraordinary severity, followed by an alarming earthquake and violent tempest, omens, as it proved, of impending disasters.

In this same month of September, Henry II. recalled his Ambassador from Augsburg. Ten days later he declared war. For some time past he had been supporting Ottavio Farnese, who was in open revolt against his father-in-law, and carrying on secret intrigues with Maurice of Saxony and the Protestant Electors. The Marquis Albert had never forgiven the Emperor for the affronts of which he imagined himself to be the victim, and, after vainly offering his sword to the English King and his hand to Princess Mary, he went to France as Maurice's emissary. Here he concluded a secret treaty, which was signed at Friedewald on the 5th of October by the German Princes, and ratified at Chambord by Henry II.[1]

Charles's affairs were in a critical state. The war

[1] Granvelle, iii. 630; Henne, ix. 162; T. Juste, 185.

354

of Parma was a heavy drain on his resources, and had swallowed up the gold of Mexico and the best Spanish soldiers, while Maurice's treachery had converted the strongest body of imperial *Landsknechten* into foes.

"The Emperor doth little yet," wrote Roger Ascham from Augsburg, "but the French be a great deal aforehand. He is wise enough, but hath many irons in the fire, and everyone alone to give him work enough, the Turk by land and sea, the French sitting on his skirts, beside Magdeburg and the rest."[1]

The discontent in Augsburg rose to the highest pitch when, one day in September, ten preachers were summarily banished. The imperial residence was besieged by crowds of furious women, clamouring to have their babes christened, and guards were doubled at every gate, while Charles sat within, enfeebled by gout and reluctant to face the coming peril.

In vain Mary of Hungary warned him of Maurice and Albert's intrigues with France, and told him that his incredulity was like to cost him very dear, and that if he did not take care he would lose, not only Germany, but also the Netherlands, which were not the meanest feather in his cap. Both he and Arras refused to listen. Instead of following his sister's advice and remaining at Worms or Spires to control Germany and protect Lorraine, Charles lingered on at Augsburg after war was declared, and persisted in taking refuge at Innsbruck. After protracted delays, he at length left Augsburg on the 21st of October, dragging the reluctant Ambassadors in his train, and crossed "the cold Alps, already," sighed Ascham, "full of snow," to descend on Tyrol.[2]

---

[1] Ascham, ii. 313; Papiers d'État, viii., Archives du Royaume, Bruxelles.   [2] Lanz, iii. 75; Granvelle, iii. 527.

Meanwhile his niece was watching the course of events with increasing anxiety. All the French King's fine promises could not allay Christina's fears, as the autumn months went by, and the din of warlike preparations sounded louder in her ears. In her terror she clung to the Guises, hoping that their influence might save her son and his realm from ruin. On the 20th of July she went to Joinville to meet the Dowager Queen of Scotland and stand proxy for Queen Catherine at the christening of Francis of Guise's daughter, afterwards the notorious Duchess of Montpensier. When, in October, the young Duke of Longueville died suddenly, on the eve of his mother's departure, Christina once more went to condole with Antoinette on the loss of her " Benjamin."[1] Both she and Anne, who came to Nancy at her earnest request, were full of sympathy for the venerable Duchess in the trials that clouded her declining years. A fresh proof of Christina's anxiety to gratify her powerful relatives appears in a letter which she wrote to her uncle from Pont-à-Mousson on the 28th of October, begging him to grant a request of the Cardinal regarding the Abbey of Gorzes, which he had lately annexed to his vast possessions.

" I could not refuse this petition," she adds, " as my Lord Cardinal is so near of kin to my children, and has always treated me and my son with so much kindness and affection. And I humbly beg Your Majesty to show him favour, in order that he may see that I do all that is possible to please him and his house."[2]

As the year drew to its close, the insolence of the French increased, and their incursions and depredations

[1] Pimodan, 375, 381.
[2] Lettres des Seigneurs, iii. 104, Archives du Royaume, Bruxelles.

were a perpetual source of annoyance to the people of Lorraine. At the same time their intrigues fomented discontent among the nobles, some of whom were annoyed at the appointment of Monsieur de Montbardon to be the young Duke's tutor. This French Baron had originally followed the Constable of Bourbon into exile, and, after being for many years in the Emperor's service, had by his wish accompanied Christina to Lorraine. And both the Regents had good reason to doubt the loyalty of one of the Lorraine magnates, Jean de Salm, a son of the late Marshal, commonly known as the Rhinegrave, who had lately received the Order of St. Michel from Henry II. All Christina could do in this critical state of affairs was to keep Mary of Hungary and the Emperor fully informed of current events.

On the 7th of January the Sieur de Tassigny, an agent whom the Queen had sent to Nancy, received a command from a Court page to come to the Duchess's rooms that night, in order that she might tell him certain things which she dared not write. Tassigny obeyed the summons, and had a long talk with Christina in the privacy of her own chamber. She told him that the French were assembling in great force on the frontier, and that Lorraine would be the first country to be attacked. And she further informed him that certain great personages in Germany, the Marquis Albert, Duke Maurice, and others, were in secret communication with the King, and were about to take up arms against the Emperor, and join the French when they crossed the Rhine. The Rhinegrave had been often seen going to and fro in disguise between the King and Duke Maurice. Moreover, a German had lately told the Duchess that he had been

24

at table with the Elector the day before, and had heard him vow that he would release his father-in-law, the captive Landgrave of Hesse, were he at the Emperor's own side ! When another guest warned Duke Maurice to be more careful, lest his rash words should be repeated, he replied defiantly: " What I say here is meant for all the world to hear."

This confidential conversation was faithfully reported to Mary of Hungary by Tassigny, who concluded his letter with the following words:

" *En somme*, Madame complains that she is in a terrible position, seeing that Lorraine will be entirely at the mercy of the French, and that there is not a single person in whom she can trust and who is loyal to His Imperial Majesty, excepting Monsieur de Bassompierre, her chief Councillor, and Monsieur de Vaudemont, who is quite alienated from France, and entirely devoted to the Emperor, saying that it is impossible to serve two masters."[1]

By Christina's wish, Tassigny went on to Nomény the next day, and had a long interview with Vaudemont, who assured him that every word spoken by Her Excellency was true, that at Candlemas there would be a great revolt in Germany, and that the French King meant to seize the three bishoprics— Toul, Verdun, and Metz. The only way to prevent this would be for the Emperor to place strong garrisons in these cities, and thus defeat his enemies' plans. The Count's information, as time showed, was perfectly accurate, and, in spite of all that has been alleged to the contrary, he was probably loyal to the Duchess, who never doubted his honesty, and to whom he seems to have been sincerely attached. But he was timid

---

[1] Lettres des Seigneurs, iii. 90.

and vacillating, and lacked courage and firmness to
face the crisis when it came.

Mary, to whom Christina turned in this extremity,
was powerless to help. Every available man was
needed to defend the Low Countries, and she could
only advise her niece to claim the protection of the
Empire for her son's State, and, if Lorraine were
actually invaded, retire with her children to the Palatinate. Even Charles began to wake up from his
lethargy, and to realize too late that Mary had been
right all the time. At Christmas Stroppiana wrote
from Innsbruck:

" We begin to suspect the existence of a plot against
the Emperor, hidden under the cloak of a military
revolt. Maurice is not a stranger to this conspiracy,
and Albert has let his soldiers loose and is ravaging
Germany."[1]

A few weeks later Christina's secretary, who kept
Arras informed of all that was happening in Lorraine,
sent the Emperor a message to say that the King was
collecting his forces at Châlons, and that Maurice was
marching on Augsburg at the head of his *Landsknechten*,
although no one knew whether he meant to fight for
the King or the Emperor.[2]

On the 5th of February Henry issued a manifesto,
stamped with the cap of liberty, proclaiming himself
the protector of the Germans and their deliverer from
the Emperor's yoke, and, after solemnly invoking
St. Denis's help, set out for Reims with the Queen and
Dauphin. The gilded youth of France all flocked to
the camp at Châlons, eager to start on the *voyage
d'Austrasie*, as the expedition was termed by these

[1] Bulletins, etc., série 2, xii. 189.
[2] Lettres des Seigneurs, iv. 108 ; Granvelle, iii. 613.

gay spirits, and drive Charles of Austria out of Germany. The Constable was appointed to the chief command, Aumale was made Captain of the horse, and the Rhinegrave Colonel of the German infantry.

As soon as the news reached Nancy, the Duchess sent Bassompierre to Brussels, and told the Queen that terror reigned everywhere, although it was doubtful if Henry would march on Germany or turn aside to invade Lorraine. The alarm which filled the hearts of these two defenceless women is reflected in the letters which Anne and Christina wrote during these anxious days. The wildest rumours were abroad, and death and ruin seemed to be staring them in the face. Bassompierre soon returned with a letter from Mary, thanking Anne for her valuable information, and begging her not to desert the sorely-tried Duchess at this crisis. Since Madame was good enough to honour her with her commands, Anne asked nothing better than to obey. She wrote daily to Brussels, giving minute details of the King's advance. On the 15th of March he left Reims, and reached Joinville on the 22nd. From here he sent Commissioners to Nancy to inform the Duchess that her towns would not be attacked, and that there was no need to fortify them. The Regents only raised a sufficient body of men under the Governor of Nancy, Baron d'Haussonville, to protect the Duke's person. Following her aunt's advice, Christina sent one of her secretaries to Innsbruck to ask the Emperor for assistance; but Charles could only lament his inability to come to her help, and advise her to ask the French King to respect the neutrality of Lorraine. This was her only hope, and, encouraged by the Cardinal of Guise,

she and Anne went to Joinville on the 1st of April,
and sought an audience from the King.[1]

Here they were received in the kindest manner
by the old Duchess, and conducted into Henry's
presence by the Constable. The King received them
courteously, and conversed some time with them in
a friendly manner. Christina begged him to take her
son under his protection, and reminded him that his
grandmother, Renée de Bourbon, was a Princess of
the blood royal; then, gathering courage, she told him
that she had been accused of designs against him by
slanderous tongues, and asked nothing better than to
show that she was absolutely innocent of these charges.
" So great a lady," remarked the Sieur de Rabutin,
who witnessed the interview, " must have been very
reluctant to plead so humbly, and I doubt if she would
ever have taken a step so contrary to her natural
inclination if her uncle had been able to give her
help."[2] The King listened civilly, and replied that
he bore her no ill-will whatsoever, but was obliged to
secure the frontier and protect himself from danger on
the side of Lorraine. As for her son, he cherished
the most friendly feelings for him, and was anxious to
see him affianced to his own daughter, if the Duchess
were agreeable. This kind language and the
affection shown her by the Cardinal and his mother
relieved Christina's worst fears. She begged the
King to do her the honour of staying under her roof
if he came in that direction, and returned to Nancy
with the Constable, who escorted the two Duchesses
home, in the most amiable fashion, and then went
on to take possession of Toul.

[1] Lettres des Seigneurs, iv. 42, 108.
[2] Calmet, ii. 1290; F. de Rabutin, " Collection de Mémoires,"
xxxvii. 185.

On her return, Christina wrote the following letter to the Emperor:

> " MONSEIGNEUR,
>   " I have been to Joinville in accordance with Your Majesty's advice, and have sent full particulars of my interview with the King to Monsieur d'Arras. I beg you, Monseigneur, to give me your commands as to my future conduct, as my only wish is to obey Your Majesty to the end of my life.
>   " Your very humble and very obedient niece,
>   " CHRESTIENNE.
> " From Nancy, April 5, 1552."[1]

A few days of anxious suspense followed. The French Queen fell ill of quinsy, and was in danger of her life. Solemn prayers and litanies were chanted for her recovery in all the churches, and Diane of Poitiers hastened to Joinville, where she found the King " playing the good husband at his wife's bedside."[2]   But by Palm Sunday Catherine recovered sufficiently for Henry to leave her in the charge of Duchess Antoinette and continue his march. On Monday, the 11th of April, he joined the Constable before Toul, which opened its gates the next day. On the 13th the King left the bulk of the army to go on to Metz with the Constable, and, taking the household cavalry and a few companies of men-at-arms under the Duke of Guise, turned his steps towards Nancy.

II.

Eastertide, 1552, was a sad and memorable epoch in the annals of Lorraine. At two o'clock on Maundy Thursday, Henry II. entered Nancy at the head of

    [1] Lettres des Seigneurs, iv. 19.
    [2] A. de Ruble, " La Jeunesse de Marie Stuart," 73.

his troops, with trumpets blowing and banners flying. For the first time in the last hundred years, foreign soldiers were seen within the walls of Nancy. The Cardinal and the Duke of Guise rode on before, to inform the Duchess of the King's coming and see that due arrangements were made for his reception. Christina nerved herself for a final effort, and with splendid courage prepared to welcome the enemy of her race within her palace gates. Salutes were fired from the bastions as the King entered the town, and the young Duke rode out to meet him at the head of the nobles and magistrates, and escorted him to the church of St. Georges. Here Henry alighted, and the citizens held a canopy of state over him as he entered the ancient shrine of the Lorraine Princes, and, after kissing the relics of the saints on the altar steps, prayed by the tomb of King René. Then the young Duke led him through the stately portal, under his grandfather's equestrian statue, to the hall where his mother was waiting to receive her royal guest, with the Duchess of Aerschot and the young Princesses. Henry, the Duke of Guise, the Cardinal, the Marshal St. André, and 200 gentlemen of the royal household, were sumptuously lodged in the ducal palace, while the troops were quartered in the town, and French guards were stationed at the gates, not without a protest from Baron d'Hausson-ville.[1]

That evening the Duchess entertained her guests at a magnificent banquet in the Galerie des Cerfs, and the brilliantly-lighted hall, with its vaulted fret-work of blue and gold, frescoed walls, and rich tapestries, excited the admiration of all the French.

[1] Calmet, ii. 1199.

François de Rabutin, the young Captain in Monsieur de Nevers's corps of archers, walked through the streets of the " fine, strong little town," lost in wonder at the splendour of the palace, the prosperity of the citizens, and their affection for the ducal family. More than all he was struck by the young Duke himself, who appeared to him " the handsomest and cleverest boy in the world," and who evidently made the same impression on the King. Henry paid the Duchess many compliments on her son's good looks and intelligence, and expressed so much pleasure at his reception that her worst alarms were allayed. Late in the same evening she wrote a letter to her aunt, telling her of the kind expressions used by His Majesty, and of her hopes that all might yet be well. But a rude awakening was in store for her. Early on Good Friday morning Vaudemont appeared at the door of her room with consternation written on his face. The King had sent him to inform the Duchess that her son was to leave Nancy the next day for Bar, in charge of one of the King's captains, while she was deprived of all share in the government, which was henceforth to be administered by Vaudemont as sole Regent. On receiving this unexpected message, Christina hastily summoned as many members of the Council as could be brought together, and with their help and her brother-in-law's support, drew up a protest couched in respectful and dignified language, reminding the King of the terms of the late Duke's will, and of her own rights both as mother and Regent. Henry's only reply to this appeal was to send the Duchess a copy of the agreement to which she was expected to conform. It was as follows:

PALAIS DUCAL, NANCY (1627)

" The Duke is to start to-morrow for Bar before
the King leaves Nancy. His mother may accompany
him, or go elsewhere, if she prefers. She may retain
the administration of her son's property, but will no
longer have any authority over the fortresses in Lorraine. All subjects of the Emperor who hold any
office in the government or in the Duke's household
are commanded to leave Lorraine without delay. A
French garrison of 600 men will be left in Nancy under
Monsieur de Thou, but Monsieur de Vaudemont will
remain Governor of the city, and take an oath to observe the conditions laid down by the King. A French
garrison of 300 men will also be placed in Stenay
under the Sieur de Parroy."[1]

These hard conditions filled Christina with dismay.
She begged the Cardinal to defend her rights, but he
could only advise her to submit to the inevitable.
Both he and Francis of Guise have often been blamed
for not opposing Henry II.'s arbitrary proceedings,
but there seems little doubt that the King originally
intended to reduce Lorraine from the rank of an independent State to that of a fief of the Crown, and
that it was only the opposition of the Guises which
saved the duchy from this fate. In her despair
Christina made a last attempt to soften the King's
heart. Clad in her black robes and flowing white
veil, she entered the Galerie des Cerfs, where Henry
and his courtiers were assembled, and, throwing
herself on her knees at the King's feet, implored
him, for the love of Christ who died on the cross
that day, to have pity upon an unhappy mother.
The sight of her distress, and the touching words
in which she begged the King to take everything
else, but allow her to keep her son, moved all
hearts, and there was not a dry eye in the whole

[1] Lettres des Seigneurs, iv. 101, f. 320.

assembly. Even Henry was filled with compassion, and, raising the Duchess from her knees, he assured her that he only wished to confirm the friendship between the two houses. Far from intending any harm to the young Duke, he proposed to bring him up with his children, and to treat him as if he were his own son, but Lorraine was too near the frontiers of Germany, and too much exposed to attacks from his enemies, for him to be able to leave the boy there. With these consoling words, he took the weeping Duchess by the hand and led her to the doors of the gallery, but, as Anne afterwards told the Queen of Hungary, the King vouchsafed no reply to her sister's entreaty that she might not be deprived of her boy, and Christina's prayer remained unanswered.[1]

Early the next morning Vaudemont and the Councillors renewed their oaths of allegiance to Duke Charles III., after which the young Prince left Nancy in charge of the French captain Bourdillon and an escort of fifty men-at-arms. The parting between the Duchess and her son was heartrending. The poor mother gave way to passionate tears, in which she was joined not only by Vaudemont and Anne, but by all the nobles and people who had assembled at the palace gates to see the last of their beloved Duke. Nothing but the sound of weeping and lamentation was to be heard, and Rabutin, with all his hatred of the House of Austria, was filled with compassion at the sight of the Duchess's grief.

On Easter Day Christina wrote the following letter

---

[1] Calmet, ii. 1300; Pfister, ii. 188; Brantôme, xii. 110; Lettres des Seigneurs, iv. 101; Ravold, iii. 780.

to her aunt, enclosing a copy of the articles drawn up
by the French King:

" MADAME,
    " The extreme grief and distress which the
King's violence has caused me prevents me from
writing to you as fully as the occasion requires; but
I must tell you what has happened since my last
letter, in which I told you of the King's arrival.
Now, in reward for the good cheer which I made him,
he has carried off my son by force, with a violence
which could not have been greater if I had been a
slave. Not content with this, he has deprived me
of the chief part of my authority, so that I can hardly
remain here with honour and reputation, and, what
is worse, I shall no longer have the power of doing
Your Majesty service, which is one of my greatest
regrets. Have pity, Madame, on a poor mother,
whose son has been torn from her arms, as you will
see more fully by this copy of the King's final resolutions, which he has sent me in writing. These have
been carried out in every particular. Before he left, my
brother, Monsieur de Vaudemont, and all the members
of the Council, except myself, were made to take an
oath, pledging themselves to defend the strong places
in this land against all his enemies, and to open their
gates to him whenever required. The same oath was
taken by the garrison who are to guard this town,
and I was asked to give up the keys of the postern
gate. So that I, who was first here, and could once
serve Your Majesty, am now deprived of all power,
and am little better than a slave. I foresee that I
shall soon be stripped of everything, in spite of the
treaties and agreements formerly made between Your
Majesties and this State. This ill-treatment and the
evident wish shown by the French that I should
leave this house have made me decide to retire to
Blamont, where I will await Your Majesty's advice
as to my future action. . . . I must warn Your
Majesty, with regard to Stenay, that the new Captain,
Sieur du Parroy, although of Lorraine birth, belongs
to the King's household, and is devoted to French
interests, as is also the second in command. Madame,

I have written all this to the Emperor, but he is so
far away and in so remote a place that I felt I must
also tell Your Majesty what had happened here,
begging her humbly to let me know her good pleasure.
"Your humble and obedient niece,
"CHRESTIENNE.
"Nancy, April 17, 1552."[1]

The letter which Anne addressed to the Queen the
next day is still more graphic in the details it supplies:

"I cannot help writing to inform you, Madame, of
the utter desolation and misery to which my poor
sister is reduced owing to the great rudeness and
cruelty with which she was treated by the King of
France on Good Friday. He came here under pretence of good faith and true friendship, as he had
lately given us to understand. On his arrival he
was received with all possible honour and entertained
in the most hospitable manner. On Good Friday
he told Madame that, in order to satisfy the conditions
of his league with the Germans, he must secure all
the fortified posts in Lorraine, as well as the Duke's
person, and with this end must take him to Bar. In
order to prevent this, Madame, Monsieur de Vaudemont
and I, with all the members of the Council, drew up
a remonstrance couched in the most humble terms,
to which he only replied by sending us a written copy
of his resolutions. Upon this my sister went to find
him in the Grande Galerie, and begged him humbly,
even going as far as to fall on her knees to implore
him, for the love of God, not to take her son away
from her. He made no reply, and, to make an end
of the story, Madame, on Easter Eve they took the
boy, escorted by a band of armed men, in charge of
the Sieur de Bourdillon and the Maréchal de St.
André, who did not leave his side until he had seen
him well out of the town. It was indeed a piteous
thing to see his poor mother, Monsieur de Vaudemont,
and all the nobles and this poor people, in tears
and lamentation at his departure. Madame, Your
Majesty can imagine the terrible grief of my poor

---

[1] Lettres des Seigneurs, iv. 101, f. 320.

sister at this outrage, and will understand that her
sorrow at losing her son is still so great that I have
been obliged to abandon my intention of returning
home, and feel that I cannot leave her. The King
allows her to keep the charge of her daughters and
the administration of her children's estates, excepting in the case of the fortified towns, which remain in
the hands of Monsieur de Vaudemont.... And since,
Madame, I am still as ever very anxious to do Your
Majesty service, I beg you to lay your commands
upon me, and they will be obeyed by one who is the
most affectionate servant that Your Majesty will ever
have.
                                " ANNE DE LORRAINE.
"From Nancy, the day after Easter,
              April 18."[1]

In a postscript Anne further informed Mary that
her sister had just received a letter from the King,
telling her that, hearing an attempt would be made
to carry off the young Duke, he had ordered Bourdillon to take him to join the Queen at Joinville.
Henry's letter was written from Pont-à-Mousson,
where he spent Easter Day, after sleeping at the
Duke's country-house at Condé on Saturday:

" MY SISTER,
        " After leaving you I received warnings from
several quarters that the Burgundians were going to
make an attempt to surprise Bar and carry off my
cousin, the Duke of Lorraine; and as I am anxious to
prevent this, I ordered Monsieur de Bourdillon to take
him straight to Joinville, which is sufficiently remote
to escape this danger, and where both you and he would
be quite at home in his own family. And you will
find good company there and be given the best of
cheer, just as if I were there myself. I hope, my
sister, that this may be agreeable to you, and that
you will believe that my anxiety for his person is

[1] Lettres des Seigneurs, iv. 101, f. 330 (see Appendix).

the reason why I wish to avoid any risk of injury, which would be a cause of grave displeasure to those who love him, as you and I do. Farewell, my sister, and may God have you in His holy keeping.

" Your good brother,
" HENRY.

" Written at Pont-à-Mousson,
April 17, 1552."[1]

The tone of the letter was kind. Henry had evidently been touched by Christina's distress, and tried to soften the blow. Fortunately, the little Duke himself was too young to realize the meaning of these startling events. The ride to Joinville and the welcome which he received from the kind old Duchess amused him, but at bedtime he missed the familiar faces, and asked for his mother and tutor, Monsieur de Montbardon. When he was told that they had stayed at Nancy, the poor child burst into incontrollable sobs, and refused to be comforted.[2]

III.

The invasion of Lorraine and the harsh treatment which the Duchess suffered at the French King's hands were keenly resented by her imperial relatives. Mary wrote indignantly to Charles at Innsbruck, complaining justly of Henry's violation of the neutrality of Lorraine and of the young Duke's[3] capture. To Christina herself she expressed her anger at the King's wicked act, at the same time advising her to bow to the storm and retire to Blamont for the present. This the Duchess did three days after her son's departure, taking the two Princesses as well as her

---

[1] Lettres des Seigneurs, iv. 101, f. 319.
[2] Bulletins de la Commission d'Histoire, série 2, xii. 213.
[3] Bucholtz, ix. 539.

faithful sister-in-law. Anne's pen was never idle, and on the following Sunday—that of *Pâques-fleuries*—she sent the Queen a list of all the Princes who were members of the League. But they had not been many days at Blamont, when their peace was disturbed by the arrival of the French King and the Constable, who, after taking possession of Metz, marched through the Vosges on their way to Strasburg, and took up their quarters in the castle. The Duchesses left hurriedly to avoid another meeting with the King, and moved to Denœuvre, where they remained during the next three months. But the strain of recent events had been too much for Christina's strength; she became seriously ill, and her condition was a grave cause of anxiety to Anne and her ladies.

Count Stroppiana, who heard the details of the French invasion from Belloni's own lips at Innsbruck, wrote the following account of the Duchess's wrongs to his master, the Duke of Savoy:

" The King of France, we hear, has occupied Lorraine, and sent the young Duke to Châlons, guarded by 100 men-at-arms, contrary to the promises which he made to the Duchess his mother. She threw herself at his feet, imploring him not to rob her of her son, her only joy and consolation, without whom she could not bear to live, with many other words which would have moved the hardest heart to pity. The King would not listen, and repulsed her with many rough words, forbidding any of the Emperor's subjects to remain in her service on pain of death. He has deprived her of the Regency, and relegated her to a remote country place, where she does nothing but weep and lament, and will certainly die before long, if her great sorrow is not comforted, as she has been ill for some time past. The poor little Duke is said to be ill, too. When he reached the first stage of his journey, he asked for his mother and tutor, and, when he did not see them, wept so bitterly that it was impossible to comfort him."[1]

The boy's tears were soon dried, and he recovered his spirits in the charge of the Duke of Longueville's old tutor, Jean de la Brousse, and the companionship of the royal children. His mother remained long inconsolable for his loss, but the affection of her son's subjects was her best solace. So earnest were their entreaties that she should remain among them that she declined her aunt's urgent invitation to take refuge in Flanders, and decided to stay at Denœuvre. On the 31st of May she wrote as follows to inform the Emperor of her intention:

" MONSEIGNEUR,
    " At the prayer of my brother Monsieur de Vaudemont, and my sister the Duchess of Aerschot, and the earnest desire of my good people, I have been bold enough to remain here, although Your Majesty had sent me orders to join the Queens. I trust you will not take this in bad part, but will understand that I have only done this at the urgent prayer of my brother and sister, and not out of disrespect to your command, since my sole desire is to obey you all my life, and I beg you to believe this and remember my son and his poor country.
        " Your humble niece and servant,
                        " CHRESTIENNE.
    " From Denœuvre, May 31, 1552."[2]

This letter found the Emperor at the lowest depth of his fortunes. On the 19th of May he was carried in his litter by torchlight over the Brenner in torrents of driving rain, and hardly paused till he arrived at Villach in Carinthia. A few hours after he left Inns-

---

[1] Bulletins, etc., série 2, xii. 213.
[2] Lettres des Seigneurs, iv. 102, f. 127 (see Appendix) ; Lanz, iii. 208.

bruck, Maurice and his troopers entered the town, plundered the Emperor's quarters, and robbed the baggage which had been forgotten in his hasty departure. The victor might easily have captured the fugitive Emperor, but, as Maurice said himself, he had no cage for so fine a bird.

The tide, however, was already turning. Strasburg closed her gates against the French invaders, and early in May an Imperial army attacked Champagne and sent Queen Catherine flying in terror from Reims. Alarmed by these reports, Henry beat a hasty retreat, and contented himself with the empty boast that he had watered his horses in the Rhine. The seat of the war was now transferred to Luxembourg, and Lorraine was once more harassed by the outposts of the two contending armies. From their safe retreat at Denœuvre, Christina and Anne watched the course of the campaign anxiously, and kept up a constant correspondence with Mary of Hungary. The bold measure of placing an Imperialist garrison in Nancy was now proposed by the Duchess, and gladly accepted by her uncle, who realized the advantages of the scheme, and wrote that Lorraine might well be occupied, on the ground of the Duke's detention, and would be restored to him as soon as he was released.[1] Early in July, Christina's trusted servant, Bassompierre, the Bailiff of the Vosges, arrived at Denœuvre with a message from Vaudemont, promising to admit the Imperialist force within the gates of Nancy on condition that the occupation was only temporary. The Duchess promptly sent a lackey to Flanders with a cipher letter to inform the Queen of his consent. But, as ill-luck would have it,

[1] Bucholtz, ix. 543; Bulletins, 2, xii. 191.

the servant fell into the hands of the French, who were besieging Luxembourg, and he was brought before the King and forced to confess the object of his errand. Henry was furious at discovering the plot, and sent a gentleman of his household, Monsieur de Rostain, to Denœuvre, with a letter to the Duchess, saying that he feared her attachment to the Emperor was greater than her maternal love, and desired her to leave Lorraine without delay. Christina sent one of her gentlemen, Monsieur de Doulans, back with Rostain to protest against this order, saying that, after robbing her of her son and depriving her of the Regency, the King would surely not be so cruel as to drive her out of her own dower-house, especially as Denœuvre was a fief of the Empire. But these passionate appeals availed her little. A week later Henry sent another gentleman, Monsieur de Fontaine, to order the Duchess to leave Denœuvre immediately, if she did not wish to feel the full weight of his displeasure. This time the messenger had orders not to return to the King's presence until he had seen the Duchess across the frontier. So with a heavy heart the two Princesses left the land of Lorraine, where they were both so fondly beloved, and took refuge in Alsace. Belloni, who sent the Queen an account of his mistress's latest troubles in his clear Italian handwriting, was desired to tell her aunt that the Duchess had many more things of importance to say, but must wait for a more convenient season. Only one thing she must add, and this was that through all Monsieur de Vaudemont had remained perfectly true and loyal to her, although he was compelled by his office to conform outwardly to the French King's tyranny.[1]

[1] Lettres des Seigneurs, vii. 603.

On receiving this bad news, Mary sent to beg her niece to come to Flanders without delay, promising the Duchess a home for herself and her little daughters. Unfortunately, as Christina found, this was no easy task. Not only was the whole countryside in peril of daily attacks from the French, but the Marquis Albert had descended like a whirlwind from the Suabian hills, and was spreading terror and destruction along the banks of the Rhine. The next letter which she addressed to her aunt from the imperial city of Schlettstadt, where she had sought refuge, gives vent to these alarms:

" MADAME,
        " I received the kind and loving letter which Your Majesty was so good as to send me on the 6th of August. It came at the right moment, for I can assure you that I was sorely troubled, but Your Majesty's kindness in saying that I shall be welcome has done me so much good that I feel I do not know how to thank you enough, and am only sorry I cannot set out at once. For the roads are very dangerous, above all for children. . . . Your Majesty will understand how distressed I shall be until I can find some way of coming to you, and certainly one year will seem to me a hundred, until I am with Your Majesty once more."[1]

This grateful letter was written from Schlettstadt on the 22nd of August, and sent to Brussels by Niccolò Belloni, the only messenger whom Christina felt that she could trust. But fresh trouble awaited her in this direction. Belloni reached Flanders safely, and came back to Lorraine with letters to the Count and Countess of Vaudemont, but disappeared in some mysterious manner two days after he reached

[1] Lettres des Seigneurs, iv. 103, f. 348.

Nancy. It seems doubtful whether he died of the plague, as Massimo del Pero wrote to his friend Innocenzo Gadio, or whether he fell into some ambush and was slain by the enemy's hand. The loss was a great one to the Duchess, whom he had served so faithfully and well for the past sixteen years, and the honest Milanese was lamented by all his colleagues. Innocenzo Gadio, sent the sad news to the Princess of Macedonia's daughter, Dejanira, the wife of Count Gaspare Trivulzio, who had formerly received Christina in his castle at Codogno. The Countess expressed her sympathy with her dearest Messer Innocenzo in the warmest terms.

" I am sure," she wrote, " that the death of so beloved a friend will cause my mother the greatest sorrow. When you return to Lorraine," she adds, " please kiss Her Excellency's hands for me, and tell her that the sufferings which she has undergone in those parts grieve me to the bottom of my soul; and tell her too that we, her servants in this country, shall always be ready to risk our lives and all that we have in her service."

"Dejanira, Contessa Trivulzio.

"From Codogno, September 29, 1552."[1]

There were still faithful hearts in this far-off land who never forgot the Duchess whom they had known in early youth, and who followed her fortunes with tender sympathy and affection.

But now help came to the sorely-tried Princess from an unexpected quarter. The Marquis Albert had haughtily declined to take any part in the conference that was being held at Passau between King Ferdinand and Maurice of Saxony, or to be included in the treaty which was signed between the Emperor

[1] Manuscript 18, Biblioteca Cavagna Sangiuliani, Zelada (see Appendix).

and the Elector on the 15th of August. Instead of
laying down his arms, he chose to continue his reckless course, and marched through the Rhineland
plundering towns and burning villages, " making
war," wrote an eyewitness, " as if he were the devil
himself."[1] But when he reached Treves he heard of
the Duchess's expulsion from Lorraine and her distressed condition, and, with a touch of the old chivalry
that made him dear to women, he promptly sent to
offer her shelter in his castle of Hoh-Königsberg, the
strongest and finest citadel in the Vosges. Christina
accepted the offer gratefully, and during the next
few weeks the red sandstone fortress which still
crowns the heights above Schlettstadt became her
abode. She was there still when the Emperor made
his way from Augsburg to the banks of the Rhine,
at the head of a formidable army.

On the 7th of September he entered Strasburg; on
the 15th he crossed the river and encamped at
Landau. A week before he sent one of his bravest
Burgundian captains, Ferry de Carondelet, to visit
her at Hoh-Königsberg and invite her to visit him
in the camp.[2] Christina obeyed the summons joyfully, and a few days after the Emperor reached Landau she and Anne of Aerschot made their way by
the Rhine to the imperial camp. The Prince of Piedmont rode out to meet them, and Anne's kinsfolk,
Egmont and D'Arenberg joined with Emanuel
Philibert and Ferrante Gonzaga in welcoming the
distressed ladies and condoling with them on the
terrors and hardships which they had undergone.
Only one thing grieved Christina. The Emperor firmly
refused to admit her trusted Councillor, Bassompierre,

[1] Lettres des Seigneurs, iv. 518 (see Appendix). [2] Ibid., iv. 103.

into his presence, being convinced that he had betrayed his mistress and played into the French King's hands. Nothing that she could say altered his opinion in this respect, and she thought it wiser to send the Bailiff to Nancy, where he was able to watch over her interests and send reports to the Queen of Hungary.[1]

Charles was suffering from gout and fever, and Christina was shocked to see his altered appearance. The fatigues and anxieties of the last few months had left their mark upon him. His face was pale and worn, his hands thin and bloodless, and he spoke with difficulty owing to the soreness of his mouth and the leaf which he kept between his lips to relieve their dryness. Only his eyes kept the old fire, and no one could divine the thoughts which lay hidden under the mask-like face. As Morosyne wrote after an interview which he had with the Emperor about this time: " He maketh me think of Solomon's saying: ' Heaven is high, the earth is deep, and a king's heart is unsearchable.' "[2] But he was full of kindness for Christina, telling her that she and her children would always find a home at Brussels. Since, however, her cousin of Guise had entrenched himself in Metz and the country round was swarming with soldiery, he advised her to remain at Heidelberg for the present.

The Duchess obeyed this advice and retired to her brother-in-law's Court. The Palatine was growing old, his beard had turned white and his strength began to fail, but his influence was as great as ever in Germany. Morosyne, who met him at Spires, pro-

[1] Bulletins de la Commission d'Histoire, série 2, xii. 232; Lettres des Seigneurs, iv. 518.
[2] "Hardwicke Papers," i. 55.

nounced him to be the wisest and best of all the
Electors, and was touched by the affection with which
he spoke of the late King Henry VIII., declaring that
his shirt never lay so near his skin as King Edward's
noble father lay near his heart. The Ambassador's
secretary, Roger Ascham, made friends with Hubert,
who sent him long dissertations on the pronuncia-
tion of Greek, and invited him to Heidelberg. Now
Frederic and his wife welcomed the Duchess and her
children with their wonted hospitality, and insisted
on keeping them until the end of the year; but Christina's heart was with her poor subjects, who suffered
severely from the ravages of the war. From Nancy,
Bassompierre sent word that the Marquis Albert had
suddenly deserted his French allies, and had captured
Aumale and carried him in triumph to the imperial
camp before Metz.[1]

Here, on the 20th of November, Charles came face
to face with the man who had wronged him so deeply.
" God knows what I feel," he wrote to Mary, " at
having to make friends with the Marquis Albert, but
necessity knows no law."[2]   At least, he accepted the
situation with a good grace. Morosyne was present
when the Emperor came riding into the camp on a
great white horse of Naples breed, and, seeing Albert,
took his hand with a gracious smile, and shook it
warmly twice or thrice.

" The Marquis fixed his eyes fast on the Emperor's
countenance, as one that meant to see what thoughts
his looks betrayed. When he saw that all was well,
or at least could not see but all seemed well, he spake
a few words, which His Majesty seemed to take in
very good part."

[1] Calendar of State Papers, Foreign, Edward VI., 230.
[2] Lanz, iii. 513.

Calling a page to his side, he took a red scarf, the Imperialist badge, from his hands, and gave it to the Marquis. Albert received it with deep reverence, saying that he had not fared badly when he wore these colours before, and trusted the Emperor's gift would bring him the same good fortune as of old.[1] The return of the wanderer saved Charles from utter ruin. His affairs were still going badly. Vieilleville, the French Governor of Verdun, seized the boats laden with provisions for the imperial camp, which Christina had sent down the Rhine, and laid violent hands on six waggons of choice fruits, wines, and cakes, which were despatched from Nancy for her uncle's table. Worse than this, he contrived to enter Pont-à-Mousson, which Fabrizio Colonna held, disguised as a messenger from the Duchess, and obtained possession of this important place by stratagem.[2] The valour of Guise and the strong fortifications of Metz were proof against the reckless courage of Albert and the might of the imperial army. The heavy rains and biting cold of an early winter increased the sufferings of the troops, and, after losing half his army by famine and dysentery, Charles was compelled to raise the siege at the New Year. " Fortune is a woman," he remarked to one of his captains; " she abandons the old, and keeps her smiles for young men."[3]   In this forced retreat the Marquis performed prodigies of valour, and succeeded in bringing his guns safely over roads rendered impassable by a sudden thaw. The bulk of the army was dismissed, only the veteran Spanish and German

---

[1] Voigt, ii. 9, 10; P. F. Tytler, " England under Edward VI.,'' 144.

[2] Vieilleville, 161, 176.   [3] Calmet, ii. 338.

forces being quartered in Artois and Luxembourg, and Charles himself set out for Brussels. His failing strength compelled him to halt on the way, and Morosyne gave it as his opinion that the Emperor would never reach the end of his journey alive. But his spirit was indomitable as ever, and on Sunday, the 6th of February, he entered Brussels in an open litter, amid scenes of the wildest enthusiasm.

" To-day," wrote the Ambassador of Savoy, " I have witnessed the safe arrival of the Emperor. He was received with the greatest transports of joy and delight by the whole people, who feared that he was dead and that they would never see him again."

And Charles himself wrote to Ferdinand that, now he was once more in his native land and in the company of his beloved sisters, he would soon recover his health.[1]

[1] Bulletins, etc., série 2, xii. 238; State Papers, Edward VI., Foreign, 236, 243; Lanz, iii. 542.

BOOK XI

CHRISTINA AT BRUSSELS

1553—1559

I.

CHRISTINA was at Brussels on the memorable day when the Emperor set foot once more on his native soil. She heard the shouts of joy which rent the air, and joined with the Queens in the welcome which greeted him on the threshold of his palace. Early in January she had left Heidelberg and travelled safely down the Rhine and through the friendly states of her Cleves cousins to Brussels. Here she occupied the suite of rooms where she had lived before her second marriage, and to a large extent resumed her former habits. She spent much of her time with her aunts and the Duchess of Aerschot, and renewed her old friendship with Countess d'Arenberg and other ladies of the Court. The deepest sympathy was felt for her by all classes, and when Charles addressed the States-General on the 13th of February, and alluded to the treachery of the French in carrying off the young Duke of Lorraine and driving his mother out of the realm, his words provoked an outburst of tumultuous indignation.[1]

Through her brother-in-law Vaudemont she still

[1] Henne, x. 13.

382

maintained close relations with Lorraine, while the Cardinal kept her informed of all that concerned her son, and the boy's own letters satisfied her that he was well and happy at the French Court. But although Charles shared all the advantages enjoyed by the King's children, and soon became a general favourite in the royal family, it was bitter for the Duchess to feel that her only son was growing up, in a foreign land, among the hereditary foes of her race. The restoration of peace between Charles and Henry was the only means by which she could hope to recover her lost child, and this became the goal of all her efforts during the six years that she spent in exile.

The Widow of Milan had been courted by Kings and Princes, and hardly was Christina settled at Brussels before she was assailed by fresh offers of marriage. Henry, King of Navarre, whose accomplished wife had died soon after her daughter's marriage, asked the Emperor for his niece's hand, but his proposals met with small favour. Far more serious was the courtship of Albert of Brandenburg, who felt this to be a favourable moment for renewing his old suit. " No one," as Thomas Hoby wrote, " had done the Emperor worthier or more faithful service " in the siege of Metz, and was better entitled to reward. His claims were strongly supported by the Palatine, who invited the Marquis to Heidelberg to confer with the other German Princes on the best means of recovering Metz. Albert himself not only aspired to the Duchess's hand, but to the Duke of Alva's post of Commander-in-Chief, and boasted that once Christina was his bride he would easily recover her father's kingdoms.

" It is supposed," wrote Morosyne from Brussels
on the 20th of February, " that the Marquis will
marry the Duchess of Lorraine and have Alva's place.
The Palsgrave would fain it were so, in order that, if
the Marquis married his wife's sister, he might help
him to recover Denmark; for besides that a slender
title is apt to set such a one to work, he should, by
being married to the Emperor's niece, and afterwards
coming, when his uncle died, to the duchy of Prussia,
be able easily to trouble Denmark. The Marquis
doth much desire it, for that the Duke of Holstein has
been and is a great suitor to the Duchess, who was
once so nigh marrying the Marquis Albert's sister that
the contracts were drawn up and put into writing, but
broke it off upon sight of the Duchess of Lorraine.
The Palsgrave would rather any did marry with her
than the Duke of Holstein, for that his brother, King
Christian, keeps his wife's father in prison. And the
Emperor, it is held certain, will help it, in order that
he may by this means trouble Denmark, which he has
never had leisure to trouble himself."[1]

Whatever her relatives may have thought of the
Marquis's suit, Christina herself never considered it
seriously, and told the Palatine plainly that such a
marriage was out of the question. The Marquis
vented his anger on the Emperor, and left Heidelberg
in high displeasure, without taking leave of the Palatine or anyone else. Hot words passed between him
and Maurice, and these two Princes, who had once been
the closest friends, were henceforth bitter enemies.
Albert returned to his life of raids and plunder,
and when, soon afterwards, he was placed under
the ban of the Empire, Maurice led an army against
him. A fiercely-contested battle was fought on the
9th of July at Sievershausen, in which Albert was
completely routed and Maurice lost his life. The

[1] Calendar of the Manuscripts of the Marquis of Salisbury,
i. 110; Lodge, " Illustrations," i. 183.

Marquis was deprived of fortune and patrimony, his ancestral home of Plassenburg was burnt to the ground, and after leading a roving life for some years, and wandering from one Court to another, he died in the house of his brother-in-law, the Margrave of Baden, on the 8th of January, 1557. So in exile and poverty this brave and brilliant adventurer ended his career, before he had completed his thirty-fifth year.[1]

While the Palatine was holding vain conferences at Heidelberg, and the Marquis and Duke Adolf were still quarrelling for the Duchess's hand, she herself was endeavouring to open negotiations with the French King through Bassompierre and Vaudemont. But nothing would induce Henry to give up Metz, and in April war was renewed with fresh vigour. The young Prince of Piedmont, who succeeded the unpopular Alva in command of the imperial army, won a series of victories, and razed the forts of Thérouenne and Hesdin to the ground. But the Emperor was too ill to take part in the campaign or even to give audiences. Sir Philip Hoby, who now succeeded Morosyne, actually believed him to be dead, until De Courrières came to dine with his English friends, and assured them, on his honour as a gentleman, that he had seen the Emperor alive that morning.[2] Upon this Sir Philip's brother Thomas, who had just arrived from Paris, where he had been spending the winter in translating Castiglione's " Cortegiano," was sent to see his old Augsburg friend, the Bishop of Arras, and beg for an audience. At length, on the 8th of June, the Englishmen were admitted into the privy chamber, and found the Emperor sitting up, with his

---

[1] Voigt, ii. 207.
[2] Calendar of State Papers, Edward VI., Foreign, 282.

feet on a stool, " very pale, weak, and lean, but nothing so ill as they had believed." His eye was lively, his speech sensible, and his manner very friendly and agreeable. But, although he expressed an earnest wish for peace, he declared that the French demands made this quite impossible.[1]

A month later an unexpected event produced a change in the Emperor's fortunes. King Edward VI. died, and, after a vain attempt on Northumberland's part to set Lady Jane Grey on the throne, Catherine of Aragon's daughter Mary succeeded peaceably to the throne. Her accession was hailed with joy at the Imperial Court, and on the Feast of St. Bartholomew the Regent celebrated the event by giving a banquet, to which the English Ambassadors were invited. " It was such a dinner," writes Hoby, " as we had seldom seen in all our lives, and greater good cheer or entertainment than Her Grace gave us could not be devised." Mary was in high spirits that evening. She toasted the Ambassadors, conversed with them after dinner for more than an hour, and told Morosyne laughingly that his French could not be worse than her Italian. Sir Philip sat next to the Duchess of Lorraine, and reminded her of the memorable morning, fifteen years before, when he brought the German Court painter to take her portrait.[2] Since then much had happened. King Henry himself, the great painter Holbein, René of Orange, and Francis of Lorraine, were all gone, and she had lost home and state and had seen her only son snatched from her arms. Yet she was still beautiful and fascinating, and counted

---

[1] " Travail and Life of Sir T. Hoby," 85; Calendar of State Papers, Edward VI., Foreign, 288.

[2] Calendar of State Papers, Mary, Foreign, 8; T. Hoby, 102.

almost as many suitors as of old. Adolf of Holstein wooed her with a constancy which no coldness could repel, and if the wild Marquis had been forced to renounce all hope of winning her hand, another hero, the young Prince of Piedmont, was ready to lay his laurels at her feet. But Christina remained the same, calm and unmoved, and was an interested and amused spectator of the matrimonial plans which now formed the all-absorbing topic in the family conclave.

Charles quickly realized the importance of securing the new Queen's hand for his son. As soon as he heard of Edward's death, he sent orders to his Ambassador at Lisbon to delay drawing up the marriage contract which had been agreed upon between Philip and Eleanor's daughter, Maria of Portugal, and wrote to his son, setting forth the superior advantages of the English alliance. Philip replied dutifully that, as his cousin the Queen was twelve years older than himself, his father would be a more suitable husband, but added that he was ready to obey the Emperor's will in all respects.[1]

On the 20th of September Charles wrote from Valenciennes, where he was directing military operations from his litter, to the English Queen. After explaining that he was too old and infirm to think of marriage, and had solemnly vowed after the Empress's death never to take a second wife, he offered her the dearest thing he had in life—his own son. He then proceeded to point out the great advantages of the proposed union, while at the same time he advised Mary to observe the utmost caution, being " well aware of the hatred with which the English, more than any other nation, regard foreigners." Mary's own

[1] Granvelle, iv. 113, 119.

mind was soon made up. In spite of protests from her subjects and remonstrances from the French King, she was determined to marry her cousin. On the 30th of October she sent for the Imperial Envoy, Renard, and, kneeling down before the Blessed Sacrament in her chapel, she said the *Veni Creator*, and took a solemn vow to wed the Prince of Spain.[1]

The most friendly letters were now exchanged between the two Courts. The holy chrism for Mary's coronation was sent from Brussels, with venison and wild-boar for her table. Charles gave his future daughter magnificent tapestries and jewels, and Mary of Hungary sent the Queen a yet more precious gift, Titian's portrait of Philip, telling her that, if she stands at some distance from the canvas, it will give her a good idea of the Prince, only that he is older and more bearded than he was when the artist painted it three years ago. The Regent took care to add that she could only lend the Queen the picture on condition that it should be returned "when the living man joined her." In reply, Mary begged her good aunt to pay her a visit; but the Regent excused herself, owing to the Emperor's ill-health, and promised to come and see her later on, it might be in the Prince's company. The same cordial invitation was extended to the Duchess of Lorraine, who sent her new *maître d'hôtel*, Baron De Silliers, to London in April, 1554, to congratulate the Queen on her marriage. Mary made Christina a present of a fine diamond, which De Courrières was desired to give her, and when, on the 20th of July, Philip landed at Southampton, and the wedding was celebrated in Winchester Cathedral, the happy spouse sent costly jewels to the Emperor and

[1] Mignet, " Retraite de Charles V.," 69, 70.

the two Queens, and a beautiful emerald to her dear cousin the Duchess.

In January Cardinal Pole, the Papal Legate, came to the monastery of Diligam, near Brussels, with proposals of peace from the Pope, on his way to congratulate Queen Mary on her accession, and help to restore Catholic rites in the kingdom. Pole was known to be averse to the Spanish marriage, and Charles had put every obstacle in the way of his journey to England. On his arrival he gave him a very cold reception, and the Cardinal complained to the Pope that the Emperor and Arras could not have used greater violence, unless they had taken a stick to drive him back.[1] The Regent and the Duchess of Lorraine, however, were much more friendly when he dined with them the next day, after attending Mass in the royal chapel. Mary told him that no one wished for peace more earnestly than herself, seeing how terribly her poor people of the Netherlands had suffered from the war, and Christina spoke to him of her son with tears in her eyes. When the Cardinal went on to Fontainebleau, he saw the young Duke, and was able to give him his mother's messages. But he found Henry II. still less amenable than Charles, and returned to Brussels convinced that his mission was a failure as far as the hope of peace was concerned.

Before the end of April the French King invaded Hainault, at the head of a large army, and took the strong citadel of Marienburg. Namur was only saved by the promptitude of Charles, who once more took the field, although he could no longer mount a horse, and showed all his old courage in this his last cam-

[1] M. Haile, " Life of Reginald Pole," 432.

26

paign. After an indecisive battle at Renty, the French retired with heavy loss, spreading famine and desolation in their track. One act of vandalism for which Henry was condemned, even by his own captains, was the destruction of Mary of Hungary's beautiful palace of Binche, with its famous gardens and treasures of art. The Queen received the news with equanimity, saying that she was proud of being the object of the French King's vindictiveness, and glad the world should know that she was the Emperor's devoted servant.

" As for the damage which has been done," she wrote to Arras, " I do not care a straw. I am not the woman to grieve over the loss of things transitory, which we are meant to enjoy as long as we have them, and do without when they are gone. That, upon my word, is all the regret I feel."[1]

In the autumn Christina made another fruitless attempt to open negotiations through Vaudemont, who after the death of his first wife, Margaret of Egmont, was induced by the Cardinal of Lorraine to marry the Duke of Nemours's daughter. This Prince came to Brussels in November to inform the Emperor and the Duchess of his marriage, and, as might be expected, met with a very cold reception at Court. But, in spite of his French alliance, he remained scrupulously loyal to Christina and her son, and complained to his sister Anne that at Brussels he was reproached for his French sympathies, while in Paris he was looked on with suspicion as an Imperialist. So hard was it to be an honest man in those troublous times.[2]

[1] Henne, x. 132; F. Juste, "Marie de Hongrie," 204.
[2] Granvelle, iv. 307; Venetian Transcript, Record Office, 99.

II.

While the war dragged on its weary course, and Mary and Christina vainly tried to bring it to an end, on the other side of the Channel the new King of England and his spouse were holding high festival. They came to London in September, and remained there through the winter, trying to win the love of their subjects by a series of popular displays and festivities. Tournaments were held at Whitehall, hunting-parties were given at Windsor and Hampton Court, and a succession of distinguished guests travelled from Flanders to pay homage to the royal pair. Philip's favourite, Ruy Gomez, and the Duke and Duchess of Alva, arrived from Spain, Ferrante Gonzaga, the Prince of Orange, and the Grand Equerry Boussu, came over from Antwerp during the autumn.[1] On the 20th of November Cardinal Pole at length crossed the Channel ; four days later he was received at Whitehall by the King and Queen in person, and crossed the river in the royal barge, to take possession of his own house at Lambeth. He was soon followed by Emanuel Philibert, who had lately succeeded to the barren title of Duke of Savoy on his father's death, and had been made a Knight of the Garter. Earlier in the summer he had paid a brief visit to London, where his white, red, and green banners of Savoy made a fine show in the Abbey on St. Peter's Day; but as his military duties rendered his presence in Flanders imperative, his Ambassador, Stroppiana, came to Windsor in October,

[1] Gachard, iv. 19.

to be invested with the Garter[1] as proxy for his master.

It was not till Christmas Eve that the Duke himself landed at Dover, after a very rough passage, and made his way to Whitehall, where Philip and Mary received him with great honour, and showed him all the sights of London. On the 7th of January the Lord High Admiral took him by water to see the great guns at the Tower, and on St. Paul's Day he accompanied the King and the Cardinal in state to the Cathedral for the patronal feast. A procession of 160 priests bearing crosses, walked round the churchyard, with the children of Paul's School and the Greyfriars, singing " Salve, Festa Dies !" and passed in through the great west doors. After Mass a state banquet was held, with great ringing of bells, and bonfires blazed in all the streets of London throughout the night.[2]

Emanuel Philibert's visit revived the rumour of a marriage between him and the Princess Elizabeth, which the Emperor had suggested some months before. Whether from policy or genuine regard, Philip had espoused his sister-in-law's cause and refused to allow Mary to send her abroad or keep her away from Court. The Duke of Savoy was a pleasant and good-looking Prince, whose martial appearance and genial manners made him very popular in England. But Elizabeth herself quite declined to listen to this proposal, saying that she would never marry a foreigner, and, since there now seemed good hope of the birth of an heir to the crown, the question of the succession was no longer of the first importance. Something,

[1] Ashmole, " The Order of the Garter," 383.
[2] Machyn, " Diary," 66, 79, 81.

however, must be done to pacify the Duke, who complained bitterly of the Emperor's neglect, and, seeing little chance of recovering Savoy, asked the King for the viceroyalty of Milan, which Ferrante Gonzaga, on his part, refused to surrender. Philip could think of no better plan to gratify his cousin and retain his services than to give him the hand of the Duchess of Lorraine, a Princess whom he was known to regard with great affection.[1]

Accordingly the King and Queen sent pressing invitations to Christina, begging her to come to England as soon as possible. Before she could comply with their request, she had to keep an old engagement to be present at the christening of Count Egmont's infant daughter, which took place on the evening of the 19th of January. The Queen of England had graciously consented to be one of the godmothers, while the Duchess of Lorraine was the other, and the Palatine Frederic stood godfather to his kinswoman's little daughter. Mary wrote to the Duchess of Aerschot, begging Anne to represent her on this occasion, and sent a costly gold cup containing forty angels to her godchild by the new Ambassador, Sir John Masone. The Palsgrave, not to be outdone, sent the child a diamond cross, and another one, set with rubies, diamonds, and emeralds, to the mother. Anne and Christina were both present at the christening, which was attended by all the Court, " everything," wrote Masone, " being very richly ordered, the supper and banquet right stately, and Her Majesty's cup so walked up and down, from man to woman, and woman to man, as I dare answer few were there that did not go full freighted to bed."

[1] Granvelle, iv. 341; F. de Noailles, " Ambassades," v. 42.

Sir John further told the Countess in what good part her request to make her daughter a Christian woman had been taken by his royal mistress, who would willingly have done the same in person, had the distance not been so great, and Sabina sent her most humble thanks to the Queen, saying that, as she already had one daughter called Mary, she had decided to name the infant Mary Christina, after her two godmothers.[1]

When this function was over, Christina began to prepare for her journey to England, but the weather was so tempestuous that she did not cross the Channel until the first days of March. She rode from Dover, by way of Canterbury, to London, where the King and Queen received her in the most cordial manner, Philip made no secret of his affection for his cousin, the only woman in his family with whom he had ever been intimate, and Mary, in the first flush of her wedded happiness and in the proud expectation of soon being a mother, welcomed Christina warmly. Unluckily, we have no particulars of the Duchess's visit to this country, over which she might have reigned herself as Queen. We know that she was present with the rest of the Court at the great joust held on Lady Day in the tilting-yard at Whitehall, when Philip and a band of knights, armed with falchions and targets, and clad in blue and yellow, rode out against two other troops in red and green, and some 200 lances were broken.[2] But the only record that we have of this her first visit to England is a letter which she wrote to Mary on returning to Flanders. She thanked the Queen for the great

1 Calendar of State Papers, Mary, Foreign, 150.
2 Machyn, 82, 84.

honour and kindness which she had shown her, and commended the captain of the ship in which she sailed, who, as Her Majesty would doubtless learn, had rendered her notable service on this troublesome passage:

" I will say no more," she adds, " except to regret that I am no longer in Your Majesty's presence to be able to render you some small service in return for all the goodness which I have received at your hands. I beg God, Madame, to send you good health and long life, and give you a fine boy, such as you desire.

" Your very humble and obedient cousin
and servant,
" CHRESTIENNE.

"A la Royne."[1]

This letter bears no date, but the Duchess certainly left London before the King and Queen went to Hampton Court on the 4th of April, to spend Easter and prepare for the happy event which all England was anxiously expecting. She was at Antwerp with her aunt a month later, when, on the 3rd of May, " great news came over the seas." A messenger from the English ships in the port brought the Regent word that the Queen of England had been " brought to bed of a young Prince," upon which all the guns in the harbour were fired, and Mary ordered the big bells in the Tower to be rung, and sent the English sailors a hundred crowns to drink the royal infant's health. " I trust in God," wrote Sir Thomas Gresham, " that the news is true." The Emperor was more incredulous, and summoned Masone to his bedside at 5 a.m. the next morning, to know what

---

[1] Record Office Manuscripts; State Papers, Foreign, vi. 351 (see Appendix).

he thought of the matter, but soon satisfied himself that the news was false.[1]

The Savoy marriage, which Philip was so anxious to bring about, also ended in smoke. During Christina's visit, the matter was brought forward and eagerly urged both by the King and Queen. Charles was no less anxious for the marriage, and Mary of Hungary proposed to appoint the Duke, Governor of the Low Countries when she resigned the office. The plan would have been very popular in Flanders, where the Duchess was beloved by all classes, and was warmly supported by Egmont and Orange. On the 1st of May, Badoer, the Venetian Ambassador at Brussels, announced that the marriage contract had already been drawn up by De Praet, and that the Duke had started for Italy, disguised as a German, and only attended by one servant, to arrange his affairs in Piedmont before the wedding.[2]

The Venetian's news was apparently premature, but a fortnight later a Piedmontese noble, Count Avignano, came to London to consult Philip as to the marriage and arrange further details on his master's behalf. He talked freely at table to the French and Venetian Ambassadors, Noailles and Michieli, saying that the Emperor had offered his master the government of the Netherlands with the hand of Madame de Lorraine, an arrangement which he for his part regretted, thinking that the Duke would be more likely to recover his dominions if he married in France. But, since the friendship between

---

[1] Venetian Calendar, vi. 1, 69; Calendar of State Papers, Mary, Foreign 165; J. W. Burgon, " Life of Sir Thomas Gresham," i. 168.

[2] Record Office Manuscripts, Venetian Transcripts, 1555, No. 99.

his lord and the Duchess was so great, he saw no hope of any other alliance, and the marriage was, in fact, considered by the Emperor and all his family to be practically settled.[1]

Emanuel Philibert, like many others, evidently felt the power of Christina's fascination, and enjoyed a large share of her intimacy. But he does not seem to have shown any great eagerness for the marriage, whether it was that, as Avignano said, it would be a bar to the recovery of his States, or whether he recognized the Duchess's own insuperable objection to matrimony.

When, towards the end of May, a party of English Commissioners met the French and Imperial deputies at Marck, a village near Calais, to treat of peace, an offer was made by the French to give Henry II's. sister Margaret to the Duke of Savoy. The Imperial deputies expressed a doubt if this were possible, as the Duke's word was already pledged; but Cardinal Pole replied that the Prince was quite free, and ready to agree to any proposal by which he could recover his realm. These negotiations, however, were soon broken off, and on Philip's return to Brussels in September the old scheme of the Lorraine marriage was revived with fresh ardour. When the Duke of Savoy returned from Italy in August, the Regent made him attend the meetings of the Council, and treated him in all ways as her future successor, hoping by this means to obtain his consent to her wishes. But both Emanuel Philibert and Christina remained of the same mind, and neither Philip's entreaties nor Mary of Hungary's angry reproaches could alter their resolution. The Duke pleaded poverty as an excuse,

[1] Noailles, v. 74, 80; Venetian Calendar, vi. 1, 151.

lamenting his inability to offer his wife a home and
station worthy of her rank, and was evidently determined to sacrifice his affections to political ex-
pediency, although, as the French Ambassador reported, " he still made love through the window to
Madame de Lorraine."[1]

III.

Charles V.'s intention to abdicate his throne had
long been declared. For many years he had looked
forward to the time when he should lay down the
burden of public affairs and retire from the world, to
end his days in some peaceful cloister. The increasing infirmities under which he groaned, his
inability to attend either camp or council, and finally
the death of his mother, Queen Joanna, in April,
1555, all helped to hasten the execution of his resolve.
Only the continuation of the war and the absence
of his son still made him hesitate.

The same indecisive warfare as before was carried
on through the year. The Prince of Orange, who
now held the chief command, succeeded in keeping
the foe at bay, and built the citadels of Charlemont
and Philippeville for the defence of the frontier.
But everyone was heartily tired of the campaign,
and both parties gladly availed themselves of the
opportunity afforded by an exchange of prisoners,
to renew negotiations in the autumn. Christina
once more exerted herself in this direction, and
Vaudemont, who came to Brussels in October to
take leave of the Emperor, was employed to make

[1] Noailles, v. 191; Venetian Calendar, vi. 1, 211; P. Friedmann,
" Les Dépêches de Michieli," 42.

fresh overtures to the French King. But many
months passed before any conclusion was reached.[1]
Charles had always hoped that his sister would
remain at her post when he left the Netherlands,
feeling how invaluable her help would prove to Philip.
But Mary was inflexible on this point. In a noble
letter which she wrote at the end of August, she
reminded him that fifteen years before she had begged
to be released from her arduous post in order to
devote herself to the care of her unhappy mother,
and that, now this privilege could no longer be hers,
she wished to spend the rest of her life in Spain with
her sister, Queen Eleanor.

" And however great," she adds significantly, " my
affection for the King my nephew may be," in
Badoer's graphic phrase, " he hates and is hated by
her "—" Your Majesty will understand that at my
age it would be very hard to begin learning my ABC
over again. A woman of fifty, who has held office
twenty-four years, ought, it seems to me, to be content
to serve one God and one Master for the rest of her
life."[2]

There was nothing more to be said, and Charles
agreed to Philip's wish that for the present the Duke
of Savoy should be appointed Lieutenant-Governor
of the Low Countries. At length Philip succeeded
in tearing himself from the arms of his sorrowful
Queen, promising to be back in a fortnight or three
weeks. From her palace windows at Greenwich,
Mary waved her last farewells to the King, as he
sailed down the Thames. He for his part was nothing
loth to leave his fretful and melancholy wife, and
was satisfied that she would never bear him a child.

[1] Calendar of State Papers, Mary, Foreign, 189.
[2] Granvelle, iv 469.

On the 8th of September he reached Brussels, and went straight to see his father in the Casino, near the Louvain gate of the park, where he was spending the hot weather. Charles embraced his son tenderly, and after an hour's conversation Philip went on to sup with Queen Mary and Christina on their return from hunting. On the 17th and 18th he attended the Requiem Masses held in S. Gudule for the late Queen Joanna, and afterwards joined in a grand hunting-party given by the Regent in his honour.

The nobles now flocked to Brussels to be present at the Emperor's abdication. The Prince of Orange arrived from the camp near Liége, and his young wife, Anne of Egmont, was hospitably entertained by the Duchess of Aerschot. Friday, the 25th of October, was the day fixed for the great ceremony. On this afternoon, at three o'clock, the Emperor left the Casino with Philip and the Duke of Savoy, and rode to the palace on his mule. An hour later he entered the great hall, hung with the tapestries of Gideon's Fleece, wearing his mourning robes and the collar of the Order, and leaning on the Prince of Orange's arm. He was followed by Mary of Hungary, Philip, and the Duke of Savoy, who took their places on the daïs at the Emperor's side, while the Knights of the Fleece, the great nobles and Ambassadors, occupied seats below. The deputies, over a thousand in number, who thronged the hall, rose to their feet to receive the Emperor, and then sat down to hear the chief Councillor, Philibert of Brussels, deliver a speech, explaining the reasons for His Majesty's abdication. Then Charles himself addressed the vast assembly. In moving words he recalled the day, forty years before, when, a boy of fifteen, he had been declared of age by his grandfather, the Emperor Maximilian, and glanced briefly at the long record of wars and journeys, and the other chief events of his reign. Finally he commended his successor to them, asking them to serve his son as well as they had served him, and begging his loyal subjects to pardon him for any injustice which he might unwittingly have done them. Tears rolled down the great Emperor's cheeks as he spoke these last words, and Sir Thomas Gresham, who was present, says that there was not a dry eye in the whole assembly.

Christina was present on this memorable occasion. In contemporary prints she is represented standing by the side of the Regent's chair, listening with breathless attention to every word that fell from her uncle's lips. She saw the pathetic scene between the father and son, when Charles, raising Philip from his knees and clasping him in his arms, gave him the investiture of the Provinces, and, turning to the deputies, in a broken voice asked them to excuse his tears, which flowed for love of them. And she listened with still greater emotion to the touching words in which Mary begged the Emperor and the States to forgive whatever mistakes she had made out of ignorance or incapacity, and thanked them from the depth of her heart for their unfailing love and loyalty. Her speech produced a fresh burst of tears, after which Charles thanked his sister for her long and faithful services, and Maes, the Pensionary of Antwerp, bore eloquent testimony to the undying love and gratitude which the States felt for the Queen who had governed them so well.

There were still many formalities to be gone through, many farewells to be said, before Charles could lay down the sovereign power. On the day after his abdication, the Archduke Ferdinand, his favourite nephew, arrived with affectionate messages from his father, who found it impossible to leave Vienna as long as the war with the Turks lasted. The next day he went hunting with the King, Mary, and Christina, and dined with them and Eleanor. On the 3rd of November he left Brussels again after all too short a visit, as Charles wrote to his brother.

Another guest who took leave of the Emperor in the same week was Edward Courtenay, Lord Devonshire. This young nobleman of the blood royal had been exiled from England lest he should marry Elizabeth, and had been so often seen in the palace during the last few months that rumour said he was going to wed Madame of Lorraine. Now he came to thank her for the " gentle entertainment " which she had shown him, and bid her a reluctant farewell before he left for Italy. In the following spring another old friend, Adolf of Holstein, came to Brussels and took leave of the Emperor. The Danish Prince, hearing that all idea of the Savoy marriage was abandoned, took this opportunity to make a last attempt to win Christina's hand. But not even the Duke's constancy could induce her to change her mind, and he went away disconsolate.[1]

A fresh sorrow awaited her in the death of her brother-in-law, the Elector Palatine, who breathed his last at Alzei, in the Lower Palatinate, on the 26th of February, 1556. The fine old man was in his seventy-third year, and had been tenderly nursed all through a long illness by his wife. Three weeks before his death Dorothea sent for his nephew and successor,

[1] Venetian Calendar, vi. 603.

Otto Heinrich, who remained with him to the end, and brought his body to Heidelberg. Here he lay in state for three days in the Court chapel, after which his remains were borne down the castle slopes by eight noblemen, and laid with his forefathers in the church of the Holy Ghost. By order of the new Elector, he was buried with Lutheran rites. Dorothea and Countess Helene followed on foot with a long train of nobles and students of the University, bearing lighted tapers, and German hymns were sung by the Canons and school-children.[1]

Christina's first impulse was to hasten to her widowed sister, but neither the Emperor nor his sisters would allow her to leave the Netherlands before their departure, saying that she was as dear and indispensable to them as a daughter.[2] She was present at the Casino in the park on the 16th of January, when Charles resigned the kingdoms of Spain and Sicily and his dominions in the New World to Philip, and she accompanied Mary to Antwerp when Philip held his first Chapter of the Fleece. Among the new Knights elected at this meeting were William of Orange, Philip, Duke of Aerschot, and Christina's old friend Jean De Montmorency, Sieur de Courrières, whose whole life had been spent in the Emperor's service, and who had deserved well of Philip by helping to arrange his marriage with Mary Tudor.[3]

On the 5th of February, 1556, the long-protracted peace negotiations were brought to a happy conclusion, and a five years' truce was signed at the Abbey of Vaucelles, near Cambray, by Lalaing on Philip's part and by

---

[1] L. Haüsser, i. 630.   [2] Venetian Calendar, vi. 197.
[3] De Reiffenberg, " Histoire de la Toison d'Or," 451.

Coligny on that of Henry.   Both parties were to retain their conquests, and the chief prisoners on both sides were to be released.   On Lady Day the French Admiral brought the treaty to be confirmed by the King at Brussels, and was received by Philip in the palace. By an unlucky chance, the great hall in which the reception took place was hung with tapestries representing the defeat of Pavia and surrender of Francis I. This wounded the vanity of the French lords, and the King's jester, Brusquet, who had accompanied Coligny, determined to have his revenge on the haughty Spanish Prince.   So the next morning at Mass in the Court church, when Philip was in the act of taking his oath on the Gospels to keep the truce, Brusquet suddenly raised a cry of " Largesse !" and, taking a handful of French crowns from a sack which his valet carried, flung them to the crowds who had collected in the great hall adjoining the chapel.   The King looked round in surprise at Coligny, who stood dumbfounded, while men, women, and children, rushed to pick up the coins on the floor, and had to be warned off by the archers' pikes.   The King was about to ask angrily by what right the French did largesse in his palace, when both Queen Mary and Madame de Lorraine burst into uncontrollable fits of laughter, in which Philip joined so heartily that he had to cling to the altar to save himself from falling.

This absurd incident was related to Charles when, on the following Sunday of *Pâques-fleuries*, Coligny went to visit him in the Casino.   " Well, Brusquet," he said to the jester, " how are you ?   I hear you have been doing me fine largesse with your crowns." " Sire," replied Brusquet, dropping on one knee, " you take the words out of my mouth in condescending to notice a worm like myself." And the poor fool went home to boast of his interview with the great Emperor to the end of his life.[1]

A grand tournament was held in the park at Brussels to celebrate the conclusion of the truce, and Egmont distinguished himself above all competitors by his prowess. But a quarrel arose between Philip and his aunt, Mary of Hungary, who complained of the disrespect with which her nephew and his Spanish courtiers treated her, saying that, although she had laid down the Regency, she expected to be treated with the honour due to a Queen. She retired to her own domain at Turnhout, but had her revenge a few weeks later, for the States proved so unwilling to grant the aids demanded by the King that Philip was forced to send Arras to beg for his aunt's help. Mary consented to return as soon as she had despatched her most urgent private affairs, and so invaluable was her influence with the Council, that Philip joined his father in entreating her to remain at Brussels during his absence in England. This, however, Mary quite refused to do, saying that the Duke of Savoy would no doubt prove an excellent substitute.[2]

The King and Queen of Bohemia, whom Charles was very anxious to see before his departure, and whose journey had been repeatedly delayed, at length reached Brussels on the 18th of July. Their presence was the signal for a last series of festivities. There were jousts on the Grande Place, banquets in the hôtel-de-ville, hunting-parties at Groenendal in the forest of Soignies, and suppers at the Villa Laura,

[1] G. Ribier, " Lettres et Mémoires d'État," ii. 634; T. Juste, 94; Venetian Calendar, vi. 369.

[2] Venetian Calendar, vi. 421, 443, 457; T. Juste, 101; Gachard, " Retraite," etc., i. 41.

where Mary entertained her nephews and nieces at an open-air concert. King Max was in high spirits. He made great friends with the Venetian Badoer, and frankly avowed his dislike of the Spaniards, saying, with a ringing laugh, that he was glad to hear the English had taught them a lesson or two. The visit was not without its political intention, and Maximilian succeeded in persuading his uncle to consent to Ferdinand's entreaty, and retain the imperial title for the present, in order to avoid any dispute on the question of the succession.[1]

When his daughter and her husband left Brussels, on the 8th of August, Charles felt himself a free man. At half-past four in the afternoon he set out for Ghent, after receiving the farewells of the chief nobles and Bishops. Many were in tears, but the Emperor remained calm and serene until he rode out of the gates, escorted for the last time by his faithful archers. Then, turning round, he took a last long look at the city towers and wept bitterly. " Everyone about him was in tears," says Badoer, " and many wept when he was gone."[2] Christina accompanied her aunts to Ghent a few days later, and went on at the end of the month with the Queens and Emperor to Zeeland, to wait for a fair wind. On the 15th of October Charles embarked at Flushing, and his sisters followed on another ship. Two days later an easterly breeze sprang up and the fleet set sail. Christina stood on the shore till the ship which bore the great Emperor from his native land dropped below the horizon. Then she retraced her steps sorrowfully to join her children at Ghent.

[1] Lanz, iii. 709; Venetian Calendar, vi. 537.
[2] Venetian Despatches, 90 (Record Office).

IV.

When her uncle and aunts were gone, Christina
felt that there was nothing more to keep her at
Brussels. She had already thought of retiring to her
dower city of Tortona, but the castle was occupied
by a Spanish garrison, and while the war lasted the
Lombard city was hardly a safe place. This being
the case, she asked Philip's leave to take up her
residence at Vigevano, the summer palace of the
Sforzas, which the Duke had bequeathed to her,
but was told that this house was required for the
Viceroy's use. After the Palatine's death she was
seized with a longing to join Dorothea, and proposed
to go to Heidelberg, and then on to Lorraine, in the
hope that, now peace was signed, the French King
would allow her son to enjoy his own again. But
there were more difficulties in the way than she had
anticipated.[1]

Simon Renard and the other delegates to the conference at Vaucelles were especially charged to
include the Duke of Lorraine's restoration among
their demands; but the French, while professing the
utmost friendship for both the Duchess and her son,
pointed out that her guardianship would expire in
another year, and that the Regent Vaudemont and
the Guises, who were the Duke's nearest kinsmen,
agreed to his residence at the French Court. In vain
Renard and Lalaing protested at the strange kindness
shown to the Duchess in detaining her son. This
only led to a long wrangle, which almost caused the
rupture of peace negotiations, and eventually no

[1] Venetian Calendar, vi. 197, 362.

mention was made of Lorraine in the articles of the truce.

In May Christina's alarm was aroused by an intimation from the French Court that the King was going to Nancy to celebrate his daughter Claude's wedding with the Duke, and occupy the capital of Lorraine. Fortunately, Vaudemont opposed this measure, saying that as Regent he had sworn never to give up his post until his nephew was of age, and begged the King to allow Charles to return to Nancy and take possession of his State before his marriage.[1] This unexpected firmness on Vaudemont's part produced the desired effect. Henry's journey to Lorraine was put off for a year, and at the Duchess's urgent request the Cardinal of Lorraine obtained the King's leave to bring the boy to meet her at the Castle of Coucy, near his own house at Péronne. But when Philip was asked to give the Duchess permission to cross the frontier, he made so many irksome conditions, that Henry withdrew his promise, and the long-desired meeting was again deferred. Christina was cruelly disappointed, and could only take comfort from Vaudemont's assurances that before long her son would be free from control and able to decide for himself.[2]

Philip on his part was extremely anxious to keep the Duchess at Brussels. As Brantôme tells us, the King not only cherished great affection for his cousin, but relied implicitly on her tact and wisdom, and, in compliance with his entreaties, she consented to remain at the palace and do the honours of his Court.[3] Her popularity with the nobles made her

[1] Granvelle, iv. 574, 577.   [2] Ibid., iv. 701.
[3] Brantôme, xii. 114.

presence the more desirable, while the King himself
found her company far more to his taste than that
of the faded and fretful wife who awaited him in
England. Every post brought bitter reproaches and
passionate prayers from the unhappy Queen, whose
hopes of her lord's return were doomed to perpetual
disappointment. Already more than a year had
passed since he had left England, and there still seemed
no prospect of his return. First the peace conferences, then the King of Bohemia's visit and the
Emperor's departure, were pleaded as excuses for
these prolonged delays. When the fleet that bore
the Emperor to Spain was seen off Dover, the
Admiral who visited His Majesty on board, brought
back messages to say that the King would shortly
cross the Channel. On hearing this, Mary's spirits
rose, and it was only by Philip's express desire that
she refrained from going to meet him at Dover. In
October the royal stables and equerries arrived, but
Philip himself wrote that the war which had broken
out in Italy between Alva, the Viceroy of Naples, and
Pope Paul IV., compelled him to return to Brussels.
Then Mary broke into a passion of rage mingled with
sobs and tears, and shut herself up in her room, refusing to see any visitors. The dulness of the Court
had become intolerable; there were no fêtes and few
audiences, and the Ambassadors with one accord
begged to be recalled. The Queen's ill-temper vented
itself on all who approached her presence, and even
in public she occasionally gave way to paroxysms
of fury.[1] Suspicions of her husband's fidelity to his
marriage vows now came to increase her misery.
When she heard of Philip going on long hunting-

[1] P. Friedmann, 254-267; Noailles, v. 355, 362.

parties with the Duchess of Lorraine, and dancing with her at masques, she was seized with transports of rage, and, rushing at the portrait of her husband which hung over her bed, was with difficulty restrained from cutting it to pieces.[1]

Meanwhile a rival to Christina appeared at Court in the person of the King's half-sister Margaret, Duchess of Parma. This Princess, the illegitimate daughter of Charles V. and Margaret Van Gheynst, a beautiful maiden in the Countess Lalaing's service, was born at Oudenarde in 1522, and brought up under the eye of the Archduchess Margaret. At thirteen she was married to Alessandro de' Medici, Duke of Florence, with whom she led a miserable life until this worthless Prince was murdered by his cousin in 1537. Her second union, with Ottavio Farnese, Pope Paul III.'s grandson, proved little happier. Ottavio was an intractable boy of thirteen when he married her in November, 1538, and the quarrels of the young couple fill pages of the Emperor's correspondence in the archives of Simancas. After the Duke's return from the expedition to Algiers, a reconciliation was effected, and Margaret bore a son, who became the famous captain Alexander of Parma. But the Farnese were always a thorn in the Emperor's side, and, by joining with his foes at a critical moment, involved him in the gravest disaster of his life. Now harmony was restored in the family circle, and when the war with Paul IV. broke out, Philip secured Ottavio's alliance by giving him the citadel of Piacenza. Margaret and her young son came to the Netherlands to pay their respects to the King and

[1] Friedmann, 56; Noailles, " Affaires Étrangères : Angleterre," xix. (Bibliothèque Nationale).

thank him for this mark of his favour. They arrived at Christmas, in the depths of the severest winter that had been known for many years. The Scheldt was frozen over at Antwerp, and the Court was busy with winter sports, in which Philip and Christina took an active part, playing games and sleighing in the park, and attending a masked ball given by Count Lalaing on the ice.[1]

The Duchess of Parma was received with due honour at Court, and was cordially welcomed by Christina, who had known her as a child. A handsome woman of thirty-five, she resembled her Flemish mother more than her imperial father, and bore few traces of her Habsburg origin. She had none of Christina's distinction and refinement, while her manners were too haughty to please the Flemish nobles. But she had a keen eye to her own interests, and the atmosphere of deception and intrigue in which her married life had been spent had taught her to adapt herself to circumstances. She contrived to make herself agreeable both to Philip and Christina, with whom most of her time was spent. The new Venetian Ambassador, Soranzo, paid his respects to the two ladies on his arrival, and found both of them very friendly and pleasant. The Duchess of Lorraine, as Badoer had frequently remarked, was always particularly cordial to the Venetian Signory, to whom her first husband, the Duke of Milan, owed so much. At the same time the Queen of England, anxious to show civility to her husband's family, sent Sir Richard Shelley to give the Duchess of Parma a sisterly welcome, and invite her to come to London.[2]

[1] Venetian Calendar, vi. 863.   [2] Ibid. vi. 914, 932.

In the midst of the Christmas festivities, news reached Brussels of a treacherous attempt of the French, under Coligny, to surprise Douay. Fortunately the plot was discovered in time; but the truce was broken, and every day fresh incursions were made by the French, which naturally produced reprisals. The rupture was complete, and, in his anxiety to secure the help of England in the coming struggle, the King at length crossed the Channel, and joined Mary at Greenwich on the 21st of January, 1557. Political exigencies had done more to hasten his return than all his wife's prayers and tears, but in her joy she recked little of this, and guns were fired and *Te Deums* chanted throughout the realm. Before leaving Brussels, Philip had made arrangements for the two Duchesses to follow him in a few days. Their society, he felt, would help to dispel the gloom of Mary's Court, and Margaret's coming would allay any jealousy which Christina's visit might excite. Another and more important motive for his cousin's presence in England at this moment was his anxiety to revive the old scheme of a marriage between the Princess Elizabeth and the Duke of Savoy. Mary's state of health made her sister's marriage a matter of the highest importance, and the new quarrel with France had put an end to the Duke's hopes in that quarter. As both the French and Venetian Ambassadors constantly affirmed, Emanuel Philibert was the only foreign Prince whom the English would tolerate, and Christina herself told Vaudemont that she was going to England, by the King's wish, to bring back Madame Elizabeth as the Duke of Savoy's bride.[1]

[1] Venetian Calendar, vi. 1015, 1080.

PHILIP II. (1554)
By Jacopo da Trezzo (British Museum)

MARY, QUEEN OF ENGLAND (1554)
By Jacopo da Trezzo (British Museum)

MARGARET OF AUSTRIA
DUCHESS OF PARMA
By Pastorino

ANTOINE PERRENOT
CARDINAL GRANVELLE
By Leone Leoni

To face p. 412

The King had a calm passage to Dover, but the ladies were less fortunate, for an equinoctial gale sprang up when they were halfway across the Channel.

" The Duchesses," wrote Philip's secretary, Jean de Courteville, " had to dance without music between Dover and Calais, and the results were such as are commonly the case with travel' rs unaccustomed to the sea. The great festivities we are having here this Lent will grieve them the less."[1]

But if the passage was disagreeable, nothing was lacking in the kindness of their reception. The Queen sent her litter to meet them at Dover, with chariot and hackney horses for their suite, and at Gravesend, Lady Lennox and Lady Kildare were waiting to conduct them in the royal barge to Whitehall. Here Philip received them at the water-gate, and led them up the steps into the great hall, where Mary welcomed her guests. The King and Queen who had only arrived from Greenwich the day before rode in state through the city, with the Lord Mayor carrying the sceptre at the head of the guilds and crafts of London, while a salute was fired from the Tower and bells rang from all the churches.

Both the Duchesses were lodged in the Palace of Westminster, Christina in rooms on the ground-floor, looking on the gardens, and Margaret in an apartment on the upper floor, commanding a view of the Thames.[2] Soon after their arrival another visitor was brought by the Bishop of London to see Their Majesties—an Envoy from the Czar of Muscovy, who was lodged in Fenchurch Street, as the guest of

[1] Kervyn de Lettenhove, " Relations des Pays-Bas avec l'Angleterre," i. 67.   [2] Gachard, iv. 25.

the Company of Muscovite Merchants. Englishmen
and Spaniards, Lorrainers and Italians, alike looked
with curious eyes at this stranger from the shores of
the Polar Sea, who was clad in robes of Oriental
splendour, and whose turban glittered with gems.
He brought the Queen a present of magnificent sables
from the Czar, and saluted her by bowing his whole
body down and touching the ground with his hand.
In spite of his strange clothes and barbarous language,
he was a cultivated person, as keen to see the sights
of London as Christina herself. One day he dined
with the Lord Mayor in gorgeous attire, another he
attended Mass at Westminster and saw St. Edward's
shrine, with the relics which had been fortunately
preserved when the Abbey was plundered.[1]

After spending a fortnight at Whitehall, Philip
and Mary took their guests to spend Easter at
Greenwich. On Maundy Thursday the King and
Queen washed the feet of a number of poor beggars,
and blessed the cramp rings, which were as much
prized in Spain and Flanders as in England. Easter
Day witnessed fresh balls and banquets, dog and
bear fights, bull-baiting and horse-races, after which
a large hunting-party was given in the park for the
Duchess of Lorraine's amusement. On the 22nd of
April the royal party returned to Whitehall for St.
George's Feast. High Mass was celebrated in the
Abbey by the Bishop of Winchester, and all the
Knights of the Garter, in their mantles of royal blue,
walked in procession round the inner court of the
palace, while the Queen and her guests looked on from
a window on the garden side. The King and Queen
and all the Knights of the Order attended vespers in

[1] Machyn, 130-134.

the Abbey, after which the Muscovite Envoy came
to take leave of Their Majesties, and delivered a long
farewell speech, which was translated by an interpreter into English and Spanish, expressing his hope
that these mighty Sovereigns might live to see their
children's children. Six English ships were in readiness to escort the stranger across the Northern seas,
and prevent him falling into the hands of the Norsemen, who were jealous of English interference with
the trade of Muscovy.

On Sunday the Queen gave a grand banquet, and
appeared resplendent in cloth of gold and jewels.
Christina sat on her right, and Margaret, with her
little son, on the King's left hand. The next morning
the Duchess of Parma left for Italy, but Christina,
at Philip's entreaty, remained in London another
ten days. She was already very popular with the
English, and made friends with Lord Arundel, Lord
Pembroke, and several other nobles and ladies at
Court, while her splendid robes and jewels, her
numerous suite and fine horses, excited general
admiration. In the midst of the Court fêtes, she
found time to visit several shrines and places of
interest, and, while the King was holding the Chapter
of the Garter on St. George's Day, went by water to
the Tower, and was shown its treasures and antiquities.
But in one respect her visit proved a failure. Mary
refused to entertain any idea of the Savoy marriage,
and would not even allow Christina a glimpse of
Princess Elizabeth, who was kept at Hatfield in
strict seclusion during her visit. What was worse,
the Duchess's presence revived all the Queen's
jealousy, and, in spite of the King's protests, Christina
found it prudent to hasten her departure. All manner

of stories about Mary's dislike of the Duchess found
their way to the French Court, and King Henry had
many jokes with Soranzo on the subject, and told
him he heard that the Queen flew into a frantic
passion when the King led out his cousin to dance
at Greenwich.[1]

Philip did his best to atone for his wife's ill-humour,
and, when Christina expressed a wish to visit Ghent
on her return, wrote to ask the Duke of Savoy to see
that she and her daughters were well lodged and
entertained in the old Prinzenhof. On the 11th of
May the Duchess wrote a formal letter of thanks to
the Queen from Dover, acknowledging the attentions
which she had received from Her Majesty and all
her subjects, and on the 8th of June she sent her a
second letter from Ghent, on behalf of the widow
and daughter of Sir Jacques de Granado, a Brabant
gentleman who had been Equerry to Henry VIII.
and Edward VI., and had met his death by accident
during the Duchess's visit. As he rode into the
privy garden at Whitehall before the Queen's
chariot, his bridle broke, the horse shied violently,
and dashed his rider's head against the wall. Sir
Jacques was killed on the spot, and buried at St.
Dunstan's in the East two days afterwards with a
great display of torches and escutcheons. On Christina's recommendation, the Queen granted a pension
of £50 to the widow, and saw that she and her children
were amply provided for.[2]

From Ghent the Duchess went to meet her sister
Dorothea at Jülich, the Court of the Duke of Cleves

[1] Venetian Calendar, vi. 1154; Kervyn de Lettenhove, i. 68.
[2] Machyn, 135, 136; Calendar of State Papers, Mary, Foreign,
305, 314.

and the Archduchess Maria. The reformed faith was now firmly established in the Palatinate, and Dorothea's well-known Lutheran leanings were a great source of annoyance to her own family. " The Electress Dorothea," wrote Badoer from Brussels in 1557, " is known to be a Lutheran and against the Emperor, and is as much hated here as her sister Christina is beloved." From his retreat at St. Yuste, Charles begged Philip to invite Dorothea to settle at Brussels, " lest one of our own blood should openly forsake the faith." When the Princess declined this proposal, Philip and Arras desired Christina to use her influence to bring her sister to a better mind. But Dorothea resisted all these attempts obstinately, and went back to Neuburg to live among her husband's kindred and worship God in her own way.[1]

On the 1st of June England declared war against France, and Philip returned to Brussels, having accomplished the object of his journey. Here he was joined by the Duchess of Lorraine and the Count of Vaudemont, who came to Flanders to try and reopen peace negotiations. But the moment, as Arras told him, was singularly inopportune, since Philip was armed to the teeth and had England at his back. On the 11th of August the King left Brussels for the camp before St. Quentin, where he arrived just too late to claim a share in the brilliant victory gained by the Duke of Savoy and Egmont over the French on St. Lawrence's Day. The Constable Montmorency, the Marshal St. André, Admiral Coligny, and the Rhinegrave, were among the prisoners made on this memorable day, together with all the guns and fifty-six colours. The news

[1] Granvelle, v. 86-113.

of this decisive victory was celebrated with great joy both in Brussels and across the Channel. *Te Deum* was sung in St. Paul's, and the loyal citizens of London lighted bonfires and sat up drinking through the livelong night; while in Paris the King and Queen went to Notre Dame in sackcloth, and Henry II. carried the Crown of Thorns in procession from the Sainte Chapelle. In the lonely monastery far away on the heights of Estremadura, the news sent a thrill to the great Emperor's heart, and he asked eagerly in what route his son was marching on Paris. Had Philip followed this course, had he, in Suriano's words, " taken Fortune at the flood," he might have brought the campaign to a triumphant close. But, with characteristic timidity, he confined himself to capturing St. Quentin, and then returned to Brussels, throwing away such an opportunity as comes but once a lifetime.[1]

[1] Venetian Calendar, vi. 1287; Machyn, 147; Gachard, " Retraite," etc., 176.

BOOK XII

THE PEACE OF CÂTEAU-CAMBRÉSIS

1557—1559

I.

THE lull that followed the decisive battle of St. Quentin afforded the Duchess of Lorraine a favourable opportunity for resuming her efforts to open negotiations between the contending monarchs. The Constable, after fighting like a lion and receiving a severe wound, had been made prisoner, and was taken to the Castle of Ghent, where Christina and her daughters were staying. The Duchess paid him daily visits, and brought him letters of condolence from her aunt Eleanor, who wrote that she wished she were still in Flanders to nurse her old friend. More than this: Christina obtained leave for his wife to visit him, and even proposed that the prisoner should be allowed to go to France on parole. These good offices gratified the French King, who was very anxious for his favourite's release, and whose behaviour towards the Duchess now underwent a marked change.[1]

The young Duke Charles was almost fifteen, and his marriage to the Princess Claude was fixed for the following spring. With the King's leave, he sent his

[1] F. Decrue, " Montmorency à la Cour de Henri II.," 207.

steward to Ghent to invite his mother to the wedding, and at the same time make proposals of peace through Montmorency. These letters were laid before Philip by Christina, and a brisk correspondence was carried on between her and the Constable. In December Vaudemont came to Brussels, bringing portraits of Charles and his bride as a gift from Henry II. to the Duchess, and negotiations were actively pursued.[1] But just when the wished-for goal at length seemed to be in sight, and Christina was rejoicing to think of once more seeing her son, all her hopes were shattered by the Duke of Guise's capture of Calais. The surprise had been cleverly planned and brilliantly executed. The new fortifications of the town were unfinished, and after a gallant resistance the little garrison was overpowered and forced to capitulate, on the 8th of January, 1558. This unexpected success revived the courage of the French, and strengthened the Guise brothers in the determined opposition which they offered to peace. The star of their house was at its zenith, and on the 24th of April the marriage of their niece, the young Queen of Scots, to the Dauphin, was celebrated with great splendour at Paris. In deference to his mother's wishes, the Duke of Lorraine's wedding was put off till the following year, when he should have attained his majority; but he figured conspicuously in the day's pageant, and led his lovely cousin in her lily-white robes and jewelled crown up the nave of Notre Dame.[2]

The French King now gave his consent to Vaude-

---

[1] Venetian Calendar, vi. 1346, 1363.

[2] Ruble, "La Jeunesse de Marie Stuart," 153; Bouillé, i. 455; Pimodan, 173-180.

mont's request, that a meeting should be arranged between the Duke and his mother in the neighbourhood of Péronne. Philip, after his wont, raised many difficulties, and insisted that the Bishop of Arras must be present at the interview.[1] At length all preliminaries were arranged, and on the 1st of May Charles left Paris with his uncle Vaudemont and Guise's eldest son, Henri, Prince of Joinville, attended by an escort of 200 horse. The Duchess had already arrived at Cambray with her daughters and Anne of Aerschot, accompanied by Egmont, Arras, and a great train of courtiers, and had prepared a splendid reception for her son. But at the last moment fresh difficulties arose. The Cardinal of Lorraine sent Robertet, the King's secretary, to tell the Duchess that, although her son was most anxious to see her, it would be derogatory to his master's dignity for him to enter King Philip's territories as a suppliant for peace. Would Her Highness therefore consent to come as far as his castle at Péronne ? This Philip quite refused to allow, and eventually the village of Marcoing, halfway between Cambray and Péronne, was fixed upon as the meeting-place. An old manor-house which had been partly destroyed in the late military operations was hastily repaired for the occasion, and here, on the 15th of May, the much-desired meeting at length took place.[2] The Frenchmen, who came in riding-clothes, were amazed to find the splendid company awaiting them. The Duchess with the young Princesses, Anne of Aerschot, and the Princess of Macedonia, stood under a bower of leafy boughs, and Egmont and the other courtiers were all richly clad and mounted on fine horses. The

[1] Venetian Calendar, vi. 1471, 1488. [2] Granvelle, v. 168.

coming of the guests was greeted by a gay fanfare
of trumpets and roll of drums, together with salutes
of artillery. Then the young Duke, springing from
his horse, rushed into his mother's arms. At the
sight of her boy, Christina burst into tears and almost
fainted away. For some minutes she remained
unable to speak, and the spectators were deeply
moved by her emotion. After repeatedly embracing
his mother, Charles kissed his sisters and aunt, and
proceeded to salute Egmont and the rest of the company with charming grace; while the happy mother
followed his movements with delight, and could not
take her eyes off the tall and handsome youth whom
she had last seen as a child, and who had grown up
the image of his father.

During the conversation which followed, Charles
spoke to his mother with great good sense and wisdom,
telling her how kindly he was treated at the French
Court, and how it would be hard for him to feel at
home anywhere else. But directly after his marriage
he and his wife intended to return to Nancy, where he
hoped that his mother would join them and live among
their own people. The Duchess and her children now
sat down to an exquisite *déjeuner* with the Duchess
of Aerschot and the Cardinal, while Egmont and Arras
entertained Vaudemont and the Prince of Joinville,
and the other French gentlemen dined with the
members of Christina's suite. After dinner three
Spanish jennets which King Philip had sent the
young Duke were led out, and Charles mounted a
spirited charger given him by the French monarch,
and performed a variety of feats of horsemanship
before the company, to his mother's great delight.
Then the Duchess and her sister and children retired

to enjoy each other's company in private, leaving the Cardinal to confer with Arras and Egmont.

The Cardinal produced the royal mandate, and Robertet read out Henry's proposals, offering to restore Savoy to the Duke, but only on condition of receiving Milan in exchange. All Arras would say in reply to these demands was that they must be referred to his master, upon which the Cardinal exclaimed with some heat that these were the only terms which the King of France would accept. " Thus," remarks the Venetian Ambassador, " this meeting, which began with such a beautiful outburst of motherly love and tenderness, ended in mutual recrimination."[1] The Cardinal then took leave of the company, after presenting the young Princesses and their mother with gifts of gold bracelets, rings, and brooches, and receiving a box of choice gloves, perfumed, and embroidered in Italian fashion from the Duchess. As he rode back to Péronne, he saw the flames of a burning village which had been destroyed by the Imperialists, and, in spite of his safe-conduct, was seized with so great a panic that he hurried back to Paris, fearing his château might be surprised by the foes. The young Duke and Vaudemont spent another day with the Duchess, and only returned to Compiègne on the 18th of May. Here Charles received the warmest of welcomes from the royal family, who had feared that he might be induced to remain with his mother. The King threw his arms round the boy's neck, the Queen and Dauphin, the Princesses Elizabeth and Claude and the young Queen of Scots, all embraced him affectionately, telling him how much they had missed him. In fact,

[1] Venetian Calendar, vi. 1496-1498.

as Soranzo remarks, this short absence served to show how much b 'oved the young Prince was by the whole Court.[1]

Meanwhile Arras and Egmont returned to Brussels, satisfied that the French had no real wish for peace, and Philip declared his conviction that they had made a plot to capture the Duchess, which had only been defeated by the strong escort with which she was attended. But Christina herself was radiant with happiness, and received congratulations from all her friends. The French had done her many cruel wrongs, but they had not been able to rob her of her son's heart, and the future still held the promise of some golden hours.

For a while the war still raged fiercely. The capture of Thionville by Guise in June was followed a month later by Egmont's fresh victory at Grave-lines, when the Governor of Calais, De Thermes, and his whole force, were cut to pieces. The Count had always been a splendid and popular figure; now he was the idol of the whole nation. His brilliant feat of arms had saved Flanders from utter ruin, and made peace once more possible. Both sides were thoroughly weary of the long struggle, the resources of both countries were exhausted, and the unhappy inhabitants of Picardy and Artois were crying out for a respite from their sufferings. Christina made use of the opportunity to renew her correspondence with the Constable and the Marshal St. André, his companion in captivity.[2] A new recruit now came to her help in the person of William of Orange. This young Prince had enjoyed the favour of Charles V. and his sister Mary from his boyhood, and had been

---

[1] Venetian Calendar, vi. 1500.   [2] Ibid., vi. 1528.

treated with especial kindness by the Duchess of Aerschot and her sister-in-law. The death of his young wife, Anna, Countess Büren, in the spring of 1558, had thrown him much into the company of these ladies, and it was already whispered at Court that he would certainly marry Madame de Lorraine's elder daughter, Renée, who was growing up a tall and attractive maiden. The Prince himself was a handsome youth with fine brown eyes and curly auburn locks, and a charm of manner which few could resist. If the cares and anxieties of his later life made him taciturn, in youth he was the most genial and pleasant of companions, and Arras, who never loved him, said that he " made a friend every time that he lifted his hat." His attire was always as faultless as it was splendid, he was renowned for his skill as a rider and jouster, and had greatly distinguished himself in the recent campaigns. Both in his home at Breda and in the stately Nassau house at Brussels the Prince kept open house, and the worst faults of which his enemies could accuse him were his reckless hospitality and extravagant tastes.

Christina had always taken especial interest in William of Orange, for the sake of the kinsman whose name and wealth he inherited, and he on his part became deeply attached to her. So intimate was their friendship, that the Duchess one day told Count Feria's English wife, Jane Dormer, in speaking of the Prince's intended marriage with her daughter, that she would gladly have married him herself.[1]

The Prince now joined his personal exertions to

[1] Groen van Prinsterer, " Archives de la Maison d'Orange et de Nassau," i. 1; Kervyn de Lettenhove, ii. 257.

those of the Duchess, and was the frequent bearer of letters between Brussels and the camp near Amiens, where the two Kings and their rival armies were drawn up face to face. At length, on the 9th of September, a ten days' armistice was proclaimed, and a few days later the Prince of Orange, Ruy Gomez, and Arras, met the Constable and St. André at Lille, to discuss preliminaries of peace.[1] The two French prisoners were eager for peace, and had the secret support of Henry II. and Diane de Poitiers; but the Guises, who had everything to lose and nothing to gain by the cessation of war, were still strongly opposed to a truce, and Renard told Philip that the only way of gaining their good-will would be to give Mademoiselle de Lorraine's hand to the Prince of Joinville. In the end, however, their opposition was overruled, and on the 30th of September William of Orange was able to bring the Duchess news that a Conference had been arranged, and would take place at the Abbey of Cercamp, near Cambray, in October. He found Christina at Douai, where she and her daughters were attending a marriage in the d'Aremberg family. She had just heard of her son's return to Nancy, where he had been received with acclamation by his subjects, and where her own presence was eagerly expected. But at Philip's earnest entreaty she consented to remain in Flanders for the present, and preside at the coming Conference. This proposal was strongly supported by the Cardinal of Lorraine, who hastened to send the Duchess a safe-conduct, saying that her presence would do more than anything to bring the desired peace to perfection.[2]

[1] Granvelle, v. 171.   [2] *Ibid.*, v. 227.

Christina herself was very reluctant to accept the post, as we learn from the following letter which she wrote to Philip from Douai on the 12th of October. Her delicate child, Dorothea, was ailing, and her faithful companion, the aged Princess of Macedonia, was hardly fit to be left alone.

" I have received the letter which Your Majesty has been pleased to send me, and thank you humbly for your affectionate expressions. As to the inconvenience of the place selected for this Conference, I should never allow my comfort or pleasure to interfere with your commands, and will accordingly go to Arras to-morrow and await your further orders. I have been very unwell lately, and must beg Your Majesty to provide for my safety, not only because I am a woman, but because, as you know, I am not in the good graces of the French. My daughters must remain here a few days longer, as Dorothea is indisposed, and the Princess of Macedonia is in a very feeble state. I will follow Your Majesty's advice as to Bassompierre's mission and my son's affairs, and cannot thank you enough for your kind thought of me and my children. I kiss Your Majesty's hands.
" Your very humble and obedient cousin,
" CHRÉTIENNE."[1]

Some further difficulties—chiefly the work of Silliers, poor Belloni's hated rival and successor—delayed the Duchess's journey for another week. On the 16th Arras wrote to tell her that the Commissioners had already arrived at Cercamp, and beg her to come as soon as possible. The Cardinal was very anxious to see her, and hoped that she would not fail to bring his young cousins, " Mesdames your daughters," with her. Christina could delay no longer, and hastened to Cercamp the following day.

[1] Granvelle, v. 231.

II.

On the 17th of October, 1558, a fortnight's truce was proclaimed. Both armies remained encamped on their own territories, while the two Kings withdrew respectively to Arras and Beauvais. The next day the Commissioners met at one o'clock in the Duchess's lodgings. The Prince of Orange, Alva, Ruy Gomez, Arras, and Viglius, the President of the Council, represented Philip; while the Constable, the Cardinal of Lorraine, St. André, the Bishop of Orleans, and Secretary l'Aubespine, were the five French deputies. Stroppiana represented the Duke of Savoy, and the English deputies, Lord Arundel, Dr. Wotton, and Thirlby, Bishop of Ely, arrived a few days later. The Duchess welcomed the Commissioners in a brief speech, explaining that, as for several years past she had endeavoured to make peace between these two illustrious monarchs, it was their pleasure that she should continue her good offices, adding that she would count herself too happy if her services could help to attain this blessed end, and relieve the people of both countries from the awful miseries of war.[1]

During the next fortnight conferences were held daily in the presence of Christina, who herself read aloud each different proposal that was made, and showed infinite tact in smoothing over difficulties and suggesting points of agreement. Each morning the deputies met at Mass in the parish church, and often discussed separate questions after service. In the evenings, private interviews took place in Christina's

[1] Granvelle, v. 266.

rooms, and the Prince of Orange held long conversations with Montmorency and the Cardinal, which contributed not a little to their mutual understanding. " Loving entertainments," in Suriano's phrase, " were exchanged," and one night the Duchess gave a banquet in honour of the Constable's wife and daughter, who paid a visit to Cercamp. As the Cardinal complained jestingly, Montmorency was too good a Christian and all too ready to make peace with his country's enemies. But King Henry supported him secretly, and sent private notes and messages, telling him to take no notice of the Guises, and do all he could to make peace.[1]

The great difficulty which had hitherto stood in the way of all attempts at negotiation was the restitution of Savoy. The Constable now proposed that the Duke should marry the King's sister, Madame Marguerite, with a dower of 300,000 crowns, and be placed in possession of the chief portion of his dominions. At first the Duke demurred to this offer, and begged that the King's daughter Claude should be substituted for her aunt, who was five years his senior. But the Cardinal replied that this Princess was already pledged to his nephew, Charles of Lorraine, and laid stress on Margaret's charms and learning. The Duke yielded, and a long wrangle ensued as to the towns and citadels to be retained by the French. But there was a still more thorny question to be decided. This was the restoration of Calais, which the English demanded with the utmost pertinacity, while the French were no less determined to keep their conquest. The English pleaded

[1] Venetian Calendar, vi. 1537; Ruble, " Traité de Câteau-Cambrésis," 12.

that they had held the town during two centuries; the French replied that it had been unjustly snatched from them in the first place. Old treaties, going back to the days of the Black Prince, were produced, and Arras and his colleagues supported the English claim loyally, knowing that, if Philip consented to abandon Calais, he would lose all hold on his wife's subjects. In vain Christina proposed that, as the marriage of the French King's elder daughter with the Infant Don Carlos had been agreed upon, Calais should form part of Elizabeth's dower. The Cardinal told the Duchess that the possession of the town, which his brother had conquered, touched his honour too closely for him to agree to the surrender, and King Henry sent word that he would rather lose his crown than give up Calais. So stern and intractable were the French that the only thing to be done was to adjourn the Conference and refer the matter to the two monarchs.[1]

The Constable was allowed to go to Beauvais with the Cardinal to consult King Henry, Alva and Orange went to Brussels to see Philip, and Christina took three days' holiday with her children at Douai. Before she went to Cercamp, a report of Charles V.'s death had reached Brussels. Now this was confirmed by letters from St. Yuste, announcing that the great Emperor had passed away on the 21st of September. The sudden death of his sister Eleanor, seven months before, had been a great shock to him, and when the Queen of Hungary entered his room without the accustomed figure at her side he burst into tears. The recent events of the war, and Philip's difficulties in the administration of the provinces,

[1] Calendar of State Papers, Mary, Foreign, 402-404.

troubled him sorely, and he was very anxious for Mary to resume the office of Regent. When, in August, the Archbishop of Toledo brought a letter from the King, imploring the Queen to come to his help, Charles used all his influence to induce her to consent. In vain Mary pleaded her advancing years and failing health; the Emperor replied that her refusal would bring ruin and disgrace on their house, and adjured her by the love of God and her sisterly affection to do him this last service. This appeal decided the noble woman. On the 9th of September she wrote to tell Philip that, in obedience to his father's orders, she would start for the Netherlands as soon as possible. The knowledge of the Queen's decision was a great consolation to Charles in his last moments, and as soon as she had recovered from the first shock of his death she prepared to obey his last wish. But before she embarked at Laredo, a fresh attack of the heart trouble from which she suffered ended her life, and on St. Luke's Day she passed to her well-earned rest.[1]

Her death was deeply lamented throughout the Low Countries, where her return had been daily looked for, and no one mourned her loss more truly than the niece to whom she had been the best of mothers. It was with a sad heart that Christina came back to Cercamp to preside at the second session of the Conference, which opened on the 7th of November. Alarming accounts of their mistress's health now reached the English Commissioners, and Count Feria, whom Philip sent to London, wrote that the Queen's life was despaired of, and that

[1] Gachard, " Retraite," etc., i. 44-48; Venetian Calendar, vi. 1544.

Parliament was in great alarm lest, if she died, the King would cease to care for the recovery of Calais. But, although Arras and Alva still declared that they would never consent to any treaty which did not satisfy the English, the French remained obdurate, and the Commissioners were at their wits' end. The Bishop of Ely was in tears, and on the 18th of November Lord Arundel wrote home that

" it seemed very hard that all others should have restitution of their owne, and poore England, that began not the fray, should bear the burthen and loss for the rest, and specially of such a jewel as Calais."[1]

The next day came the news of the Queen's death. The French, who, Wotton remarked, " have ears as long as those of Midas," were the first to inform Her Majesty's Envoys that their mistress had breathed her last, on the morning of the 17th of November, after sending a message to Elizabeth, recognizing this Princess as her successor, and begging her to maintain the Catholic religion. The new Queen at once sent Lord Cobham to announce her accession to Philip, and assure him of her resolve to hold fast the ancient friendship between England and the House of Burgundy.

The news of Mary's death decided the Commissioners to adjourn the Conference. The truce was prolonged for two months, and on the 2nd of December they all left Cercamp. Arundel had already started for England, and Wotton was longing to get away, saying " that he was never wearier of any place than he was of Cercamp, saving only of Rome after the sack." The Constable was set at liberty, and received a promise that his 200,000 crowns

[1] Kervyn de Lettenhove, i. 257.

ransom should be reduced by half, if peace were finally made. Arras, Alva, and Orange, went to the Abbey of Groenendal to see Philip, who had retired to pray for his father's soul, and there received the tidings of his wife's death. Christina returned to Brussels to assist at a succession of funerals. On the 22nd of December a requeim for the Queen of England was chanted in S. Gudule, the Duke of Savoy acting as chief mourner in the King's absence, and on the following day solemn funeral rites for the late Queen of Hungary were performed in the Court chapel, which she and the Emperor had built and adorned. The Duchess of Lorraine was present at this service, together with the Duke of Savoy, the Prince of Orange, and all the chief nobles and Crown officials, while the palace gates were thronged with a crowd of sorrowing people.[1] But the grandest funeral ceremonies ever known in Brussels were those that were celebrated on the 29th of December, in memory of the late Emperor.

Great preparations had been made for this solemnity during the last few weeks. A *chapelle ardente* was erected in S. Gudule, rising in tiers to the lofty roof, adorned with golden diadems and shields emblazoned with the dead monarch's arms and titles, and lighted with 3,000 candles. Here, on a couch draped with cloth of gold, an effigy of the Emperor was laid, clad in robes of state and wearing the collar of the Order. On the morning of the 29th a long procession wound its way through the narrow streets leading from the palace on the heights of the Caudenberg to the cathedral church, and a stately pageant

[1] Venetian Calendar, vi. 1568.

unfolded the glorious .story of Charles of Austria's deeds. A richly carved and gilded ship, drawn by marine monsters, bore the names of his journeys and battles and armorial bearings of the kingdoms over which he reigned, while banners of the Turks and of the other foes whom he had vanquished were plunged in the waves below, and white-robed maidens sat in the stern, bearing the cross and chalice, the symbols of the faith by which he had conquered the world. This imposing group was followed by a representation of the Pillars of Hercules with Charles's motto, *Plus oultre*, and twenty-four horses decked in coloured plumes and trappings to match the banners of his different States. Each of these pennons was borne by a noble youth, while four Princes supported the great standard of the Empire. Then came the officers of the imperial household, leading Charles's war-horse, and bearing his armour and insignia; the Prince of Orange with his master's sword, Alva with the orb of the world, and the Grand Commander of Castille with the imperial crown. Last of all King Philip himself appeared on foot, clad in a mourning mantle five yards long, and followed by the Duke of Savoy and a long train of Knights of the Golden Fleece, Councillors and Ministers, with the Archers of the Guard bringing up the rear. The procession left the palace at nine, and the funeral service, which included a lengthy oration by the Bishop of Arras's coadjutor, Abbé Richardot, was not over till five o'clock. The next day Philip and all his nobles attended High Mass, and at the end of the celebration the Prince of Orange, standing before the funeral pile, smote his breast three times, repeating the words: " He is dead, and will remain dead; and there is another risen up in his place, greater than ever he has been." So the solemn function ended.

" It was a sight worth going 100 miles to see," wrote Richard Clough, an English apprentice who had been sent by Sir Thomas Gresham from Antwerp, and counted himself fortunate to witness this imposing ceremony. " The like of it, I think, hath never been seen. The Lord give his soul rest !" [1]

The Duchess of Lorraine had been anxious that her son should attend his great-uncle's funeral, but the tardy invitation which Philip sent to Nancy arrived too late, and the young Duke could not reach Brussels in time to take part in the ceremony. To console herself for this disappointment, Christina went to meet Charles at Treves on the 6th of January, and spent two days in his company, before he returned to France for the wedding. His loyal subjects presented him with a marriage gift of 200,000 crowns, double the amount which any Duke of Lorraine had received before. Charles who inherited his mother's lavish generosity, spent most of the money in costly jewels for his bride, and presented the King and Dauphin, Vaudemont and the Guises, with superb robes embroidered with the arms of Lorraine and lined with lynx fur. The wedding was solemnized at Notre Dame on the 22nd of January, with as much splendour as that of the Dauphin in the previous spring. The Guises held open house for ten days in their palatial abode, the " Hôtel de Lorraine et de Sicile," near the royal palace of Les Tournelles, and gave a grand tournament in which the young Duke appeared at the head of a troop splendidly arrayed

[1] Kervyn e Lettenhove, i. 384 ; Gachard, " Voyages," iv. 35-62.

in corslets of gold and silver, with the *alérions*, or eagles, of Lorraine on the crest of their helmets. Ronsard celebrated the union of the eagles of Lorraine and the golden lilies of France, and sang the praises of the " Fair Maid of Valois and her bridegroom, the beautiful Shepherd who feeds his flock in the green pastures along the banks of Meuse and Moselle."[1]

The French King and Queen had invited the Duchess in courteous and affectionate terms to be present at the wedding, but she declined on the plea of her deep mourning, as well as of the promise which she had made to preside at the Peace Conference, which was shortly to meet again.[2]

III.

The Commissioners who had attended the Conferences at Cercamp were unanimous in refusing to return to this unhealthy and inconvenient spot, and at the Duchess of Lorraine's suggestion the small town of Câteau-Cambrésis, belonging to the Bishop of Cambray, was chosen for their next meeting-place. The Bishop's manor-house at Mon Soulas, which had been damaged in the war, was hastily repaired by the Duchess's *fourriers*, the rooms were furnished anew, and paper windows were inserted in place of the broken glass. The Bishop of Arras, who arrived with the Prince of Orange's servants, secured a decent lodging and good cook for himself and his colleagues in the neighbouring villas of Beau Regard and Mon Plaisir, while Wotton and the Bishop of Ely found very indifferent quarters in a

[1] Calmet, ii. 1, 351; Pfister, ii. 244; Venetian Calendar, vii. 19, 20.

[2] Venetian Calendar, vii. 8, 10.

ruinous house belonging to the Bishop of Cambray. The French complained that the accommodation was no better than at Cercamp, if the air was healthier, and, after a good deal of grumbling, fixed on two houses, known as Mon Secours and Belle Image, outside the gates.[1] The dilapidated country - house, with its patched-up walls and paper windows, could hardly have been a pleasant residence in the cold days of February, but Christina made light of these discomforts, and threw herself heart and soul into the difficult task before her. The Commissioners all recognized the tact and patience which she showed in conducting the negotiations, and the courtesy which the Ambassadors of other nationalities received at her hands, during the next two months.

The French delegates were delayed by the fêtes for the Duke of Lorraine's wedding, and did not reach Câteau-Cambrésis until late on the evening of the 5th of February. On the following afternoon they held their first meeting with the King of Spain's Commissioners in the Duchess's rooms at Mon Soulas. They seemed very cheerful, and, the next day being Shrove Tuesday, were all entertained at dinner by the Constable. On Ash Wednesday, Mass of the Holy Ghost was sung in church, after which business began in earnest, and various points regarding the Duke of Savoy's marriage were decided. The next evening Lord William Howard, who had been made Lord Chamberlain by the new Queen, and advanced to the peerage with the title of Lord Howard of Effingham, arrived from England. He was received with great civility by Alva and his colleagues, and conducted by the Prince of Orange to salute the

[1] Granvelle, v. 420-426; Kervyn de Lettenhove, i. 420.

Duchess. Christina welcomed him graciously, asked after Queen Elizabeth with great interest, and kept him talking of England " for a pretty while " in the most friendly manner.

" This assembly," wrote Howard to his mistress, " hath been entirely procured by the Duchess's labour and travail; and she being a Princess not subject to the King of Spain or France, the Commissioners are content to use her as one that is indifferent betwixt all parties, and she is continually present at all meetings and communications."[1]

But the Frenchmen, Lord Howard complained, behaved in a very strange fashion, and quite refused to meet him and his colleagues if they persisted in their demand for Calais, pretending that this question had been finally settled at Cercamp. At Christina's entreaty, however, the Cardinal consented to an interview, and at one o'clock on Saturday, the 11th of February, the whole body of Commissioners met at Mon Soulas. The Duchess sat at the head of the table, the English on her right, the French deputies opposite, and Alva and his companions at the other end. A long wrangle followed; all the old arguments were revived, and the Cardinal, as Howard noticed, did his best to stir up a quarrel between the English and the King of Spain's servants. After the meeting broke up, the members stood about in little knots, conversing amicably with each other and the Duchess. On Sunday the Constable had a long private interview with Howard, and, as the latter afterwards discovered, caught Alva and Stroppiana as they left church, and tried to induce them to abandon the English. But Philip's servants stood loyally by their

---

[1] Kervyn de Lettenhove, i. 422, 444.

allies, and the Prince of Orange and Alva discussed the matter with Howard until a late hour. During the next two days the debate was continued with ever-increasing acrimony, until on Tuesday afternoon Howard broke into so violent a passion that the Cardinal and his friends rose and walked out of the house, saying that it was impossible to argue with such people. As Arras remarked shrewdly: " The French are better advocates of a bad cause than the English are of a good one."[1]

Presently a page brought the Duchess word that the French Commissioners had ordered their horses, and were preparing to pack up and leave. Upon this Christina followed them into the garden, and by dint of much persuasion prevailed upon the Cardinal to listen to her suggestion that Calais should remain for eight years in the hands of the French, and that a yearly sum should be paid to Queen Elizabeth as a security for its ultimate surrender. Meanwhile the outer world was becoming very impatient. Philip wrote to the Prince of Orange, saying that he could get no more supplies from Spain, and that the greatest service he could do him would be to obtain peace at any cost; and Henry sent an autograph letter to the Constable, complaining of the Guises' opposition, ending with the words: " Never mind what these men say; let them talk as they please, but make peace if possible !" It was accordingly decided to refer the Duchess's proposal to Queen Elizabeth and her Council, while the Constable went to consult the French King at Villers-Cotterets.[2]

[1] Granvelle, v. 454.
[2] Ruble, " Traité de Câteau-Cambrésis," 23; Venetian Calendar, vii. 39; Granvelle, v. 495.

Late this same evening the Duke of Lorraine arrived from Court, with two of the Guise Princes, the Grand Prior of Malta, and the Marquis of Elbœuf, and was met by the Prince of Orange, and taken to Mon Soulas. The Duchess was overjoyed to see her son, and the next three days were devoted to hunting-parties. Howard was invited to join in one of these, and he and the Prince of Orange accompanied Christina and Margaret of Aremberg out hunting. As they rode home together, the ladies began to talk of Queen Elizabeth, and Christina expressed her wish that she would marry the King of Spain.

" Why ?" returned Howard. " What should my mistress doe with a husband that should be ever from her and never with her ? Is that the way to get what we desire most—that is, children ? I think not."

At this both the Duchess and Madame d'Aremberg laughed, and Christina, remembering her unlucky experiences at the English Court, observed that the late Queen was too old to bear children, and had not the art of winning her husband's affections. Howard was entirely of the same opinion, but assured her that whoever the present Queen chose to marry, " would be honoured and served to the death by every one of her subjects, and all the more so if he make much of his wife."[1] This conversation was duly reported to Elizabeth by Howard, who begged his royal mistress to forgive his boldness, and not impute it to him as folly. All the world knew that Philip was paying assiduous court to his sister-in-law, and Christina's remarks were no doubt prompted by the wish to do him a good turn. But three weeks after this conversation

[1] Kervyn de Lettenhove, i. 457.

the Queen told Count Feria that she was determined
to restore the Church of the land to what it was in
her father's time, and that, being a heretic, she could
not become his master's wife.[1]

Christina had long sought an opportunity of
presenting her son to the King, and at her request
Philip agreed to come to Binche for hunting, and
meet the Duke at Mons.   On the 22nd of February, the Duchess and her son, accompanied by
Madame d'Aremberg, the Prince of Orange, and
the Guise Princes, rode to Mons, where they
were hospitably entertained by the Duke of
Aerschot, and received a visit from the King, who
came over on St. Matthias's Feast from Binche to
spend the day with his cousins.   He showed himself
unusually amiable to the young Duke, and delighted
the boy with the gift of a richly carved and jewelled
sword, in memory of the great Emperor, whose
birthday fell on this day.   On the 25th, Marguerite
d'Aremberg wrote to inform Arras that the Duchess
hoped to be back in a few days, and thanked

" him for having her hall put in order, promising
the Bishop that, if he were seized with a wish to
dance when the ladies from the French Court arrived,
he should have the best place."[2]

Three days afterwards Christina returned to Mon
Soulas, bringing both her daughters to meet their
brother's wife, who was expected in a few days.   The
conferences were resumed on the 2nd of March, but
there seemed little prospect of a settlement.   The
Cardinal made more difficulties than ever, and even
ventured to question Queen Elizabeth's right to the

[1] Kervyn de Lettenhove, i. 475.
[2] Granvelle, v. 487, 495, 502.

crown, saying that she was a bastard, and Mary, Queen of Scots was the true Queen of England. Here Christina intervened once more, and succeeded in soothing down her irascible kinsman. But the leading part taken by the Duchess in these debates annoyed Arras seriously. He blamed her for playing into the hands of the French, and complained to the Duke of Savoy that there were too many ladies at Mon Soulas, and that their absence would be of more advantage than their presence. This last remark was aimed at the young Duchess of Lorraine, who, on the 5th of March arrived from Court with the Duchess of Guise, Anna d' Este, and a numerous suite of ladies. An innocent, simple girl, devoted to her young husband, Claude responded warmly to the affectionate welcome which she received from her mother-in-law and sisters; and Christina thus surrounded by her children, declared herself to be the happiest of mothers. Everyone, as Arras complained, was given up to amusement. Lord Howard went out hunting with his old friend the Constable, and the Prince of Orange and the Cardinal spent their evenings with the Duchess and her joyous family circle.[1]

On Saturday, the 12th of March, there was another stormy meeting in the Duchess's rooms. This time the French and Spanish Commissioners quarrelled violently, and Alva and Arras left the room in anger, declaring they had been fooled, and retired to their own lodgings. In a private letter to the Duke of Savoy, the Bishop complained bitterly of the Frenchmen's insolence, saying that nothing could be " done with such people by fair means, and the only way

[1] Venetian Calendar, vii. 54; Granvelle, v. 520, 525.

was to show your teeth."[1]   The next afternoon, however, at the Duchess's earnest entreaty, he and Alva returned to the Conference.   This time the Cardinal was in a more amiable mood, and the terms originally proposed by Christina were accepted by all parties. Calais was to remain in the hands of France for eight years, and hostages were to be given for the payment of a yearly ransom of 500,000 crowns.   There was great rejoicing at this agreement, and the young Duchess and her ladies returned to Court on the 19th of March, full of the goodness and generosity of the Duke's mother, who loaded them with costly presents, and gave her daughter-in-law the magnificent jewelled necklace which had been the Emperor's wedding gift on her marriage to the Duke of Milan. Christina herself was now so convinced of the certainty of peace that she begged her son to delay his departure a few more days, in order that he might take the good news to the Most Christian King.   The end of the Conference seemed really in sight, and Lord Howard wrote to inform Queen Elizabeth of the treaty regarding Calais, only to receive a sound rating from his mistress for having dared to allow the French and Spaniards to call her title in question.[2]

IV.

The question of Calais having been settled, the French and Spanish Commissioners met again on the 13th of March, and conferred for six hours on their own affairs.   The Duke of Savoy's marriage treaty was the chief point under discussion.   Madame Marguerite's own eagerness for the union was well

[1] Granvelle, v. 529.   [2] Kervyn de Lettenhove, i. 460.

known. She had repeatedly asked her friend the Constable to press the matter, and on the 25th of March she sent her *maître d'hôtel*, Monsieur de l'Hôpital, to Câteau-Cambrésis to sign the contract on her behalf. The Duke's original reluctance had been overcome, and he sent Margaret word through a friend that she must not think him ill-disposed towards her, but that, on the contrary, he counted himself fortunate to win so noble and accomplished a bride, adding, with a touch of irony :

" I believe that the fate with which you have often threatened me is really in store for me, and that I shall submit to be governed by a woman whom I shall try to please."[1]

But there still remained some troublesome details to arrange. All through Holy Week, Christina stayed at her post, while the French and Spanish delegates wrangled over the citadels to be given up by Henry and Philip respectively. On Maundy Thursday a sharp contest arose between Ruy Gomez and the Cardinal on this point. Both parties left the room angrily, and a complete rupture seemed imminent.

" They fell suddenly to such a disagreement," wrote Howard, " that they all rose up, determined to break off and depart home the next morning, being Good Friday."[2]

The Cardinal ordered his rooms to be dismantled and his beds and hangings packed, and on Good Friday morning he and his colleagues had already put on their riding-boots, when Christina appeared at the door and made a last appeal.

[1] V. de St. Génis, " Histoire de Savoie," iii. 181.
[2] Kervyn de Lettenhove, i. 485.

" The Duchess," wrote the Venetian Tiepolo, " regardless of personal fatigue, went to and fro between the Commissioners, with the greatest zeal, ardour, and charity, imploring them to come together again."[1]

Seven years before, on another Good Friday, in her own palace, Christina had knelt in an agony of grief at the King of France's feet, asking to be allowed to keep her only son. To-day she pleaded with tears and prayers, in the name of the same Christ who died on the cross, for the suffering thousands who were sighing for peace. This time her prayer was heard. The Cardinal was induced to meet the Spanish delegates once more, and, after a conference which lasted over seven hours, it was decided that King Philip should keep Asti and Vercelli, and surrender all the other citadels which he held in Savoy. Ruy Gomez hastened to the Abbey of Groenendal to obtain his master's consent to this plan, and, to the amazement of the whole Court, the Cardinal appeared suddenly at La Ferté Milon, at dinner-time on Easter Day. Happily, there was little difficulty in arranging matters. Madame Marguerite told her brother plainly that he ought not to let her marry the Duke, if he treated him with suspicion, and Henry bade her be of good cheer, for all would be well.[2]

On Easter Tuesday the Commissioners held another meeting at Mon Soulas, and by the following evening the terms of the treaty were finally arranged. The Cardinal embraced the young Princesses of Lorraine, and the Duke bade his mother farewell, and rode off as fast as his horse could take him to bear the good

[1] Venetian Calendar, vii. 56; J. F. Le Petit, " Grande Chronique de Hollande," ii. 20.

[2] Venetian Calendar, vii. 57

news to the French King. All the Commissioners attended a solemn *Te Deum* in the church, and bonfires were lighted in the town. " Thanks be to God !" wrote the Constable to his nephew, Coligny: "Peace is made, and Madame Marguerite is married."[1] One point still awaited settlement. The Princess Elizabeth's hand had been originally offered to Don Carlos, but the Constable brought back word that Henry would greatly prefer his daughter to wed King Philip himself. The plan had already been mooted at an earlier stage of the Conference, but it was not until Philip saw that there was no hope of marrying the Queen of England that he consented to wed the French Princess. On the 2nd of April, when the articles of the treaty were being drafted, the Constable made a formal proposal from his master to the Duchess, who, after a few words with Arras and Ruy Gomez, graciously informed him that King Philip was pleased to accept his royal brother's offer.[2]

" It seems a bold step," wrote Tiepolo, " for the Catholic King to take to wife the daughter of the Most Christian King, who had been already promised to his son, especially as marriage negotiations with the Queen of England are still pending. But, seeing how this Queen has already alienated herself from the Church, he has easily allowed himself to be brought over to this plan, which will establish peace more effectually, and will no doubt please the French, who are above all anxious to keep him from marrying the Queen of England."[3]

On the next morning the Commissioners met for the last time, and signed the treaty, after which they heard Mass and all dined with the Duchess, who

[1] Ruble, 26; Venetian Calendar, vii. 67, 77.
[2] Granvelle, v. 577.   [3] Venetian Calendar, vii. 62.

received the thanks and congratulations of the whole body. Then they went their several ways, rejoicing, in Arras's words, " to escape from purgatory." Howard and his colleagues hastened home to make their peace with the offended Queen. In spite of her affected indifference, Elizabeth was by no means gratified to hear of Philip's marriage. " So your master is going to be married," she said with a smile to Count Feria. " What a fortunate man he is !" Presently she heaved a little sigh, and said: " But he could hardly have been as much in love with me as you supposed, since he could not await my answer a few months." [1]

Before leaving Câteau-Cambrésis, Christina sent letters of congratulation to the French King and Queen and to Madame Marguerite, expressing her joy at the conclusion of the treaty, and the pleasure which she had received from her son's presence. To Henry II. she wrote:

" It has pleased God to set the seal on all the joy and content which I have experienced here—chiefly owing to Your Majesty's kindness in allowing me to see my son, and, after that, Madame your daughter and her company—by bringing those long-drawn negotiations to a good end, and concluding, not only a lasting peace, but also the marriage of the Catholic King with Madame Elizabeth. For all of which I thank God, and assure Your Majesty that I feel the utmost satisfaction in having been able to bring about so excellent an arrangement, and one which cannot fail to prove a great boon to Christendom."

In her letter to Catherine, Christina dwells chiefly on her gratitude to the Queen and her daughter for allowing her to keep her son so long.

[1] Calendar of Spanish State Papers, i. 49, Archives of Simancas; Kervyn de Lettenhove, i. 494.

" I thank you, Madame," she writes, " very humbly for your kind interest in our son, who is very well, thank God, and I hope that the pleasure of seeing you will prevent him from feeling the fatigues of the journey. And I am greatly obliged to Your Majesty and our daughter for having lent him to me so long. I praise God that our negotiations have ended so happily, and that these two great monarchs will henceforth not only be friends, but closely allied by the marriage of the Catholic King and Madame Elizabeth, which, as you will hear, was frankly and joyfully arranged after all the other articles of the treaty had been drawn up. I rejoice personally to think that by this happy arrangement I shall often have the pleasure of seeing your Majesties, our daughter, and my son, and take this opportunity of wishing you joy on this auspicious event, hoping that in future you will not fail to make use of me as of one who is ever ready to do you service."[1]

The Duchess now returned to Brussels with her daughters and the Prince of Orange. All the towns and villages through which she passed were hung with flags and garlands of flowers, and her coming was hailed with shouts of joy. The prison doors were thrown open, and the poor French soldiers, who had languished in captivity for years, called down blessings on her head.[2] When she reached Brussels, the King himself rode out to meet her, at the head of his nobles, while courtiers and ladies flocked from all parts to welcome her return and offer their congratulations on the triumphant success of her labours. For Christina it was a great and memorable day. The bitterness of past memories was blotted out, and peace and good-will seemed to have come back to earth.

At Whitsuntide the Treaty was ratified. The Duke of Lorraine came to Brussels with the Cardinals of

---

[1] Granvelle, v. 582, 583.   [2] Venetian Calendar, vii. 64.

Lorraine and Guise and the Constable, and spent a fortnight with his mother. They were present in the Court chapel, with Cardinals and Princes, when the King, laying his hand on a relic of the True Cross, took a solemn oath to keep the articles of the Treaty. And Christina occupied the place of honour at Philip's right hand at the state banquet in the great hall, while her son and daughters and the Duchess of Aerschot were all at table.[1] The King gave the Cardinal of Lorraine a service of gold plate and a wonderful ship of rock-crystal studded with gems, and bestowed similar presents on the Constable; while the Marshal St. André, being a poor man was excused his ransom. They all left Flanders on the following Sunday, except the Duke of Lorraine, who remained another week with his mother. Before he left Brussels, letters from Denmark were received, confirming a report which had already reached the Court of his grandfather King Christian II.'s death. The old King had died in the Castle of Kallundborg, after forty-five years of captivity, on the 25th of January, 1559, at the ripe age of seventy-seven. He was buried with his parents in the Franciscan church at Odensee, and Duke Adolf of Holstein followed his kinsman's remains to their last resting-place. When her son left Brussels, Christina put her household into mourning, and retired to the Convent of La Cambre to spend a month in retreat. After the strain and stress of the last six months, she felt the need of rest sorely, and the shelter of convent walls was grateful to her tired soul.[2]

[1] Gachard, iv. 67; Venetian Calendar, vii. 87-90.
[2] Schäfer, iv. 445.

BOOK XIII

THE RETURN TO LORRAINE

1559—1578

I.

DURING the last year the Duke of Savoy had repeatedly begged to be relieved of his post as the King's Lieutenant in the Low Countries. By the Treaty of Câteau-Cambrésis he recovered his dominions, and set out on the 15th of June for Paris with a great train of gentlemen and servants, to celebrate his marriage with King Henry's sister. At the same time, the death of the Emperor made Philip's return to Spain necessary. The appointment of a new Regent of the Netherlands became imperative, and everyone expected the Duchess of Lorraine would be chosen to fill the vacant office. A Habsburg by birth, she inherited the capacity for governing which distinguished the women of her house, and had proved her fitness for the post by the wisdom with which she administered her son's State during seven years. Her popularity with all classes of people in the Netherlands was an additional advantage, and when, in the summer of 1558, it had been doubtful if Mary of Hungary would consent to return, the Duchess was the first person whose name was suggested. The Venetian Suriano remarked that the only doubt as to her fitness for the office was that she hardly possessed her aunt's extraordinary vigour and energy.[1] But these doubts had been dispelled by the admirable manner in which she had conducted the negotiations at the recent Conference and the immense credit which she had acquired on all sides. Unfortunately, she had made an enemy of the Bishop of Arras, and excited his jealousy by her private consultations with the Cardinal and Constable, and still more by her friendship with the Prince of Orange. Both Orange and Egmont disliked the Bishop almost as much as they hated the King's Spanish favourites, and lost no opportunity of showing their contempt for the " meddling priest," as they called Philip's confidential counsellor. And both of these proud nobles, seeing no hope of themselves obtaining the Regency, supported the Duchess's claims strongly.[2] But the very popularity which Christina enjoyed, the acclamations which greeted her return from Câteau-Cambrésis, had the effect of arousing Philip's jealousy. He lent a willing ear to Arras and Alva when they spoke scornfully of the Duchess's French connection and of the influence which the Prince of Orange would gain by his marriage with her daughter. Then, in an evil hour both for himself and the Netherlands, the Bishop suggested the name of the Duchess of Parma. Margaret was closely related to the King, and would be far more pliable and ready to follow his counsels than Christina. Philip liked his sister, and shared the Spaniards' jealousy of the great Flemish nobles, more especially of the Prince of Orange, whose intimacy

[1] Venetian Calendar, vi. 1533.
[2] T. Juste, " Philippe II.," 209 ; Gachard, " Correspondance de Guillaume d'Orange," i. 431 ; Granvelle, v. 628.

with Christina he regarded with growing suspicion. His mind was soon made up, and when the French Commissioners came to Brussels in May, the appointment of the Duchess of Parma to be Governess of the Low Countries was publicly proclaimed.[1]

The announcement was the signal for an outburst of popular discontent. Orange and Egmont protested loudly at this affront to the Duchess of Lorraine, and complained of the indignity offered to the nation by giving them a ruler of illegitimate birth, whose interests and connections were all foreign, and whose husband had actually borne arms against the late Emperor.

" There is great discontent here," wrote Tiepolo, " at the Duchess of Parma's appointment. The common folk use very insolent language, and say that if a woman is to reign over them they would far rather have the Duchess of Lorraine, whom they know and love and hold to be one of themselves. Every one, indeed, would have greatly preferred this Princess, who is of royal lineage on both sides, and has long dwelt in these provinces, besides being far more gracious and affable to the nobles."[2]

To Christina herself the blow was heavy. She had suffered many trials and disappointments at her enemies' hands, but had never expected to be treated with such ingratitude by the King, who had always professed so much affection for his cousin, and was so deeply indebted to her.

" The Duchess of Lorraine," wrote Tiepolo, " feels the injustice of the King's decision more deeply than any of her past adversities, and naturally thinks that, after her long and indefatigable exertions in negotiating this peace, taking part in every Conference

[1] T. Juste, 206; Venetian Calendar, vii. 83.
[2] Venetian Calendar, vii. 83.

and adjusting every dispute, she deserved to be treated with greater regard. Everyone here admits that peace was concluded chiefly owing to her wisdom and efforts, and this is all the reward which she has received."[1]

It is scarcely to be wondered at if Christina never wholly forgave Philip for the cruel wrong which he had done her, and if in all her future correspondence with him we trace a strain of reproachful bitterness. Her resolve to leave the Netherlands was now fixed. She could not bear to see another Regent at Brussels, and was not even sure if she cared to live as a subject at her son's Court. Her thoughts turned once more to Italy, and, since the Castles of Tortona and Vigevano were not available, she addressed a petition to Philip through her Italian secretary, asking him to give her the duchy of Bari in Calabria. This principality, once the property of Lodovico Sforza, had been lately bequeathed to Philip by the late Queen Bona of Poland, on condition that he would discharge a considerable debt owing to her son, King Sigismund. The beauty and salubrity of the spot, as well as its association with the Sforzas, probably prompted Christina's request, which ran as follows:

" The Duchess of Lorraine in all humility begs Your Majesty, in consideration of her close relationship and of the great affection which she bore the late Emperor, and of the services which she has rendered both to His Majesty of blessed memory and to yourself, to do her the favour of granting her and her children the duchy of Bari, with the same revenues and independent liberties as were enjoyed by the Queen of Poland. She will undertake to pay the King of Poland the sum of 100,000 crowns due to him, and humbly begs Your Majesty to grant her half of this amount in ready

[1] Venetian Calendar, vii. 83.

money, the other half in bills on merchants' houses, in order that she may be able to pay the creditors who annoy her daily. Her revenues for the next year are already mortgaged, owing to the necessity laid upon her of supporting her daughters, during the last seven years, and the repeated journeys which she has undertaken to England, and across the French frontier to treat of peace, all of which have involved her in great and heavy expenses. . . ."

Here the petition breaks off abruptly, the rest of the page being torn off; but we see by Philip's reply that it contained a bitter complaint of the injustice which he had done Christina by refusing to make her Regent. He wrote to Arras, desiring him to see that the Duchess ceased to repeat these perpetual recriminations on the subject of the Regency, which were as derogatory to her dignity as they were injurious to his interests. He regretted that his own pressing needs made it impossible for him to do as much as he should wish to help her. At the same time he said that, besides the revenue of 4,000 crowns which he had already offered her, and which she had neither refused nor accepted, he was ready to give her another yearly allowance of 10,000 crowns, to be charged on Naples and Milan, pointing out that she could raise money on this income to satisfy her creditors.

" The sincere affection which the King has always felt for the Duchess, and the closeness of their relationship," added the writer, " impels him to advise her to retire to her dower lands of Lorraine and live near her son, in order that she may foster the loyalty and devotion which this young Prince owes her, and give him advice and help that may conduce to his welfare and that of the House of Lorraine. Any other action on her part, the King is convinced, will only excite public suspicion and slander. If, however, the

Duchess prefers to live in the kingdom of Naples, the King is ready to offer her the town of Lecce, the most important next to the capital, where she can enjoy all the comforts and amenities of Italian life, together with the respect due to her exalted birth and rank."[1]

This offer, however, did not commend itself to Christina. In spite of its ancient castle and beautiful situation, Lecce was not an independent principality, and had no connection with her family. She replied curtly that she would follow His Majesty's advice and return to Lorraine, as soon as her creditors were satisfied and her affairs sufficiently arranged for her to leave the Netherlands with honour. Upon this, Philip sent the Duchess a sum of 21,000 crowns to defray the expenses of her journeys, and a further substantial advance on the additional revenues which he had assigned her.[2]

But while he was outwardly endeavouring to atone for one act of injustice, he was secretly doing the Duchess another and a more serious injury. The marriage of the Prince of Orange with her daughter Renée had been practically arranged at Câteau-Cambrésis, but some difficulties had arisen regarding the settlements already made by the Prince on his two children by his first marriage, and the heavy debts which he had incurred by his extravagance, amounting, it was said, to 900,000 crowns. Up to this time Philip had openly encouraged the Prince's suit, but both he and Arras looked with alarm on a marriage that would make Orange more powerful and more dangerous than he was already, and were secretly plotting against its conclusion. One day, when Philip was walking in the park at Brussels with the Prince,

[1] Granvelle, v. 625-627.   [2] Venetian Calendar, vii. 112.

he told him how much he regretted to find that
Madame de Lorraine was strongly opposed to his
marriage with her daughter, and had begged him to
inform the Prince that she must decline to proceed
further with the matter. The King added, in a
friendly way, that he had told him this in order that
he might look about for another wife while he was
still young. The Prince was naturally much annoyed
at this unexpected communication, and replied
proudly that, if this were the case, he would promptly
seek another alliance in Germany, where he had
already received several offers of marriage. He was
deeply wounded, not without reason, and went off to
Paris a few days later, with Egmont and Alva, to
remain there as hostages until the conditions of the
treaty had been fulfilled. It was not until many
months afterwards that he discovered how he had
been duped. Christina meanwhile remained in her
convent retreat, unconscious of what was happening
in her absence, and heard with some surprise that the
Prince of Orange had left Court without informing
her of his departure.

All eyes were now turned to the Palais des Tournelles in Paris, where the Catholic King's marriage to
Elizabeth of France, and that of the Duke of Savoy
to Margaret, were about to be celebrated. Alva
represented his master at the wedding, which was
solemnized at Notre Dame on the 22nd of June, and
his old enemy Guise proclaimed the new Queen's
titles at the church doors, and flung handfuls of gold
to the applauding crowds. But their joy was soon
changed into mourning. King Henry was mortally
wounded by a splintered lance in the tournament that
followed, and, after lingering for ten days, breathed

WILLIAM, PRINCE OF ORANGE, ÆTAT 23

By Adriaan Key (Darmstadt)

To face p. 456.

his last on the 10th of July, two days after the marriage of his sister and the Duke of Savoy had been quietly solemnized in the neighbouring church of St. Paul.

The news of his father-in-law's death reached Philip at Ghent, where he was preparing for his departure. Here Christina joined him on the 19th, and was greeted with the liveliest demonstrations of affection from both Court and people. Before leaving Brussels, she saw an English gentleman, who was on his way to Italy, and brought her a pressing invitation from Queen Elizabeth to pay a visit to England.[1] Elizabeth had evidently not forgotten the Duchess's friendly intentions on her behalf when she came to London in Mary's reign, nor her more recent conversation with Lord Howard. After her arrival at Ghent, she received frequent visits from Chaloner, the newly appointed Ambassador, and from the French Envoy, Sébastien de l'Aubespine, who had been one of the delegates to the Conference, and could not speak too highly of Madame de Lorraine's goodness and ability. Through him she sent affectionate messages to the young King Francis II. and his Scottish wife, thanking them in the warmest terms for their kindness to her son. Nor was Philip lacking in his attentions. He met the Duchess on her arrival, paid her daily visits, and seemed to fall once more under the old spell. On the 24th he and Christina were both present at a Requiem for the King of France, and dined together afterwards. The same afternoon Philip rode out to receive the Duchess of Parma.[2] The next day the Duke of Savoy

---

[1] Calendar of State Papers, Elizabeth, i. 82.

[2] Sébastien de l'Aubespine, " Négociations au Règne de François II.," 43, 66.

returned from Paris, bringing with him the Prince of
Orange and Egmont, who were released on parole, and
attended the Chapter of the Fleece held by the King
in the Church of St. John. On the 7th of August the
States met, and the new Regent was formally presented to them. But many voices were raised to
protest against the powers conferred upon her, and
the States refused to grant the aids demanded unless
the Spanish troops were withdrawn. This act of
audacity roused Philip's anger, and in his farewell
interview with William of Orange he accused him of
being the instigator of the measure.

Before leaving Ghent, the King arranged a meeting
between the two Duchesses in the garden of the
Prinzenhof, and afterwards invited Christina to visit
him at Flushing, where he spent some days before he
embarked. They dined together for the last time
on the 12th of August, and seem to have parted
friends.[1] Then Christina returned to Brussels to
prepare for her own departure, and Chaloner wrote
home:

" I heare say the Duchess of Lorraine repaireth
shortly hence into Lorraine, smally satisfied with
the preferment of the other, for old emulations'
sake."[2]

During the next two months Christina had much
to endure. She found a marked change in the Prince
of Orange. He treated her with profound respect
and courtesy in public, but kept aloof from her in
private, and appeared to have transferred his attentions to Margaret of Parma. All idea of his marriage
with Renée—" the Duchess of Lorraine's sound-

---

[1] Venetian Calendar, vii. 119, 121; Gachard, iv. 72.
[2] Kervyn de Lettenhove, i. 583.

limbed daughter," as she was called by Chaloner—
seemed to be abandoned, and in September he left
Court to attend the French King's coronation at Reims.
There was a general feeling of discontent abroad.

" The new Regent is greatly disliked," wrote John
Leigh, an English merchant of Antwerp, " by all
estates, who wished to have the Duchess of Lorraine
for their ruler, and some of her own ladies have
told her that she is a bastard, and not meet for
the place."

The States refused to grant the subsidies asked for,
and the people clamoured for the removal of the
Spaniards. The nobles showed their displeasure by
retiring to their country-houses, and the ladies ab-
sented themselves from Margaret's receptions to meet
in the Duchess of Lorraine's rooms.[1] This naturally
provoked quarrels and jealousies, which, as Arras
remarked in his letters to Philip, might easily prove
serious.

" Then there is rivalry between the Duchess of
Lorraine and her of Parma," wrote the Bishop on the
4th of October, at the end of a long tale of troubles.
" The best way would be to keep them apart, for all
these comings and goings can produce no good result.
Fortunately, the former is about to go to Lorraine.
We shall see if she leaves her daughters here, or takes
them with her. What is certain is that, wherever
she and her daughters may be, it will be better for
Your Majesty's service they should be anywhere but
here, as long as Madame de Parma remains in these
parts, and discord prevails between her and the
Duchess."[2]

When Arras wrote these words, Christina was already on her way to Lorraine. Philip received a
letter from her at Toledo, informing him of her final

[1] Groen, i. 49; Kervyn de Lettenhove, ii. 8; Venetian Calendar,
vii. 112.   [2] Groen, i. 35; Granvelle, v. 652.

departure, and wrote to tell Arras that all strife between the Duchesses was now at an end.[1] In the same month a marriage was arranged between William of Orange and Anna of Saxony, the Elector Maurice's daughter. Arras was greatly alarmed when he heard of this alliance with a Protestant Princess, and used all his powers of persuasion to induce the Prince to return to his old suit and marry Mademoiselle de Lorraine. But it was too late. The Prince knew that the Duchess would never forgive the studied neglect with which he had treated her, and, as he told the Bishop, his word was already pledged. A year later he married the Saxon Princess, but lived to repent of this ill-assorted union, and to realize that he had been the dupe of Philip and his astute Minister.[2]

II.

Christina's return to Lorraine took place at an eventful moment. The death of Henry II. and the accession of Francis II. placed the supreme power in the hands of the Guise brothers. As the saying ran, " So many Guise Princes, so many Kings of France." The elder branch of the House of Lorraine shared in the triumphs of the younger. The reigning Duke, Charles, had grown up with the young King and Queen, and was tenderly beloved by them. Francis could not bear his brother-in-law to be absent from his side, and after his coronation at Reims, on the 18th of September, he and Mary accompanied the Duke and Duchess on a progress through Lorraine.

---

[1] Granvelle, v. 672, vi. 29.
[2] Groen, i. 49, 52; " Correspondance de Granvelle," iii. 529.

The festival of the Order of St. Michel was held at Bar, where Charles kept open house for a week, and his aunt, Anne of Aerschot, came to join the family party and meet the daughter of her old companion, Mary of Guise. The charms of the young Queen won all hearts in her mother's native Lorraine, and Francis indulged his passion for sport in the forests of Nomény and Esclaron.[1]

Here, at this favourite hunting-lodge of the Guises, the royal party were joined by the Duke's mother. Christina reached Esclaron on the 11th of October, and was received with every mark of respect and affection. At first, if Brantôme is to be believed, the Duchess - mother was inclined to stand on her dignity, and refused to yield precedence to the youthful Queen; but Mary's grace and sweetness soon dispelled all rivalry, and Christina became the best of friends with both the King and Queen. General regret was expressed at the absence of the young Princesses, whom their mother had left at Brussels; but Christina was aware of the Cardinal's anxiety to arrange a marriage between Renée and the Prince of Joinville, and had no intention of consenting to this arrangement.

" She left her daughters behind her," wrote Throckmorton, the English Ambassador, " because she is unwilling to satisfy the hopes of the House of Guise, and makes not so great an account of their advances as to leave the old friendship of King Philip and his countries. The French, in fact," he adds, " are doing all they can to make the Duchess Dowager a good Frenchwoman, but they will not find it as easy as they think."[2]

[1] Calmet, ii. 1552; Pfister, ii. 246; Calendar of State Papers, Elizabeth, i. 562.
[2] Calendar of State Papers, Elizabeth, Foreign, ii. 55.

At the end of the week Christina went on to Nancy
with her son and daughter-in-law, leaving the King
and Queen to proceed to Joinville, where Mary was
anxious to see her beloved grandmother. She had
already appointed Antoinette and her three daughters-
in-law to be her ladies-in-waiting, and, as a further
proof of affection, had given her grandmother the
present which she received from the city of Paris on
her state entry. From Blois, where the royal pair
spent the autumn and winter, Francis II. sent his
brother-in-law the following letter, which throws a
pleasant light on the happy relations existing between
the two families:

"My dear Brother,
    "I am longing for news of you and my sister,
and have not heard from either of you since you
reached Nancy. Next week I take my sister, the
Catholic Queen, to Châtelhérault on her way to Spain,
after which I shall return to Blois, and not move
again before Easter. As you may imagine, I cannot
be in this house without missing you very much. I
shall await your return with the utmost impatience,
and wish you were here to enjoy the fine rides which
I have made in my forest. I must thank you for
the good cheer that you are giving my sister, which
is the best proof of your perfect love for me. And I
am quite sure that in this you are helped by my aunt
your mother, Madame de Lorraine, for whom I feel
the deepest gratitude, and whom I should like to
assure of my readiness and anxiety to do her every
possible service. And I pray God, my dearest
brother, to have you in His holy keeping."[1]

The young Duke and Duchess were both of them
longing to accept this pressing invitation and return
to the gay French Court. Charles as yet took little

[1] A. de Ruble, 308; Bibliothèque Nationale, 123, 4, f. 40.

interest in public affairs which required serious attention. Confusion reigned in every department. In many instances the ducal lands had been seized and their revenues appropriated to other uses, while the whole country had suffered from the frequent incursions of foreign troops, and famine and distress prevailed in many districts. Under these circumstances the help of the Duchess-mother was sorely needed. Vaudemont, having neither health nor capacity to cope with these difficulties, had retired into private life, and by degrees Christina resumed most of her old functions. She applied herself to reforming abuses and restoring order in the finances, and at the same time helped her son and daughter-in-law in entertaining the nobles who flocked to Nancy to pay them homage. Her daughters came to join her at Christmas, and she settled once more in her old quarters in the ducal palace. In March the Duke returned to the French Court, and his mother was left to act as Regent during his absence.[1]

After visiting Remiremont and Bar, Charles and his wife went on to spend the summer with the King and Queen at Amboise, where they gave themselves up to hunting and dancing, and enjoyed suppers at Chenonceaux and water-parties on the Loire. But this joyous life was rudely disturbed by the discovery of a Huguenot conspiracy, which was put down with ruthless severity, and was followed by continual alarms. The King and Duke had to be escorted by 500 men-at-arms on their hunting-parties, and the Cardinal of Lorraine never left his room without a guard of ten men bearing loaded pistols. On the 10th of June Mary of Guise died in Edinburgh Castle,

[1] Calmet, ii. 1353; Pfister, ii. 246.

and her remains were brought back to her native
land and buried in her sister's convent church,
St. Pierre of Reims. The whole Court went into
mourning, and Throckmorton was so moved by the
young Queen's tears that he declared " there never
was a daughter who loved her mother better."[1]
Meanwhile the aspect of affairs grew daily more
threatening. There were riots in the provinces, and
rumours of plots at Court. The Duke of Lorraine was
present at the Council held at St. Germain for the
defence of the realm, but left for Nancy when the Court
moved to Orleans in October.

Two months later the young King died there very
suddenly. He fainted at vespers one evening, and
passed away at midnight on the 5th of December,
1560. His brother Charles, a boy of ten, was proclaimed King in his stead, and his mother, Catherine
de' Medici, assumed the Regency. Three days afterwards Throckmorton wrote that the late King was
already forgotten by everyone but his widow, who,
" being as noble-minded as she is beautiful, weeps passionately for the husband who loved her so dearly,
and with whom she has lost everything." The young
Queen behaved with admirable discretion. On the
day after the King's death she sent the Crown jewels
to her mother-in-law, and, as soon as the funeral had
been solemnized, begged leave to go and visit her
mother's grave at Reims. After spending three weeks
with her aunt, Abbess Renée, Mary went to stay with
her grandmother at Joinville, where she was joined
by Anne of Aerschot, the one of all her mother's
family to whom she clung the most closely, calling

[1] Venetian Calendar, vii. 163; Calendar of State Papers,
Elizabeth, Foreign, iii. 224.

her " ma tante," and consulting her in all her
difficulties.[1]

Christina herself was full of sympathy for this
young Queen, whose early widowhood recalled her
own fate, and she joined cordially in the invitation
which the Duke sent Mary to pay a visit to Nancy.
" The Queen of Scotland," wrote Throckmorton to
Elizabeth on the 1st of May, 1561, " is at Nancy with
the Dowager, whom here they call Son Altesse."
Christina rode out with her son to meet their guest
on the frontiers of Lorraine, and her uncles, the two
Cardinals, Aumale, Vaudemont, and the Duchess of
Aerschot, all accompanied her to Nancy.

The touching beauty of the young widow created
a profound sensation at the Court of Lorraine. Brantôme describes her as " a celestial vision "; Ronsard
sang of the charms which transfigured *son grand
deuil et tristesse*, and made her more dangerous in this
simple white veil that rivalled the exquisite delicacy
of her complexion than in the most sumptuous robes
and dazzling jewels; and Clouet drew his immortal
portrait.[2] The Duke arranged a series of fêtes to
distract the young Queen's mind and help to dry her
tears. There were masques and dances at Nancy,
hunting-parties and banquets at Nomény, where
Mary stood godmother to the Count Vaudemont's
youngest child; and the Court was gayer than it had
been for many years. But intrigue was once more rife
at the French Court, and all manner of proposals
were made for the young widow's hand. The King of
Denmark, Frederic III., the Prince of Orange, the

[1] Calendar of State Papers, Elizabeth, Foreign, iv. 91; Venetian
Calendar, vii. 290.

[2] A. de Ruble, 210; Brantôme, xii. 116; Aubespine, 752.

Archduke Charles, the Dukes of Bavaria and Ferrara, were all suggested as possible husbands. The fascination which Mary had for the boy-King Charles IX. was well known, and Catherine de' Medici, who had never forgiven Mary for calling her a shopkeeper's daughter, was secretly plotting to keep her away from the Court, and yet prevent her marriage to Don Carlos, whom she wished to secure for her youngest daughter, Margot. The Cardinal of Lorraine was known to be eager for the Spanish marriage, and both Christina and Anne did their best to forward his scheme, which was the subject of many letters that passed between Granvelle, the Duchess of Aerschot, and Mary herself. But Philip, without actually declining the offer, always returned evasive answers, whether he shrank from placing his sickly and wayward son in an independent position, or whether he feared the power of the Guise faction.[1]

In the midst of the festivities at Nancy, Mary fell ill of fever, and as soon as she was fit to travel returned to Joinville, to be nursed by her grandmother; while Christina accompanied her son and his wife to Reims for the new King's sacring on the 15th of May. The magnificence of the Duchess-mother's appearance on this occasion excited general admiration. Grief and anxiety had left their traces on her face, but, in spite of advancing years and sorrow, Christina was still a very handsome woman. Among all the royal ladies who met in the ancient city, none was more stately and distinguished-looking than Madame de Lorraine. As her chariot, draped with black velvet fringed with gold, and drawn by four superb white horses of Arab breed, drew up in front of the Cardinal's palace, a

---

[1] Aubespine, 80-84; Bouillé, ii. 74; Venetian Calendar, vii. 290

Mary Stuart as Queen of France
in widow's dress
From the drawing in the Bibliothèque Nationale at Paris.

murmur of admiration ran through the crowd. The Duchess sat at one window, clad in a long black velvet robe, and wearing a jewelled diadem on her head, with a flowing white veil and cap of the shape that became known at the French Court as *à la Lorraine*, and was adopted by Mary, Queen of Scots, for her habitual use. At the other sat her lovely young daughter Renée, the coveted bride of many of the Princes who were present that day, while on the opposite seat was the Princess of Macedonia, an august white-haired lady, with the chiselled features of the proud Greek race to which she belonged. The Queen-mother, Catherine de' Medici, stood at a window of the Archbishop's palace to watch the entry of the Lorraine Princes, and as she saw the Duchess alight, she exclaimed: " That is the finest woman I know !" Then, descending the grand staircase, she advanced to meet Christina with a stately courtesy, and thanked her for the honour she was doing her son.

" Herself a very proud woman," writes Brantôme, " she knew that she had her match in the Duchess, and always treated her with the highest honour and distinction, without ever yielding one jot of her own claims."[1]

The Duke of Lorraine bore the sword of state at the great ceremony on the morrow, while Francis of Guise held the crown on the boy-King's head, and his brother, the Cardinal, anointed his brow with the holy chrism. " Everything," as Charles IX. wrote to the Bishop of Limoges, " passed off to the great satisfaction of everyone present;"[2] and when all was over, Madame de Lorraine and her children accompanied the King and his mother to a country-house

---

[1] Brantôme, xii. 117.   [2] Aubespine, 867.

belonging to the Cardinal in the neighbourhood, and enjoyed a week's repose in delicious spring weather. Then the Court went on to St. Germain, where the Queen of Scots came to take leave of her husband's family, and with many tears bade farewell to the pleasant land of France, which she had loved all too well for her own happiness.

III.

On the death of Christian II. of Denmark, his elder daughter, Dorothea, the widowed Electress Palatine, assumed the royal style and title. But as she was childless herself, and lived in retirement at Neuburg, in the Upper Palatinate, the faithful subjects who still clung to their rightful monarch's cause turned to Christina, the Duchess-Dowager of Lorraine, and begged her to assert her son's claims to the throne, saying that they regarded him as their future King. Chief among these was Peder Oxe, an able public servant who had been exiled by Christian III., and came to visit the Duchess in the convent of La Cambre at Brussels in 1559, soon after the captive monarch's death. Peder tried to enlist her sympathies on behalf of her father's old subjects, and assured her that the recovery of Denmark would be an easy matter, owing to the unpopularity of the new King, Frederic III. At first Christina lent a willing ear to these proposals, but her friend Count d'Aremberg succeeded in convincing her of the futility of such an enterprise, while both Philip and Granvelle firmly refused to support the scheme.[1] Peder Oxe, however, followed Christina to Nancy, where he be-

----

[1] Schlegel, 253; Granvelle, vi. i.

came a member of the Ducal Council, and did good service in restoring order in the finances.

Other Danish exiles sought refuge at the Court of Lorraine, where their presence naturally revived Christina's dreams of recovering her father's throne. All manner of rumours were abroad. In March, 1561, Chaloner heard that the French King and the Duke of Lorraine were about to invade Denmark. Three months later Mary, Queen of Scots' faithful servant, Melville, wrote from Heidelberg that the Duchess-Dowager of Lorraine had come there to persuade her sister, the old Countess Palatine, to surrender her rights on Denmark to her nephew, the Duke of Lorraine. Christina spent some time with her sister, and was joined in September by the Duke, who came to escort her home.[1] The Palatine Frederic's successor, Otto Heinrich, had died in 1559, and his cousin, the reigning Elector, Frederic of Zimmern, the brother of the Countess Egmont and her sister Helene, was deeply attached to Dorothea, and, like his predecessor, professed the Lutheran faith. A year after Christina's visit Dorothea died suddenly at Neuburg, and was buried by her husband's side in the Church of the Holy Ghost at Heidelberg. The Palatine Frederic erected a fine monument over her grave, with the following inscription:

" To the most noble Lady, Dorothea, Countess Palatine, and Queen of Denmark, Sweden, and Norway, the beloved consort of the Elector Frederic II., this tomb was raised by Frederic III., by the grace of God Elector Palatine, in the year 1562, as a token of love and gratitude to this his most dear and excellent kinswoman."

[1] Calendar of State Papers, Elizabeth, Foreign, ii. 458, iii. 328.

31

Dorothea's tomb was destroyed with that of her husband and many others when Louis XIV.'s armies sacked and burnt Heidelberg in 1693, but an English traveller who visited the castle and Church of the Holy Ghost thirty years before, preserved this in-scription in his diary.[1]

Christina came to Heidelberg with her son and both her daughters in the autumn of the year 1562, and was present at Frankfurt on the 24th of November, when her cousin Maximilian was crowned King of the Romans. On this occasion the Emperor Ferdinand collected as many of the imperial family as possible around him. The Dukes and Duchesses of Bavaria and Cleves were present, as well as most of the Electors and Princes of the Empire; while Ibrahim Bey, the Sultan's Ambassador, brought camels and rugs and Persian jars as gifts from his master. Among the old friends whom the Duchess met at Frankfurt were the Prince of Orange, Counts Egmont and Jacques d'Aremberg. They greeted her with renewed friendliness, and from their lips she heard how badly things were going in the Low Countries, and how unpopular the Regent and her Minister, the newly-created Cardinal de Granvelle, had become with all classes of people.[2] The Emperor and all his family returned to Heidelberg after the coronation, and were splendidly entertained by the Palatine, who was anxious to arrange a marriage between one of his sons and Mademoiselle de Lorraine. But Frederic's strong Lutheran tenets were a serious obstacle to this plan. At the recent corona-

[1] A. Churchill, " Collection of Voyages and Travels," vi. 458.

[2] Calendar of State Papers, Elizabeth, Foreign, v. 554; Granvelle, vi. 683.

tion he had refused to attend Mass, and had remained in the vestry of the cathedral until the service was over.

Meanwhile religious strife was raging in France, and Christina returned to Nancy to find that civil war had broken out. Earlier in the year the massacre of a peaceable congregation at Wassy, near Joinville, had excited the fury of the Huguenots, and a fierce struggle was being waged on the frontiers of Lorraine. The Duke's own kindred were divided. Condé was the leader of the revolted party, while his brother Antoine, King of Navarre—l'Échangeur, as he was called, because he was said to change his religion as often as he did his coat—was mortally wounded, fighting on the King's side, in the siege of Rouen. A month later the Constable de Montmorency was made prisoner in the Battle of Dreux, by his own nephew Coligny. On the 21st of February, 1563, Christina and her son were attending the baptism of the Duke of Aumale's son Claude, when a messenger arrived with the news that the Duke of Guise had been stabbed by a Huguenot fanatic in the camp before Orleans. After a public funeral in Notre Dame, the remains of Antoinette's most illustrious son were buried at Joinville, amid the lamentations of the whole nation.[1]

Fortunately, the duchy of Lorraine escaped the horrors of civil war. On the 18th of May, 1562, Charles made his long-deferred state entry into Nancy, and took a solemn vow to observe the rights of his subjects before he received the ducal crown. But he still consulted his mother in all important matters, and treated her with the utmost respect

[1] Pimodan, 215.

and affection.[1] His own time and thoughts were chiefly occupied in enlarging and beautifying the ducal palace. He extended the Galerie des Cerfs, and built a fine hall, adorned with frescoes of the Metamorphoses of Ovid, a translation of which had been dedicated to his grandfather, Duke Antoine, by the poet Clement Marot. At the same time he rebuilt the old Salle du Jeu de Paume on the model of one at the Louvre, and made a picture-gallery above this new hall, which he hung with portraits of the ducal family.[2]

Christina also devoted much attention to the improvement of her estates. She rebuilt the salt-works at Les Rosières, which had been abandoned in the last century, and placed an inscription on the gates, recording that in February, 1563, these salt-works were erected by

" Christina, by the grace of God Queen of Denmark, Sweden, and Norway, Sovereign of the Goths, Vandals, and Slavonians, Duchess of Schleswig, Dittmarsch, Lorraine, Bar, and Milan, Countess of Oldenburg and Blamont, and Lady of Tortona."[3]

Several indications of the active part that she took in affairs of State appear in contemporary records. In 1564, with the Pope's sanction, she concluded an agreement with the Bishop of Toul, by which he made over his temporalities to the Duke of Lorraine. Christina, as she explained to Granvelle, had taken this step to avoid the see from becoming the property of France; but her action roused the indignation of her uncle, the Emperor Ferdinand, who rebuked his

---

[1] Granvelle, vii. 488.
[2] Pfister, ii. 184; H. Lepage, " Le Palais Ducal de Nancy," 3.
[3] Calmet, iii. 30.

DVC DE LORRAINE

CHARLES

Grand Duc le Prince Ayné, des Princes de tú Race,
Le Lorrein etonné de tés exploits guerriers,
Ne peut assez trouuer en son cloz de Lauriers,
Pour ombrager ton front, tes Temples, et ta face.

Thomas de leu Fe: et excud:

CHARLES III., DUKE OF LORRAINE

To face p. 472

good niece sharply for venturing to meddle with the affairs of the Imperial Chamber.[1]

On the 8th of November, 1563, the Duchess Claude gave birth to her first child, a boy which was named Henry, after her father, the late King of France. Both Charles IX. and Philip II. consented to stand godfathers, and the French King announced his intention of attending the child's christening in person. His visit, however, was put off, as the young Duchess fell seriously ill of smallpox, and was eventually fixed to take place at Bar after Easter. There was even a rumour that King Philip, whose presence in the Low Countries was earnestly desired, would visit Lorraine on his journey, and meet the French monarch on the 1st of May. The prospect of seeing Catherine and her son with an armed force in Lorraine filled Christina with alarm. The Queen-mother, as she knew, was very jealous of the Duchess-Dowager's influence with her son, and neglected no means of placing French subjects in positions of authority at the Ducal Court;[2] while her recent intrigues with the Huguenot leaders might lead to the introduction of Protestant rites at the ceremony. Before the date fixed for the christening, however, Christina received an unexpected visitor in the person of Cardinal Granvelle, who had been compelled to bow to the storm and leave the Netherlands. In a private note which he sent to Granvelle on the 1st of March, 1564, Philip had desired the Cardinal to retire to Besançon on plea of paying a visit to his mother, whom he had not seen for nineteen years. The desired permission was readily granted by the Regent, and, to the great satisfaction

[1] Granvelle, vii. 344; Calmet, iii. 434, 438.
[2] Granvelle, vii. 488.

of the nobles, the hated Minister left Brussels on the
13th of March. " Our man is really going," wrote
William of Orange to his brother Louis. " God grant
he may go so far that he can never return !"[1]

The Cardinal had by this time recognized his fatal
mistake in persuading the King to appoint the
Duchess of Parma Regent instead of Madame de
Lorraine, " by which action," as he himself wrote,
" I made the Prince of Orange my enemy."[2]   He
was the more anxious to recover Christina's good
graces, while she on her part does not appear to have
borne him any grudge for his share in the transaction.
His way led him through Lorraine, and when he
reached Pont-à-Mousson he found a messenger from
the Duchess begging him to come and see her at
Nancy.   On his arrival he was received by the
Duke's *maître d'hôtel*, and conducted to lodgings in
the palace.   This " very fine house," and the hospitality with which he and his companions were entertained, gratified the Cardinal, and after supper he
was received by the Duchess-Dowager, with whom he
had a long interview in the Grande Galerie.[3]   They
conversed freely of the troubles in the Netherlands.
Christina was anxious to justify herself from the charge
of fomenting these dissensions, and declared that
she had nothing to say against the Duchess of Parma,
and only complained of her refusal to allow a Mass
for her father, King Christian II., to be said in the
Court chapel on the anniversary of his death.   But
she had many complaints to make of the King, who
had only written to her five times in the last five
years, and who insisted on keeping her Castle of

---

[1] Gachard, " Correspondance de Guillaume, Prince d'Orange,"
ii. 67; Groen, i. 214.   [2] " Mémoires de Granvelle," xxxv. 19.
[3] Granvelle, vii. 437-440..

Tortona in his own hands, and employed the revenues
of the town to pay the garrison, without giving her
any compensation. Granvelle could only allege the
unsettled state of Lombardy and the disorder of
Milanese finances as excuses for Philip's behaviour.
The Duchess further confided to him her fears regarding the French King's visit, and the intrigues of
Catherine, who was always endeavouring to destroy
the harmony that prevailed between herself and her
daughter-in-law. Granvelle did his best to allay
these alarms, and assured her that the rumours as
to the large force that was to accompany him to
Lorraine were absolutely false.

Another subject on which Christina consulted the
Cardinal was her designs against Denmark. The
young King Frederic III. at first professed great
friendship for her, and opened negotiations for his
marriage with her daughter Renée—a proposal which
she was reluctant to accept.[1] This idea, however, was
soon abandoned, and the outbreak of war between
Denmark and Sweden seemed to afford an opportunity for advancing her own claims.   Peder Oxe and
his companion in exile, Willem von Grümbach, urged
her to raise an army and invade Jutland, assuring her
that the discontented Danish nobles were only longing
for an excuse to rise in a body and dethrone the
usurper. But Christina realized that it would be
useless to make any attempt without Philip's support,
which she begged Granvelle to obtain.   The Cardinal,
however, quite declined to approach the King on the
subject, and told the Duchess that a rupture with
Denmark would make him more unpopular in Flanders
than he was already, saying that he had no wish to be

[1] Schäfer, v. 111. 112.

stoned by the Dutch. Before leaving Nancy he discussed the situation at length with the Duchess's
latest friend, Baron de Polweiler, the Bailiff of
Hagenau, a brave and loyal servant of Charles V.,
who had warmly espoused Christina's cause and
was in correspondence with the Danish malcontents.
The Baron was a wise and practical man, and agreed
with Granvelle that the best course of action would
be to keep up the agitation in Denmark, without
taking further measures until the coming of King
Philip, which was now confidently expected.[1]

After the Cardinal's departure, Christina fell ill at
Denœuvre, and was unable to accompany the Duke,
who came to fetch her, and insisted on putting
off the child's christening until his mother was fit
to travel. At length, on the 2nd of May, the
Duchess and her daughters started for Bar, where the
christening was celebrated on the following day, and
Christina held her grandson at the font. There was
no display of armed force, nor was any attempt made
to introduce Lutheran rites. On the contrary, the
Queen-mother and all her suite were most amiable,
the greatest good-will prevailed on all sides, and the
whole party spent the next week in feasting, jousting,
and dancing, while Ronsard composed songs in honour
of the occasion. On the 9th of May the young King
resumed his progress to Lyons, and the aged Duchess
Antoinette, who had come to Bar at the Cardinal of
Lorraine's prayer, returned to Joinville with her son.
Christina's worst alarms had been dispelled, but
her suspicions were to some extent justified by the
revival of the French King's old claims to Bar, and
the advance of certain new pretensions, which were

[1] Granvelle, vii. 533, 671, viii. 522.

eventually referred to a court of justice in Paris. What annoyed her scarcely less was the inferior quality of the ring sent by the King of Spain to Duchess Claude, which excited more than one unpleasant comment, although Count Mansfeldt, who stood proxy for Philip, informed her privately that Margaret of Parma had spent double the sum named by His Majesty on his christening present.[1]

IV.

In July, 1564, Christina fell dangerously ill, and Silliers told Polweiler that his mistress was suffering from a grave internal malady. In November she had a severe relapse, and her death was hourly expected. Her children and servants nursed her with untiring devotion, and her friends at Brussels were deeply concerned. Anne d'Aerschot, Margaret d'Aremberg, Egmont, and the Prince of Orange, made frequent inquiries; and even Queen Mary wrote from Scotland to ask after the Duchess's health. Philip alone took no notice of her illness, and his indifference was keenly resented by Christina and her whole family. " For the love of God," wrote Silliers to Polweiler, " do your best to see that Madame is consoled, or she will certainly die of grief and despair." And he poured out a passionate complaint, setting forth his mistress's wrongs, and saying how, after cheating her out of Vigevano, the King kept both the castle and revenues of her dower city in his hands, and allowed her subjects to be exposed to the depredations of the Spanish garrison. " To my mind," he adds, " this is a strange proof of the singular

[1] Calmet, iii. 1359; Granvelle, viii. 46.

affection which he professes to have for my Lady !"[1]
Granvelle himself was much concerned, and, when
Polweiler wrote to report an improvement in the
Duchess's condition, expressed his thankfulness, saying
that the loss of such a Princess would be a heavy
blow to the cause of religion, as well as the greatest
calamity that could befall Lorraine. He owned that
Madame had been harshly treated, and could only
counsel patience and assure her of Philip's good-will;
but he confessed that the task was a disagreeable one.
When Philip wrote at last, it was merely to exhort
the Duchess to be patient, as the whole world was
in travail, and to promise that her claims should be
settled by the Cardinal.[2] Meanwhile fresh appeals
reached Christina every day from her Danish partisans, while King Eric of Sweden, who had declared
war on Denmark, opened negotiations with her
through his French Minister, Charles de Mornay. A
marriage between this young King and Renée was
proposed, and Eric offered to support the Duchess's
rights to Denmark if she could obtain the help of the
Emperor and of the Netherlands. Ferdinand, however, quite declined to countenance any attack on his
ally, and begged his dear niece not to stir up strife in
Germany, although he assured her of his paternal
love and readiness to help her in the recovery of her
rights by peaceable methods. A few weeks after
writing this letter the good Emperor died, and, as
Christina knew, she could expect little from his successor Maximilian, who had never forgiven her friend·
ship with Philip in bygone days, and did not even
send her the customary announcement of his father's
death.

[1] Granvelle, viii. 345.   [2] *Ibid.*, viii. 472.

Another ally whose help the Duchess tried to enlist was the old Landgrave, Philip of Hesse, whose daughter Christina, after being wooed for some years by the King of Sweden, was finally married to Duke Adolf of Holstein on the 20th of January, 1565. As Granvelle remarks, it was a strange ending to this Prince's long courtship of Madame de Lorraine, but he probably still hoped to support her cause in Denmark. And as the Prince of Orange was asked to represent King Philip at the marriage, Christina would have an opportunity of consulting him about her Danish expedition.[1]   But the Prince refused to leave Flanders, and a serious relapse prevented the Duchess from attending the wedding. As soon as she had recovered sufficiently, Christina dictated a letter to her beloved sister Anne, who was still her most faithful friend:

" Your letter was most welcome, as I had not heard from you lately, and I thank you warmly for all that you say. I am getting better, but am not very strong yet. As to the Swedish business, I am anxious to know the name of the person whom you mention as having the greatest affection for me and mine, and who might help me with the King. And as I know that you only desire my good, I beg you to keep your eyes open, and tell me who are my best friends at Court. I quite agree with you that it is useless to fish in troubled waters. Monsieur d'Egmont's journey to Spain is a surprising event ! The cause is unknown to me, but it must be some matter of importance. Thank you again with all my heart for the love that is expressed in your letters."[2]

The friends to whose influence at Court Anne had referred were the Count and Countess of Aremberg, who stood high in favour with the King and the

[1] Granvelle, viii. 609.   [2] Ibid., viii. 637.

Regent, and were in constant correspondence with Christina.

" Would to God," wrote Margaret of Aremberg, " that Madame de Lorraine could obtain the King's favour ! She would then be easily able to regain her own, as the Danes hate their King, and he has no power over them. But I confess I have lost all hopes of this ever coming to pass."[1]

By the advice of these friends, the Duchess now decided to send Baron de Polweiler to Spain to beg the King for the 300,000 crowns due to her, in order that she might avail herself of the opportunity presented by the war between Sweden and Denmark, and open the campaign in the summer. Upon this Granvelle felt it his duty to inform his master of the Duchess's plans, which might, he thought, be successful if the King could help her with subsidies, since she had several allies in Germany.[2]   Duke Eric of Brunswick offered to raise an army and take the command of the expedition, and the Landgrave of Hesse promised to help on condition that she gave her daughter Renée in marriage to one of his sons; while, by way of removing Philip's objections, the Cardinal dwelt on the advantages of restoring the true faith in these Northern kingdoms. But this plan was frustrated by the Archduke Ferdinand's refusal to give Polweiler leave of absence, and as Silliers, who offered to go in his stead, would only have made matters worse, Christina resolved to ask Count Egmont to plead her cause at Madrid. Even Granvelle, who had no love for the Count, approved of this plan. Egmont was known to be devoted to the Duchess, and his great

---

[1] Granvelle, viii. 637.
[2] Granvelle, ix. 22, 28; Schäfer, v. 114.

popularity in the Low Countries would go far to remove the objections to a breach with Denmark in those provinces. Unfortunately, in spite of his goodwill, Egmont effected no more for Christina than he did for the liberties of the Netherlands. He was royally entertained by Philip and his courtiers, and loaded with presents and flatteries, but, when he came to business, received nothing but vague words and empty promises.

On his return to Flanders in April, his house was crowded with visitors, and the Duchess, finding that she could obtain no answer to her letters, determined to go to Brussels herself. In June she set out on her journey, saying that she was going to kiss the Holy Coat at Treves and pay her devotions to the Blessed Sacrament of the Miracle at Brussels, in fulfilment of a vow made when she had been at the point of death.[1] Her pilgrimage excited great curiosity, and even Polweiler was in the dark as to its object, but felt convinced that she meant to see Egmont and Eric of Brunswick, and that they would soon hear of a sudden call to arms.

" I hear from a trustworthy source," wrote the Landgrave to Louis of Nassau, " that the old Duchess of Lorraine is going to Brussels with both her daughters. She has raised 400,000 crowns at Antwerp to make war on Denmark, and is to be helped by the Netherlands with ships, money, and men. Her daughter Renée is to marry King Eric, and a close alliance against the Danish King is to be formed between Sweden, Lorraine, the States, and the Holy Empire. Although I do not hold popular rumours to be as infallible as Holy Gospel, I count them more worthy of belief than Æsop's fables or the tales of Amadis de Gaul. Of one thing I am quite sure: The

[1] Granvelle, ix. 373.

Duchess does not travel to Flanders or send an Ambassador to Sweden to roast pears or dance a galliard. The latest report is that the Duchess is going to sell her claims on Denmark to the King of Spain, but I can hardly think His Majesty will be anxious to buy these barren rights which bring a war in their train. Do not take my gossip unkindly, but let me know what you hear of this business."[1]

A cloud of mystery surrounds this visit which Christina paid to Brussels in the summer of 1565. She declined the Regent's invitation to occupy her old quarters in the palace, but stayed in the religious house known as the Cloister of Jericho, and afterwards with the Duchess of Aerschot at Diest. She received visits from Duke Eric, who professed himself ready to raise troops to serve her at the shortest notice, and also from Count Egmont. But all that she could learn from this noble was that, when he urged her claims on the King, and begged him to see that the arrears due to her were paid, Philip replied that Her Highness was the wisest and most virtuous of women, and would always take the best course possible.[2] By August Christina was back in Lorraine, and attended the christening of Nicholas de Vaudemont's new-born daughter, who received the name of Christina.[3]

Whatever others may have felt about the Duchess's designs on Denmark, the King of Sweden was evidently in earnest. Four Ambassadors arrived at Nancy on All Saints' Day, 1565, and went on to Denœuvre. They brought offers from Eric to conquer Norway and Denmark in the Duchess's name and leave her in possession of the latter kingdom, and asked for Madame Renée's hand, in order to confirm the alliance between Lorraine and Sweden. During a whole year the Swedish Envoys remained at Nancy, and prolonged conferences were held between them and the Duke and his mother. A new ally also came to her help in the person of the Czar of Muscovy, who was profuse in his offers of assistance. Christina's hopes rose high, and a medal was struck in 1566, bearing her effigy as Queen of Denmark, with the motto: *Me sine cuncta ruunt* (Without me all things perish).[1] But one ally after the other failed her. Both the Emperor Maximilian and the Elector of Saxony, who had married a Princess of Denmark, were strongly opposed to her schemes; while the ancient feud between the Danes and Swedes, who, in Silliers's words, " hated each other as much as cats and dogs or English and French," helped to complicate matters.[2] At the same time, she felt reluctant to give her daughter to a man of Eric's unstable character, who had been courting Queen Elizabeth and Christina of Hesse at the same time, and was known to have a low-born mistress. She had good reason to be afraid that the story of King Christian and Dyveke might be repeated, and her fears were justified when, a year later, the King of Sweden raised this favourite to the throne, and was soon afterwards deposed by his subjects. The defection of Peder Oxe, who made his peace with the King of Denmark and returned to Copenhagen at the close of 1566, was another blow, and the ultimate defeat of the Swedes in the following year extinguished her last hopes.[3] Cardinal Granvelle, who had been sent to Italy by Philip to keep him away from the Netherlands, wrote

---

[1] Schäfer, v. 116-118; Calmet, ii. 26.
[2] Granvelle, ix. 661-664; Groen, i. 303.   [3] Schäfer, v. 167.

that the Viceroy, with the best will in the world, found it impossible to pay the arrears due to the Duchess, and could not withdraw the garrison at Tortona without the King's leave. As for the Danish expedition, Granvelle told Polweiler that it was more hopeless than ever, and he could only advise Her Highness to abandon the idea.[1]

" Madame de Lorraine," replied the Baron, " is in great perplexity, abandoned by all her relatives, and, like Tantalus, is left to die of thirst, looking down on a clear and beautiful stream."

But a few faithful friends were still left. In May, 1566, the Duchess of Aerschot came to Lorraine with her young son, and spent the summer in her old home. The troubles in the Netherlands filled her with the utmost anxiety, and her family, like many others, was divided. All her own sympathies were with William of Orange and Egmont in the struggle for freedom, but her stepson, Philip of Aerschot, and her cousin, Count d'Aremberg, were among the few nobles who refused to join the League, and stood fast by the Regent. Margaret of Parma looked coldly on her, owing to Anne's connection with Christina and the Prince of Orange, and did not even send her an invitation to her son Alexander's wedding. With her wonted good sense, Anne refused to notice this affront, and told her friends that she was too unwell to attend the festivities, which excited much discontent by their profuse extravagance.[2]   But the situation was painful, and she was glad to retire to Lorraine and enjoy the company of Christina and her venerable aunt, Duchess Antoinette. Together they read the affectionate letters

---

[1] Granvelle, "Correspondance," i. 126, 178.   [2] *Ibid.*, i. 43, 524.

which Mary Stuart wrote from her Northern home, and sighed over the perils surrounding the young Queen. In spite of her relatives' advice, she had married Darnley, the handsome Scottish boy whom her uncle the Cardinal of Lorraine termed " that great nincompoop of a girl," and was already learning to her cost the mistake that she had made.

Terrible news now came from Flanders. Riots broke out in Antwerp and Ghent, and spread rapidly through the provinces. The great church of St. John was plundered, Hubert van Eyck's famous Adoration was only saved by the presence of mind of the Canons, and the tomb of Christina's mother, Queen Isabella, was hacked to pieces.[1] In Brussels S. Gudule was stripped of its pictures and statues, and the cry of " Vivent les Gueux!" rang through the courts of Charles V.'s palace. The Regent tried in vain to escape, and was forced to turn for help to the Prince of Orange and her most bitter enemies. Anne returned home to find public affairs in dire confusion, and retired to her dower-house at Diest. After her departure Christina became seriously ill, and in the spring of 1567 her daughters entreated the Countess of Aremberg to come to Lorraine, saying that her presence would be the best medicine for their mother. Margaret obeyed the summons and spent three months at Nancy and Denœuvre.[2] On her return she told Granvelle's friend, Provost Morillon, that the King made a great mistake in being so unfriendly to the House of Lorraine, and that if Madame died the Duke would become altogether French, and his duchy might at any moment fall into the hands of France. Charles was Catholic to his finger-tips, and

[1] Granvelle, "Correspondance," i. 444.   [2] *Ibid.,* i. 494.

entirely devoted to his mother, but after her death
no one could tell what might happen.[1]   These representations were not without effect.   Philip wrote in
a more kindly strain to the Duchess, and sent one of
his Chamberlains—Don Luis de Mendoza—to wait
upon her at Nancy, and remain in Lorraine until the
arrival of the Duke of Alva, who was now despatched
from Spain to replace Margaret of Parma as Captain-
General of the Netherlands.   In July he crossed the
Mont Cenis, and marched through Lorraine at the
head of a force of picked Spanish and Italian soldiers
Brantôme rushed to Nancy to see this " gentle and
gallant army," with their fine new muskets and pikes,
but the sight filled many of the spectators with profound misgivings.[2]

The Prince of Orange had already resigned all his
offices and retired to Germany, but Egmont and his
friend Count Horn were caught in the fatal snare, and
were both arrested at a banquet in Alva's house on
the evening of the 9th of September.   The news filled
Europe with consternation.   In her distress Christina
wrote several letters to the King of Spain, pleading
passionately for the Count's release, and recalling his
great deeds and the devotion which he had always
shown to the King's service.[3]   Her appeals were
seconded by the Duke and his wife, by Vaudemont,
—Egmont's own brother-in-law—by the Duke and
Duchess of Bavaria, the Elector Palatine, and all the
Princes of the Empire.   Maximilian himself addressed
two autograph letters to Philip, praying for the Count's
release, and the Knights of the Golden Fleece protested against this violation of the rules of their Order.

[1] Granvelle, " Correspondance," ii. 494.   [2] Brantôme, i. 104.
[3] Gachard, " Correspondance de Philippe II.," i. 18.

But all was in vain. Philip vouchsafed no answer to any of these appeals, saying he would not change his mind if the sky were to fall on his head,[1] and on the 6th of June, 1568, the Grande Place witnessed the execution of the hero of Gravelines. A fortnight before this shocking event, Anne, Duchess of Aerschot, breathed her last at Diest, thankful to escape from a world so full of misery, and only grieving to think that her vast dower and fine estates would not pass to their rightful owner, William of Orange.[2] In the same month of May the first battle was fought between the revolted nobles and the Spanish forces, and Margaret of Aremberg's husband fell fighting valiantly in the mêlée. Meanwhile civil war had broken out again in France, and in November, 1567, the Constable Montmorency, the old Nestor of France, was killed in a battle at St. Denis, fighting against the Huguenots, with Condé and his own nephew Coligny at their head. Old friends were falling on every side, and before Christina's tears for her sister-in-law were dried, she and the aged Duchess of Guise were mourning the sad fate of Antoinette's luckless granddaughter, the Queen of Scots, who had been compelled to abdicate her throne, and was now a captive in the hands of her rival, Queen Elizabeth.

V.

While civil war was raging all round, and Christina's best friends were dying on the scaffold or the battle-field, the marriage of her daughter Renée brought a ray of light into her life. The tale of Renée's court-ships almost rivals that of her mother's. The Kings

---

[1] Gachard, " Correspondance de Philippe II.," i. 588, 738, 762.
[2] Granvelle, " Correspondance," iii. 235.

of Sweden and Denmark, William of Orange and
Henri de Joinville, were only a few among the candi-
dates who sought her hand.   Granvelle once proposed the Duke of Urbino as a suitable match, and
Philip was anxious to marry her to his handsome and
popular half-brother, Don John of Austria.   But
the Duchess declined this offer repeatedly, saying
that no child of hers should ever wed a bastard.
When in the summer of 1567, Don Luis de Mendoza
again urged this suit on the King's behalf, the Duchess
informed him that her daughter's hand was already
promised to Duke William of Bavaria, the eldest son
of the reigning Duke Albert and his wife, the Archduchess Anna.   The contract was signed in September, and the marriage took place early in the following
year,[1] and turned out very happily.   Throughout his
life the Bavarian Duke maintained worthily the strong
Catholic traditions of his house, and proved a dutiful
and affectionate son-in-law.   Christina spent the
following winter at the Castle of Friedberg in Bavaria,
where she was once more dangerously ill, and Silliers
as usual complained bitterly of Philip's neglect and
unkindness in never making inquiries after her health.
But, in spite of all rebuffs, neither the Baron nor his
mistress had abandoned their dreams of conquering
Denmark, and in April, 1569, Cardinal Granvelle
wrote to the King from Rome:

" Madame de Lorraine is still trying to recover her
father's kingdom, and both she and her Councillor,
Silliers, are continually begging me for help in this
matter.   In vain I have replied for the hundredth
time that I am too far from Madrid and the Low
Countries to know if the affair is practicable, and have

[1] Calmet, i. 265.

pointed out that, in the first place, the Dutch will
never break with Denmark; secondly, that the
Emperor would object to any attempt of this kind;
and, thirdly, that Your Majesty's hands are full.   In
fact, I have told her that I cannot see any solid
foundations for her hopes.   But she returns to the
charge again and again."[1]

It was the last flicker of an expiring flame. After
this, even Christina seems to have recognized the
futility of her schemes, and the death of Silliers finally
decided her to abandon them altogether. This " vain,
insupportable, and foolish man," as the Cardinal
called him, and whom her son, the Duke, also detested
cordially, lost his life in Bavaria, in September, 1572,
being killed by a shot from a crossbow, which was
said to be accidental, but which Granvelle and his
other enemies ascribed to a paid assassin.[2]   During
the last twenty years, it must be owned, Silliers had
been the Duchess's evil genius; but, in spite of all
his faults, he was sincerely attached to his mistress,
and his devotion to her interests cannot be questioned.

Christina spent the next six years chiefly at Nancy
or Denœuvre, in the company of her children and
grandchildren. The Duke had a large family of
three sons and six daughters, the eldest of whom,
Christina, bore a strong likeness to her grandmother
both in face and character. This Princess and her
cousin Louise de Vaudemont, the daughter of Nicholas
by his first wife, Margaret of Egmont, were great
favourites with the Duchess-mother, and spent much
time in her society. Louise was a fair and gentle
maiden, whose charms captivated Henry, Duke of
Anjou, when he came to Lorraine in 1573, on his way
to take possession of the throne of Poland.   He was

[1] Granvelle, " Correspondance," iii. 463.   [2] *Ibid.*, v. 418.

accompanied by his mother, Queen Catherine, who spent a week at Nancy, and after her son's departure remained some days at Blamont with Christina. When, two years later, Henry succeeded his brother, Charles IX., the new King's first thought was to make the Princess of Lorraine his wife. Christina was too ill to leave her bed, but Duchess Antoinette, still young in spite of her eighty years, brought the bride to Reims, where the wedding was celebrated two days after Henry III.'s coronation. The Duke and his sister Dorothea were present at the ceremony, as well as all the Guise Princes.[1] Five days afterwards, on the 20th of February, 1575, the Duchess Claude, whose health had long been failing, and who had lately given birth to twin daughters, died in the ducal palace, at the age of twenty-eight, leaving the Duke an inconsolable widower. He was only thirty-two, and although he lived till 1608, never married again. Soon after Claude's death, her eldest daughter, Christina, went to live with her grandmother, Catherine de' Medici, at the French Court. This masterful lady, who quarrelled with her own daughter Margaret, was very fond of Christina, and kept this young Princess constantly at her side during the next fourteen years.

In the following December, Elizabeth of Austria, the widow of Charles IX., and daughter of the Emperor Maximilian II., visited Nancy on her way back to Vienna, and was escorted on her journey by Renée and her husband, the Duke of Bavaria. They were all three present at the wedding of the Princess Dorothea, who was married in the Church of St. Georges, on the 26th of December, to Duke Eric of Brunswick.[2] This wild and restless Prince had

---

[1] Pimodan, 254.   [2] Calmet, i. 265; Pfister, ii. 256.

always been on friendly terms with Christina and her family, and was one of King Philip's favourite captains and a Knight of the Golden Fleece. He had lately lost his first wife, and succeeded his father in the principalities of Göttingen and Calenberg, although his roving tastes made him prefer foreign service to residence on his own estates. Now, at the age of forty-seven, he became the husband of Christina's younger daughter. In spite of her lameness, this Princess inherited much of her aunt Dorothea's charm and gaiety, and was fondly beloved by her brother and all his children. She took especial interest in the improvements which the Duke was never tired of making at Nancy, and helped him in laying out the beautiful terraced gardens, adorned with fountains and orangeries, in the precincts of the ducal palace. And the bell in the new clock-tower, which the Duke built in 1577, was named Dorothea, after the Duchess of Brunswick.[1] Charles himself, like his father, was a Prince of cultured tastes, who studied the Latin and Italian poets and took delight in Ronsard's verses. The foundation of the University at Pont-à-Mousson bore witness to his love of learning, while he employed scholars to collect precious books and manuscripts, and sent his gardeners to inspect the royal palaces at Fontainebleau and St. Germain, and to bring back rare plants and exotics.[2]

In these last years of Christina's life at Nancy, new hopes and interests were suddenly brought into her life by Don John of Austria's arrival in the Low Countries. When terrorism and massacre had failed

[1] Pfister, ii. 246; H. Lepage, " La Ville de Nancy," 63, " Palais Ducal," 3.

[2] Pfister, ii. 496.

to crush the revolted provinces, the hero of Lepanto was appointed Governor, in the hope that he might succeed in restoring order, by appealing to his illustrious father's memory and ruling the Netherlands according to his example. In October, 1576, Don John travelled through France in the disguise of a Moorish servant, and, after spending one night in Paris, came to Joinville to consult the Duke of Guise on a romantic scheme which he had formed to release and marry the captive Queen of Scots. Then he hurried on to Luxembourg and proclaimed his intention of withdrawing the Spanish troops and granting a general amnesty. The coming of this chivalrous Prince, with his message of peace, filled the people of the Netherlands with new hope. Don John was received with open arms by the Duke of Aerschot and his half-brother, Anne of Lorraine's son, Charles de Croy, Marquis of Havré. His first act was to restore the lands and fortune of the late Count Egmont to his widow, the Countess Palatine Sabina, and her innocent children. This rejoiced the heart of Madame d'Aremberg, who had been spending the winter at Nancy with the Duchess, and Christina's nephew, Charles de Croy, told Don John frankly that the Low Countries would gladly have him, not only for their Governor, but for their King. Christina herself was deeply stirred, and sent a member of her household to Luxembourg with a letter welcoming the Prince in the warmest terms, and thanking him for the cheering news which he had sent her.

" I can only praise God," she wrote, " for your appointment to the government of the Low Countries, and trust that the same success that, thanks

to your great valour and prudence, has everywhere
attended you will continue to crown your efforts.
       " Your very loving and more than
              very affectionate cousin,
                            " CHRÉTIENNE.
"Blâmont, November 12, 1576."[1]

In her anxiety to see Don John, the Duchess set
out for Pont-à-Mousson; but when she reached Nancy,
on the 12th of December, she heard that the Prince
had already left Luxembourg for the Netherlands,
and sent him the following letter by a confidential
servant, who was to tell him many things which she
could not commit to paper:

" MY COUSIN,
       " The singular wish that I have to see Your
Highness, and confer with you on many points of the
highest importance, induced me to leave Blamont
and come to Pont-à-Mousson, in order to be near you
and to have an opportunity of seeing you and conversing together, as you will learn more fully from
this gentleman whom I am sending to wish you all
prosperity and success in your noble designs and
enterprises, as well as to tell you many things which
I beg you to hear and believe."[2]

Don John replied in the same friendly spirit, telling
her his plans and thanking her most warmly for her
advice.

" As for me," he wrote, " I am exceedingly obliged
to Your Highness for your offers, and shall always
be most grateful for your advice and help, knowing,
Madame, your great experience and wisdom in affairs.
God knows how anxious I was to come and see Your
Highness on my journey here, and kiss your hands,
but it was impossible owing to the urgency of affairs

---

[1] Gachard, " Correspondance de Philippe II.," v. 29.
[2] *Ibid.,* v. 92.

requiring my presence here. I am very glad indeed,"
he adds in a postscript, " to hear that you are in good
health."[1]

The Prince was evidently impressed by the sound-
ness of the Duchess's judgment and by her great
popularity in the Netherlands, for when, a few weeks
later, he began to realize the hopeless nature of his
task, and begged for his recall, he repeatedly told
Philip that, in his opinion, the Duchess of Lorraine
would be the best person to take his place.

" The Duchess of Lorraine," he wrote on February
16, 1577, " has all the qualities necessary for the
government of these provinces, which she would
administer far better than I can, because they are
beginning to hate me, and I know that I hate them."

Again, a little later:

" I find in Madame de Lorraine a real desire to
serve Your Majesty. She has come to Pont-à-
Mousson to see if she can be of help to me, and I am
sure would gladly execute any orders that she may
receive."

Christina heard with delight of Don John's joyous
entry into Brussels on May Day, and received with
deep thankfulness his letter informing her of the
departure of the hated Spanish troops. But these
high hopes were doomed to disappointment. The
war soon broke out again, and after Don John's
victory of Gembloux in January, 1578, Madame de
Lorraine was one of the first persons to whom he
announced the news by letter.[2] Both of the Duchess's
sons-in-law joined in supporting Don John, and in
May, 1578, the Duke of Brunswick brought a force
of 3,000 Germans to join him at Namur. Dorothea

---

[1] Granvelle, " Correspondance," vi. 521.   [2] *Ibid.*, vii. 572.

accompanied her husband, and was about to pay the Prince a visit, when she received a message from her brother Charles, informing her of their mother's serious illness, and left hastily for Nancy.[1]

Five months afterwards a premature death closed the brilliant adventurer's career, and Christina was left to grieve over the tragic end of this Prince, of whom so much had been expected.

[1] Granvelle, vii. 638.

BOOK XIV

THE LADY OF TORTONA

1578—1590

I.

THE marriage of her last remaining daughter, and the removal of her granddaughter to the French Court, loosened the ties that bound the Duchess-mother to Lorraine. The failure of the high hopes which Don John's coming had aroused were a grievous disappointment, and, after her dangerous attack of illness in the spring of 1578, Christina decided to follow her doctor's advice and seek a warmer climate. Her thoughts naturally turned to her dower city of Tortona, whose inhabitants still paid her allegiance, in spite of Philip's invasion of her privileges. Since the Spanish garrison still occupied the castle, the magistrates begged her to inhabit the Communal palace, and Christina, touched by their expressions of loyalty and affection, resolved to accept the offer.

Before settling at Tortona, however, she decided to make a pilgrimage to Loreto, the shrine for which the Lorraine Princes had always cherished especial veneration. Early in August, 1578, she left Nancy and travelled across the Alps, and through Savoy, by the route which she had taken as a bride, nearly half a century before. Her old friend, the Duchess Margaret, whose marriage had been one of the happiest results of the Treaty of Câteau-Cambrésis, had already been dead four years, and her lord of the Iron-head was a confirmed invalid; but he sent his son, Charles Emanuel, to meet the Duchess and escort her to the citadel of Turin.

From Savoy, Christina proceeded to Milan, where she arrived on the 20th of August, and was hospitably entertained in the Castello by the Spanish Viceroy, the Marquis d'Ayamonte.[1] Once more she drove in her chariot through the streets where her coming had been hailed by rejoicing multitudes, once more she prayed by her husband's tomb in the Duomo and saw Leonardo's Cenacolo in Le Grazie. Her old friends, Count Massimiliano, the Trivulzi, and Dejanira, were dead and gone, and at every step the ghosts of bygone days rose up to haunt her memory. Then she travelled on by slow stages to Loreto, on the Adriatic shore, where she paid her vows at Our Lady's shrine, and offered a massive gold heart set with pearls and precious gems, to the admiration of future pilgrims.[2] But the long journey had overtaxed her strength, and when, on her return to Lombardy, she reached Ripalta, she was too ill to go any farther. Here she remained throughout the winter to recover from her fatigues and give the citizens of Tortona time to prepare for her reception.

At length, on the 17th of June, 1579, the Duchess made her state entry into the city. The magistrates met her at the gates with a stately baldacchino fringed

---

[1] Granvelle, " Correspondance," vii. 149.
[2] A. Villamont, " Voyages," 70 (1589).

with gold and silver, and escorted their Sovereign Lady to the house of Bartolommeo Busseto, where she alighted to partake of the banquet which had been prepared. Afterwards the loyal citizens accompanied her to the Palazzo Pubblico, halfway up the hill above the town, which had been splendidly fitted up for her occupation. The beauty of the view delighted the Duchess as much as the enthusiastic warmth of her reception, and the health-giving breezes of the Lombard city proved even more beneficial than her physicians had expected. " She came to our city of Tortona a dying woman, and lived there in health and comfort for more than ten years."[1] So wrote Niccolò Montemerlo, the historian whose chronicles of Tortona were published in 1618, when Christina had not yet been dead thirty years. His contemporaries joined with him in praising the Duchess's wise and beneficial rule, the strictness with which she administered justice, her liberality and benevolence.

" The Duchess Christina of Milan," wrote Campo of Cremona in 1585, " celebrated for her beauty and gracious manners, for her affability and generosity, has lately come to spend her widowhood in the city of Tortona, and lives there in great splendour, beloved by all."[2]

Christina's administrative powers found ample scope in the government of the city, and under her rule Tortona enjoyed a brief spell of peace and prosperity. She reformed abuses, obtained the restitution of lost privileges, and healed a long-standing feud with the city of Ravenna. At her prayer, Pope

[1] Niccolò Montemerlo, " Nuove Historie di Tortona " (1618), 247-253.
[2] A. Campo, " Storia di Cremona," 107; C. Ghilino, " Annali di Alessandria," 166; Hilarion de Coste, " Les Éloges," etc., i. 406.

Gregory XIII. repealed a decree exacting a heavy fine from every citizen of Tortona who entered Ravennese territory, and friendly communications were restored between the two cities. Before her coming, the Spanish Viceroy had incurred great unpopularity by building a new citadel on the heights occupied by the ancient Duomo and episcopal palace, and converting these into barracks and powder-magazines. In 1560 the foundations of a new Cathedral were laid by Philip's orders in the lower city, but this could not atone in the eyes of the citizens for the desecration of the venerated shrine founded by St. Innocent in the fourth century, and adorned with priceless mosaics and marbles. When, in 1609, the lofty campanile was struck by lightning, and 400 barrels of gunpowder stored in the nave exploded with terrific force, the accident was regarded as a Divine judgment, and the panic-stricken Spaniards joined in the solemn procession that bore the relics of the martyrs from their old resting-place to the new sanctuary.[1]

But if Christina could not atone for this indignity, or deliver Tortona from the presence of the hated Spaniards, she protected her subjects from their outrages, and rigidly enforced the observance of the law. Many were the petitions and remonstrances on behalf of her own rights and those of the citizens which she addressed to her dear and illustrious cousin, Don Carlos of Aragon, Duke of Terranuova, who reigned over the Milanese as Viceroy from 1583 to 1592. The Duchess was in frequent correspondence with her children beyond the Alps, and many requests for passes for horses which she is sending to Lorraine and Bavaria, as well as for privileges for

[1] Montemerlo, 260; N. Viola, " Il Santuario di Tortona," 5.

her Equerries, Signor Alfonso and Gaspare Visconti, are to be found in the archives of Milan.[1]

Many were the illustrious guests, remarks Montemerlo, who came to visit the Duchess at Tortona. In October, 1581, the Empress-Dowager Maria, widow of Maximilian II., passed through Lombardy on her return to Spain, and was received at Alessandria by Madame de Lorraine. Together they drove through streets hung with tapestries and adorned with triumphal arches, until, after three days' festivities, they went on to Tortona, and thence to Genoa. The families of the old Milanese nobles who had remained loyal to the House of Sforza welcomed Christina's return to Lombardy with joy. The nephew and heir of Count Massimiliano Stampa placed his superb pleasure-house at Montecastello, in the fief of Soncino, at her disposal, and named his eldest son Christian in her honour. The Guaschi of Alessandria, the Counts of Oria, the Trivulzi, the Somaglia and Visconti, vied with each other in entertaining her sumptuously.[2] The saintly Archbishop of Milan, Carlo Borromeo, visited her more than once, and the excellent Bishop of Tortona, Cesare Gambara, sought her help and advice in all that concerned the welfare of his people. From the day when, hardly more than a child herself, she begged Cardinal Caracciolo's protection for the destitute ladies at Pavia, Christina always cared for the poor and needy, and in her old age she was busy with active works of mercy. One of her last good actions was to send to Paris for Madame Castellani, a daughter of her old friend the Princess

[1] Feudi Camerali, Tortona, Archivio di Stato, Milano.

[2] Autografi di Principi: Sforza, Archivio di Stato, Milano; G. Porta, "Alessandria Descritta," 161; Merli e Belgrano, "Pal. d' Oria," 55.

of Macedonia, who was living in reduced circumstances
at the French Court, and bring her to Tortona to
spend the rest of her life in peace and comfort. So
she earned the love and gratitude of all around her,
and thousands blessed the good Duchess's name long
after she was dead.

II.

This last phase of Christina's life was on the whole
peaceful and happy. Brantôme pitied this great
lady, a daughter of Kings and niece of Emperors,
and the rightful Queen of three kingdoms, who,
after reigning over Milan and Lorraine, was reduced
to hold her Court in an insignificant Lombard town,
and was known in her last years as " Madame de
Tortone."[1]   But after her troubled life Christina was
grateful for the peace and repose which she found at
Tortona, and would have been perfectly content if it
had not been for the continual annoyances to which
she was exposed by Philip and his Ministers.   From
the moment that she settled in her dower city, the
King began to dispute her right to its sovereignty,
and insisted that, since Tortona had been settled
upon her as an equivalent for the dower given her
" out of pure liberality " by the late Emperor, she
was bound to surrender her claims on payment of
the sum in full.   Christina, on her part, maintained
with good reason that her claim to the city had never
before been questioned, and that it was settled on her
at her marriage, and belonged to her and her heirs of
the House of Lorraine in perpetuity.   The assertion
of this claim roused Cardinal Granvelle to the highest
indignation.   " So dangerous a thing," he wrote to

---

[1] Brantôme, xii. 120.

Philip, " cannot possibly be allowed." But, as he
confessed, what made the situation awkward was that
Madame de Lorraine's claims were strongly supported,
not only by her son, Duke Charles, but by the Emperor
Rudolf, the Duke of Bavaria, the Archdukes Ferdinand
and Charles, and all the Princes of the Empire.[1] A
long wrangle ensued, which ended in a declaration on
the King's part that he would consent to Tortona
being retained by the Duchess for her life, and afterwards held by her son-in-law and daughter, the Duke
and Duchess of Brunswick.

Dorothea and her husband were, in fact, the only
members of Christina's family for whom Philip showed
any regard. In 1578 Duke Eric was summoned to
Spain to join in the contemplated invasion of Portugal, and served in the campaign led by Alva two years
later. Dorothea accompanied her husband, and spent
most of her time at Court. The King evidently liked
her, and when, after the successful termination of the
war, the Duke and Duchess came to take leave of
him at Madrid, Granvelle was desired to draw up a
secret convention by which Tortona and the revenues
were assigned to Eric in lieu of the yearly pension
allowed him. But Dorothea was not to be out-
witted by the Cardinal. She insisted, on the arrears
due to her husband being paid in full, and Philip
himself told Granvelle to see that two or three thousand crowns of the Duke's salary were given to the
Duchess, since she was short of money, and this seemed
to him only reasonable. He also gave Dorothea two
fine horses, which she wished to send to her brother-
in-law, the Duke of Bavaria, and granted her a patent
for working certain gold-mines, which the Cardinal

[1] Granvelle, " Correspondance," x. 65.

promised to forward either to her mother at Tortona,
or else to the care of the Prince of Orange in Germany.[1]
This last direction sounds strange, considering that
the famous ban against the Prince, setting a price of
30,000 crowns on his head, had already been issued
at Granvelle's suggestion.[2]

The Duke and Duchess now returned to Göttingen,
after visiting Christina at Tortona, and remained in
their own dominions for the next few years, among
their long-neglected subjects. But Eric soon became
restless, and in April, 1582, Dorothea wrote to beg
Granvelle's help in obtaining the Viceroyalty of Milan
or Naples for her husband. The Cardinal promised
to do his best, and two years later actually recommended the Duke for the Viceroyalty of Sicily. But
a few weeks afterwards, on the 15th of December,
1584, Eric of Brunswick died at Pavia, and was buried
in the crypt of Bramante's church of S. Maria
Canepanova, where his tomb is still to be seen.[3]
The Duke's death released Philip from his promise
regarding the succession of Tortona. But he had
already taken the law into his own hands.

In June, 1584, when Christina and her ladies were
enjoying the delights of the Marchese Stampa's
beautiful villa at Montecastello, the Viceroy suddenly
appeared on the scene, and presented her with two
letters from His Catholic Majesty. These were to
inform her that, after long and mature deliberation,
the King and his Council had come to the conclusion
that her rights to the sovereignty of Tortona were
extinct, and reverted to him as Duke of Milan. But
since Madame de Lorraine was closely bound to him

[1] Granvelle, vii. 225, xii. 581.   [2] Groen, vii. 165.
[3] Granvelle, ix. 141, xi. 338.

by ties of blood, and still more by the singular affection which he had always borne her, His Majesty was pleased to allow her to retain the enjoyment of Tortona and its revenues for the remainder of her life, which he hoped would be long and prosperous. In vain Christina protested that her dowry had never been paid, and that this city was granted to her in its stead by the terms of her marriage contract. The Viceroy replied in the most courteous language that Madame was no doubt right, but that this was not his affair, and he could only recommend that on this point her claims should be referred to the Treasury.[1] He then proceeded to take possession of Tortona in the King's name, and hoisted the Spanish standard on the citadel and the Duchess's palace. Christina could only bow to superior force, but she forwarded a protest to the Catholic King and his Council, both of whom refused to receive it, on the flimsy pretext that the writer assumed the title of Queen of Denmark, which they could not recognize. Certainly, as Brantôme remarked, and as Polweiler and Silliers often complained, Philip showed his great affection for his cousin in a strange manner.[2]

Before the Duchess left Montecastello, she received the news of the Prince of Orange's assassination at Delft on the 10th of July, 1584. The hero and patriot had fallen a victim to the plots of Philip and Granvelle, and had paid the price with his life. Three years afterwards Christina shared in the thrill of horror that ran through Europe when Mary, Queen of Scots, died on the scaffold. In that hour she could only be thankful that the good old Duchess Antoinette was

[1] Feudi Camerali, Tortona, Archivio di Stato, Milano.
[2] Granvelle, x. 551; Brantôme, xii. 114.

spared this terrible blow, and had died four years before, at the advanced age of eighty-nine. To the last Antoinette kept up friendly relations with her niece, and in a letter written with her own hand in November, 1575, the venerable lady expressed her sincere regret that owing to her great age she was unable to welcome Christina in person on her return to Nancy, but that in the spring she quite hoped to come and see her once more before she died.[1]

In 1586 Christina's old rival, Margaret of Parma, and this Princess's stanch supporter, Cardinal Granvelle, both died. Friends and foes were falling all around, and young and old alike were passing out of sight. But the Duchess still enjoyed fair health and was so happy at Tortona that she often said she never wished to leave home. As a rule, however, she spent the summer months at the Rocca di Sparaviera, in the mountains of Monferrato, " more," writes the chronicler, " to please others than herself."[2] Each year she obtained permission from the Viceroy to send 250 sacks of wheat, free of duty, for the use of her household to the Rocca, and her *maggiordomo* went beforehand to prepare the rooms for her arrival.[3] The presence of the Duchess Dorothea, who joined her mother at Tortona after the Duke of Brunswick's death, was a great solace in these last years, and consoled Christina for many losses and sorrows.

Meanwhile the war of the League had broken out in France, and the three Henries were contending for the mastery. Since Henry III. was childless, Catherine now tried to put forward the claims of a fourth

[1] Pimodan, 322.   [2] Montemerlo, 250.
[3] Feudi Camerali, Tortona, Archivio di Stato, Milano.

Henry, the eldest son of her daughter Claude and the Duke of Lorraine, and a party in France maintained his claims to be at least as valid as those which Philip II. advanced in virtue of his wife Elizabeth. Christina's heart was moved at the thought of her grandson succeeding to the throne of France, and in 1587 she sent a Lorraine gentleman, De Villers, to Rome to beg the Pope for his support in this holy cause. The Pope, however, merely replied that he advised the Duke to live at peace with his neighbours. The Duchess, nothing daunted, sent De Villers to Nancy with letters bidding her son be of good cheer and persevere in his great enterprise. Unfortunately, the messenger fell into the hands of Huguenot soldiers, who took him into the King of Navarre's camp. All that could be found on him was an almost illegible letter from Her Highness the Duke's mother, containing these words:

" I am very glad to hear of the present state of your affairs, and hope that you will go on and prosper, for never was there so fine a chance of placing the crown upon your head and the sceptre in your hand."[1]

The Béarnais smiled as he read this characteristic effusion, and bade his soldiers let the man go free. Charles, on his part, expressed considerable annoyance at his mother's intervention, which only aroused the suspicions of King Henry III., and made him look coldly on his brother-in-law. The Duchess's last illusion, however, was soon dispelled, and after the murder of the Guise brothers at Blois, and the assassination of the last Valois, Henry of Navarre was recognized as King by the greater part of France.

Christina did not live to see the end of the civil war,

[1] S. Goulart, " Mémoires de la Ligue," ii. 213

and the union of Henri Quatre's sister with her own grandson. But the last year of her life was cheered by the marriage of her granddaughter Christina with the Grand - Duke Ferdinand of Tuscany. Several alliances had been proposed for this Princess since she had gone to live at the French Court with her grandmother. Catherine was very anxious to marry her to Charles Emanuel, who in 1580 succeeded his father as Duke of Savoy; but Spanish influences prevailed, and the young Prince took the Infanta Catherine for his wife.[1] In 1583 the Queen-mother planned another marriage for her granddaughter, with her youngest son, the Duke of Alençon, who had left the Netherlands and lost all hope of winning Queen Elizabeth's hand; but, fortunately for Christina, the death of this worthless Prince in the following June put an end to the scheme.[2] When, in October, 1586, the King of Navarre divorced his wife Margot, Catherine proposed that her son-in-law should marry her granddaughter; but this plan fell through, as Henry refused to abjure the Huguenot religion. On the death of the Grand-Duke Francis in 1587, his brother Ferdinand exchanged a Cardinal's hat for the ducal crown, and made proposals of marriage to the Princess of Lorraine. Catherine was overjoyed at the thought of her beloved Christina reigning in Florence, the home of her ancestors, and promised her granddaughter a dowry of 600,000 crowns, with all her rights on the Medici estates in Florence, including the palace of the Via Larga. Orazio Rucellai was sent to France to draw up the contract, which Bassompierre signed on the Duke of Lorraine's part, on the 20th of

---

[1] Ed. Armstrong, " Cambridge Modern History," iii. 413.

[2] Granvelle, " Correspondance," x. 411.

October, 1588.[1] But the state of the country was so unsettled that the Queen would not allow her granddaughter to travel, and the fleet which sailed to fetch the bride was detained for months in the port of Marseilles. The murder of the Duke of Guise at Blois in December threw the whole Court into confusion, and a fortnight later Catherine herself died, on the 5th of January, 1589. It was not till the 25th of February that the marriage was finally celebrated at Blois. In March the bride set out on her journey, attended by a brilliant company of French and Florentine courtiers. Dorothea of Brunswick came to meet her niece at Lyons, and accompanied her to Marseilles, where Don Pietro de' Medici awaited her with his Tuscan galleys, and on the 23rd of April Christina at length landed at Leghorn. Ferdinand met his bride at the villa of Poggio a Caiano, and conducted her in triumph to Florence.[2] When the prolonged festivities were over, Monsieur de Lenoncourt, whom Charles of Lorraine had sent to escort his daughter to Florence, went on, by his master's orders, to Tortona, " to kiss the hands of the Duke's mother, the Queen of Denmark, and receive her commands."[3]

Unlike her mother and grandmother, the Grand-Duchess Christina enjoyed a long and prosperous married life, and after her husband's death was Regent during the minority of both her son and grandson. There is an interesting triptych in the Prado at Madrid, with portraits of the bride, her mother and grandmother, painted by some Burgundian artist at the time of the wedding. The

---

[1] A. J. Butler, " Cambridge Modern History," iii. 42.
[2] A. v. Reumont, " Geschichte Toscana's," i. 327-329.
[3] H. Lepage, " Lettres de Charles III.," 93.

CHRISTINA OF DENMARK   CLAUDE OF FRANCE   CHRISTINE OF LORRAINE
DUCHESS OF LORRAINE   DUCHESS OF LORRAINE   GRAND DUCHESS OF TUSCANY

(Madrid)

To face p. 508

young Grand-Duchess, a tall, handsome girl of four-
and-twenty, wears a high lace ruff, with ropes of pearls
round her neck and a jewelled girdle at her waist.
She carries a fan in her hand, and the Medici *palle*
are emblazoned on her shield with the lilies of France
and the eagles of Lorraine.   Her mother, the short-
lived Duchess Claude, bears a marked resemblance to
Catherine de' Medici, but is smaller and slighter in
build, and altogether of a gentler and feebler type.
She too holds a fan, and wears a gown of rich brocade
with bodice and sleeves thickly sown with pearls.
Christina, on the contrary, is clad in mourning robes,
and her white frilled cap and veil and plain cambric
ruff are without a single jewel.   But the fine features
and noble presence reveal her high lineage.   Instead
of a fan, she holds a parchment deed in her hand, and
on her shield the arms of Austria and Denmark are
quartered with those of Milan and Lorraine, while
above we read the proud list of her titles—Queen of
Denmark, Sweden, and Norway, Duchess of Milan,
Lorraine, Bar, and Calabria, and Lady of Tortona.

This was the last portrait of Christina that was
ever painted.   In the following summer she went as
usual to the Rocca of Sparaviera with her daughter
Dorothea, to spend the hot days of August in the
hills.   But she had not been there long before she
fell dangerously ill.   In her anxiety to return home,
she took boat and travelled by water as far as Alessandria.   There she became too ill to go any farther,
and died on the 10th of August, 1590, in the house of
her friend Maddalena Guasco.[1]

The Duchess's corpse was borne by night to Tortona,
where a funeral service was held in the new Duomo,

[1] Montemerlo, 250.

after which the body was embalmed and taken by her daughter Dorothea to Nancy. The news was sent to King Philip in Spain, and he and his greedy Ministers lost no time in laying hands on her city and revenues. " We are informed," wrote the Viceroy to the President of the Senate, two days after Christina's death, " that Her Most Serene Highness Madame de Lorraine has passed to a better life, and accordingly we claim the pension of 4,000 crowns assigned to Her late Highness, on the quarter of the Castello, and enclose a list of the revenues of Tortona, which now revert to the Duchy of Milan."[1]

III.

The good citizens of Tortona were sorely distressed when they learnt that the remains of their beloved liege Lady were not to rest among them. But Christina's heart was in Lorraine, and her children laid her body in the crypt of the Cordeliers' church, in the grave of the husband whom she had loved so faithfully and so long. Twenty-one years later her ashes were removed with those of Duke Francis and his parents, Antoine and Renée, to the sumptuous chapel begun by her son Charles in 1607, and completed by his successors. The Rotonde, as it was called in Lorraine, was built on the model of the Cappella dei Principi, which the Duke's son-in-law, Ferdinand de' Medici, had lately reared in Florence, and was dedicated to Our Lady of Loreto. It was the work of a Tuscan architect, Gianbattista Stabili, and of Jean Ligier Richier, the son of the famous Lorraine sculptor, and was lined throughout with rich marbles and adorned

---

[1] Feudi Camerali, Tortona, Archivio di Stato, Milano.

with a mass of carving.[1] The cupola was added in
1632 by Simon Drouin, and the internal decorations were only completed in 1743, by order of the
husband of Maria Theresa, afterwards the Emperor
Francis I. By this Prince's pious care Latin inscriptions were placed over each sarcophagus, and the
following words were carved on the tomb of Christina
and her husband:

Francisco I . Lotharingiæ . Duci . Bari . Calabriæ . virtuti
bellicæ . natus . quas . ei . mors . immatura . præripuit . laurus
reddidit . nativa . benignitas . senilis . prudentia . semper . sibi
similis . sapientia . mortuus . anno . MDXLV.
  Christianæ . a . Dania . Ducis . memorati . thoro . sociatæ
pupilli . Caroli . Ducis . rebus . regendis . strenua . existimatione
supra . famam . maxima . fata . subiit . anno . MDXC.[2]

Christina's son, Charles III., died, after a long and
prosperous reign, on the 14th of May, 1608, and was
tenderly nursed during his last illness by his youngest
daughter, Catherine, and his sister Dorothea. After
her mother's death, the Duchess of Brunswick never
left Lorraine again, and became the wife of a Burgundian noble, Marc de Rye, Marquis of Varembon.[3]
She only survived her brother four years, and was
buried in the Jesuit church of St. Stanilas at Nancy.
Her remains and the heart of Duke Charles, which had
been interred in the same chapel, were removed to the
ducal mausoleum in 1772, when some fresh improvements were made in the Rotonde, by order of Marie
Antoinette, the daughter of the last Duke of Lorraine and of the Empress Maria Theresa.[4] At the
Revolution, in 1793, these tombs were destroyed and
their contents rifled by the mob, and the ashes of the

[1] Calmet, iii. 153.   [2] Pfister, i. 640-647; Calmet, ii. 87.
[3] Granvelle, " Papiers d'État," vii. 619.   [4] Pfister, i. 652.

dead Princes were flung into a common grave. In 1818 they were replaced in their original tombs, the sarcophagi were restored, and the old inscriptions once more carved in the marble.

Charles III.'s second daughter, Elizabeth, married her first cousin, Maximilian, who succeeded his father in 1598, as Duke of Bavaria, and played a memorable part in the Thirty Years' War. Her next sister, Antoinette, became Duchess of Cleves, while Catherine, the youngest and most interesting of the whole family, took the veil after her father's death. This beautiful and accomplished Princess refused all the suitors who sought her hand, among them the scholar-Emperor, Rudolf II., who found in her a kindred spirit. A mystic by nature, Catherine assumed the grey Capucin habit while she lived at her father's Court, and, after he died, founded a Capucin convent in Nancy. The Pope appointed her Abbess of Remiremont, a Benedictine community of high-born ladies, which she endeavoured to reform. She was much attached to her aunt Dorothea, and after her death spent most of her time at the Court of France with her niece Margaret, the wife of Gaston, Duke of Orleans. Catherine took an active part in French politics in the stormy days of Louis XIII., and died in Paris in 1648, at the age of seventy-five.[1]

The seventeenth century witnessed the gradual dismemberment of the duchy of Lorraine, and in Richlieu's days Nancy was again occupied by French invaders. At length, in 1736, the last Duke, Francis III., was compelled to surrender Lorraine in exchange for the grand-duchy of Tuscany, on his marriage with Maria Theresa, the only child of the

[1] Calmet, ii. 153; Pfister, ii. 734.

Emperor Charles VI. From that time Lorraine ceased to exist as an independent State, and became a province of France, while the ex-King Stanislas of Poland fixed his residence at Nancy and transformed the ancient capital into a modern city. By this marriage the House of Lorraine became merged in the imperial line of Habsburg, and the blood of King René still flows in the veins of the Austrian Emperor and of the royal families of Savoy and Spain.

Christina would have rejoiced to know that this union—a love-match like her own—was followed shortly by the elevation of Maria Theresa's husband to the imperial throne, and that by this means the House of Habsburg was raised to a height of power and splendour which it had never attained since the days of Charles V. For although she married twice into princely houses, and was much attached both to Milan and Lorraine, Christina was before all else a Habsburg, and the glory and welfare of the imperial race remained throughout her life the first object of her thoughts. Like Mary of Hungary and Eleanor of France, she grew up in absolute obedience to the Emperor's will, and wherever she went in after-years his word was still her law. In the darkest hours of her life, when she lost son and State at one blow, it was her greatest sorrow to feel that she could no longer be of service to the Emperor and his house. After the abdication of Charles V., this love and loyalty were transferred to Philip II., and her one fear was lest her son should be drawn into the opposite camp, and become French in his sympathies. And to the end she was always quick to obey the call of blood and respond to any appeal from a member of the House of Austria.

This strong family affection gave an added bitterness to the neglect and injustice which she suffered at Philip's hands during the last thirty years of her existence. One reason for his persistently harsh usage was, there can be no doubt, that Christina represented the national feeling and aspirations after freedom, which Philip and his ministers, Alva and Granvelle, did all in their power to crush. Both in the Netherlands, where the popularity of the great Emperor's niece made her dangerous in their eyes, and in Lombardy, where she filled an important position as Lady of Tortona, she came into collision with the same all-reaching arm. To the last she strove valiantly to resist the tyranny of Spanish officials and to protect her subjects from the rapacity of foreign soldiers, and a century after her death the citizens of Tortona still cherished the memory of the noble lady who, as long as she lived, had preserved them from the yoke of Spain.

Christina's lot was cast in troubled times, when crime and bloodshed were rife, and religious convictions only served to heighten the violence of men's passions; but her name shines pure and unsullied on these dark pages of history. She was naturally hasty and impulsive, she made some mistakes and met with many failures, but she was always generous and high-minded, faithful and affectionate to her friends, and full of ardent charity for the poor and downtrodden. Above all, her unceasing labours in the cause of peace justly earned the gratitude of her contemporaries, and deserve to be remembered by posterity.

At the close of this long and eventful life we turn back once more to Holbein's portrait of the youthful

Duchess. As we look at the grave eyes and innocent face, we ask ourselves what was the secret of this woman's power, of the strange fascination which she possessed for men and leaders of men. What made heroes like René of Orange, and daredevils like Albert of Brandenburg, count the world well lost for love of her? Why were brave captains and brilliant courtiers—Stampa, Vendôme, De Courrières, Polweiler, Adolf of Holstein—all of them her willing slaves from the moment that they saw her face and heard the sound of her voice? What drew thoughtful men like William of Orange and Emanuel Philibert into the circle of her intimate friends, and brought even the cold-hearted Philip under her spell? It was hardly her beauty, for she had many rivals, or her superior intellect and exalted birth. Rather was it the rare and indefinable quality that we call charm, the sweet womanliness of nature, the gentle sympathy and quick response of heart and eye, ready at any moment to listen and to help, to comfort and to cheer. This, if we mistake not, was the secret of Christina's wonderful influence, of the attraction which she possessed for men and women alike, an attraction which outlived the days of youth and endured to the last hour of her life. Ever loving, she was therefore ever beloved.

APPENDIX

A SELECTION OF UNPUBLISHED DOCUMENTS

I.

Christina, Duchess of Milan, to Francesco II., Duke of Milan.

MONSIGNORE mio cordialissimo marito : Ho bene veduto voluntieri, come sempre sono accostumata, le sue care littere del 20, ma di molto megliora voglia haveria voluto veder la presentia sua, come speranza mi fu data di breve esser, et per dire la vera verita ormai quelli Signori cominciano haver puì che torto. Pur mi voglio contentar di quello che la ragione consiglia che si faci, et quella dimora che V. S. judicara esser bene per tutti, lo havero anche io per accepto, ringratiandola de le sue cortese excusationi per la tardezza del ritorno, ma non savendogli gratia di quello che la mi scrive, ch'io nō prende pena di scriverli di mia mano, perchè questo e solo ben speso tempo, et a me agredable quanto cū V. S. parla, almeno per scriptura di propria mano, non potendo la per hora partialmente goder. In bona gratia sua senza fine riccoman[mi] cum ricordo del presto e sano ritorno, cosi N. S. Dio degni di conservarlo longamente. Mlo. li 7. Zugno. 1535.

Vostra très humble consorte,

CRISTIERNA.

A Monsignore cordiall[mo] mio consorte
le Duca de Millano.

[Autografi di Principi, Sforza, Archivio di Stato, Milano.]

II.

Christina, Duchess-Dowager of Milan, to Cardinal Caracciolo, Governor of Milan.

Quello affettione chio conosco V. R[ma] S[ria] portarmi, et il buon conto che la tene di me fa ch'io non possi cessar de desiderar' ogn' hora la salute et comodo lei: Ver ho la prego esser contento darmi nova come la si è portata in questa sua andata et di prēste si trova. Che di resto maggior consolatione no' potreî havere che saper di sua bona valetudine. Appresso: benchè sappia non essere bisogno, nondimeno no' cessero di' ricordar à V. R^ma Sig^ria el caso mio. Per il quale pregola a far presso la Cæs^rea M^tà mio supremo S^ro quello che de la singulari bontà sua sumāmento mi prometto; Et perchè tra tutte l' altre cose molto desidero il ben et honor della S^ra Dorothea. Perho la sara contenta per il particolar sua operar con Sia M^tà tanto efficamente quanto glie sia poss^le, acciò che col bon meggio lei me venghi essere esauditi; assicurando V. R^ma S^ra chio stimavo il comodo dessa S^ra Dorothea mio proprio. Parmi anchora non solamente ragionevole ma ex debito, che essendo compito il corso del integro anno che'l Illmo et Exmo di felicissima memoria, S^re Duca, già mio Consorte passeva di questa vita, si ne debbi anch' io tener memoria et fargli far il debito anniversario. Perho prego V. R^ma Sig^ra esser contenta supplicar Sua M^tà in mio nome, che commetti et ordino acciò che detto anniversario sia fatto nel modo che debitamente si conviene e son certiss^na che Sua M^tà nomo negar di fare cosi exequire. Non me occorrendo per hora altro, a V. R^ma S^ra molte me ricom^o et offero. Pregando N. S. Dio che gli doni presto et bon ritorno. Di Mlo. el xiiii. de' Ottobre, MDXXXVI.

Vostra buona figliola,

CHRESTIENNE.

Al R^mo et Ill^m S^ro Car^le Caracciolo,
Locoten^te generale di Sua M^tà nel
Stato de Mlo. come Patre osser^sso.
In Corte di Sua M^ta a Genoa.

[Autografi di Principi, Sforza, Archívio di Stato, Milano.]

III.

Christina, Duchess-Dowager of Milan, to Cardinal Caracciolo, Governor of Milan.

R^mo et mio quanto Patre honorando: Ho presentito per certo che in la hosteria de la Fontana se gli ritrova una bellissima chinea learda, manco bona che di apparenza bella, et perchè me ritrova haverne bisogno de una per la Persona mia, ho voluto cū ogni confidenza indrizzar' questa et el presente mio lachayo a V. S. R^ma pregandola che se consensi di conten-

34

tarme che l' habia; et cometti el pagamento fuori di la spesa ordinario del rollo stabilito, perchè se potea mettere nel numero de li debiti ch' andarano pagati per altro conto, et questo recevero per singular piacer da V. S. R^{ma}, in bona gratia de la quelli me reco^{do}. Dal Castello de Pavia, al 3º di Genaro, nel 1537. De V. S. R^{ma} comme bonne fille,

CRESTIENNE.

Al R^{mo} Car^{le} Caracciolo, Governator
de Mlo. quanto p^{re} honor^{do}. *Cito*,
cito.

[Autografi di Principi, Sforza, Archivio di Stato, Milano.]

IV.

Antoinette de Bourbon, Duchesse de Guise, to Mary, Queen of Scotland.

. . . La santé de votre petit fils est aussi bonne que lui fut onques. Il mange fort bien, et l'on le mène souvent a les ébats que me semble lui fait grant bien. Il me semble vous trouverez cru et devenu gras. Quant au reste de n're ménage, v're sœur est toujours malade de sa fièvre et a été cette semaine passée bien mal d'un flux de ventre qui l'a fort affoiblie. Il y a bien huit jours qu'elle ne bouge point du lit. Depuis hier le flux com̃ãse a passer, de la fièvre je ne vois pas grant amendement. . . . V^{re} frère Claude a été aussy malade jusqu'à la mort. . . . V^{re} sœur Anthoinette est aussy malade d'une fièvre et d'un rhume. . . . Je vous avise quo Madame v^{re} tante est mandée pour aller à la cour à la venue de la Reyne de Hongrie, qui doit bientost estre à Compiègne, ou le Roy et toute la Court doit estre en peu de jours. Je m'en suis excusée pour l'amour de mes malades. Il n'y a que deux jours que le gentilhomme du Roy d'Angleterre qui fût au Havre et le paintre, a été ici. Le gentilhomme vint vers moi, faisant semblant venir de trouver l'Empereur, et que ayant su Louise malade, il n'avait voullu passer sans la voir, afin d'en savoir dire de nouvelles au Roy son maistre, me priant qu'il la peut voir, ce qu'il fit, et c'estait le jour de sa fièvre. Il lui tint pareil propos qu'a moi, puis me dit qu'estant si près de Lorrayne, il avait envye d'aller jusques à Nancy, voir le pays. Je ne me donte incontyment il y allait voir la demoy-selle peur la tirer comme les aultres et pour cela j'ai envoyé à leur logis, voir qui y était, et j'ai trouvé le dit paintre y était, et de la ils ont esté à Nancy et y ont resté un jour, et ont été fort festés, et le Maistre d'hôtel venait à tous les repas manger avec eux, avec force présents, et ils etaient très bien traités. Voilà ce que j'ay entendu, donc au pis aller, si vous n'avez pour voisine v^{re} sœur, ce pourrait estre v^{re} cousine. Il se tient quelque propos que l'Empereur offre récompense pour le duché de Gueldres, et que ce faisant, se pourrait faire quelque mariage de la fille de Hongrie et de Monsr le Marquys. Monsr vre père entend bien, ce faisant, avoir sa part en la dite récompense. Je voudrais qu'il en fust bien récompensé. Voilà tout ce que j'ay de nouveau . . . je me doute que vous ne ferez de si bonne diligence que moi, car je sais bien que vous tenez de Monsr v'tre père, et qu'estes paresseuse à ecrire, si l'air d'Ecosse ne vous a changé. Je n'ai encore eu que vos premyères. Il me tarde bien savoir comme depuis vous vous serez porté, cela me sera grant joye quand je pourrait ouir de vos nouvelles. Ce sera toujours quant N^{tre} Seigneur le veuille, et je prie, Madame, qu'il vous donne longue et bonne vie. Ce premier de Septembre, de v'tre humble et bonne mère,

ANTHOINETTE DE BOURBON.

À la Reyne d'Écosse.

[Balcarres MSS., ii. 20. Advocates' Library, Edinburgh.]

V.

Antoinette de Bourbon, Duchesse de Guise, to Mary, Queen of Scotland.

Madame: J'ay tardé plus longuement que je ne pensais à vous escrire, mais les noces de Mademoiselle de Lorraine nous ont tant ameusées que jusque à cette heure on a peut avoir le loisir. Nous departismes hier de la compaignye qui a esté bien grosse. Les noces furent Mardy passé. Monsr le Prince y est venu bien accompaigné et je vous assure c'est un bien honeste Prince et de bonne grâce. Il se contente fort de sa mye, et aussi elle de lui. Ils s'entendent aller chez eux dans xv. jours. La feste a esté à Bar, il n'y a eu guères d'estrangers, fors la Marquise de Baulde et Madame de Baçin, et des Comtesses et dames voisines. Vous en saurez quelque jour plus au long. Nous sommes en chemin pour aller à Guise, pensant en estre de retour pour la Toussaint. Nous laissons n'tre petit fils à Roche. Il court tant de maladie que nous n'avons osé

le mettre en chemin, mais je vous assure il se porte bien. . . .
Je vous avais escrit par Saint-Genould, du mariage de v're
frère, mais j'entens qu'il ne part pas si tost comme il m'avait
dit, pourquoi je veulx vous dire ce qui en est et co^me le Roy
veult faire le mariage de luy et de la nyèce du Pape, fille du
Duc de —— je ne puis retrouver son nom, mais elle est belle
et honeste et a bonne grâce, et est d'ancienne maison, de
l'age de xv. ans. L'on luy donne trois cent mille francs en
mariage, elle n'a que ung frère, s'il meurt elle serait heritière de
quarante mille livres et d'un Duché et aultre terres. Je pense
entre ceci et la Toussaint il en sera fait ou failli. Je prends
grand plaisir entendre par vos lettres le bon portement du Roy,
de vous et du petit prince. . . . Nous sommes prêts à
monter à cheval, pourquoi ferais fin. . . . Ce penultième
d'Aoust.

V^re humble et bo^ne mère,
Anthoinette de Borbon.

À la Reyne d'Écosse.

[Balcarres MSS., ii. 15. Advocates' Library, Edinburgh.]

VI.

*Antoinette de Bourbon, Duchesse de Guise, to Mary, Queen of
Scotland.*

Madame: L'on m'a tant assuré qu'on envoye les lettres
sûrement par le moyen des Marchands d'Anvers, que je les
ai mis à l'entrée pour en apprendre le chemin. Vostre sœur
en doit estre la messagère. Je vous ai escrit la conclusion de
son mariage et envoyé les articles et depuis ses noces par
vostre brodeur. Je viens de la mener en ménage, en une
belle et honneste maison et aultant bien meublée qu'il est
possible, nommé Beaumoult. Son beau-père la receuillit tant
honorablement et avec tant de gens de bien et grosse compaignye que l'on ne sait plus souhaiter; la Reyne de Hongrerie
entre les aultres s'y trouvait et la Duchesse de Myllan, aussi
Monsr et Madame la Princesse d'Orange, qui l'on tient grosse,
toute fois la chose n'est pas fort sure, et pour ma part j'en
doute. Il me semble v're dite sœur est bien logée. L'on luy
a fait de beau présens, et elle a de belles basques. Son Mary
est jeune, mais il a bon vouloir d'estre du nombre des gens de
bien. Il ne paraissait point qu'il fût Caresme, car les armes et
les tambours ne cessaient point; il s'y est fait de beaux joustes

là bas. A la fin il a fallu departir, qui n'a pas esté sans larmes. Je regagne ce lieu de Guyse, où je ne reste qu'une nuit, et demain à la Fère, où Monsr le Cardinal mon frère et mon père et ma sœur de St Pol seront mercredy, et vendredy recommencerai me mettre en chemin pour gagner Joinvylle le plus tost que je pourrais. Je pense trouver encore Monsr v^{re} père, et nos enfans, savoir les petits et les prètres. . . . Ce xiiii Mars, à Guise. . . .

ANTHOINETTE DE BOURBON.

À la Reyne d'Écosse,

[Balcarres MSS., ii. 5. Advocates' Library, Edinburgh.]

VII.

Louise de Lorraine, Princesse de Chimay, to Mary, Queen of Scotland.

Madame: Depuys que Dieu a tant faict pour moi que de me donner un bon Mary, je n'ai point eu loisir de vous en faire la part. Vous pouvez estre assurée que je me tiens en ce monde heureuse d'estre en la maison ou je suis, car avec la grandeur qu'il y a en tout, j'ai un seigneur et beau-père que je vous puis nommer bon, car il me faict un bien bon traitement, accompagné de tant de beaux présents, qu'il me faudroy employer trois feuilles de papier avant que je vous pourrais en rendre bon conte et qui sera, s'il vous plait, occasion de prendre contentement du bien de votre sœur, qui a commandement de vous offrir les très humble services des maistres et seigneurs de cette maison, vous suppliant a tout endroit les employer. Nous avons une très sage et vertueuse Reyne, et je ne puis vous dire l'honneur qu'elle me faict, car estant venue exprés à cette maison—la sienne et nôtre—elle m'a voulu prendre pour sa très humble fille et servante, et veulst que pour l'avenyr je dois estre toujours en sa compagnye, où pour le peu que j'y ai este m'a fayct fort grant chère. Madame la Duchesse de Mylan m'a dit le semblable, qui est la meilleure, et nous ésperons bientost la voir en Lorayne, car le maryage de Monsr le Marquys et d'elle, est en très bon train. Depuis que Madame ma mère est retournèe, elle m'a envoyée une lettre pour essayer si le chemin de ça luy sera plus aise que l'autre, et si'il vous plait de m'apprendre de vos nouvelles, je serai merveilleusement aise. Mais il faudra, Madame que a la lettre que vous m'enverrez, vous mettiez sur le paquet, "*Au Duc d'Aerschot*," et par les marchands qui viennent d'Ecosse, il vous sera aisé, car en les laissant à Anvers ou à Bruges, ou autre endroit du Pays, ne failleront point, en s'adressant à Monsr mon beau-père, de tomber entre mes mains, car il est grandement craint et aimé par deça, qui sera l'endroit où je supplye Dieu qu'il vous donne très bonne vie et longue. De Beaumont, ce xxv. jour de Mars.

V're très humble et très obeissante sœur,

LOUISE DE LORRAYNE.

[Balcarres MSS., ii. 153. Advocates' Library, Edinburgh.]

VIII.

Antoinette de Bourbon, Duchesse de Guise, to Mary, Queen of Scotland.

Madame: Je suis très aise que ce porteur soit venu par ici, pour s'en retourner vers vous, car je vous voullais escrire et envoyer un paquet. . . . Je desire bien fort savoir comme vous vous serez porté en v're couche et aussi comme le Roy et v're petit prince se portent. Je prie a N. S. à tous donner bonne santé et longue vie. Quant à notre costé, tout se porte bien, Dieu mercy ! Mon^r v're père est revenu depuis huit jours pour quelques bastyments et fortifications que le Roy lui a ordonné faire en cette frontière. J'ay esté très aise il ait cette charge, afin de l'avoir plus tost de retour. Quant à v're petit fils, il se porte bien et devient grand ; il commence très bien apprendre, et sait quasi son Pater noster, il est joli et bon enfant. J'ai esté cause qu'il n'est venu en ce lien, dans la pour des Rougeolles, qui régnent si fort, et je crains il les prends par les champs, ou il ne peut estre si bien traisté qu'à Joinvylle, et aussi que ne devons demeurer dans ce lieu que huit jours. . . . Nous attendons M. le Cardinal de Lorraine le iii d'Août. Il vient pour nous tous ensemble trouver au Pont-a-Mousson le huitième du dit mois, on se doit faire le premyer recueil de n'tre nouvelle Dame, pour la mener à Nancy. V're frère aussi vient avec M. le Cardinal, l'on doit faire grande chere a cette bien venue, et force tournois. Les noces furent il y a Dimanche huit jours. S'il s'y fait rien digne de vous faire part vous en serez avertie. J'ai bonne envye de voir si Monsr le Marquis sera bon Mary ! L'on se jouit fort au pays recevoir une si honneste Princesse . . . ce xx. Juillet de . . . ec.

ANTHOINETTE DE BOURBON.

À la Reyne d'Écosse.

[Balcarres MSS., ii. 4. Advocates' Library, Edinburgh.]

IX.

Christina, Duchess-Dowager of Lorraine, to Mary, Queen of Hungary.

18 Avril, 1552.

Madame: J'ay escrit une letter à votre Majesté pour avoir moyen d'avertir celle-ci et la Reine vostre sœur de la méchancetè que le Roy de France m'a faict, que sur ombre de bonne foy me emmène mon filz avecque grande rudesse, comme Vostre Majesté entendra par ce présent porteur plus au long. Suppliant Vostre Majesté ne prendra de mauvaise part sy je ne faict ceste lettre plus longue, car la grande fâcherie que j'ay, m'en garde. Sy esté, Madame, que je supplie à Vostre Majesté avoir pitié de moy, et m'assister de quelque conseil, et je n'oublyerai à jamais luy faire très humble service et vous obèir toute ma vie, comme celle quy desire demeurer à jamais,

Vostre très humble et très obeissante nièce et servante,

CHRESTIENNE.

[Lettres des Seigneurs, 101, f. 332. Archives du Royaume, Bruxelles.]

X.

Anne, Duchess-Dowager of Aerschot, to Mary, Queen of Hungary.

18 Avril, 1552.

Madame: Je ne saurais vous escrire la grande désolation en laquelle est presentément Madame ma sœur, constitué par la grande rudesse et cruauté que le jour du grand Vendredy luy a esté faicte par le Roy de France, qui est qu'il esté venu icy sous ombre de bonne foy et vrai amitié, comme dernièrement il nous avoit fait entendre. À son arrivée, il a esté reçu avecque tous les honneurs possible, et le meilleur traistement, et le dit jour du grand Vendredy il fit entendre à Madame comme pour satisfaire au capitulations de la Ligue, il falloit qu'il s'assurait de Monseigneur le duc de Lorraine, et de ses places, et que pour ce faire il falloit qu'il fust transporté à Bar, pour à quoy obvier, Ma dicte dame, Monseigneur de Vaudemont et moy, et tous ceux de son conseil, luy fust faicte une rémonstrance la plus humble qu'il estoit possible. A quoy il e répondit aultre chose sinon qu'il hâteroit sa resolution par escrit, ce qu'il a faict, comme votre Majesté pourra voire par les articles que je vous envoye. Ce voyant, elle et moy l'allâmes trouver en la Grande Galerie où ma dite dame parla encore a luy, jusqu'à se mettre à genoux, luy requérant pour l'amour de Dieu ne transporter son filz, et ne le luy ôter. A quoi ne fit response, et pour conclusion, Madame, le lendemain Samedy, veille de Pâques, il l'ont emmené, accompagné de force gens de guerre, sous la charge du Sr de Bourdillon, mais le Maréchal de Saint André n'a bougé qu'il ne l'ait mis hors de la ville, et c'étoit pitié voire Madame sa mère, Monseigneur de Vaudement et toute la noblesse et le pauvre peuple faire leur lamentation. Et voyant Madame ma sœur en telle pitié, étant en telle douleur, Madame, que votre Majesté peult estimer pour ly avoir faict une telle outrage que de luy oter son filz, et la voyant porter tel desplaisir, moy que m'estait deliberé m'en partir, ne la puis delaisser. Le Roy luy laisse Mesdames ses filles et l'administration des biens, comme elle avait auparavant, reservé les places fortes, qui demeurent à la charge de Monseigneur de Vaudemont, à condition que Votre Majesté pourra voire, toutefois n'y demeurra que Lorrains. Et par ce que Madame j'ai toujours envie de faire service à Votre Majesté tel que j'ai toute ma vie desiré, il luy plaira me commander ce que je fasse, et vous serez obéy comme la plus affecionée servante que Votre Majesté aura jamais. Suppliant Notre Seigneur donner à celle très bonne et longue vie, me recommandant toujours très humblement, en sa bonne grâce. De Nancy, ce lendemain de Pâques.

ANNE DE LORRAINE.

Madame: Depuis avoir escrit à Votre Majesté, le Roy de France a escrit une lettre à Madame ma sœur comme il a eu avertissement que les Bourgnignons faisaient une entreprise pour aller à Bar, afin d'y surprendre Monsieur de Lorraine, et que pour obvier à cela, il a ordonné au Sr de Bourdillon le mener à Joinville, où la Royne de France est encor là.

[Lettres des Seigneurs, 101, f. 330. Archives du Royaume, Bruxelles.]

XI.

Christina, Duchess-Dowager of Lorraine, to the Emperor Charles V.

A l'Empereur. Monseigneur: A la prière de Monseigneur de Vaudemont mon frère et de la Duchesse d'Aerscot ma sœur, j'ay pris la hardiesse de demeurer, encore que Vostre Majesté m'avait escript et commandé que je me retirasse vers les Roynes, ce que j'éspère que Vostre Majesté n'aures pas pris de mauvaise part. Car la grande instance et prière que mon dit frère et sœur m'ont faict, ont esté la cause, non pas pour aller contre son commandement, le voulant obéir toute ma vie, et je vous supplie, de toujours le croire, et avoir mon filz et son païs pour recommandé, et je supplieray le Créateur, Monseigneur, de donner à Vostre Majesté bonne santé et très longue vie. De Denœuvre, ce 26ᵉ May, 1552.

Vostre très humble et très obéissante
nièce et servante,

CHRESTIENNE.

[Lettres des Seigneurs, 102, f. 127. Archives du Royaume, Bruxelles.]

XII.

Christina, Duchess-Dowager of Lorraine, to the Emperor Charles V.

A l'Empereur. Monseigneur: J'ay reçu la lettre qu'il a plu à Vostre Majesté m'èscrire par le Seigneur de Carondelet, et par luy ay entendu la bonne souvenance qu'il a plu à Vostre Majesté avoir de moy et mes filles, de la bonne visitation, dont très humblement la remercie, et aussi de la charge que Vostre Majesté luy a donné pour me dire ce qu'il me faudra ensuivre. Votre Majesté m'oblige tant de l'honneur qu'elle me faict, que toute ma vie je seray preste à obéir à ses commandements, comme celle entendra s'il luy plait plus au long par le dit Seigneur de Carondelet, et aussi d'autres choses que luy ay donné charge de dire à Vostre Majesté, pour ne pas la fâcher de longue lettre. Et toute ma vie je suppliray le Créateur de donner à Vostre Majesté très bonne santé, et longue vie et de demeurer toujours à la bonne grâce d'icelle. De Hoch-Königsberg, ce 4e Septembre, 1552.

Vostre très humble nièce et servante,

CHRESTIENNE.

[Lettres des Seigneurs, 103, f. 518. Archives du Royaume, Bruxelles.]

XIII.

Dejanira Commena Contessa Trivulzio to Messer Innocenzio Gadio.

Magnifico Signore, Innocenzio: Ho ricevuto un altra vostra, inteso la morte del Magnifico Signor Belloni, che certo mi ha dato molto fastidio. Io sono certa che la Signora mia madre me haverà havuto grandissimo dispiacere, come risentirà la morte e privatione di tale amico. Però non si può resistere al Divino volere. Mi maraviglia molto non habbiati avuto la littera mia qual mandai alli di passati, in mane di Barile, però di novo vi dico che ho ricevuto la corona ed altre cose per Andronica, et le littere della Signore Madre, et così vi rimandò la risposta. Sareti contenti basare le mane in mio nome a Sua Excellentia, dicendoli che mi duole fino all' anima, dalle travaglie che patisse Sua Excellentia in quelle bande, et che siamo sempre apparentiati come servitori che li giurano esponere la vita et quanto tenemo in suo serviggio. Non mi occorrente altro a Vostra Signoria mi raccomando. De Codogno all. 29. Sett, 1552. Di Vostra Sig. Dejanira, Contessa Trivultia.

À Messer Inn. Gadio, amico carissimo.

[MS. No. 18, Biblioteca di Zelada, Pavia.]

XIV.

Christina, Duchess-Dowager of Lorraine, to Mary, Queen of England.

April, 1555.

Madame: Je supplie V^{tre} Maj^{té} me pardonner si je prends tant d'audace que d'escrire à icelle, mais tant d'honneur et de faveur que je recois de V^{tre} Maj^{té} en est cause. Car je ne puis laisser d'avertir que le Capitaine de mon vaisseau qui me mène a si bien faict son devoyr, sans nul hasart, comme V^tre Maj^tè lui a faict commande, que je ne puis laisser d'en avertir V^tre Maj^tè et la supplier de l'avoyr en souvenance. Et puis j'assure V^tre Maj^tè, que je n'en ai reçu que d'entier bon service, et connaissant cela, n'ay su laisser de le recommander à V^tre Maj^tè et pensant que le Capitaine Bont vous fera entendre ce qui s'est passé à mon passage, je n'en ferai plus propos, si non de vous assurer combien je regrette de ne plus estre dans la prèsence de V^re Maj^tè et que je ne puis estre auprès d'icelle, pour luy pouvoir faire quelque service, pour la satisfaction que je me ferais a tant de mercis que j'ay reçu, dont je demeure sans espoir d'y satisfaire. Et cependant je supplie très humblement à V^re Maj^tè me tenir en sa bonne grâce, a la quelle humblement me recommande, et baisant ses mains, priant Dieu, Madame, vous donner bonne santé, très longue vie et ung beau filz, comme le désire.

V^re très humble et très obeissante
cousine et servante,
CHRESTIENNE.

À la Reyne.

[MS. State Papers, Foreign, Mary, vol. vi., 351.   Public Record Office.]

BIBLIOGRAPHY

MANUSCRIPT SOURCES

ARCHIVIO DI STATO, MILANO: Autografi di Principi; Carteggio Diplomatico, 1533-1535; Carteggio con Montmorency, Conte di Corea, 1537-1538; Feudi Camerali, Tortona; Potenze Sovrane, 1533-1534.

BIBLIOTECA AMBROSIANA : Continuazione della Storia di Corio, O. 240.

MUSEO CIVICO DI STORIA PATRIA, PAVIA: No. 426, Lettere dell' Oratore, 1535; No. 546, di B. d. Corte, 1536.

BIBLIOTECA DEL CONTE ANTONIO CAVAGNA SANGIULIANI A ZELADA, PRESSO PAVIA : Archivio Sezione Storico, Diplomatico. Mazzo n. 127, Tortona; Lettere di Niccolò Belloni, etc., i.-xviii.

ARCHIVES DU ROYAUME, BRUXELLES: Lettres des Seigneurs, iii.-vii.; Papiers d'Etat de l'Audience, No. 82; Correspondance de Charles V. avec Jean de Montmorency, Seigneur de Courrières, 1537; No. 8, 26, 1178, etc., Lettres de Marie de Hongrie, Charles Quint, etc.; Régistre des Revenus et Dépenses de Charles V.; Régistre de Marguerite d'Autriche, 1799, 1800, 1803.

BIBLIOTHÈQUE NATIONALE, PARIS: Affaires d'Angleterre, xix.; F.F. 123, 20,467, 20,468; Oudin, Histoire des Guises; MS. Gaignières 349; Marillac MS. 8,625 ; Coll. de Lorraine, 27-33, etc.

ADVOCATES' LIBRARY, EDINBURGH: The Balcarres Manuscripts, ii., iii.; Correspondance de Madame de Guise, etc., avec la Reine d'Écosse.

BRITISH MUSEUM: Additional Manuscripts, 5,498; Harleian Manuscripts, 3,310, 3,311; F. Roddi, Annali di Ferrara.

PUBLIC RECORD OFFICE: State Papers, Foreign, Mary, vi. 351; Venetian Despatches, 1553-1558; Brussels Transcripts, 1553-1558.

PRINTED SOURCES

ALBERI, E.: Le Relazioni degli Ambasciatori Veneti nel Secolo XVI. Serie 2. 5 vols. Florence, 1839-1863.

ALTMEYER, J.: Isabelle d'Autriche. Brussels, 1842.

ALTMEYER, J.: Relations Commerciales des Pays-Bas. 1840.

ARCHÆOLOGIA, vols. xxxix., xl. (Society of Antiquaries). Brussels. 1865.

ARCHÆOLOGIA CAMBRENSIS, xxiii. 1877.
ARETINO, P.: Lettere. 6 vols. Paris, 1609.
ARMSTRONG, E.: The Emperor Charles V. 2 vols. 1902.
ASCHAM, R.: Works, ed. Giles. 1864.
ASHMOLE, E.: The Order of the Garter. 1672.
AVENATI, P.: Entrata Solemne di Cristina di Spagna, 1534. Milan, 1903.
BARACK, K.: Zimmerische Chronik. 4 vols. Freiburg, 1881.
BAUMGARTEN, H.: Geschichte Karl V. 3 vols. Stuttgart, 1885-1892.
BELTRAMI, L.: Il Castello di Milano, 1450-1535. Milan, 1894.
BERGH, L. v. d.: Correspondance de Marguerite d'Autriche, Gouvernante des Pays-Bas, 1506-1528. Leyden, 1845.
BOUILLÉ, R. DE: Histoire des Ducs de Guise. 4 vols. Paris, 1849.
BRADFORD, W.: Correspondence of Charles V. and his Ambassadors, with Itinerary, 1519-1551. 1850.
BRANTÔME, P. DE: Œuvres Complètes, ed. Mérimée et Lacour. 13 vols. Paris, 1895.
BUCHOLTZ, F. v.: Geschichte der Regierung Ferdinand I. 9 vols. Vienna, 1831-1838.
BULLETINS de la Commission d'Histoire, Séries ii., v., vii., xi., xii. Brussels, 1852.
BURGON, J. W.: Life and Times of Sir T. Gresham. 2 vols. 1839.
BURIGOZZO, G.: Cronaca Milanese, 1500-1544. Arch. Stor. Italiano, vol. iii. Florence, 1842.
CALENDAR of Letters and State Papers, Foreign and Domestic. of the Reign of Henry VIII., 1509-1547. 21 vols. 1862-1912.
CALENDAR of State Papers during the Reign of Henry VIII. Record Office Commission. 11 vols. 1831-1852.
CALENDAR of State Papers, Foreign Series, of the Reign of Edward VI., 1547-1553. 1861.
CALENDAR of State Papers, Foreign Series, of the Reign of Mary, 1553-1558. 1861.
CALENDAR of State Papers, Foreign Series, of the Reign of Elizabeth, 1558-1577. 11 vols. 1863-1901.
CALENDAR of State Papers in the Archives of Simancas, Series 1, 1485-1544. 7 vols. 1862-1899.
CALENDAR of State Papers in the Archives of Simancas, Series 2, 1558-1580. 3 vols. 1892-1899.
CALENDAR of State Papers in the Archives of Venice, 1202-1607. 10 vols. 1864-1900.
CALENDAR of Manuscripts of the Marquis of Salisbury, vol. i. Historical Manuscripts Commission. 1883-1899.
CALMET, A.: Histoire Ecclésiastique et Civile de Lorraine. 3 vols. Nancy, 1728.
CAMBRIDGE Modern History, The. Vol. II.: The Reformation; Vol. III.: The Wars of Religion. 1903-1904.
CAMPO, A.: Storia di Cremona. Cremona, 1585.
CHURCHILL, A.: Collection of Voyages and Travels. 6 vols. 1744-1746.

CIMBER, L., ET DANJOU, F.: Archives Curieuses de l'Histoire de France. III. Histoire Particulière de la Cour du Roi Henri II. Paris, 1835.

CONWAY, SIR MARTIN: The Literary Remains of A. Dürer. 1889.

CORTILE, L.: Ragionamenti. Venice, 1552.

CORYAT, T.: Crudities. 3 vols. 1611.

COURNAULT, C.: Ligier-Richier. Paris, 1887.

CROWE, J. A., AND CAVALCASELLE, G. B.: Titian—his Life and Times. 2 vols. 1877.

CUST, L.: Burlington Magazine, xix. August, 1911.

CUST, MRS. HENRY: Gentlemen Errant. 1909.

DAHLMANN, F.: Geschichte der Europäischen Staaten: Dänemark. 3 vols. Hamburg, 1840-1843.

DECRUE, F.: Anne de Montmorency à la Cour de François I.

DECRUE, F.: Anne de Montmorency à la Cour de Henri II., François II., et Charles IX. 2 vols. Paris, 1885-1889.

DU BELLAY, M. ET G.: Mémoires (Petitot Coll., Série i., 17-19). Paris, 1819.

FÖRSTEMAN, C.: Neues Urkundenbuch z. Gesch. d. Reformation. Hamburg, 1842.

FRIEDMANN, P.: Les Depêches de G. Michieli, 1554-1557. Venice, 1869.

FRIZZI, A.: Memorie per la Storia di Ferrara, iv. Ferrara, 1791.

GACHARD, L.: Analecta Belgica. Brussels, 1855.

GACHARD, L.: Collection des Documents Inédits conc. l'Histoire de la Belgique. 3 vols. Brussels, 1853.

GACHARD, L.: Collection des Voyages des Souverains des Pays-Bas. 4 vols. 1876-1882.

GACHARD, L.: Relations des Ambassadeurs Vénitiens sur Charles V. et Philippe II. 1855.

GACHARD, L.: Relation des Troubles de Gand sous Charles V. 1846.

GACHARD, L.: Retraite et Mort de Charles V. 2 vols. 1855.

GARDNER, E.: The King of Court Poets. 1906.

GAYE, G.: Carteggio Inedito di Artisti dei Secoli XV., XVI., e XVII. 3 vols. Florence, 1840.

GHILINO, C.: Annali di Alessandria. Milan, 1666.

GOULART, S.: Mémoires de la Ligue. 6 vols. Amsterdam, 1758.

GRANVELLE, CARDINAL DE: Correspondance, 1565-1586, publié par E. Poullet et C. Piot. 12 vols. Brussels, 1896.

GRANVELLE, Cardinal de, Mémoires pour servir à l'Histoire du Par P. Levesque. Brussels, 1753.

GRANVELLE, Cardinal de, Mémoires du. L. d'Esnans, Brussels, 1761.

GRANVELLE, CARDINAL DE: Papiers d'État, publié par C. Weiss. 9 vols. 1852.

GROEN VAN PRINSTERER, G.: Archives de la Maison d'Orange-Nassau. Série i. 8 vols. Leyden, 1847.

GUAZZO, M.: Historie, 1524-1552. Milan, 1552.

GUICCIARDINI, L.: Descrittione di Tutti i Paesi-Bassi. Antwerp, 1588.

HAILE, M.: Life of Reginald Pole. 1910.

HARDWICKE PAPERS, The, 1501-1726. 2 vols. 1778.
HAÜSSER, L.: Geschichte der Rheinischen Pfalz. 2 vols. Heidelberg, 1856.
HENNE, A.: Histoire du Règne de Charles V. en Belgique. 10 vols. Brussels, 1860.
HOBY, T., The Travail and Life of, 1547-1564. Camden Miscellany, x. 1902.
HUGO, L.: Traité de l'Origine de la Maison de Lorraine. Berlin, 1711.
JUSTE, T.: Les Pays-Bas sous Charles V. Brussels, 1861.
JUSTE, T.: Les Pays-Bas sous Philippe II. Brussels, 1884.
JUSTE, T.: Marie de Hongrie. 1867.
KAULEK, J.: Correspondance Politique de Castillon et de Marillac. Paris, 1885.
KERVYN DE LETTENHOVE, J. DE: Relations Politiques des Pays-Bas et de l'Angleterre sous le Règne de Philippe II. 10 vols. Brussels, 1892.
KÖSTLIN, J.: Leben Luthers. Tübingen, 1882.
LANZ, K.: Correspondenz des Kaisers Karl aus d. K. Archiv. 3 vols. Leipzig, 1844.
L'AUBESPINE, S. DE: Négociations au Règne de François II. Paris, 1841.
LAVISSE, E.: Histoire de France, vol. v. Paris, 1903.
LE GLAY, E.: Correspondance de Maximilien I. et de Marguerite d'Autriche. 2 vols. Brussels, 1839.
LEPAGE, H.: Les Archives de Nancy, Le Palais Ducal, La Galerie des Cerfs, La Ville de Nancy; Lettres de Charles III., Duc de Lorraine. Nancy, 1844-1865.
LE PETIT, J.: La Grande Chronique de Hollande, etc., jusqu'à 1600. Dordrecht, 1601.
LEVA, G. DE: Storia Documentata di Karl V. in Italia. 5 vols. Venice, 1863.
LITTA, P.: Famiglie Celebri, vol. ii. Milan, 1839.
LODGE, E.: Illustrations of British History, Henry VIII. to James I., in Papers of the Families of Howard, Talbot, and Cecil. 3 vols. 1830.
MACHYN, H.: Diary of a Citizen of London, 1550-1563, ed. J. S. Nicholls. Camden Society, No. 42. 1848.
MAGENTA, C.: I Visconti e gli Sforza nel Castello di Pavia. 2 vols. Milan, 1883.
MAITLAND MISCELLANY, i. Maitland Club. Edinburgh, 1834.
MERRIMAN, R. B.: Life and Letters of Thomas Cromwell. 2 vols. 1902.
MIGNET, F.: Charles Quint—son Abdication et Séjour à Yuste. Paris, 1857.
MIGNET, F.: Rivalité de François I. et de Charles V. Paris, 1875.
MOELLER, C.: Éléonore d'Autriche, Reine de France. Paris, 1893.
MONTEMERLO, N.: Nuove Historie di Antica Città. Tortona, 1618.
NOTT, G.: The Works of Surrey and Sir T. Wyatt. 2 vols. 1815.
NUBILONIA: Cronaca di Vigevano.
PIMODAN, G. DE: La Mère des Guises. Paris, 1889.
PORTA, G.: Alessandria Descritta, Illustrata, Celebrata. Milan, 1670.

PUTMAN, R.: William the Silent, Prince of Orange. 2 vols. New York, 1895.

RABUTIN, F. DE: Commentaires des Dernières Guerres. Petitot Coll., No. 37. Paris, 1819-1829.

RATTI, N.: Della Famiglia Sforza. 2 vols. Rome, 1794.

RAVOLD, J. B.: Histoire Démocratique de Lorraine. 4 vols. Paris, 1890.

REIFFENBERG, F. DE: Histoire de la Toison d'Or. 2 vols. Brussels, 183 .

REUMONT, A. V.: Geschichte Toscanas. 2 vols. Gotha, 1876.

RIBIER, G.: Lettres et Mémoires d'État. Paris, 1666.

RUBLE, A. DE: Antoine de Bourbon et Jeanne d'Albret. 4 vols. Paris, 1881.

RUBLE, A. DE: La Jeunesse de Marie Stuart; 1891. Le Traité de Câteau-Cambrésis; 1887.

SAINT-GÉNIS, V. DE: Histoire de Savoie. 3 vols. Chambéry, 1869.

SANUTO, M.: Diarii, 1496-1533, vols. liii., liv., lv., lvi., lvii. Venice, 1879-1902.

SCHÄFER, D.: Geschichte v. Dänemark. 4 vols. Gotha, 1893.

SCHLEGEL, J. H.: Geschichte d. Könige v. Dänemark aus d. Oldenburg Stamme. 2 vols., folio. Kopenhagen, 1769-1777.

THOMAS, H.: Annalium de Vita et Rebus Gestis Illustrissimi Principis Frederici II., Elect. Pal. Frankfort, 1624.

THOMAS, H.: Spiegel d. Humors Grosser Potentaten. Leipzig, 1629.

TYTLER, P. F.: England under Edward VI. and Mary. 2 vols. 1839.

ULMANN, H.: Kaiser Maximilian I. 2 vols. Stuttgart, 1884-1891.

VAISSIÈRE, P. DE: Charles de Marillac, 1510-1560. Paris, 1896.

VERRI, P.: Storia di Milano. 2 vols. Florence, 1851.

VERTOT, R. DE: Ambassades de MM. de Noailles en Angleterre. 5 vols. Paris, 1762.

VIEILLEVILLE, F. DE SCÉPEAUX, MARÉCHAL DE: Mémoires. Coll. Petitot, Série i., 26-28. Paris, 1819-1829.

VILLAMONT, A.: Voyages. Urbino, 1589.

VIOLA, N.: Il Santuario di Tortona. Tortona, 1675.

VOIGT, J.: Albert - Alcibiades, Markgraf von Brandenburg. 2 vols. Berlin, 1852.

WALPOLE, H.: Anecdotes of Painting, vol. i. 1826-1828.

WORNUM, R.: Life and Works of Holbein. 1867.

YOUNG, COLONEL G.: The Medici. 2 vols. 1909.

GENEALOGICAL TABLES

35

I. HABSBURG.

Maximilian I., d. 1519, =(1) Mary of Burgundy ; (2) Bianca Sforza.

Philip, d. 1506. =Juana of Spain, d. 1555.   Margaret, d. 1530. =(1) John, son of Ferdinand and Isabella. (2) Philibert II. of Savoy.

Eleanor, =(1) Emanuel of Portugal.   Charles V., =Isabella of Portugal,   Don John, d. 1578.   Isabella, d. 1526.=Christian II. of   Mary, = Louis of Hun-
d. 1558.   (2) Francis I. of France.   1500-1558.   d. 1539.   Denmark, d. 1559.   d. 1558.   gary, d. 1526.
(See II.)

Margaret,=(1) Alessandro de' Medici.   Philip II., =(1) Mary of Portugal.   Mary = Maximilian II.
d. 1586.   (2) Ottavio Farnese.   1527-1598.   (2) Mary of England.   (a)
Alessandro, Duke of Parma, d. 1592. = Mary of Portugal.   (3) Elizabeth of France.
(4) Anne of Austria.
Sebastian of Portugal.
d. 1578.

Don Carlos, d. 1568.   Philip III., = Margaret of Austria.   Katherine = Charles Emanuel,   Isabella, d. 1633. = Albert of Austria,
d. 1621.   Duke of Savoy.   d. 1621.
(b)

Ferdinand I., d. 1564.=Anne of Bohemia, d. 1547.   Katherine=John III. of Portugal, d. 1557.

(a)   (a)   John, d. 1554.=Juana of Spain.   Mary, d. 1539 = Philip II. of Spain.
Sebastian, d. 1578.

Maximilian II.,=Mary   Mary = William of   Ferdinand,=Philippina   Charles=Anne.   Anne=Albert III.
d. 1576.   Cleves.   d. 1595.   Welser.   of Bavaria.
(b)

Rudolf II.,   Anne = Philip II.   Albert.   Elizabeth = Charles IX.,   Matthias,=Anne.   Ferdinand II.,=Maria Anna.   William II.,=Renée of
d. 1612.   King   d. 1619.   d. 1637.   d. 1626.   Lorraine.
of France.

Mary = Philip IV.   Leopold I.,=(1) Margaret of Spain.   Eleanor = Charles Leopold   Ferdinand III., d. 1657.=Mary of Spain.   Maximilian, = Elizabeth of
of Spain.   d. 1705.   (2) Claude of Tyrol.   of Lorraine.   d. 1651.   Lorraine.
(3) Eleanor, d. of Elector Palatine.

Joseph I., d. 1711.= Wilhelmina of Hanover.   Charles VI., d. 1740.=Eliz. Christina of Brunswick.

Maria Theresa, d. 1780. = Francis III., Duke of Lorraine ; el. Emperor 1745 ; d. 1765.

II. DENMARK, 1481—1588.

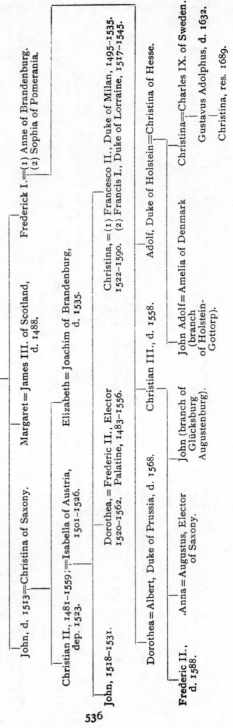

Christian I., King of Denmark, Norway=Dorothea of Brandenburg, widow of Christopher,
and Sweden ; d. 1481. King of Denmark ; d. 1448.

John, d. 1513==Christina of Saxony.   Margaret=James III. of Scotland,   Frederick I.==(1) Anne of Brandenburg.
                                                   d. 1488.   (2) Sophia of Pomerania.

Christian II., 1481–1559;==Isabella of Austria,   Elizabeth = Joachim of Brandenburg,
dep. 1523.   1501–1526.   d. 1535.

John, 1518–1531.   Dorothea, = Frederic II., Elector   Christina, = (1) Francesco II., Duke of Milan, 1495–1535.
                      1520–1562. Palatine, 1483–1556.   1522–1590.   (2) Francis I., Duke of Lorraine, 1517–1545.

Dorothea=Albert, Duke of Prussia, d. 1568.   Christian III., d. 1558.   Adolf, Duke of Holstein==Christina of Hesse.

Anna = Augustus, Elector   John (branch of   John Adolf=Amelia of Denmark   Christina=Charles IX. of Sweden.
of Saxony.   Glücksburg   (branch
                              Augustenburg).   of Holstein-   Gustavus Adolphus, d. 1632.
                                                  Gottorp).
Frederic II.,
d. 1588.   Christina, res. 1689.

536

III. SFORZA.

Francesco, 1401-1466; Duke of Milan, 1450 = Bianca Maria Visconti, d. 1468.

- **Galeazzo Maria, 1444-1476 = Bona of Savoy.**
  - **Gian Galeazzo, 1469-1494 = Isabella of Aragon, d. 1524.**
    - Francesco, 1490-1512; Abbot of Noirmoutiers.
    - Bona, d. 1557 = Sigismund I., King of Poland; d. 1548.
    - Ippolita, d. 1501.
  - Caterina, d. 1509 = (1) Girolamo Riario. (2) Giacomo Feo. (3) Giovanni de' Medici.
  - Ermes, 1470-1504.
  - Ottaviano, Bishop of Lodi.
  - Carlo = Bianca Simonetta.
  - Anna, 1473-1497 = Alfonso d'Este.
  - Ippolita = Alessandro Bentivoglio.
- **Ippolita, 1446-1484 = Alfonso of Calabria, afterwards King of Naples.**
- **Filippo, 1448-1492 = Costanza Sforza.**
- **Sforza, Duke of Bari, 1449-1479.**
- **Lodovico Maria, 1451-1580 = Beatrice d'Este, 1475-1497.**
  - Massimiliano, 1493-1530; abd. 1515.
  - Francesco II., 1495-1535; last Duke of Milan = Christina of Denmark, 1522-1590.
  - Cesare.
  - Leone, Protonotary.
  - Bianca, d. 1497 = Galeazzo di Sanseverino, d. 1525.
  - Gian Paolo, 1497-1535.
  - Line of Caravaggio extinct 1697.
- **Ascanio, Cardinal, 1455-1505.**
- **Tristano, d. 1477 = Beatrice d'Este da Correggio.**

IV. LORRAINE, 1300—1736.

Frederic IV., d. 1328=Elizabeth, daughter of the Emperor Albert I.

Raoul, killed at Crécy, 1346.

John, d. 1391.

Charles II., d. 1431=Margaret, daughter of the Emperor Rupert III.

Frederic, killed at Agincourt, 1415=Margaret, heiress of Joinville and Vaudemont.

Anthony=heiress of Aumale and Mayenne.

Isabella, d. 1453=Réné I. of Anjou, d. 1480.

Frederic, Count of Vaudemont, d. 1472.

René II., d. 1508=Philippa of Guelders, d. 1547.

Margaret=Henry VI. of England.

Yolande, 1428-1483=Frederic, Count of Vaudemont, d. 1472.

John, d. 1470.

Claude, Duke of Guise. (See Table V.)

John, Cardinal, 1498-1550.

Francis, Count of Lambesque, 1503-1525.

Louis, Count of Vaudemont, 1506-1527.

Anthony, 1489-1544=Renée de Bourbon, d. 1539.

Nicolas, Count of Vaude-mont, 1524-1577.==(1) Margaret of Egmont. (2) Joanna of Savoy. (3) Catherine of Aumale.

Francis I.=Christina of Denmark, 1517-1545. 1522-1590.

Anne, 1522-1568==(1) René, Prince of Orange. (2) Philip, Duke of Aerschot.

Charles de Croy, Marquis of Havre, b. 1549.

a

b

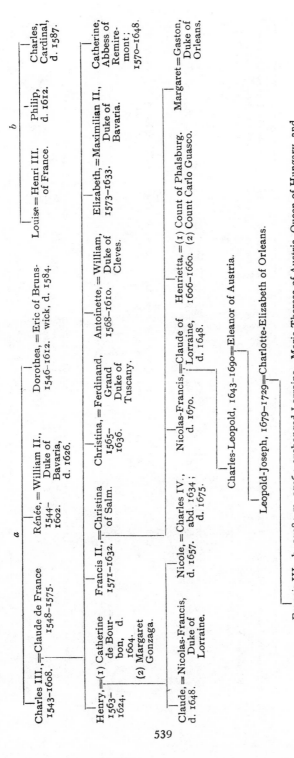

a

b

Charles III., = Claude de France
1543–1608.   1548–1575.

Rénée, = William II., Duke of Bavaria, d. 1626.
1544–1602.

Dorothea, = Eric of Brunswick, d. 1584.
1546–1612.

Louise = Henri III. of France.

Philip, d. 1612.

Charles, Cardinal, d. 1587.

Henry, = (1) Catherine de Bourbon, d. 1604.
1563–1624.   (2) Margaret Gonzaga.

Francis II., = Christina of Salm.
1571–1632.

Christina, = Ferdinand, Grand Duke of Tuscany.
1565–1636.

Antoinette, = William, Duke of Cleves.
1568–1610.

Elizabeth, = Maximilian II., Duke of Bavaria.
1573–1633.

Catherine, Abbess of Remiremont; 1570–1648.

Claude, = Nicolas-Francis, Duke of Lorraine.
d. 1648.

Nicole, = Charles IV., abd. 1634; d. 1675.
d. 1657.

Nicolas-Francis, = Claude of Lorraine, d. 1648.
d. 1670.

Henrietta, = (1) Count of Phalsburg. (2) Count Carlo Guasco.
1606–1660.

Margaret = Gaston, Duke of Orleans.

Charles-Leopold, 1643–1690 = Eleanor of Austria.

Leopold-Joseph, 1679–1729 = Charlotte-Elizabeth of Orleans.

Francis III., b. 1708; m. 1736; exchanged Lorraine = Maria Theresa of Austria, Queen of Hungary, and
for Tuscany; elected Emperor 1745; d. 1765.   daughter of the Emperor Charles VI.; d. 1780.

V. GUISE, 1500—1600.

René II., Duke of Lorraine and Bar, King of Sicily, etc.; d. 1508=Philippa of Guelders, d. 1547.

Claude, Duke of Guise, 1496-1550=Antoinette of Bourbon, 1494-1583.

Mary,=(1) Louis, Duke of Longue-ville; d. 1537. 1515-1560. (2) James V., King of Scotland; d. 1542.

Francis,=Anna d' Este, Duke of Guise, 1531-1607. 1520-1563.

Louise,=Charles, Prince of Chimay. 1521-1542.

Renée, Abbess of S. Pierre, Reims, 1522-1586.

Charles, Cardinal, 1523-1574.

Claude, Duke=Louise de of Aumale, Brézé, 1526-1573. m. 1545.

Louis, Duke of Longueville, 1536-1551.

Mary, Queen=(1) Francis II., of Scots, King of France; 1542-1587. d. 1560. (2) Henry, Lord Darnley; d. 1567.

Catherine,=Nicolas, Count of Vaudemont. m. 1569.

Louis, Cardinal, 1527-1578.

Charles, Duke=Marie of Aumale; d'Elbœuf. b. 1556.

Antoinette, Abbess of Far-moustiers, 1531-1561.

Claude, Abbot of Bec; b. 1563.

Diana, =Francis, m. 1576. Duke of Piney.

James VI. of Scotland=Anne of Denmark, and I. of England d. 1619. (1603) 1567-1623.

Louis, Cardinal, 1555-1576.

Francis, Prior of Malta, 1534-1563.

Réné, Marquis=Louise de of Elbœuf, Rieux. 1535-1576.

Charles, Marquis of Elbœuf; created Duke 1581.

Marie, m. 1576.=Charles of Aumale.

Henri le Balafré,=Catherine of Prince of Cleves. Joinville, etc., Duke of Guise, 1549-1588.

Charles, Duke=Henrietta of Mayenne, of Savoy. 1554-1611.

Louis, Archbishop of Reims and Cardinal of Guise, 1555-1588.

Catherine,=Louis, Duke of 1552-1596. Montpensier, 1513-1582.

Francis, 1558-1573.

Charles, Duke of=Henriette de Joyeuse, Guise, Duchess of Mont-1571-1640. pensier; d. 1656.

Louis, Cardinal and Arch-bishop of Reims; b. 1575.

Claude, Duke of=Marie de Chevreuse; Rohan. b. 1578.

Louise,=Francis, Prince of Conti; m: July 24, 1605.

540

INDEX